1997

HEALTH CARE
AND
REFORM IN
INDUSTRIALIZED
COUNTRIES

Edited by

MARSHALL W. RAFFEL

HEALTH CARE AND REFORM IN INDUSTRIALIZED COUNTRIES

The Pennsylvania State University Press
University Park, Pennsylvania

Library of Congress Cataloging-in-Publication Data

Health care and reform in industrialized countries / edited by
    Marshall W. Raffel.

            p.   cm.
    Includes bibliographical references and index.
    ISBN 0-271-01620-5 (cloth : alk. paper)
    ISBN 0-271-01644-2 (paper : alk. paper)
    1. Medicine, State.   2. Insurance, Health.   3. Medical care, Cost
of.   I. Raffel, Marshall W.
RA411.H42   1997
362.1—dc20   96-13824
                                                        CIP

It is the policy of The Pennsylvania State University Press to use acid-free paper for the first printing
of all clothbound books. Publications on uncoated stock satisfy the minimum requirements of American National Standard for Information Sciences—Permanence of Paper for Printed Library Materials, ANSI Z39.48-1992.

Contents

Introduction

This is a book concerned with the health systems of ten industrialized countries, all democratic and affluent with well-educated populations and high health standards. They are countries that have interacted with each other extensively over the years in commercial, cultural, and scientific affairs. For some time now all of these countries have faced pressures from their health sectors for additional resources to improve or maintain the health of their populations. The pressures stemmed from the availability of useful new technologies, a direct result of scientific advances. The pressures also came from increased utilization because of the growing needs of their aging populations and from all age groups who could now be treated better than before. The health sectors were thus demanding, and sometimes getting, a greater share of each nation's wealth. This created a problem for all of these democratic countries: how to maintain some balance in their economies while at the same time maintaining their current high health standards and providing the resources to attain even higher standards. Where is the money to come from? The agricultural sector? Defense? Social welfare? Education? Debt service? Decreased consumer spending? The countries continue to struggle and search for ways to respond to these seemingly unending pressures. Some reforms have been instituted—some incremental, some more radical—but the search process is never ending.

The chapters in this book are designed to provide a baseline of information about each country's health system: the structure of the health system's organization, operation, finance, and efforts at reform. More specifically, the various chapters describe the training, pay, and work conditions of each country's physicians, the influences of the medical profession, how hospitals are organized and financed, the provisions for care of the frail elderly and mentally ill, public health services, the role of private health insurance, detailed information on national health expenditures and efforts at cost containment, and the roles of both central government and lower governmental units. Most important is the patient: here the various chapters deal with waiting lists, patient choices in selecting physicians and hospitals, quality assurance, and how much patients have to pay out of pocket and for health insurance. Each chapter has a wealth of statistical data relevant to that country.

The various countries not only have similar problems; they appear to be addressing them in similar ways. Readers will note many instances where the countries are influencing each other, borrowing and adapting ideas in terms of health system organization and finance. Though each country's health system is unique, a product of its past history and both its political and social culture, the international influences come primarily from the works of individual scholars or from the successful steps taken by one or more of the countries. Coupling the ideas from another country with ideas from their own, nations have been experimenting, incrementally adjusting, and in some countries proposing radical overhauls. To cite a few examples, America has had periodic flirtations with the health systems of Sweden, the United Kingdom, and in recent years with Germany and Canada; health system reform proposals typically draw upon the experiences from one or more of those countries. American influence in recent times on Europeans is evident from the work of Stanford University's Alain Enthoven on market competition, which has influenced reform in—at least—Sweden, the Netherlands, the United Kingdom, and New Zealand. American influence is also evident by the widespread captivation with DRGs (Diagnosis Related Groups) in Sweden, Germany, the United Kingdom, France, and other countries, a pioneering system for financing hospital care developed by Robert Fetter and the late John Thompson at Yale University. New Zealand has historically been heavily influenced by what the British have been doing. The final chapter deals with some of the major issues faced by the countries, including some that relate to international influences.

It is not the objective of this book to provide or suggest some grand solution to national health system problems but rather to provide information for readers as they examine and address the organizational and financial problems in their own countries. This book emphasizes, therefore, the ways in which ten industrialized nations organize and finance their health systems, and deal with the problems they encounter. Written by residents of each country, each author was asked to include specific information and statistical tables. It is hoped that their efforts will provide new insights as we continue to adapt and change our health systems to meet current demands.

Brief comment might be made regarding the statistical data employed by each of the authors, and the use of those data when comparing countries. Statistics across national boundaries have to be treated with great care. The Danish authors, Allan Krasnik and Signild Vallgårda, note that nursing homes for the sick, disabled elderly, and handicapped are not considered part of the health sector, but rather part of the social welfare system. They go on to note that as a consequence many of the figures in official Danish statistics are not comparable to those of other countries. For the purposes of this book they adjusted the figures and made them part of the health sector. But their point is well taken. A similar situation exists in Sweden. Countries do count and classify differently; therefore we should treat data cautiously when making international comparisons. Both Peter Hatcher and Toshitaka Nakahara also make this point: in the United Kingdom where long-term care expenditures are divided between the health and social sectors, and in Japan where medical care expenditure figures announced by the Japanese ministry are different from those announced by the OECD (Organization for Economic Cooperation and Development). U.S. data can also be misunderstood if one does not know what is included and what is not. Drug expenditures, for example, do not include drug and drug sundries used in hospitals; those expenditures appear as a hospital expenditure in national health accounts. Similarly in the United States, national health expenditures for physician services do not include physicians employed by hospitals; their costs appear as part of hospital costs.

About the Authors

CANADA

Peggy Leatt is professor and chair of the Department of Health Administration at the University of Toronto. Dr. Leatt teaches courses in organization theory and behavior. Her current research interests are concerned with the design of alternative organizational structures, decentralization of decision-making, strategic alliances, and other integrated delivery systems; she has recently published a book of case studies on innovations in health care management. She has provided consulting services on organizational issues to a wide range of health service organizations internationally, including Mexico, the Bahamas, Britain, and Hungary.

Department of Health Administration
University of Toronto
McMurrich Building, 2d Floor
12 Queens Park Crescent-West
Toronto, ON   M5S 1A8
Canada

Tel: (416) 978-2736
Fax: (416) 978-7350
e-mail: p.leatt@utoronto.ca

A. Paul Williams is associate professor of health administration at the University of Toronto. He specializes in Canadian health politics and policy. His particular interests are the extent to which organized medicine has influenced the evolution of Canadian Medicare, and the implications for professions, consumers, and governments of the shifting balance between public and private interests in the health system. His papers have appeared in leading Canadian and American professional journals.

Department of Health Administration
University of Toronto
McMurrich Building, 2d Floor
12 Queens Park Crescent-West
Toronto, ON   M5S 1A8
Canada

Tel: (416) 978-8327
Fax: (416) 978-7350
e-mail: paul.williams@utoronto.ca

DENMARK

Allan Krasnik, Ph.D., M.P.H., M.D., is professor of social medicine at the University of Copenhagen. He is engaged in health services research and graduate and postgraduate teaching of health policy analysis and health administration.

Department of Social Medicine
University of Copenhagen
Panum Institute
Blegdamsvej 3
DK-2200 Copenhagen
Denmark

Telephone: 45 35 32 79 71/45 35 32 79 00
Fax: 45 31 35 11 81
e-mail: Krasnik@iabvs.ku.dk

Signild Vallgårda, M.A., D.M.Sc., is senior research fellow in the Department of Social Medicine, University of Copenhagen. Her research focuses on the history of the health services and perinatal epidemiology. She is engaged in pre- and postgraduate teaching of medical sociology, health policy analysis, and health administration.

Department of Social Medicine
University of Copenhagen
Panum Institute
Blegdamsvej 3
DK-2200 Copenhagen
Denmark

Telephone: 45 35 32 79 68
e-mail: S.Vallgarda@socmed.ku.dk

FRANCE

Marie-Pascal Pomey, M.D., is *assistant hospitalo-universitaire* in public health, University Hospital of Brest, and lecturer in public health, University of Western Brittany. Between June 1993 and

May 1995 she was adviser in the private office of the French Minister of Health. In 1993 she published a report on the Dutch health system reform.

Service de Santé Publique
Hospital Morvan
5, avenue Foch
F-29200 Brest
France

Telephone: 33-9-82-23-308 / 33-9-80-16-936
Fax: 33-9-80-16-431

Jean-Pierre Poullier is head of a comparative health policy unit at OECD, and a lecturer in health economics at the University of Paris IX–Dauphine. He has authored a number of studies on the health systems of the industrialized countries.

2, rue du Conseiller Collignon
F-75016 Paris
France

Telephone: 33-1-45-24-91-86
Fax: 33-1-45-24-90-98
e-mail: Jean-Pierre.Poullier@oecd.org

GERMANY

J.-Matthias Graf v. d. Schulenburg is professor of business administration and director of the Institute for Insurance Economics at the University of Hannover. In addition, he is managing director of the North-German Centre of Health Services Research, one of the largest public health research institutions in Germany. He has published many books and articles in scholarly journals in the fields of risks and insurance, health economics, and empirical microeconomics. He has worked in particular on health insurance issues and methodological questions of economic evaluations of health services.

Fachbereich Wirtschaftswissenschaften
Universität Hannover
Königsworther Platz 1
Wunstorferstrasse 14
D-30167 Hannover
Germany

Telephone: 49-511-762-5083
Fax: 49-511-762-5081
e-mail: jms@ifvb.uni-hannover.de

Wolfgang Greiner is currently at the Department of Economics at the University of Hannover and managing director of a major project about the social cost of kidney and liver transplantation. His special interest of research is the evaluation of health services and health care programs. He was graduated from the University of Hannover.

Fachbereich Wirtschaftswissenschaften
Universität Hannover

Königsworther Platz 1
Wunstorferstrasse 14
D-30167 Hannover
Germany

Telephone: 49-511-762-5084
Fax: 49-511-762-5081
e-mail: WG@insurance.ifvb.uni-hannover.de

JAPAN

Toshitaka Nakahara, M.D., Ph.D., M.P.H., is the director of the Department of Public Health Administration, Institute of Public Health. He was engaged in public health administration as a medical officer in the Ministry of Health and Welfare, the prefectural governments of Yamanashi and Kagoshima, and the Ministry of Labor after becoming a medical doctor in 1974. In 1992 he was appointed to his present position, which Professor Masami Hashimoto had occupied from 1958 to 1982. Hashimoto contributed a chapter on the health care system of Japan to *Comparative Health Systems* (ed. Raffel, Penn State Press, 1984); Nakahara's chapter draws upon Professor Hashimoto's earlier contribution.

6-1 Shiroganedai 4
Minato-ku
Tokyo 108
Japan

Telephone: 81-3-3441-7111, ext. 306

NETHERLANDS

J. A. M. (Hans) Maarse has been professor of health care policy analysis at the University of Limburg in Maastricht, Faculty of Health Sciences, since 1986. In August 1995 he was appointed dean of the Faculty of Health Sciences. He studied political science at the Catholic University of Nijmegen. His main interests are health care finance, hospital budgeting, political decision-making in health care, and international comparative analysis of health care systems.

Programme in Health Policy and Management
University of Limburg
Beleidswetenschap
Postbus 616
6200 MD Maastricht
The Netherlands

Telephone: 31-43-388-1571
Fax: 31-43-367-0944

NEW ZEALAND

Claudia D. Scott is professor of public policy and director of the Master of Public Policy Programme at Victoria University, Wellington, New Zealand. She holds a B.A. from Mount Holyoke College and a M.A. and Ph.D. in economics from Duke University.

Public Policy Group
Faculty of Commerce and Administration
Victoria University
P.O. Box 600
Wellington
New Zealand

Telephone: 64-4-471-5377
Fax: 64-4-471-2200
e-mail: claudia.scott@vuw.ac.nz

SWEDEN

Stefan Håkansson, Ph.D., is associate professor and director of the Department of Health Economics at the Swedish Institute for Health Services Development (Spri), Stockholm. He has been working with care of the elderly, evaluation of screening activities, technology assessment, economic evaluations, and DRGs. He had participated in more than thirty expert commissions for WHO, the Council of Europe, and OECD.

Spri
Box 70487
S-10726 Stockholm
Sweden

Telephone: 46 8 702 46 60
Telefax: 46 8 702 47 99
e-mail: stefan.hakansson@spri.se

Sara Nordling received her B.Sc. in Economics from the Lund University in 1992 and has worked as an assistant secretary for the Swedish Committee on Funding and Organisation of Health Services and Medical Care (HSU 2000). Since the beginning of 1995 she has been a research officer in the Department of Health Economics at the Swedish Institute for Health Services Development (Spri), Stockholm

Spri
Box 70487
S-10726 Stockholm
Sweden

Telephone: 46 8 702 46 76
Telefax: 46 8 702 47 99
e-mail: sara.nordling@spri.se

Spri (Swedish Institute for Health Services Development) is an independent research and development institute. Its research and development activities are in health economics, quality development, medical informatics, and dissemination of information. Spri is jointly funded by the national government and the county councils.

UNITED KINGDOM

Peter R. Hatcher was trained in health administration at the University of Toronto and has worked in Ontario in senior hospital management positions. His interest in international health issues led to an appointment with a major health development organization in eastern Africa, the African Medical Research Foundation. In 1990 the National Health Service reforms were being introduced when he moved to the United Kingdom to work as a consultant to various health provider organizations and universities. He joined the faculty of the Health Services Management Centre at The University of Birmingham as a senior fellow in 1993. His consulting and teaching activities currently involve work in Europe, North America, Africa, and Asia.

Health Services Management Centre
The University of Birmingham
40 Edgbaston Park West
Birmingham B15 2RT
United Kingdom

Telephone: 44-121-414-7050
Fax: 44-121-414-7051

UNITED STATES

Marshall W. Raffel is professor emeritus of health policy and administration at The Pennsylvania State University. He is a graduate of the University of Illinois and has a Ph.D. in political science from Victoria University of Wellington, New Zealand. He was senior lecturer in political science at Victoria University. In the United States he has worked in health care planning in government both at the state and federal levels. He has been a WHO consultant in Southeast Asia. Recently he served as a consultant on health care reform in Poland, the Czech Republic, the Slovak Republic, and Hungary. He is co-author of a leading text, *The U.S. Health System: Origins and Functions* (Albany, N.Y.: Delmar; 4th ed., 1994).

610 Glenn Road
State College, PA 16803
U.S.A.

Telephone: (814) 237-3462
Fax: (814) 231-2077
e-mail: mwr2@psu.edu

Norma K. Raffel holds an M.S. and Ph.D. from the University of Maryland. She has held appointments at the University of Maryland School of Medicine, and has taught biological sciences at Goucher College and The Pennsylvania State University. She has served as a consultant to state education agencies and universities on educational policy. More recently she was a consultant on health care reform in Poland, the Czech Republic, and Hungary. She is co-author of the text, *The U.S. Health System: Origins and Functions* (Albany, N.Y.: Delmar; 4th ed., 1994).

610 Glenn Road
State College, PA 16803
U.S.A.

Telephone: (814) 237-3462
Fax: (814) 231-2077
e-mail: mwr2@psu.edu

International Exchange Rates, July 7, 1995

	Foreign currency in U.S. $	U.S. $ in foreign currency
Canada (dollar)	.7361	1.3586
Denmark (krone)	.1844	5.4240
France (franc)	.2060	4.8535
Germany (mark)	.7181	1.3925
Japan (yen)	.01153	86.750
Netherlands (guilder)	.6414	1.5591
New Zealand (dollar)	.6777	1.4757
Sweden (krona)	.1378	7.2560
United Kingdom (pound)	1.5955	.6268

NOTE: References to ''dollars'' in the Canadian and New Zealand chapters are to dollar ($) amounts in their respective currencies unless otherwise stated. References to dollars ($) in other chapters are to U.S. dollars unless otherwise stated.

The Health System of Canada*

Peggy Leatt and A. Paul Williams

Introduction

Like health systems in other industrialized countries, the Canadian system faces tremendous challenges. In Canada there is sustained and clearly articulated public and political support for the principles of universality, accessibility, and comprehensiveness that underlie the federal-provincial health insurance plan, and that qualify it in the minds of most Canadians as among the best in the world. However, because of declining economic growth, Canadian governments are unable or unwilling to finance further increases in health costs.

At the same time an aging population, biomedical advances, declining social networks, and changing values and expectations about health and health services generate pressures for reform. In particular, there is an increasing emphasis on community-based health promotion and support services in contrast to more traditional bed-based, institutional acute care. Individuals and communities are demanding a greater role in decisions about their health and the use of health resources. There are increasing calls from governments and the health professions to move toward more cost-effective, "evidence-based" care. The health system itself is increasingly seen as only one, and perhaps not even the most important, determinant of health.

To understand the dynamics of the Canadian health system, it is important to appreciate the social and political context in which it exists. We begin by describing key characteristics of Canadian society and government, and then provide details of the health system. In a final section we discuss emerging initiatives and possibilities for health system reform.

*We acknowledge the contributions of Karen Atkin in researching and formatting this chapter.

Canadian Government and Society

Canada is a federal state comprised of ten provinces and two territories. Geographically, it is the largest land mass in the Western Hemisphere and the second largest in the world. In 1994, its population was 29 million people; as a result, its overall population density was just under three persons per square kilometer, among the lowest in the world. However, more than 75% of the population is located in urban centers within two hundred kilometers of the United States border to the south and 60% live in the two largest provinces of Ontario and Quebec. This distribution poses special problems for providing equal access to health services for all Canadians, particularly those living in remote areas of the north.

Canada was founded on a partnership of French and English colonial cultures. However, successive waves of immigration since the turn of the century, particularly from Europe, Asia, and the Caribbean, have produced a ''multicultural'' society that values ethno-cultural diversity. Such diversity is apparent in the health system in different culturally based attitudes to health and health services and in an increasing trend, especially at the community level, to tailor services for specific ethno-cultural needs (Levine, Leatt, and Poulton 1993).

Canada's political system, modeled on the traditions of British parliamentary democracy, was defined by the British North America Act of 1867. This Act established the organizational structure for the new nation and divided legislative powers between federal (national) and provincial governments. The federal government, composed of an elected House of Commons and an appointed Senate, was given jurisdiction over areas seen to be of ''national'' importance, such as railways and canals, trade and commerce, taxation, defense, international relations, currency and banking, and health services for First Nations (aboriginal) people. The provinces, also governed by elected assemblies, were given power in areas seen to be of a more ''local'' and less costly nature, including property and civil law, natural resources, education, and agriculture. They were also given authority for the ''establishment, maintenance and management of hospitals, asylums, charities, and eleemosynary institutions in and for the province, other than marine hospitals.'' Municipal governments have powers delegated to them by the provinces in areas such as public health (Hastings 1971).

Canada's federal constitution, and the division of powers it establishes, reflects the political reality of a country characterized by diverse regional interests, resources, and patterns of development. Conflicts between federal and provincial governments over issues of jurisdiction and fiscal resources have been central to Canadian politics and health policy since Confederation. Although health has been seen as a natural extension of hospitals and thus a provincial responsibility, federal control over the considerable fiscal resources required to finance health services gives it significant leverage in this policy field. Thus, the national government in Ottawa has had a substantial role in the health care field despite its lack of constitutional authority (Mahtre and Deber 1992). Federal-provincial relations, and jurisdictional conflicts, have become increasingly important as governments have taken on a greater health care role, a role that has been widely accepted and supported by the Canadian public. However, the extension of government's activities in the health field has been a source of conflict with the organized medical profession, which has seen health as a field of private and professional control.

Evolution of the Canadian Health System

Universal government health insurance was first proposed in Canada in 1919, but it was the massive social and economic dislocation of the Great Depression of the 1930s that pushed it onto the national political agenda. Prior to that, health and health services were considered to be primarily private matters, the responsibility of individuals, their families, and self-governing professions, with minimal services available, often as a last resort, through charitable, religious, and municipal organizations; governments had only limited involvement in the health field.

One of the first government health-related policy initiatives was the Workmen's Compensation plan introduced in the industrial province of Ontario in 1915. This plan provided injured workers with cash compensation for lost wages as well as necessary medical and rehabilitation services. Saskatchewan, a western agricultural province, was the first to allow its municipalities to levy taxes "covering" physician services and municipal hospitals. In Newfoundland, an Atlantic province heavily dependent on the fishing industry, a Cottage Hospital and Medical Care Plan was introduced in 1934 (prior to its becoming a province of Canada) to provide services to individuals living in isolated fishing "outports."

A federal role in the health field became an issue in 1934 as part of an attempt by the ruling Conservative government to gain support from an electorate battered by the Great Depression. Although this government had steadfastly resisted earlier pleas from the provinces and municipalities for federal involvement in the provision of relief services to the poor and unemployed, dwindling electoral support on the eve of a national election motivated the introduction of a comprehensive package of social reforms modeled along the lines of the Roosevelt "New Deal" in the United States. This package included pensions, public works, and health and unemployment insurance. However, in spite of this "deathbed conversion" to the cause of social justice, the Conservative party lost the ensuing national election, and the proposed reforms were subsequently struck down by the courts as outside of federal constitutional jurisdiction.

It was not until after World War II that health again took its place on the national political agenda. Following the war, bureaucratic energies in Ottawa, previously directed at winning the conflict in Europe, were directed at issues of social reform. The experience of the war, including the process of mobilizing an effective military effort, heightened awareness of health problems in the country including high infant and maternal mortality rates, and high rejection rates for armed forces service caused by poor health. The war also generated a public sense that government could and should act on behalf of its citizens, and that it had an obligation to prevent the catastrophic consequences to individuals of accidents, illness, and disability.

At the Dominion-Provincial Conference on Reconstruction held in 1945 the federal government again proposed a national program of comprehensive health insurance that would be cost-shared with the provinces and phased in gradually. However, disputes over cost-sharing arrangements caused these proposals to fail. The federal government subsequently moved ahead unilaterally to offer grants-in-aid to the provinces for hospital construction; the grants were within federal jurisdiction as the provinces were not obliged to accept. These grants produced an enormous expansion of hospital facilities across the country, institutionalizing the acute care, institutional focus that still characterizes the Canadian health system. These grants also marked the first acceptance of the principle of federal-provincial cost-sharing for health services, a principle that has substantially influenced all subsequent health policy.

During this period, a number of provinces took the first steps toward establishing health insurance systems. In 1947 the Social Democratic government of Saskatchewan introduced a plan, financed by general tax revenues and compulsory premiums, covering all medical services provided in hospitals (Hastings 1971). A similar plan was introduced by the province of British Columbia in 1949; Alberta introduced a plan based on existing municipal hospital plans in 1949; and with its entry into Confederation in the same year, Newfoundland brought with it its existing Cottage Hospital Plan.

These provincial developments, combined with the national government's desire to establish a hospital insurance plan covering all Canadians, led to the Hospital Insurance and Diagnostic Services Act of 1957. Under the terms of the Act, the federal government paid the provinces roughly half the costs of all inpatient services provided. The plan was widely supported by Canadians and it generated little opposition from the medical profession: although government became the major funding source for hospital services, physicians retained control over medical decision-making and their own private practices. Moreover this new funding further stimulated the growth of the hospital system, which physicians supported. By the beginning of 1961, all of the provinces had initiated hospital insurance plans (Hastings 1971).

In 1962 the Social Democratic government of Saskatchewan once again took the initiative and introduced a public health insurance plan covering all medically necessary services whether or not they were provided in a hospital setting. While politically popular, this policy was strongly opposed by the medical profession, which viewed it as an intrusion into its field of private control. Since the end of World War II, the medical profession had sponsored the establishment of a number of commercial plans that had demonstrated the financial and administrative viability of health insurance, but also demonstrated that many Canadians could not afford insurance on their own. The result was the month-long Saskatchewan physicians' strike, which resulted in physicians being ceded the right to bill patients for services above the fees insured under the provincial plan.

Following the successful Saskatchewan initiative, the federal government introduced the Medical Care Act in 1966. This Act offered provinces federal payments roughly equal to half of provincial costs if the provinces established insurance plans that met certain criteria: plans must be publicly administered and nonprofit; they must cover virtually all residents; they must cover all medically necessary services; and residents must be covered regardless of where they received services in Canada (Hastings 1971). This Act, which established Canadian Medicare, was strongly supported by the Canadian public. However, it was strongly opposed by the organized medical profession, even though, in effect, the Act equated ''health care'' with physicians' services, retained the prevailing fee-for-service system and fee schedules negotiated under the former private plans, and guaranteed physician payments for every service, producing windfall economic gains especially during the early years of the plan's operation (Taylor 1986).

Several factors contributed to changes in federal-provincial financing arrangements for Medicare. On the one hand, because of the open-ended nature of the federal funding commitment, costs were not under federal control, and spurred by what were in effect 50-cent dollars, provincial expenditures increased rapidly. On the other hand, the provinces complained of the degree of federal government control and scrutiny inherent in the shared cost-funding arrangements. A new financing system was implemented in 1977 under the Fiscal Arrangements and Established Programs Financing Act, which tied federal contributions to population and economic growth and not to provincial spending. These arrangements involved ''block'' cash transfers to the provinces, and a shift of federal ''tax room'' to provincial jurisdiction. The federal government was thus afforded increased predictability and control over its expenditures, and the provinces were afforded more flexibility in policy development (Taylor 1986). At the same time, however, this formula is seen to have begun a progressive ''balkanization'' of provincial health insurance plans, some of which began to levy higher health plan ''premiums'' on residents, while others allowed physicians to ''extra-bill'' for services above those insured under Medicare.

Continuing profession-government tensions, coupled with growing public concerns over escalating health costs and a possible erosion of access to medical care because of extra-billing, led to the establishment in 1979 of a federal Royal Commission. The Commission affirmed the Medicare principles of universality, access, and comprehensiveness, and criticized extra-billing by physicians as a threat to those principles (Hall 1980; Touhy 1988).

The outcome was the Canada Health Act of 1984, which added an additional principle to Medicare: Canadians must have "reasonable access to health services without financial or other barriers" (Taylor 1986:33). The Act provided federal financial penalties for provinces permitting hospital user fees or extra-billing; penalties would be deducted from the cash portion of federal transfers to the provinces.

Declining economic growth during the 1980s posed significant challenges for Canadian Medicare. As a response to increasing budget deficits, the federal government introduced the Expenditures Restraint Act in 1991, which capped federal cash contributions to provincial programs including Medicare; such contributions are expected to decline to nil by the year 2000 although the provinces will be able to generate revenues through added powers of taxation. However, this development undermines the federal government's ability to enforce the provisions of the Canada Health Act and to maintain a universal, comprehensive, and accessible Medicare system with uniform terms and conditions for all Canadians.

These developments have generated increasing public concern about the future of Medicare. Currently, provincial governments are considering alternative means of controlling health costs, some of which are potentially in conflict with federal conditions. These include reduction of out-of-province coverage, limits on drug benefits, possible delisting of some insured services, physician and hospital user fees, and Medicare deductibles.

There is also increasing public debate about the role of the private sector in the Canadian health system. Under Medicare, funding for health services has been public, but most services have been provided by private physicians and hospitals run by semi-autonomous boards. Questions are now being raised about whether governments should permit private entrepreneurs to provide services on a for-profit basis outside of government Medicare (e.g., in specialized clinics). Critics argue that private services will undermine Canadian Medicare and produce a "two-tier" system based on the ability to pay; proponents see privatization as a means of reducing financial pressures on the public system.

Currently, the Canadian health insurance system provides patients free choice of physicians. Patients also have free choice of hospitals though it is the norm for individuals to be admitted to a hospital to which their physician has admitting privileges. Emergency care is also easily accessible in urban centers, although there are efforts to reduce the unnecessary use of emergency rooms, and to utilize less expensive methods such as after-hours clinics or crisis hotlines. The challenge is, how to maintain this system as it continues to encounter increasing demand and declining fiscal resources.

Health Costs

In 1993, Canada spent 10.1% of their GDP (gross domestic product) on health. This places Canada second only to the United States among the OECD (Organization for Economic Cooperation and Development) countries for health expenditures.

As discussed above, Canada's health services are financed by a mix of federal and provincial dollars (which make up the major contribution) along with some local and private expenditures. From 1977 to 1993, total federal contributions to health decreased from 33.0% to 23.5% of the total, posing problems for provincial governments that provide services and pushing issues of private funding onto the political agenda. Just over seven-tenths (71.9%) of health expenditures were financed by the public sector in 1993 as compared with 76.8% in 1977. During this time period, private expenses rose from 23.2% to 28.1%.

In Canada the major categories of health expenditure are hospitals, drugs, and physician payments. Hospital expenditure accounted for 38.0% of health expenditures in 1993 (a 5.8% decrease from 1977); drug expenditures, 15.1% (an increase of 8.3%); and physicians' services, and additional 15.1%.

The largest spending increases occurred in the private sector, with the increase mainly attributable to drugs, institutional care other than acute care hospitals (e.g., long-term care facilities), and other expenditures, such as home care and out-of-country health premiums. Out-of-pocket or third-party insurance drug expenditures constituted one of the fastest growing categories in 1993, increasing by 9.1% over 1992 figures.

Although universal health insurance covers most hospital and physician services, many Canadians also have private insurance coverage through employer group plans, unions, or professional associations, which extends the range of insured services. Such services often include semiprivate or private accommodation in hospitals, rehabilitation, cosmetic procedures, dental care, private care nursing, prescription drugs, and wheelchairs. Private disability plans help to replace lost income, and can supplement income from public workers' compensation or unemployment insurance plans.

Typically, there is a deductible for extended health care and dental benefits, after which the insurer covers a fixed percentage of the costs. The Canadian Life and Health Insurance Association

Figure 1   Distribution of Health Expenditures by Sector of Finance, 1993 (%)

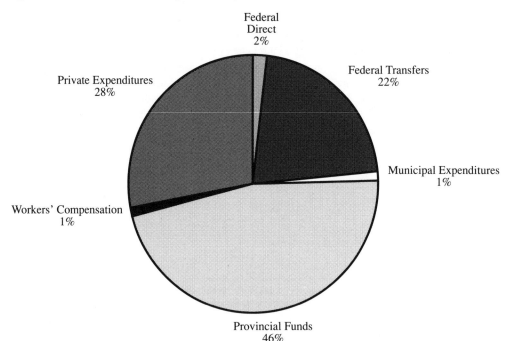

Figure 2   Distribution of Health Expenditures by Category of Expenditure, 1993 (%)

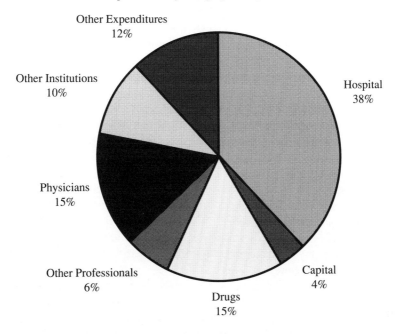

views its members as being very competitive in terms of premiums and coverage. Benefits are paid either directly to the provider, or to the insured person who has paid for the cost of care. Government regulation of the life and health insurance companies requires them to maintain adequate forms of capital and liquidity.

The Canada Health Act requires coverage of all "medically necessary services." However, such services are not well defined, so that the provinces have flexibility of interpretation. Under fiscal pressure, some provinces have moved to "de-insure" procedures and services not thought to be vital to health. For instance, Ontario introduced a list of services in 1994 that will no longer be covered under the provincial health insurance plan including routine circumcision, in vitro fertilization except where there is complete fallopian tube blockage, and removal of acne pimples. Other provinces have discontinued or changed eligibility requirements for their Children's Dental Health Plans, making the age limit lower. In cases where such services are required, patients must seek coverage from a private insurance company, or pay out-of-pocket.

Physicians

Physicians play a central role in the Canadian health system. As individuals, they act as "gatekeepers" to the system, primary providers of medical services, patient advocates, and resource allocators. Although physicians' fees accounted for just 15% of total health expenditures in Canada in 1993, physicians exerted a substantial influence over an additional 50% to 70% of health costs through hospital admissions, referrals, prescribing decisions, and orders for tests and treatments.

As organized and self-governing professionals, physicians have also had a significant influence over the development of the Canadian health system. Although provincial governments have authority to regulate health providers, they delegate control over physicians to professional ''colleges'' whose duty it is to set and enforce standards for licensure and practice in the public interest. Recently, in an effort to make the colleges more accessible and accountable to the public, provincial governments have required lay representation on governing councils and forced publication of disciplinary hearings.

Physicians also have national and provincial medical associations that represent their political interests and negotiate insured fee schedules with provincial health ministries. For instance, the nationally based Canadian Medical Association views its role as physician (as opposed to patient) advocate, health policy advocate, catalyst for maintaining high standards of medical training and practice, and ethical and legal adviser to the profession. Historically, these associations have actively defended professional interests and resisted government policies perceived to limit economic and clinical freedom, sometimes provoking overt profession-government conflict. The monthlong physicians' strike in Saskatchewan following the introduction of that province's health insurance plan in 1962, and a twenty-five-day strike by physicians in Ontario in 1986 following the introduction of legislation forcing physicians to end the practice of extra-billing above insured fee schedules, are the most dramatic examples of such conflict.

More recently, physicians have sought to influence policy through forms of political accommodation with government. In Ontario, an important example of such accommodation is the Joint Management Committee on Physician Services, a body with equal representation from the Ontario Medical Association (OMA) and the Ministry of Health. Except for hospitals, which also enjoy co-representation with government on a parallel committee considering the future of hospital services, no other health profession or interest has such direct and institutionalized access to government.

Although physicians have historically enjoyed considerable economic and clinical freedom in Canada, newer physicians are entering practice in the context of what has been seen as a general decline in the historical status and dominance of the medical profession in Canada as in other industrialized countries. Such a decline is seen to involve an attenuation of professional control over the conditions and content of medical work, including the work of other health professions, as well as control over broader issues of how health care is organized and funded (Coburn, Torrance, and Kaufert 1983). While the medical profession's claims to self-governance and self-accountability have been justified historically on the basis of mastery of the curative technology of scientific medicine, such claims have been increasingly challenged by governments and by the public (Evans 1987).

Indeed, the status of scientific medicine has itself been challenged by a series of reports in Canada and internationally that have suggested that the formal health system, including physicians' services, constitutes only one factor, and perhaps not even the most important factor, in achieving health (Evans 1987; Lalonde 1974). Medical dominance has also been challenged by the burgeoning professionalization and legitimation by governments of new health professions, including midwifery in Ontario; by the increasing primary care roles of other health professionals, such as nurse practitioners; and by the progressive recourse of provincial governments to cost-controlling measures including limited increases to insured fee schedules, caps on physicians' incomes, and restrictions on medical school enrollments.

Partly as a response to these challenges, Canadian physicians have begun to broaden their managerial roles in the health system. Physicians are now routinely involved in hospitalwide issues such as strategic planning, budgeting, and quality improvement, in addition to their clinical responsibilities. More frequently, physicians are being appointed to hospital boards of trustees and senior management committees (Leatt 1994).

Physicians have also taken a lead in developing practice guidelines to ensure that clinical decisions are based on the best available scientific evidence. Organizations such as the Canadian Institute for Health Information (CIHI), which collects Canada-wide data, and the Institute for Clinical Evaluative Sciences (ICES) are actively studying ways of improving physicians' decisions. For instance, ICES has conducted research into hospital specific surgical rates as a means of establishing clinical benchmarks.

However, there is still considerable controversy within the profession about the extent to which individual physicians should be constrained in their decision-making; to this point practice guidelines are voluntary. Only in a relatively small number of cases are physicians' practices subject to review or audit by the professional colleges. Indeed, although there is a general expectation that physicians will engage in continuing medical education as a means of assuring the highest quality of care possible, there are currently no requirements for recertification. The recently proclaimed Regulated Health Professions Act (RHPA) in Ontario requires that professional colleges must have quality assurance programs, as well as standards for continuing professional education, but the Act does not specify what such programs and standards should entail.

The general prerequisites for entering medical school are two years of undergraduate study combined with successful completion of the Medical College Admission Test (MCAT). The medical school curriculum in Canada consists of four years in a university setting, during which there is clinical experience, followed by two years of postgraduate training. Only after these two years, and the Medical Council of Canada Qualifying Examinations have been passed, can an individual obtain a license to practice through the provincial college. For specialty training the duration of this period is variable. Training for general surgery, for example, lasts from five to seven years. As with any other course of study, students are able to obtain loans from federal and provincial governments.

A trend toward forms of medical group practice may facilitate greater peer review and quality assurance apart from government or professional regulation. Historically, traditional solo practice has been the dominant form of practice organization in Canada, reflecting a professional culture that emphasizes the autonomy and discretion of the individual physician. However, growing numbers of physicians, particularly younger general practitioners and women, are now working in forms of collaborative practice involving shared patient care and formal financial arrangements (Vayda 1994). In addition to providing greater opportunities for workload management, group practices also foster increased peer interaction and review.

However, the structure of Canadian Medicare itself does not support experimentation with different forms of practice organization of the type seen in the Health Maintenance Organization movement in the United States or the polyclinics in other countries. Under Medicare, fee-for-service remains the dominant method of physician payment in Canada; most physicians are paid on what amounts to a piecework basis for the services they provide. Alternatives such as salaries or fixed per capita payments to physicians for patients registered under their care (capitation) have not been widely tried or accepted in most provinces. This reflects both resistance on the part of physicians who wish to retain the economic discretion that fee-for-service provides, and because of the Canadian tradition of free choice of providers by patients, which would be restricted under payment methods like capitation (Vayda 1994).

There are a number of concerns about the persistence of fee-for-service medicine. First, it is essentially an open-ended payment system; physicians determine the mix and volume of services provided and thus their incomes. Recently, some restrictions have been put in place by provincial health insurance plans. For instance, some provinces have placed "caps" on individual physicians' incomes as income thresholds are reached, but these thresholds tend to be high (e.g., $400,000 per year in Ontario). Second, fee-for-service has been seen to generate a tendency on the part of physicians to maximize service volume and to bill for more expensive services. Since 1984 when the federal government banned the practice of "extra-billing" by physicians above Medicare insured fee schedules, services per physician increased at significantly higher rates than the rate of population growth. While some provinces responded by capping total annual expenditures for physicians' services, there is evidence that some physicians have simply begun to bill more aggressively to maintain their incomes. Third, current fee-for-service schedules tend to reward "curative" services at a higher rate than "preventive" services such as counseling, thus supporting a tendency in the health system as a whole toward "illness" as opposed to "wellness." Finally, fee-for-service produces wide variations in physician remuneration by specialty and causes inequities among physicians in terms of average lifetime earnings.

On the whole, however, physicians enjoy relatively high incomes, higher than those of other professionals, and from three to five times as high as those of average workers. For instance, in 1992 the average before-tax income for self-employed physicians was $133,000, compared to $109,000 for dentists, $96,000 for lawyers, $67,000 for self-employed accountants and $38,000 for self-employed engineers. The average salary for all workers was about $25,000.

A related issue concerns the size and distribution of the physician population. At the time of the introduction of Canadian Medicare in the 1960s, planners predicted an undersupply of physicians. However, growth in the number of physicians in Canada has actually exceeded population growth since that time by a factor of about three or four, and has only recently begun to plateau, in part because of provincial policies limiting the number of students in Canadian medical schools. Nevertheless, this historic growth did little to correct a geographic maldistribution of physicians throughout the country; most newly graduated physicians still establish practice in urban areas, and Canadians living outside of these areas may experience problems gaining access to specialized care. Part of the problem is that there is little consensus around what would constitute an optimal physician to population ratio; this reflects difficulty defining the underlying concepts of "need," "demand," and "productivity." Need is seen to be a function of the epidemiology of illnesses and the sociodemographic characteristics of the population; demand is related to socioeconomic factors

Table A   Population and Population per Active Physician in 1992 by Province

Province	Population (in thousands)	GP's and Family	Certified Specialists	All *excluding* Interns and Residents	All *including* Interns and Residents
Newfoundland	576.6	1,024	1,753	646	526
Prince Edward Island	131.4	1,251	1,932	760	760
Nova Scotia	909.1	938	1,151	517	425
New Brunswick	729.9	1,204	1,746	713	713
Quebec	6,968.8	966	952	479	419
Ontario	10,212.7	965	1,032	499	431
Manitoba	1,099.7	1,048	1,162	551	462
Saskatchewan	992.0	1,063	1,771	664	574
Alberta	2,584.1	1,048	1,308	582	499
British Columbia	3,356.8	861	1,099	483	447
Yukon	29.0	853	7,250	763	763
Northwest Territories	56.8	1,136	5,164	931	931
Canada	27,647.0	971	1,090	514	448

SOURCE: *Statistics Canada, Quarterly Demographic Statistics,* vol. 3, no. 4, (April 1993): cat. no. 91-002.

such as standard of living, education, access to medical services, and society's willingness to medicalize social problems; finally, productivity has been measured as a function of professional workloads and technology often without considering the quality or appropriateness of the care provided (El-Geubaly, Beausejour, Woodside, et al. 1991). Such issues make it difficult to specify precisely how many physicians in different specialties should be working in given geographic areas (Barer and Stoddart 1992).

An additional difficulty is that attempts by provinces to address the distribution problem have had only limited success, largely because, up until now under Canadian Medicare, physicians have been guaranteed payments regardless of where they provided their services. It has been assumed that competition with other physicians, not over pricing, but over access to patient pools, would itself guarantee a reasonable distribution of physician human resources, but this has not been the case. Some provinces have provided incentive payments to physicians locating outside of population centers. Others have tried to penalize physicians establishing in "overdoctored" areas or have refused to issue billing numbers to foreign graduates for certain specialties (e.g., obstetrics). Other provinces have restricted billing numbers to underserviced areas. Foreign medical graduates have also been encouraged to open practices in rural underserviced areas.

In a highly publicized and influential report, Barer and Stoddart (1992) suggested a number of policy options aimed at equalizing the distribution of physicians in urban (often overserviced) and rural (often underserviced) areas. These include compulsory rural area rotations and development of new residency training programs designed to prepare generalist specialists to serve as rural consultants. However, the organized medical profession has been critical of such options because of a perceived threat to physician choice of where to establish practice.

Patterns of movement in and out of the profession also impact on physician supply and distribution. Watanabe and Tholl (1986) suggest that 60% to 65% of physicians retiring in the next twenty years will be specialists, and 35% to 40% will be general/family practitioners (note that in Canada general practitioners account for roughly half of all physicians). General surgeons, obstetricians and gynecologists, laboratory medicine specialists, and internists now tend to be older than other physicians and will likely experience the highest rates of attrition due to aging. This is of particular concern in provinces such as British Columbia and Prince Edward Island, which currently have a large proportion of semiretired physicians in active practice. The fact that more women are entering medicine is also a consideration for physician supply and distribution since women are more likely to choose general/family practice over the specialties and to locate in urban areas (Williams, Domnick Pierre, and Vayda 1993). This may pose problems of access to certain specialties outside of major urban areas, and may also begin to shift the historical generalist/specialist ratio above the current 50%.

In summary, in spite of increasing challenges to its autonomy and status, medicine in Canada remains a powerful and prestigious profession. Reflecting this, the results of a recent international physicians' survey revealed that 65% of the Canadian physicians surveyed, compared to 54% of those in the United States, agreed that "it is satisfying practising under the health-care system in this country." Canadian physicians were also somewhat less likely to agree that "government intervention seriously interferes with the way I practise" (73% in Canada vs. 79% in the United States) although the role of government in the health field is much more extensive in Canada, or to support "further development" of the "private health-care system" (68% in Canada vs. 81% in the United States) although the private system is much more extensive in the United States. Canadian physicians were also more willing to accept restrictions on their economic discretion: 47% of Canadian physicians, compared to 22% of those surveyed in the United States, agreed that "physicians should be subjected to revenue limits." However, Canadians were no less likely than their

U.S. counterparts to agree that "operating as a health-care professional is financially satisfying" (79% vs. 78%).

Hospitals

In most circumstances, patients are admitted to hospital by a practitioner who has admitting privileges. Typically admissions are made by physicians who are general practitioners or specialists, or by dentists for oral procedures done under anesthetic. Arrangements are made with another physician in cases where a patient's own physician does not have privileges. Until recently, most physicians who requested them were granted privileges in hospitals near their private practices and some had multiple hospital privileges. Now, because of perceptions of an oversupply of physicians in urban areas, and pressures to control hospital beds, some physicians, particularly general practitioners, are experiencing delays in obtaining the right to admit.

In Ontario, recent changes to the Public Hospitals Act (which governs the operation of public hospitals) as well as to the Regulated Health Professions Act (which governs the self-regulating professions) have allowed licensed midwives to be granted hospital admission privileges. Under the Act, the Medical Advisory Committee (MAC) of a hospital must grant privileges to two midwives, since midwives are required to work in pairs.

The majority of Canada's hospitals are public, not-for-profit institutions. They are classified as lay, religious, municipal, provincial, and federal as an indication of ownership. There are only a few for-profit facilities providing specialty services not insured under Medicare. Most public hospitals are financed through global budgets negotiated with provincial governments, or the federal government in the case of hospitals in the Territories. In addition, hospitals derive revenues from private insurance companies and from individuals; in cases where preferred (private or semiprivate) accommodation is utilized, noninsured services are used, or a noninsured party makes use of the hospital's services. However, hospitals are not permitted to charge "user fees" for services covered under Medicare.

To control costs, and in some cases to generate additional funds, Canadian hospitals have begun to engage in a variety of nontraditional arrangements and activities. These include contracting with other facilities to provide clinical or diagnostic services, providing noninsured services such as fitness programs or smoking cessation programs, providing retail services, and contracting hospital management to private companies (Pink, Deber, Lavoie, and Aserlind 1991). In addition, most hospitals in Ontario, and a smaller number in other provinces, have charitable foundations which conduct fund-raising activities in the community (Pink and Leatt 1991).

Most Canadian hospitals use Case Mix Groups (CMGs) and Resource Intensity Weights (RIWs). CMGs group patients according to their diagnosis, whereas RIWs estimate the relative resources used by patient type. However, at present there is little direct relationship between these measures and hospital funding, except in the provinces of Ontario and Alberta where they are taken into account in negotiations with governments. A major concern about the use of RIWs in Canadian hospitals is that the measures now in use have been imported from the United States; because of differences in medical practice, use of technology, philosophy of care, funding incentives, relative labor mix, relative costs, inflation since 1985, and population demographics, however, they are not seen to be wholly applicable to Canada. CMGs also have some limitations, among them the fact that cases within a given CMG might have a similar length of stay but vary in terms of severity of illness, complications, therapies, drugs, hospital characteristics, physician training and specialization, and other factors. Increasing financial pressures are stimulating further development and use of measures of these types as a means of improving hospital management and controlling costs (Pink and Bolley 1994).

Hospitals have been and for the most part remain semi-autonomous and self-governing institutions. All Canadian hospitals have boards of trustees with broad policy and management authority. Boards have often tended, in the past, to be fairly closed, with members appointed by boards themselves. This has posed significant challenges to government health policy-makers, as individual hospitals have made important decisions about staffing, service mix, and technology without considering the actions or resources of other health providers in their areas.

However, policy reforms in a number of the provinces are aimed at increasing community representation on hospital boards and ensuring that boards plan within the context of regional policy frameworks. In Ontario, for instance, hospitals must submit operating plans to District Health Councils, which then advise government on whether they should be granted approval. In other provinces, governments will attempt to steer hospital decision-making by limiting funds available for acquiring new technologies. In an attempt to ensure more regional integration of hospital planning, the province of New Brunswick recently abolished the boards of fifty-one local hospitals and replaced them with eight regional boards responsible for planning hospital services for all hospitals in their geographic area.

To this point, however, decisions about technology acquisitions typically have been made by committees, with medical and nursing staff playing an advisory role, and administrators and the boards having final internal decision-making authority. Information concerning the true impact of a given technology has been scanty. In a survey of Canadian hospitals, it seemed more the exception than the rule that data was collected on the costs of technology: that is, additional staff, effects on operating costs, need for staff training, need for renovations, or potential savings (Deber, Wiktorowicz, and Leatt 1994).

There has been an increase in the level of equipment purchases in Canadian hospitals, though compared to their United States counterparts, numbers are small. For each of the technologies listed in Table B, except for radiation therapy, the number of units in the United States exceeds that in Canada by several orders of magnitude. Hospitals typically have a mix of ward (four to eight beds), semiprivate (two beds), and private (single bed) accommodation. Patients requiring semiprivate or private accommodation in Canadian hospitals are required to pay a charge above Medicare-insured rates either through private insurance or out-of-pocket. Exceptions can be made

Table B   Medical Technology Use Comparisons

	Canada (1991–92)		United States (1991)	
Medical Technology	Number of Hospitals	Units per Million Population	Number of Hospitals	Units per Million Population
Cardiac catheterization	49	1.84	1,457	5.80
Computer tomography scanner	200	7.50	3,633	14.42
Lithotripsy	11	0.41	370	1.47
Magnetic resonance imaging	32	1.20	1,036	4.11
Radiation therapy	127	4.79	969	3.84
Open-heart surgery	33	1.24	867	3.44
Organ transplantation	28	1.08	555	2.20

SOURCE: *Health Progress* (January–February 1994).

if the patient's medical condition warrants it and hospitals may allow preferred accommodation on compassionate grounds.

All hospitals do not have emergency rooms, especially in areas where there is a high concentration of facilities, and where individuals can be assured of easy access to a nearby facility. Emergency rooms are staffed by a combination of junior doctors (or doctors in training) and emergency medicine specialists. There are also designated regional trauma centers where the more severe cases are taken. Schwartz (1993) suggests that there are two levels of trauma centers. There are those that provide definitive trauma care. Such units usually have a director and provide a full range of specialty services including neurosurgery and orthopedics. Other centers resuscitate and refer or treat only simple cases. Emergency medicine, anesthesia, and general surgery are generally seen as the minimal services required on a 24-hour basis to cover resuscitation. Patients needing critical care are normally admitted to a multidisciplinary critical care unit.

Provincial governments license hospitals, but it is the Canadian Council on Health Services Accreditation that ensures hospital standards (CCHSA, formerly CCHFA, Canadian Council on Health Facilities Accreditation). Accreditation is a voluntary process and is not required for continued facility operation. It is seen in the hospital sector, however, as a central element of quality improvement (Ontario CQI Network 1995). The lengthiest accreditation currently offered is four years.

The process of accreditation in Canada is similar to that used by the U.S. Joint Commission on Accreditation of Healthcare Organizations. The CCHSA requires a facility to be licensed and to have been in operation for at least a year prior to an accreditation survey. The accreditation process involves a detailed documentation of the hospital's operations. First, the facility undergoes a self-evaluation and reports to the designated CCHSA surveyors. An on-site survey and interview is then carried out to determine the level of compliance with CCHSA standards. The facility's governing body and management services are examined as well as service/program areas. The CCHSA has stated its commitment to quality improvement in health care and has defined quality as doing the right thing, doing it well, and satisfying the customer. Concepts of Continuous Quality Improvement (CQI) are incorporated into the accreditation standards, including improving patient or resident care, better identifying and meeting customer needs, and improving productivity (Baker, Barnsley, and Murray 1993).

There has been a shift toward a more ''customer-oriented'' approach to service delivery in the hospitals involving a greater emphasis on public relations and some selective marketing of the hospital's services to the target community. In order to facilitate these processes hospitals are engaging in more information gathering and data collection so that they can be aware of their external environment (Fried, Worthington, Leatt, and Gelmon 1990). Many hospitals have also begun community outreach programs designed to provide services outside of the institutional setting, and to educate the public about available services.

Hospitals and physicians' organizations have expressed concern that a failure to continue to increase hospital budgets will result in unacceptably long waits for surgery. A recent study (Jacobs and Hart 1990) of three selected procedures (hip replacement, heart surgery, and cholecystectomy) revealed that waiting times for these procedures were considered unacceptable by clinical administrators. There was also considerable variation in waiting times between different procedures, different regions, and within regions. Such differences were thought to stem from inadequate planning and an unequal distribution of patient loads among surgeons. However, in virtually all cases, Canadians who need emergency or urgent care receive it in a timely fashion; it is extremely uncommon for patients on surgical waiting lists to die. Moreover, research has shown that physicians' own evaluations of the urgency of need for surgery significantly affects placement on waiting lists; patients in the most urgent need are given priority. Coyte et al. (1994) studied waiting times for knee replacement surgery and found that even though Canadian waiting times were longer, averaging 13.5 weeks in Canada versus 4.5 weeks in the United States, the mean level of acceptability of waiting time for knee replacement surgery by patients was 95.0% in the United States and 85.1% in Canada. Research into satisfaction with waiting times for general surgery revealed that 85.3% of U.S. respondents compared to 83.5% of Ontario respondents were "very or somewhat satisfied."

Dentists, Nurses, and Other Health Practitioners

Individuals who have completed at least two years of university and have taken the Dental Aptitude Test administered by the Canadian Dental Association may apply for admission to a program leading to Doctor of Dental Surgery (DDS). Upon completion of all degree requirements, students take the National Dental Examining Board of Canada's examination and, if successful, are awarded a certificate. In order to practice in a given province, dentists must also comply with regulations set out by the province's professional college. In Ontario, for example, dentists must complete a course in ethics and jurisprudence.

As indicated earlier, dentists' incomes are higher than those of any other profession in Canada with the exception of medicine. In most provinces dentists in private practice are paid on a fee-for-service basis according to a schedule established by the dental association; public health dentists are primarily salaried. Dental care is not covered by the provincial health insurance plans, except for surgical procedures performed in hospitals under anesthetic. The majority of patients pay out-of-pocket for their dental care or have coverage through private third-party insurers, often as an employment benefit. However, a number of provinces do provide in-school dental programs including education and preventive checkups.

Canadian nurses are trained in universities, community colleges, and in other institutions such as hospitals. University-trained nurses have a four-year degree, with a broad liberal education in the first two years, and clinical work concentrated in the last two years of study. Basic admission requirements to baccalaureate programs are the same as for any other Canadian university program: high school graduation or the equivalent. By contrast, diploma-prepared nurses typically have two to three years (six semesters) of training, with about forty-five weeks of clinical experience; their curriculum also includes general education and nursing science. Registered Nursing Assistants (or Registered Practical Nurses) are trained in one-year certificate programs offers by community colleges, hospitals, and secondary or regional schools predominantly in Quebec and Ontario. RNA/RPNs are typically employed in home care or long-term care settings (Levine et al. 1993).

There are a variety of other nursing programs in existence, some of which simply allow for a specialization at the certificate or diploma level, for example, in operating room nursing, or gerontological nursing. Some of these programs are offered through community colleges and others are offered at the university level (Levine et al. 1993).

Canadian nursing is attempting to enhance its professional scope and prestige. In 1982 the Canadian Nurses Association declared that by the year 2000, all nurses entering practice must be "baccalaureate prepared"; that is, they must have a university degree (Levine et al. 1993). This reflects a professional vision for the future that sees the role of nursing moving from a narrow technical skills base to take on greater responsibilities for the provision and management of primary care. As a result there has been an increase in degree program enrollment as well as an increase in the number of diploma nurses enrolling in post-RN degree programs.

There has also been an expansion of graduate nursing education. Eleven Canadian universities offer master's level training in nursing or nursing science. The programs are two years in length and provide the opportunity for specialization in areas such as maternal-child health, mental health, and community health. Typically, master's trained nurses assume positions as teachers, clinical nurse specialists, or managers. In addition, doctoral degrees are now offered at two Canadian universities (Toronto and Alberta) and are being considered by others. Nurses holding doctorates are more likely to be employed in universities or health agencies (Levine et al. 1993).

Nursing education has changed dramatically since the late 1980s by seeking to integrate a broader understanding of social-environmental factors influencing health and the changing role of the nurse as care provider, patient advocate, and resource for community development. Nurses are encouraged to acknowledge caring as a core value of this profession, and to encourage the development of critical thinking skills.

Like physicians and dentists, nurses must take registration examinations set by the Canadian Nurses Association. If successful, they can then become registered with the provincial College of Nurses (Levine et al. 1993). The vast majority of Canadian nurses are employees of health care organizations; some individuals practice as private consultants and health advisors. Public health nurses (PHNs) have been employed in health units in Canada since the 1930s to provide nursing service for all people living in defined geographic areas. Average incomes have risen steadily in recent years due, in part, to a high degree of unionization in Canadian hospitals.

The scope of practice for nursing is set out in provincial legislation. In Ontario, for example, the governing legislation is the Regulated Health Professions Act (RHPA). The Nursing Act, which is governed by the overarching legislation (RHPA), states that nursing involves the promotion of health, assessment and provision of care and treatment by supportive, preventive, therapeutic, palliative, and rehabilitative means in order to maintain optimal function. However, in most cases, nurses still require an order from a physician before they can carry out "controlled" medical acts, including those which involve blood.

Nurse practitioners (NPs) are beginning to play a more important role in the Canadian health system. NPs receive specialized training beyond the baccalaureate level in a university setting. To become a nurse practitioner in the province of Ontario, baccalaureate-trained nurses will require an additional twelve months of training, whereas diploma nurses will require an additional twenty-four months. Nurse practitioners will work in primary care settings, have their own caseloads, and admit or discharge clients from their care. They will be licensed to conduct diagnosis, to prescribe, and to perform certain invasive procedures. Increasing reliance on nurse practitioners has been strongly criticized by provincial medical associations, which argue that nurses should perform such tasks only under physician supervision. However, this fails to recognize that especially in remote areas, and in provinces like Newfoundland, nurse practitioners have routinely and competently performed such tasks for decades.

In this context there has been a growing recognition of the "multidisciplinary team" model, whereby different practitioners including physicians are seen to play an important role in providing care to patients. Potential members of this team include physiotherapists, occupational therapists, speech pathologists, dietitians, social workers, audiologists, and respiratory therapists. As consumers become more educated about health care and aware of the services available to them, other practitioners who traditionally did not fit into the medical model of care are also being utilized, including chiropractors, naturopaths, and homeopaths. It should be recognized, however, that all of these professions are not regulated or self-governing, and their services are not all covered by provincial health insurance plans.

Midwives trained in other countries can practice and have been recognized in different provinces. Alternately, individuals with no nursing background are trained as midwives. For instance, Ontario has recently begun to train midwives for direct entry into the occupation and, in December 1993, midwives in Ontario became a self-regulating profession. Midwifery's scope of practice includes hospital admission, management of delivery, and prescribing. However, midwives must work in pairs to ensure 24-hour coverage for their patients.

Nursing Homes, Care Homes, Community Ambulatory Care Programs, Mental Health Facilities, and Other Community Health Agencies

As Canada's population ages there is an increased demand for long-term care services. Such demands are compounded by a shift in social values from "warehousing" those who require support, including seniors and persons with disabilities, to enhancing functional independence and quality of life. It is compounded also by a decline of social networks, by women's changing role in the family and by their increased participation in the paid labor force, by a shift in emphasis from institutional to community-based service provision, and by the challenge of responding to the diverse needs of Canada's ethno-cultural communities.

In general, the aim in the provision of long-term care services in Canada is to provide individuals with as much autonomy as possible and to provide preventive services that enable them to stay in their homes.

In most provinces, there has been no long-term care "system" per se. Instead, there have been different mixes of informal and formal services available on different terms and conditions to those who have actively sought them. Informal services were provided for the most part by daughters, relatives, friends, and neighbors. Formal services included community-based programs, such as older adult centers, friendly visiting, meals-on-wheels, transportation, attendant outreach, home-making, and nursing home care, as well as services provided in institutional settings such as homes for the aged, nursing homes, and chronic care hospitals (see Table 9).

Currently there are wide provincial and regional variations in programs and services offered. In large urban areas like Toronto, for instance, community services available in one municipality may not be available across the road in another municipality. Funding is also complex: a mix of federal, provincial, and municipal money; charitable donations; and fee-for-service. Some services are completely free to consumers, including all medical services covered under Medicare; some require co-payments or user charges such as meals-on-wheels and nursing home care; and other services like transportation are paid for by the individual client.

Nursing homes and homes for the aged are primarily for the frail elderly who are no longer able to function independently. Clients are usually transferred from an acute care hospital, or are referred from the community by a family physician. Family physicians and geriatricians make visits to nursing homes and homes for the aged but care is generally provided by a multidisciplinary team often including physiotherapists, occupational therapists, social workers, nurses, and doctors. The ownership and operation of nursing homes and homes for the aged is varied, although the former tend to be private, for-profit, run by large corporations such as Extendicare, with the latter run mostly by municipalities and charitable organizations on a nonprofit basis.

Funding of institutional care also varies considerably. In Alberta and Ontario, for example, nursing care in institutions is provincially funded according to a patient classification system; an additional sum is allocated for programs such as recreation and rehabilitation; finally, there is a fixed per diem for accommodation, with clients generally asked for co-payments. In Nova Scotia nursing homes are municipally funded, although there is a 66.6% provincial reimbursement to the municipality in the cases where residents have no assets; residents with means exceeding the municipally approved amount pay the full cost.

A wide range of community services is available to seniors. These include meals on wheels, friendly visiting, respite care, homemaker services, visiting nurses, attendant care, and psychogeriatric outreach. Psychogeriatric outreach provides an assessment function, homemakers provide in-home non-nursing help to clients, and respite care allows family caregivers to have a break from the daily care routine. The delivery mechanism and funding for these programs varies by province, ranging from complete provincial plan coverage to out-of-pocket payments.

Canadian acute care hospitals have experienced problems in discharging elderly patients who require continuing support. Delays occur in about 14 to 24% of cases. Behavioral problems associated with dementia tend to increase the risk of delay in discharge. Utilizing a multidisciplinary team including a social worker facilitates better discharge planning.

As a response to fiscal constraint and consumer demands to make services more appropriate and uniform, several provinces have undertaken long-term care reform. In Saskatchewan, for instance, reform is motivated by a desire to decrease reliance on institutionalization, and the loss of autonomy that individuals experience as a result, by establishing a coherent network of community services designed to support individuals in their own social settings. Planned changes include a single point of entry to the system, the integration of community and institutional care budgets to ensure greater integration and coordination of services, case management based on the needs of the individual, and the establishment of expanded community housing options.

In Ontario, a focus of reform is the Multiple Service Agency (MSA), dubbed ''Neighbors'' by consumer groups to reflect a community orientation. In the final planning stages at the time of this writing, MSAs will consolidate the functions of a constellation of existing community-based service organizations; institutionalization will be treated as a last resort for individuals who have exhausted the possibilities of care in the community. MSAs will receive fixed budgets from the provincial government to provide a mandatory ''basket'' of services to all individuals in their geographic catchment areas and will be governed by community boards.

Mental health services in Canada are also quite varied. As is the case in the United States, Canada saw a large-scale deinstitutionalization of its mental health patients in the 1960s. The 1961 report of the Canadian Mental Health Association, and the 1964 report of the Royal Commission on Mental Health Services laid the groundwork for the deinstitutionalization process, which was meant to give patients greater autonomy and control over their lives. Mental hospitals decreased their beds whereas the capacity of psychiatric units in general hospitals was increased considerably. Community mental health programs were also established, among them case-managed, rehabilitation, housing, and other support services. However, available community support services have proved to be inadequate, contributing to high readmission rates to institutions. The initial housing models tended to be ''custodial'' in their focus with little rehabilitation; there were too few of them to meet demand. Newer, alternative housing models have developed, including halfway homes, group homes, co-ops, and supportive housing, which emphasize personal autonomy and responsibility (Trainor, Morrell-Bellai, Ballantyne, and Boydell 1993).

There have been various discussions around reform of provincial mental health systems paralleling long-term reform initiatives. In Ontario, for example, the provincial government has initiated a reform process involving consumer-survivors (those who have been a part of the formal mental health system) as participants in policy-making. Among the goals of the reform are decreased fragmentation of services and development of a system that supports the whole individual as opposed simply to treating illness. Some services will be planned and coordinated provincially, whereas others will be planned and delivered regionally or locally.

In addition to long-term care and mental health services, there are other important community-based health services and programs in most Canadian provinces. Community Health Centres (CHCs) in Ontario and local community service centres (CLSCs) in the province of Quebec, utilize multidisciplinary teams to provide a range of medical, dental, social, and nursing services. These agencies are funded by provincial governments through set yearly global budgets and are governed by voluntary community boards. In Quebec, CLSCs constitute the entry point into the health system.

Health Service Organizations (HSOs) and Comprehensive Health Organizations (CHOs) are modeled along the lines of Health Maintenance Organizations (HMOs) in the U.S. Generally speaking, they constitute forms of group practice that offer a range of health services provided by teams of salaried health and social services practitioners as well as in-patient hospital care, home care, and other support services. Funding is on a fixed per capita rate for each enrolled patient; patients are therefore committed to using the organization for all their health needs.

Public Health

Public health in Canada had its origins in the early nineteenth century when Medical Officers of Health (MOHs or MHOs) were appointed by local governments to establish public health services. Initially, the focus was on control of water and food-borne infections; later, with improved technology, on airborne infections. In the 1930s the role of public health departments began to change as the techniques of isolation, vaccination, inoculation, and drug therapies decreased infections. Greater emphasis was placed on maternal and child health, and environmental services.

Public health departments typically offer a wide range of services and programs including traditional services like nutrition and health education; more recently, they have established services like breast screening, family violence counseling, and counseling and support for immigrants, refugees, and racial minority women. Some health units also provide mental health services and services for the elderly and disabled. More specialized services are usually found in urban health units.

Although public health departments receive their mandate from provincial Public Health Acts or regulations, the extent of service provided is dependent upon funding, which varies within and between provinces. In some provinces, like Ontario, funding for public health departments comes from both provincial and municipal governments. For example, in Metropolitan Toronto, 40% of funding comes from the province, while 60% is provided by the municipality; in other areas of the province, the ratio is reversed. In other provinces like Alberta, the province provides 100% of the funding.

In addition to local public health departments, provincial governments have their own departments responsible for public health, with provincial health units placed on a geographical basis. Provincial health units are semi-autonomous, mandated to establish links with hospitals, doctors, universities, and other health agencies. Except for the province of Quebec, these units also have their own dedicated staff. Quebec has a director of public health for each of its Regional Boards of Health and Social Services who deals with population health needs, public health emergencies, and disease control, as well as health promotion and disease prevention.

The Lalonde Report (1974), authored by the then federal minister of health, was a catalyst for the development of the more holistic model of health promotion that now characterizes public health in Canada. Lalonde pointed out that future improvements in Canadians' health were less likely to emerge from the formal health care system, including physician and hospital services, than from changes in behavioral and socioenvironmental factors affecting health. The report was the first of a number of reports and commissions in Canada that looked beyond the curative health system (the "illness" system) to the determinants of health (Evans 1987). It also stimulated the emergence of the concept of healthy public policy, which is future-oriented, holistic, and concerned with how government actions not limited to the health field influence the creation of a healthy society. Such policies include housing, income support, social welfare, and education, all of which impact on the ability of the individuals to influence their own lives, and the lives of their communities.

Although public health has not entirely embraced the "healthy public policy" movement, there have been increased health promotion activities that are part and parcel of this concept. The Ottawa Charter for Health Promotion, which was the outcome of the 1986 International Conference on Health Promotion, gave a boost to health promotion initiatives already under way in Canada. Recent public health initiatives have been in the areas of substance abuse, including tobacco addiction, the health of disadvantaged people, and the adverse health effects of environmental pollution. Public health departments have also taken a lead role in promoting the concepts of "community development" and "empowerment," giving communities the knowledge and expert resources needed for communities themselves to plan and implement programs and services that meet their needs.

This shift from conventional modes of service delivery to community development has implications for professional roles. British Columbia nurses, for instance, have embraced the concept of primary health care and a shift from the role of provider to the role of educator, advocate, and community resource. In a recent survey, they supported a reallocation of health dollars toward prevention, better integration of public health services with the community, and research on the qualitative aspects of health and nursing outcomes.

Conclusion

What Canadians refer to as "Medicare" is in fact a series of provincial insurance plans, cost-shared with the federal government under the terms of the Canada Health Act, which requires that all Canadians must have "reasonable access," without direct charges, to all hospital and medical services deemed "medically necessary." These programs developed incrementally, first to cover hospital-based services, and then physician care, in the process embedding an emphasis on institutional acute care medical services. However, like health systems in other industrialized countries, Canada's is experiencing significant challenges due to economic constraints, demographic change, and increasingly broad definitions of health and health care. As the recognition has grown that the most appropriate services to promote health are not always those in the "medical care system," there has been growing emphasis on reform and restructuring of the Canadian system.

In a nation where powers are balanced between federal and provincial governments, and in which health has been placed clearly under provincial jurisdiction, political questions over who will pay for health services have become more pressing, opening up public debate about the future of Medicare, and generating opportunities for reform. In spite of the challenges cited above, there remains widespread public and political support in Canada for maintaining and strengthening a system that continues to provide universal access to necessary medical services for all Canadians who need them regardless of their economic means (Rachlis and Kushner 1994).

As noted earlier, directions and possibilities for reform of Canadian Medicare have been outlined by a series of royal commissions and reports conducted over the past decade (Mahtre and Deber 1992). Common themes have included broadening the definition of health underlying the system; shifting emphasis from curing illness to health promotion; focusing on community-based as opposed to institutional care; improving human resources planning; increasing efficiency in system management; and increasing funding for health services research (Mahtre and Deber 1992).

A key direction for reform at the provincial level is devolving authority for management of the health system down to local and community levels and increasing citizen participation in decision-making. Such reforms are motivated by democratic values and by a desire to make the health system more open and accountable to the people it serves. They are motivated also by the belief that communities are best able to determine their needs and ways of meeting them within available resources, leading to more cost-effective and appropriate health services.

In British Columbia, for instance, the provincial government is in the process of establishing regional health boards with broad planning powers, and local community councils that will take on management responsibility for local health services. Both regional and local bodies will be governed by boards composed of elected community representatives as well as health "experts." In Quebec, Regional Assemblies, including representatives of public and private institutions, community organizations, specific socioeconomic groups, and municipalities will set regional health and welfare priorities, engage in planning, managing, and coordinating services on a regional basis, and establish budgets to be managed by local Health and Social Services Boards.

Reflecting different political cultures, provinces have approached reform in different ways. In provinces such as Alberta and Saskatchewan, regionalization has occurred in a top-down manner with provincial governments taking the lead in the design and implementation of regional systems. In Ontario, health reform initiatives have been accompanied by wide community consultation lead by District Health Councils. In Quebec, the process of reform has been ongoing since the inception of Medicare, and has involved broad-based citizen participation as well as the development of a sophisticated and extensive health services research capacity in universities. As is always the case, there are outstanding challenges and questions that will have to be addressed in these reforms: Where will decisions be made? Who will make decisions? How will they be held accountable? In all provinces, however, the intent is the same: to make the system more accountable, to match services more closely to population health needs, to use limited resources more efficiently, and thus, to maintain the historical strengths of Canadian Medicare.

At the federal level, there is also renewed emphasis on health as a policy field. In 1994, the federal government established a National Forum on Health to consult widely across the country about issues affecting the future of Medicare and the role of government in the health field. These issues address the determinants of health; evidence-based decision-making; values, ethics, and principles that influence decision-making; and using the limited resources that are available to achieve the maximum health outcome. The twenty-two-member forum is composed of individuals who have a wide range of experiences as volunteers, professionals, and consumers in the health field.

In conclusion, the Canadian health system continues to provide Canadians with equitable access to high-quality health services. In response to multiple challenges, the system is evolving. This evolution, while driven in large part by the reality of economic restraint, increasingly involves a recognition that health is tied to the social, economic, and natural environments in which individuals live, that health care providers and the health system as a whole must be accountable to the democratic process, that services must be delivered in the most efficient fashion possible, and that Canadians should be encouraged to participate fully in their own care, and in decisions about the future of their health system (Rachlis and Kushner 1994).

REFERENCES

Baker, G. R., J. Barnsley, and M. Murray. 1993. Continuous quality improvement in Canadian health care organizations. *Leadership in Health Services* 2(3):18–23.

Barer, M., and G. Stoddart. 1992. Toward integrated medical resource policies for Canada: 8 undergraduate medical training. *Canadian Medical Association Journal* 147(5):617–23.

Coburn, David, George M. Torrance, and Joseph M. Kaufert. 1983. Medical dominance in Canada in historical perspective: the rise and fall of medicine? *International Journal of Health Services* 13(3):407–32.

Coyte, P. C., J. G. Wright, G. A. Hawker, C. Bombardier, et al. 1994. Waiting times for knee-replacement surgery in the United States and Canada. *New England Journal of Medicine* 331(16):1068–71.

Deber, R., M. Wiktorowicz, and P. Leatt. 1994. Technology acquisition in Canadian hospitals: how is it done, and where is the information coming from? *Healthcare Management Forum* 7(4):18–27.

El-Geubaly, N., P. Beausejour, B. Woodside, D. Smith, and I. Kapkin. 1991. The optimal psychiatrist-to-population ratio: a Canadian perspective. *Canadian Journal of Psychiatry* 36(1):9–15.

Evans, J. R. 1987. *Toward a Shared Direction For Health In Ontario: Report of the Ontario Health Review Panel.* Toronto: Government of Ontario.

Fried, B., C. Worthington, P. Leatt, and G. Gelmon. 1990. The nature and extent of hospital competition in a government funded health system. *Health Services Management Research Journal* 3(3):154–62.

Gellman, D. D. 1992. Growing medical income disparities threaten fee-for-service medicine. *Canadian Medical Association Journal* 147(1):1682–86.

Hall, Emmett M. 1980. *Canada's National-Provincial Health Program for the 1980's: A Commitment for Renewal.* Ottawa: Health and Welfare Canada.

Hastings, J. E. F. 1971. Federal-provincial insurance for hospital and physician care in Canada. *International Journal of Health Services* 1(4):398–414.

Health Canada, Federal/Provincial/Territorial Subcommittee on Continuing Care. 1993. *Description of long-term care services in provinces and territories of Canada.* Ottawa: Queen's Printer.

Jacobs, P., and W. Hart. 1990. Admission waiting times: a national survey. *Dimensions in Health Service* 67(1):32–34

Lalonde, M. 1974. *A New Perspective on the Health of Canadians: A Working Document.* Ottawa: Information Canada.

Leatt, P. 1994. Physicians in health care management: 1.

Physicians as managers: roles and future challenges. *Canadian Medical Association Journal* 150(2):171–76.

Levine, E., P. Leatt, and K. Poulton. 1993. *Nursing Practice in the UK and North America.* London: Chapman and Hall.

Mahtre, S. L., and R. B. Deber. 1992. From equal access to health care to equitable access to health: a review of Canadian provincial health commissions and reports. *International Journal of Health Services* 22(4): 645–68.

Ontario Constant Quality Improvement Network. 1995. *Quality improvement project inventory.* Toronto: Ontario CQI Network.

Organization for Economic Cooperation and Development (OECD). 1992. *The Reform of Health Care: A Comparative Analysis of Seven OECD Countries.* Paris: OECD Publications Service.

Pink, G. H., and H. B. Bolley. 1994. Physicians in health care management: 3 case mix groups and resource intensity weights: an overview for physicians. *Canadian Medical Association Journal* 150(6):889–94.

Pink, G. H., R. B. Deber, J. N. Lavoie, and C. Aserlind. 1991. Innovative revenue generation. *Healthcare Management Forum* 4(4):33–41.

Pink, G. H. and Leatt, P. 1991. Fund raising by hospital foundations. *Nonprofit Management and Leadership* Summer 1991, 313–27.

Rachlis, R., and C. Kushner. 1994. *Strong Medicine: How to Save Canada's Health Care System.* Toronto: HarperCollins.

Schwartz, M. 1993. Trauma centre accreditation in Canada—a proposal: 1992 presidential address, Trauma Association of Canada. *Journal of Trauma* 35(2): 241–44.

Taylor, M. G. 1986. The Canadian health care system 1974–1984. In *Medicare at Maturity: Achievements, Lessons and Challenges,* 3–40. Calgary: University of Calgary Press.

Touhy, Carolyn J. 1988. "Medicine and the state in Canada: the extra-billing issue in perspective." *Canadian Journal of Political Science* 21(2):267–96.

Trainor, J., T. Morrell-Bellai, R. Ballantyne, and K. Boydell. 1993. Housing for people with mental illnesses: a comparison of models and an examination of the growth of alternative housing in Canada. *Canadian Journal of Psychiatry* 38(7):494–501.

Vayda, E. 1994. Physicians in health care management: 5. Payment of physicians and organization of medical services. *Canadian Medical Association Journal* 150(10):1581–88.

Watanabe, M., and W. G. Tholl. 1986. *Geographic Distribution of Physicians in Canada. December. Annex to Report of the Advisory Panel on the Provision of Medical Services in Underserviced Regions.* Ottawa: Canadian Medical Association.

Williams, A. P., K. Domnick Pierre, and E. Vayda. 1993. Women in medicine: toward a conceptual understanding of the potential for change. *Journal of American Medical Women's Association* 48(4):115–21.

Table 1 Estimates of Total Population by Special Age Groups and Sex in Canada (in thousands)

Age	Male	Female	Both Sexes
0–14	3,051.0	2,913.6	5,964.6
0–15	3,251.8	3,103.7	6,355.5
0–16	3,450.4	3,291.8	6,742.1
0–17	3,650.0	3,482.4	7,132.4
15–49	7,977.8	7,824.2	15,801.9
15–64	9,969.5	9,841.5	19,810.9
16–64	9,768.7	9,651.4	19,420.1
17–64	9,570.5	9,463.3	19,033.4
18–24	1,448.3	1,403.7	2,852.0
18–64	9,370.5	9,272.7	18,643.2
18+	10,832.9	11,282.8	22,115.7
25–44	4,928.9	4,861.7	9,790.6
45–64	2,993.3	3,007.3	6,000.6
65+	1,462.4	2,010.1	3,472.5
Total	14,482.9	14,765.2	29,248.1

SOURCE: Demography Division, Population Estimates Section, Statistics Canada, 1994.

Table 1a Population by Selected Ethnic Origins and Sex in Canada[1]

Ethnic Origins	Male	Female	Both Sexes
Latin, Central, and South America	43,325	42,205	85,535
Caribbean	43,625	50,765	94,395
Black	107,195	117,420	224,620
Other European	125,755	125,385	251,140
Aboriginal	230,865	239,750	470,616
Southern European	711,295	667,735	1,379,030
Asian and African	822,260	811,395	1,633,660
Multiple Origins[2]	3,770,460	4,023,790	7,794,250

1. Categories as defined by Statistics Canada
2. Includes those who describe themselves as having more than one ethnic origin, e.g., "British, French and Canadian"
SOURCE: Statistics Canada, cat. no. 93-315.

Table 2 Crude Live Birth Rates (Births per 1,000 population), Total Fertility Rates, and Infant Mortality Rates in Canada in 1982, 1991, and 1992

	1982	1991	1992
Births	373,082	402,528	398,642
Crude birth rate (per 1,000)	14.8	14.3	14.0
Total fertility rate	1.62	1.69	1.70
Infant mortality	9.1	6.4	6.1

SOURCES: *Health Reports* vol. 5, no. 4 (1993); *Statistics Canada*, cat. no. 82-003; *Statistics Canada*, cat. no. 84-211.

Table 3   Infant Mortality Rate by Six Most Common Causes

Common Cause of Death	Deaths Per 100,000
Symptoms, signs, and ill-defined conditions[1]	108.6
External causes of injury and poisoning[2]	17.4
Disease of the nervous system and sense organs[3]	17.1
Endocrine, nutritional, and metabolic diseases and immunity disorders	7.5
Infectious and parasitic diseases[4]	6.7
Neoplasms	3.0
All causes	639.2

1. Including sudden infant death syndrome and other symptoms, signs, and ill-defined conditions
2. Including motor vehicle accidents, accidents caused by fire and flame
3. Including meningitis, hereditary, and degenerative diseases of CNS
4. Including whooping cough, meningococcal infection, septicemia, HIV infection
SOURCE: *Statistics Canada,* cat. no. 84-209.

Table 4   Estimated Death Rates for the 10 Leading Causes of Death—Male

Causes of Death	Deaths Per 100,000
Diseases of the circulatory system	228.6
Malignant neoplasms	176.1
Accidents and adverse effects	62.3
Respiratory diseases	55.7
All other causes	53.9
Diseases of the nervous system and sense organs	14.0
Diabetes mellitus	11.7
Infectious and parasitic diseases	11.2
Chronic liver disease and cirrhosis	9.3
Congenital anomalies	5.2
Certain perinatal causes (excluding stillbirths)	4.7
All causes	632.7

SOURCE: *Statistics Canada,* cat. no. 84-209.

Table 4a   Estimated Death Rates for the Ten Leading Causes of Death—Female

Causes of Death	Deaths Per 100,000
Diseases of the circulatory system	170.2
Malignant neoplasms	130.6
All other causes	49.1
Respiratory diseases	33.3
Accidents and adverse effects	24.5
Diseases of the nervous system and sense organs	13.3
Diabetes mellitus	11.1
Congenital anomalies	4.3
Chronic liver disease and cirrhosis	4.2
Certain perinatal causes (excluding stillbirths)	3.6
All causes	448.2

SOURCE: *Statistics Canada,* cat. no. 84-209.

Table 5 Rates of Selected Surgical Procedures including Number per 100,000 Population and Average Length of Stay in Days—Males

Operation	No. per 100,000	Avg. Stay in Days
Digestive system and abdominal region	1,171	9.8
Musculoskeletal system	904	9.7
Cardiovascular system	727	10.2
Male genital organs	483	8.3
Nose, mouth, pharynx	401	6.3
Urinary tract	310	10.2
Nervous system	201	12.6
Eyes	200	5.8
Skin and subcutaneous tissue	175	21.9
Respiratory system	171	16.8
Hemic and lymphatic system	75	15.3
Ears	66	3.4
Endocrine system	15	7.9
Breast	11	7.9

SOURCES: *Health Reports,* vol. 5, no. 4 (1993); *Statistics Canada,* cat. no. 82-003.

Table 5a Rates of Selected Surgical Procedures including Number per 100,000 Population and Average Length of Stay in Days—Females

Operation	No. per 100,000	Avg. Stay in Days
Obstetric procedures	2,997	4.1
Female genital organs	1,186	5.2
Digestive system and abdominal region	1,135	10.4
Musculoskeletal system	820	13.6
Cardiovascular system	430	11.6
Nose, mouth, pharynx	356	6.4
Eyes	269	5.4
Breast	263	5.3
Urinary tract	214	11.2
Nervous system	171	13.1
Skin and subcutaneous tissue	147	25.9
Respiratory system	107	18.0
Hemic and lymphatic system	66	15.4
Ears	55	4.0
Endocrine system	42	6.4

SOURCE: *Health Reports* 1993, vol. 5, no. 4, *Statistics Canada,* cat. no. 82-003.

Table 6   Average 1992 Net Income before Taxes of Selected Self-Employed Professionals

Self-Employed Profession	Number	Avg. Net Income
Medical doctors and surgeons	43,670	$133,357
Dentists	8,740	108,871
Lawyers and notaries	23,210	96,145
Accountants	15,510	66,905
Engineers and architects	6,560	37,807
All Canadians	19,437,070	25,236

SOURCE: *Statistics Canada.*

Table 6a   Ratios of Net Annual Professional Incomes of Self-Employed Full-Time Canadian Physicians by Medical Specialty

Specialty	1966	1985
General Practice	1.00	1.00
Medicine Specialties		
Internal Medicine	1.13	1.45
Neurology	—	1.28
Psychiatry	1.08	1.11
Pediatrics	1.08	1.08
Dermatology	1.36	1.32
Physiatry	—	1.69
Anesthesia	1.20	1.40
Surgical Specialties		
General Surgery	1.39	1.44
Cardiothoracic Surgery	1.51	2.11
Urology	1.55	1.71
Orthopaedic Surgery	1.85	1.86
Plastic Surgery	1.57	1.71
Neurosurgery	1.84	1.57
Ophthalmology	1.56	1.65
Otolaryngology	1.72	1.53
Obstetrics and Gynecology	1.34	1.44
Diagnostic Radiology	1.67	1.98
Laboratory Medicine	1.30	1.43

SOURCE: Gellman (1992), p. 1683.

Table 7   Number of Acute Care Public Hospitals by Number of Beds and Hospital Type

Type	Number of Beds 1–49	50–99	100–199	200–299	300+	Total No. of Beds
Lay	114	81	44	33	65	56,932
Religious	25	20	17	19	18	17,112
Municipal	193	38	22	7	10	16,549
Provincial	42	19	28	13	28	23,487
Total	374	158	111	72	121	114,080

SOURCE: *Guide des Etablissements de Santé du Canada* (1994).

Table 8   Major Indicators of Hospital Utilization

Year	Separations per 100,000	Days of Care per 100,000	Avg. Stay in Days
1971	16,587	191,610	11.6
1975	16,165	179,904	11.1
1981–82[1]	14,621	179,750	12.3
1985–86	14,524	170,037	11.7
1991–92	13,482	152,956	11.3

1. Change in method of reporting from calendar year to fiscal year.
Source: *Health Reports*, vol. 5, no. 4 (1993); *Statistics Canada*, cat. no. 82-003.

Table 9   Number of Residential Care Facilities by Type of Facilities and Number of Beds

Type of Ownership	Total No.	Total Bed	Aged Persons No.	Aged Persons Bed	Physically Handicapped No.	Physically Handicapped Bed	Developmentally Delayed No.	Developmentally Delayed Bed	Psychiatrically Disabled No.	Psychiatrically Disabled Bed
Proprietary	2,029	79,182	1,093	66,280	25	275	298	2,642	398	6,763
Religious	362	20,784	166	15,619	4	29	65	801	8	185
Lay	2,411	51,360	426	30,321	98	1,186	1,082	9,325	151	1,553
Municipal	417	37,995	386	35,949	—	—	14	814	4	193
Provincial	377	24,011	100	6,136	8	328	80	7,525	24	5,772
Other	607	31,850	294	24,652	18	415	—	—	89	2,135
Total	6,203	245,182	2,465	179,497	153	2,233	1,539	21,107	674	16,601

Source: *Statistics Canada*, Health Statistics Division, *Guide des Establissements de Santé du Canada* (1994).

Table 10   Total Health Expenditures by Category of Expenditure and Percentage of Gross Domestic Product (in $000,000)

Year	Hospitals	Other Institutions	Physicians	Other Professionals	Drugs	Capital	Other	Total	% of GDP
1975	5,443.0	1,194.1	1,927.3	731.1	1,091.2	612.4	1,265.5	12,264.6	7.1
1980	9,293.9	2,638.4	3,448.3	1,577.7	2,026.9	1,233.6	2,479.3	22,698.1	7.3
1985	16,227.7	4,259.0	6,333.3	2,744.6	4,229.6	1,862.5	4,742.3	40,399.0	8.5
1990	24,087.1	6,285.3	9,600.4	4,003.4	8,381.2	2,589.3	7,210.2	62,156.9	9.3
1993	27,392.9	7,375.1	10,904.8	4,329.2	10,911.0	2,690.1	8,468.3	72,071.5	10.1

Source: *National Health Expenditures in Canada* (1975–93), Summary Report.

The Health System of Denmark

Allan Krasnik and Signild Vallgårda

Historical Background

Denmark is a small country of five million inhabitants. It is a constitutional monarchy; men have had the right to vote since 1849, women since 1915. The participation in national elections is very high—about 85% of the eligible voters. Agriculture has played a central role in the economic development of the country; until the 1950s more than half of the exports consisted of agricultural products. The country has few natural resources and light industry has dominated in recent years: textiles, chemicals, pharmaceuticals, and electronic production. Trade unions have organized most of the workforce and together with the Social Democratic Party have been very influential in the political life of the country, especially in the development of the welfare state. The country is fairly affluent with small social class differences. It is a member of the European Union, but some exceptions to the Maastricht Treaty have been granted Denmark due to Danish resistance to elements of European integration policy.

Public welfare politics has a long tradition in Denmark, as does decentralized management of welfare tasks. Before the eighteenth century it was the responsibility of the landlords or the artisan masters to provide help for their subordinates when they were ill or in need—which did not mean that this help was always given. Change occurred gradually with the beginning dissolution of the feudal social relations and the increasing power of the central state. Most of the tasks concerning poor relief and health care was taken over by towns and counties, not the central state. The central state laid down the guiding principles but most of the welfare measures were carried out by local authorities. Even today, the Danish health sector is financed mainly by local and regional taxes and governed by counties and local communities.

In the eighteenth century political interest in the size of the population was great. A large, healthy, and industrious population was considered to constitute the richness of the nation. A number of measures were taken in order to improve the health of the population: education of midwives, smallpox inoculation, better education of physicians and surgeons, state-employed district doctors supervising public health and health care for the poor.[1] The first hospitals were built by counties and municipalities; they were very small and their purpose was to provide the sick with care and shelter. An exception was the state hospital in Copenhagen including 300 beds. It was established in 1757 as a teaching hospital for surgeons and physicians.[2]

During the nineteenth century the number of private medical practitioners increased. The relatively well-off were treated by doctors in their homes; even extensive surgery was performed in private homes. Trained midwives were employed all over the country and they helped the poor free of charge. Public health measures were taken such as sewerage, water supply, and housing improvements, and public health boards were set up from the middle of the century.

Hospitals were built in practically all Danish towns. Most of them were very small, except in Copenhagen, which had several hospitals with more than one hundred beds. The hospitals were originally intended for the poor and were so used. However, this situation began to change from the end of the nineteenth century. The lower socioeconomic classes still constitute the majority of hospital patients even today, but now it seems mainly to be due to poorer health among these groups.[3] A few Catholic hospitals had existed on a nonprofit basis; they have gradually been taken over by the counties. During the last decade a few private hospitals have been established on a profit-gaining basis, but two of them closed due to financial difficulties. A couple of private hospitals and a few clinics with available beds still exist. The private hospitals have caused some political conflicts and have been discussed several times in the Danish Parliament. They are considered by some to be a threat to the equity of the Danish health care system, while others claim that they provide a good supplement and an innovative element.

Growing out of the craft guilds, health insurance funds were established in the latter half of the nineteenth century; in 1892 a law was passed to grant state support for these funds. The health insurance funds gave the general practitioner a more secure income and were supported by the Medical Association. Until recently the supply of doctors has been very high in Denmark, compared to the other Scandinavian countries. The early establishment of health insurance funds is one factor behind the large number of doctors. In 1925, 42% of the population was covered by the insurance. Only people with an income below a certain amount could benefit from the health insurance. In 1973, when the insurance schemes were taken over by the counties, 90% of the population were enrolled as members.

A tripartite system is now in effect: (1) *private practitioners,* such as general practitioners, specialists, physiotherapists, dentists, chiropractors, etc., financed by the counties, based on a capitation and/or fee for service, including various levels of patient co-payments; (2) *hospitals,* primarily managed and financed by the counties, except for the very few private hospitals; and (3) *local health services,* such as nursing homes, home nurses, health visitors, mainly managed and financed by the local communities (municipalities). There are 14 counties and two towns responsible for hospitals and private practitioners, and 275 local communities responsible for the local health services.

Contrary to the situation in most other countries, nursing homes for the sick, disabled elderly, and handicapped are not considered to be a part of the health care sector but a part of the social welfare system. This means that the number of beds in health care institutions as well as the health care costs in the official statistics are not directly comparable to that of other countries. In this chapter we shall deal with these institutions as being a part of the health care sector.

The central government's National Board of Health is responsible for supervision of health personnel and institutions, and for advising different ministries, counties, and municipalities on health issues. The state finances vaccinations, some health campaigns, and public health doctors. Otherwise the state is scarcely directly involved when management of the health services takes place. Danish welfare politics in general, and especially health care politics, have been characterized by consensus; controversies, however, have been more frequent since the 1970s. Since a reform in 1970 the counties have considerable independence from the central state and the responsibility for the largest part of the health care sector. The laws passed on health care are mainly general guidelines, letting the local authorities decide the actual performance.

Denmark is a small country consisting of five million inhabitants. Few inhabitants are of foreign origin. The population is considered to be homogeneous socially as well as culturally. During recent years the average length of life has not increased in Denmark, as it has in most Western European countries. This has caused some concern in the government and has resulted in a commission work. The conclusions indicated that the performance of the health care sector is not responsible for the stagnation in life expectancy.[4] Lifestyle factors (such as smoking) and structural factors (such as unemployment) seem to be causes of the stagnation.

Medical Practice

The number of Danish medical doctors increased drastically during the 1960s and 1970s. This created temporary unemployment among doctors during the 1980s. The expansion of the health sector and the reduction in working hours, however, has made it possible to incorporate almost all medical doctors into the Danish health system. At present, about 14,700 medical doctors are working in Denmark (2.9 per 1,000 inhabitants). Of these, 3,300 are general practitioners (one general practitioner per 1,600 inhabitants); 400 are younger doctors employed in general practice; 8,700 are employed in hospitals, and 900 are full-time private practicing specialists. The remaining 1,400 are working in research institutions, medico-technical industries, health administration, public health, and so forth. Some 3,200 Danish doctors are not working (mainly because of old age), and 2,400 are working abroad (primarily in Sweden).

Hospital doctors are publicly employed either in permanent positions or for a limited period of time as registrars during training. Salaries are paid according to national wage agreements negotiated by the Danish Medical Association and the Danish Association of County Councils. However, specialists employed by the hospital are to some extent allowed to undertake some private practice when not working the usual hours.

In principle the general practitioner runs a private practice either on his or her own in a solo practice (32%) or in collaboration with other general practitioners (68%). The present trend is toward a decrease of solo practitioners and an increase of group practices. The income of general practitioners primarily derives from the National Health Insurance Scheme and is a mixture between fee per capita (one-third to one-half of the income), and a fee for services rendered (consultation, examination, operation, and so forth).

Details concerning fees are negotiated by the Association of General Practitioners and the Association of County Councils. Priority setting, therefore, can take place in relation to deciding the fees. The Ministry of Health can influence this process directly by refusing to recognize the agreement (this has actually happened). Such a recognition is mandatory before the agreement is valid as a consequence of the legislation on health insurance in Denmark.

The general practitioner needs a license from the county to be able to receive fees from the scheme. The number of doctors accepted by the county is limited and based on negotiations between counties and the professional association of the general practitioners. Most private practicing specialists are also remunerated through the National Health Scheme according to specific fees for services. These remunerations are restricted to doctors with a special license from the county. Only a few doctors are working on a fully private basis without special license.

As a result of the salary and fee system income does not differ very much among different groups of doctors. No differences are found across specialties concerning hospital-employed doctors, and the income of general practitioners is on the whole similar to that of hospital doctors in permanent positions. The average level of income is comparable to or slightly higher than the income of higher public employees; that is, 60,000–80,000 U.S. dollars a year. However, it is less than the level of similar professional people in private enterprises such as lawyers and engineers. Some doctors do succeed in achieving higher income than others, mainly by combining several functions or by making the most of the fee system in the National Health Scheme. The volume of activities is monitored annually by the counties; when there is substantial deviation from the average, those doctors are asked to explain the deviation. If the explanation is not convincing, the county can limit the doctor's income. The working hours are officially thirty-seven hours a week for all employees in Denmark including doctors, but many doctors have longer working hours due to overtime in their job and functions in addition to their principal occupation.

The National Health Insurance Scheme and the production of many medical doctors have secured a fair distribution of doctors across the country and across specialties, both in hospitals and within the primary health care field. The ratio of general practitioners to inhabitants (1993 figures)[5] varies little across counties: between one to 1,544 and one to 1,653 (except for the small island county of Bornholm having only one general practitioner per 1,326 inhabitants). In this way short distances to health services and reasonable equity in access to services have been achieved. In recent years, however, smaller hospitals in rural areas have experienced increasing difficulties in attracting medical doctors. This might reinforce an ongoing trend and result in closure of smaller hospitals and centralization of hospital care. Special legislation has not yet been imposed in order to ensure the distribution of doctors across geographical areas or specialties, except for restricting the number of doctors trained in each specialty—imposed by the National Board of Health to avoid overproduction of specialists.

The Danish Medical Association has previously been a very powerful body in Danish health policy in general and it still plays an important role in regard to the negotiation of salaries for the Danish doctors. The general impact of the association has, however, diminished, as regards the organization of health services as well as Danish health policy in general. This loss of influence is a consequence of the reduced general authority of doctors in the society and internal conflicts within the Medical Association between various groups of doctors.

The Danish population is entitled to free hospital care after referral from a general practitioner. It is the responsibility of the general practitioner to decide when their own competence is no longer sufficient, if the necessary technology is not available in their clinic, and so forth. After referral the general practitioner has no direct influence on the examination, treatment, and nursing of the patient. After the patient's discharge from the hospital, a "discharge certificate" is sent to the general practitioner informing about the hospital procedures and the outcome. The value of these certificates is often reduced by the delays in sending them out from the hospitals.

The general practitioner has the option to refer to specialized ambulatory care in a hospital or to a private practicing specialist registered in the insurance scheme. All major specialties are represented in private practices, with ear-nose-throat and eye specialists being the largest groups, followed by gynecology and dermatology. Referral from a general practitioner is generally required to obtain free service from specialists. However, ear-nose-throat and eye specialists are allowed to accept patients without referral in the scheme.

The scheme also includes an alternative insurance plan for the population allowing for direct access to specialists without referral. According to the Public Health Insurance Act, citizens above the age of sixteen are required to choose one of the two security groups:

Group 1   Patients choose their own general practitioners who provide free medical attention. General practitioners can refer patients to specialized medical attention, free of charge, or to physiotherapy or chiropody (partly free of charge). Patients can choose new general practitioners every six months.

Group 2   Patients are not required to have their own general practitioners and they can consult specialized practitioners without being referred by general practitioners. Patients who belong to this group have to pay part of the fees.

Less than 4% of the population has chosen the group 2 option.

The quality of doctors and other authorized health professionals (nurses, dentists) is basically presumed by the initial training. No further formal training or monitoring of quality is required. A general surveillance is performed by the National Board of Health and the regional medical officers, but only on the basis of specific complaints or reports of serious individual problems of doctors or patients. Thus, quality assurance is still mainly based on the initiative of doctors, hospital departments and administrations, and so forth. Postgraduate training after specialization is in principle seen as a professional obligation but regarded as an individual responsibility.

Hospitals

Structure, Organization, and Financing

Since the first hospitals were established in the eighteenth century they have, with few exceptions, been the responsibility of the counties. State subsidies have been given in various forms from 1930 onward, but decisions about hospitals have remained with counties. Previously, each hospital had its own board; since 1970, however, all political decisions have been centralized in the county councils. All major changes in the services and major investments are decided by the county councils.

The Danish hospital system consists mainly of general hospitals. There are 14 psychiatric hospitals and a few specialized somatic hospitals. In 1993 the total number of hospitals was 98. The number of hospitals has been decreasing since 1930, at which time the number of acute general hospitals was 166. The centralization first resulted in an increase in the average size of the hospitals. During the last decades the reduction in the number of beds has entailed a reduction in the size of the hospitals. From the late 1930s the average number of beds at acute general hospitals has been 6 per 1,000 inhabitants. During the 1980s it started to decrease and in 1993 there were 4.6 beds per 1,000 inhabitants.

A salient feature of the history of the hospitals has been specialization. The number of special departments has been increasing from 125 in 1933 to 784 in 1981; since then it has decreased to

688 in 1990 (see Fig. 1). It is not clear whether this shall be interpreted as a shift in the politics concerning specializations or an adjustment to a smaller increase in resources. Some doctors and politicians have declared that the degree of specialization has been too high and that most patients are not in need of subspecialized services.[6] Almost all acute general hospitals have emergency rooms. Some of these are "closed"; that is, a referral from a general practitioner or another doctor is required. The purpose is to restrict the use of the emergency rooms to those needing the hospital facilities.

The number of people employed in the health care sector has been increasing, even during the last years when cost containment has been on the agenda. Per bed or bed day the increase has been twofold at acute general hospitals during the years 1960 to 1990, taking the reduced working hours into account. This increase is associated (as a cause or an effect) with the increased diagnostic and therapeutic activities at the hospitals. The proportion of doctors among health workers has also increased. At nursing homes the number of employed has increased by 50% from 1970 to 1990, despite a decrease in the number of beds. This is partly explained by an increase in the number of very old and sick inhabitants who require more care.

One problem often mentioned in managing the hospitals is the desire of various employee groups, including professional groups, to define in labor agreements what they can and cannot do. An average hospital may have about two hundred different contracts with employed groups, and different tasks can only be performed by certain professionals. The few private hospitals have succeeded in changing this, and have thereby achieved more flexibility and continuity in patient

Figure 1   Number of departments in different specialties

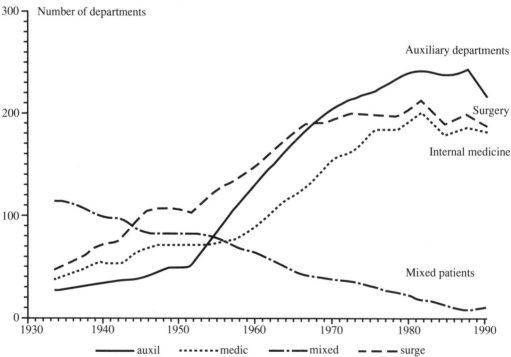

care. Negotiations with professional organizations constitute a central part of hospital management and is performed both centrally and locally.

At present, the distribution of resources to hospitals is undergoing change. Previously resources were distributed according to budgets. This is still the most used form of distribution, but contracting and fee for service is becoming increasingly common. Counties make contracts with their own hospitals and others about the price for a certain number of surgical procedures. Hospitals are paid by a per diem for treating patients from other counties. The responsibility for keeping the budget has in many hospitals been transferred to the hospital departments, which has probably made cost containment more efficient.

Hospital management is getting increased attention. The most common system is the so-called troika leadership, which consists of a hospital administrator, a chief physician, and a chief nurse constituting a leading team. Compared with those of the United Kingdom, Danish nurses have a great deal of influence within the hospitals. On January 1, 1995, a hospital company was established containing the State University Hospital in Copenhagen and the hospitals of the city of Copenhagen, including a board of politicians and health administrators, who were appointed by the state and the city. This board is expected to be acting more independently of the general political bodies than previously. The Copenhagen Hospital Company contains about one-fifth of Denmark's hospital activities.

Access to hospital treatment is limited by the requirement of a referral from a general practitioner or a specialist practitioner. Acute cases are admitted without referral. The proportion of acute admissions has been increasing from 47% in 1979 to 63% in 1993. All hospital care is free of charge at the point of use. The size of the patients' rooms varies mainly between one and four beds. In principle, access to a single room is dependent on medical criteria.

Vejle Hospital is an example of a big Danish county hospital. It has 382 beds and 18 special departments, of which 6 are auxiliary departments such as clinical genetics, clinical physiology, and clinical chemistry. It has an emergency room as well. In 1993, 160,000 patients were admitted, with the average length of stay 6.4 days. The hospital has a MRI scanner, and a CT scanner. A mobile lithotripter is shared with two other counties. In December 1993 there were 6.5 CT scanners, 0.8 PET scanners, 1.9 MRI scanners, and 1.3 lithotriptors per one million inhabitants in Denmark. No dialyses or kidney transplants take place at the hospital. In 1992 the hospital employed 984 persons; 165 of these were medical doctors and 400 were nurses.

In 1993 the right of the patient to choose a hospital irrespective of place of residence was decided by law. The county of residence is obliged to pay the hospital's county a fixed amount per diem. How this money is distributed differs: in some counties the money is forwarded to the hospital and even to the departments that treat patients from other counties; in others, the money is kept by the county, which decides how to use it. The incentive for the hospitals to attract patients varies of course with the reimbursement. In order not to be closed down, all departments have to some extent incentive to enlarge their activities. When hospitals try to attract patients they do it by sending brochures to the general practitioners, information on waiting times, and through an increasing number of articles in local papers about the hospitals. The free choice of hospital is reducing the influence of the counties on setting the priorities between different patient groups. If a general practitioner has referred a patient to hospital, the patient is entitled to go to any hospital in the country that offers the treatment, and the home county has to pay the bill. The choice is, however, limited to the level of specialization to which the patient is referred. If a patient is referred to a so-called basic department, the patient is not entitled to choose a subspecialized department. So far the patients have mainly used the freedom of choice in connection with elective surgery. In July 1994, 23% of the nonacute admissions took place outside the county of residence, as compared to 15% in July 1990 before the free choice was introduced. In total, about 4% of the admissions are considered to take place outside the county of residence due to free choice.

Activities

Since the Second World War a reduction of the care given at hospitals, as measured in bed days, has taken place. The number of bed days in acute general hospitals has been declining from more than 2,000 per 1,000 inhabitants in the 1940s to about 1,500 today. This is in spite of the increase in the number of old and very old inhabitants.

Admissions, defined as inpatient admissions of patients to a department, have increased in numbers from about 50 per 1,000 in 1930 to more than 200 in 1990. There are, however, great regional variations in admission rates, which to some extent is explained by differences in age and sex distribution and social differences, poverty, one-person households, and so forth. The increase in the admission rates has been possible because of the reduction in the average length of stay. Until the 1930s it was about one month, but since then it has declined to one week.

The distribution of different diagnostic groups such as cancer, heart disease, orthopedic disorders, among the hospital patients has been very stable since the early 1960s, despite an increase in the admission rates and a changed age distribution of the patients. A group of patients that was not registered previously is patients without diseases or symptoms. An example is healthy newborns and parents accompanying their sick children, which in 1990 constituted 9% of the admissions.

The increase in the activities can also be seen from the steep increase in the number of outpatient visits, surgical and diagnostic procedures, and from the fact that the number of auxiliary departments such as X-ray and laboratories has increased much more than the bed wards. The number of inpatient surgical procedures has increased from 40 per 1,000 inhabitants in 1945 to 102 in 1991. There is quite some variation in the procedures and lengths of stay for the same conditions at Danish hospitals. The variation in hysterectomies is sixfold.[7] Caesarean sections rates vary from 9% to 16% between the counties and even more between different hospitals.

The National Board of Health is trying to convince counties to limit the treatment of rare diseases and expensive treatment and equipment to a small number of hospitals—without much success. As an example, the Board advised the government to restrict the treatment of heart and liver transplants to one hospital. Regional interests were too strong, however, and the transplants were permitted to take place at two hospitals. Only after poor results were liver transplants restricted to one hospital.

The age distribution of the patients at acute general hospitals has changed fundamentally during the last sixty years. The proportion of older patients has increased, partly due to the increase in the number of old inhabitants. In 1930 about 11% of the population was more than 60 years old, in 1993 it amounts to 20%. Another factor is the change in admission practices. The admission rates for the old have increased much more than for the young. The cause of this is probably better health among the young and middle-aged as well as better therapeutic abilities in treating old and fragile patients. The number of bed days is decreasing in the older age groups as well as in the younger groups. Thus the hospitals provide less and less care for the elderly as measured in time. During the 1980s the number of nursing home beds has been reduced from 50,000 to 40,000 (see below); the number of acute hospital beds has declined from 31,000 to 25,500 and the beds at psychiatric hospitals even more from 9,300 to 3,600. Consequently institutional care has diminished within in all sectors.

Waiting Times

Waiting time for different surgical procedures has been a political issue that attracts some attention. In 1994 a lump sum of 300 million crowns (50 million U.S. dollars) was given from the state to counties with the explicit purpose to reduce waiting time to no more than three months. The measure was met with some criticism, maintaining that shorter waiting lists might attract more patients; thus no change in the waiting time would appear. The number of surgical procedures performed has generally not increased, and in fact some waiting times have increased. As of October 1994, the average waiting times for different surgical procedures were as follows: total hip replacement, 5.3 months; cataract, 5.4 months; knee replacement, 6.8 months; varices, 5.9 months; slipped disc, 1 month. From April 1995 a waiting time guarantee has been proclaimed by the government: less than three months for patients waiting for knee or slipped disc operations.

Patients in need of care but not of hospital treatment are causing a conflict between counties (which are responsible for the hospitals) and local communities (which are responsible for the care of the sick and disabled elderly). If the local communities are not able to provide care facilities for their hospitalized residents who no longer require hospitalization, the counties are entitled to charge the communities for their prolonged hospital stay. In Denmark, counties and local communities (municipalities) are independent authorities with their own electoral bodies and taxing authorities.

Quality Assurance

The National Board of Health has published several guidelines in order to encourage quality assurance.[8] In a recent act on hospitals and health care in general,[9] quality assurance was stated to be a fundamental responsibility of the counties and local communities. Some hospitals have employed special doctors to support the quality assurance activities, and an increasing number of articles on quality assurance projects carried out in different hospital departments are published in the national medical journal. The Cochrane Center at the University Hospital of Copenhagen collects and analyzes randomized controlled trials in order to achieve a better basis for the decisions made.

Medical Education

Three universities in Denmark provide undergraduate medical training. The Ministry of Education—after negotiations with the Ministry of Health—decides how many students are admitted, and the National Board of Health licenses the individual doctors. The training program has a planned duration of six and one-half years after secondary school. The university training is totally financed by the state and is therefore free of charge for the students.

The training programs for medical specialties (including general practice) is defined by the Ministry of Health based on the advice of the National Board of Health and the Danish Board for Medical Specialties, with members representing the Danish Medical Association, universities, medical societies, the counties, the National Board of Health, and other agencies involved in the delivery of health care. Specific objectives and requirements for each specialty include practical training as registrars in hospitals and general practice as well as courses run by the medical societies and the National Board of Health. No examinations are carried out to test the quality of the doctor—only documentation that training requirements have been fulfilled. To improve the quality of the clinical training, the National Board of Health is planning an inspection system (inspired by a similar system in Sweden) that includes surveillance and advising of the individual departments responsible for training.

The duration of the full training programs are from five to six years and the doctors receive a full salary (from the counties) and free courses (financed by the National Board of Health) during the training program. The National Board of Health decides on the number of trainees in each specialty based on protections of need, capacity for training in the country, and so forth.

Other Health Practitioners

Dentists are trained at the two health faculties of the Universities in Copenhagen and Aarhus in independent academic training programs. The majority of the dentists are working in private practices based on patient payment, but an agreement with the National Health Insurance Scheme gives the adult patients a reimbursement for part of the expenses for dental treatment. Everybody under the age of eighteen is entitled to free dental care, including preventive and curative activities, either by the private dentists (with payment by the municipalities) or by public dental services for children (also financed by the municipalities). Public dentists are employed and paid a fixed salary according to general agreements. These agreements are comparable to those of other professions in public service, but they result in wages lower than those of their colleagues in private practice.

Nurses are trained in a number of nursing schools around the country connected to hospitals and not to universities. The training program is partly theoretical and partly practical with a total duration of three and one-half years. A further theoretical program is provided for nurses training to be instructors, administrators, or public health nurses. A two-year university program is now available for postgraduate training of nurses as well.

Nurses are mainly employed by counties in hospitals, and by municipalities in nursing homes and in primary health care. The latter are home nurses, mainly delivering care to the sick and disabled elderly; and public health nurses, dealing with prevention among children. The nurses are working on the authorization from the National Board of Health, but according to health legislation, their treatments generally have to be carried out on the basis of instructions from a medical doctor. Nurses are, however, respected as important professionals, with a large amount of autonomy in daily work and they have gained a powerful role within hospital management. In spite of this they are generally badly paid as compared to doctors and other professional groups.

A new short general education of health assistants was recently established to provide training for basic nursing care functions at hospitals, nursing homes, and so forth. These institutions have so far been quite reluctant to employ these new types of staff members—mainly as a result of the competition with the traditional health professions. General practitioners can refer patients for treatment by physiotherapists, who work in private clinics under an agreement with the National Health Scheme, which partly reimburses the fees paid by their patients.

Other important health professions are midwives, who are mainly employed by obstetric departments of the hospitals; and pharmacists, mainly working in private pharmacies, which are only entitled to sell medical drugs. Lately psychologists have gained a professional, public authorization.

General practitioners can refer certain patients to privately working psychologists and the patients get a partial reimbursement by the National Health Insurance Scheme. Also treatment from chiropodists in primary health care has now been recognized for partial reimbursement for patient care—although this group has not succeeded in getting public authorization.

Nursing Homes, Community Ambulatory Care Programs, Mental Health Facilities, and Other Community Health Agents

The policy for the care of the sick and disabled elderly has changed several times during the last decades. In the 1960s and the 1970s many nursing homes were built. During the 1980s the policy changed from institutionalized care toward more care given in the home. The number of beds at nursing homes has decreased by 20%. The number of nurses caring for patients in their own homes increased from 2,000 in the mid-1970s to 7,000 in 1992. The number of home helpers has likewise increased from 14,000 in the early seventies to 32,000 in 1992. It is of course not possible to say if needs are met to a smaller or larger extent with this changed policy; needs are difficult to measure and are not stable over time. In 1987 it was decided not to build any more nursing homes, and state subsidies were given to the construction of special dwellings for the elderly. These often contain quite substantial help facilities.

With the exception of some small islands, all communities have established 24-hour domiciliary care where the handicapped and diseased who live in their own homes can call for help at any time of the day. Practically all communities also provide meals on wheels. Meals can be delivered either as primary products or as warm or frozen meals. Day centers with varying offers such as social activities, hobbies, and/or rehabilitation programs are available in most communities. Parents who care for their seriously ill children and relatives who care for dying patients are entitled to reimbursement for lost earnings by the local community.

Mental Health Facilities

Long-stay inpatient services for the mentally ill and mentally handicapped is part of general hospital services, but the capacity has been heavily reduced during recent years in favor of ambulatory care. At present the number of psychiatric beds per 1,000 population is only 1.0 (very low compared to the rate of other European countries). The increasing international emphasis on community psychiatry has also influenced the organization of Danish mental health services. Community psychiatric services have been instituted in many places in the country as part of the general psychiatric hospital-based services—in several cases in the form of experimental innovations that have been subject to external scientific evaluation. An important issue in the debate has been difficulties related to the coordination between psychiatric services run as part of the health system, and the many social services for psychiatric patients rendered by the social welfare services.

Other Community Agencies

Institutions for the physically handicapped are available as part of the social security system, which is also responsible for institutions for the elderly, day care centers, general social services, and so forth. These are organized and run by the social and health authorities of the municipality, and governed by municipal political social committees. Geriatric departments for rehabilitation of elderly hospital patients have now been established in several counties as part of the public hospital system.

Public Health

Public health programs in Denmark are partly integrated including curative services and partly organized as separate activities run by special institutions. Surveillance and general control of communicable diseases are mainly the responsibility of medical officers employed by the Ministry of Health, working on a regional level. The medical officers are informed when certain communicable diseases occur and they are in charge of individual and community interventions to control such matters. General vaccination programs, however, are performed by the general practitioners and are paid for by the counties. These include:

1. Whooping cough, diphtheria, tetanus and polio (persons under 18 years).
2. Measles, parotitis, and rubella (persons under 18 years).
3. Rubella (females over 12 years).
4. Hemophilus influenza type B (children under 6).

The first vaccinations are given in relation to health examinations by a general practitioner offered as part of a preventive program. They are also provided free of charge to children between five weeks and five years of age and paid by the county.

Antenatal services are available from general practitioners, midwives, and hospital obstetrics departments by an obstetrician according to the following schedule: from the patient's regular general practitioner, as early as possible, weeks 26 and 35; from the midwife, weeks 16, 30, 33, 37 (when needed), 38, 39, and 40 (when needed); from the obstetrician, weeks 20 and 36. Birth control measures, when requested, are provided by the general practitioner eight and twelve weeks following delivery.

Women may choose to give birth at home or at a hospital. Almost 99% of all deliveries take place at hospitals. The average length of hospital stay for uncomplicated deliveries was 3.7 days in 1991. All services are free of charge for the patient and are paid for by the county health authorities. The rates of utilization of the antenatal preventive services are very high; however, some social and ethnic differences have been found indicating lower utilization among lower socioeconomic groups and among immigrants. No special programs have yet been established to cope with these differences.

Municipal authorities are notified of all births and are responsible for the preventive care offered to parents and children by the visiting public health nurse. Each child is visited several times during the first year depending on need. The main concern of the nurse is to supervise the child's health, to give advice and support to the parents, and to provide information about supplementary health services. The municipalities are also responsible for health examination of all children at school entry; the examination is provided by school nurses and school physicians, who also participate in health education in cooperation with the teaching staff.

Schools provide sex education including the use of contraceptives as part of their general education program. This often includes a visit to a special clinic offering advice in family planning. Devices for family planning (condoms, pills, IUDs) are not covered by general health insurance, but paid totally by the consumers.

Since 1973 every woman has been able to have an abortion free of charge and on request within the first twelve weeks of pregnancy. Prior to the termination of pregnancy, the woman must be counseled as to the nature of the operation and be informed of the social benefits to which she is entitled, should she wish to have the baby. A request for abortion after the first twelve weeks will be considered by a special board.

Systematic screening programs for cervical cancer have been established by some Danish counties and not by others. The programs in various parts of the country differ and no general national program has been established. Many women do engage in preventive examinations for cervical cancer as part of a regular gynecological examination, even without the existence of an actual program. In both cases the examinations are considered to be part of the health insurance scheme; fees therefore are paid fully by the county health authorities. Breast cancer screening (mammography) has been introduced in Copenhagen for women in the age group of 50–69. Other counties are planning a similar program.

Occupational health services are not part of the general health service, but were established by the employers and employees and are financed by the employers on the basis of specific legislation on occupational health. A special state agency (the Occupational Health Surveillance Agency) is responsible for the control of occupational health by setting standards and visiting worksites.

Health Costs and Health Insurance

The health costs in Denmark have been claimed to be very low as compared to other OECD (Organization for Economic Cooperation and Development) member states and particularly compared to the United States. The level of percentage of the gross domestic product spent on health services depends, among other things, on how health services are defined. As mentioned above, nursing homes are considered a part of the social and not the health sector; consequently the expenditure of those are not contained in the health services costs. When health costs include the costs of nursing homes and care for the sick and disabled elderly, health expenditures were close to 8% in the late 1980s, which is almost at the average European Union–level.[10]

The proportion of the GDP used for health care increased until the early 1970s; since then it has decreased slightly. The proportion of public expenditures used on the health care sector has also decreased. From the middle of the 1970s the increase, in fixed prices, of hospital costs has been fairly low and almost stagnating in the late 1980s, but from the beginning of the 1990s the expenditures are increasing again. About 70% of hospital expenditures are wages and salaries. This proportion has been quite stable during the last decades. Table A indicates these recent costs.

The largest part of the health care is financed by county taxes; that is, for hospitals and general practitioners, practicing specialists, some of the dentists, physiotherapists, and drugs. Local com-

Table A   Health Care Costs in 1993 in 1,000 Danish Crowns (6 Danish Crowns = 1 U.S. dollar)

Hospitals	34,700
GPs, dentists, drugs, etc.	13,300
Local health schemes	3,600
Nursing homes	10,100
Administration, etc.	800
Patient payments*	7,700

*Estimates[11]

munity taxes finance local health care schemes and nursing homes. The central state is only financing public health doctors and some campaigns directly. Many former state tasks, such as mental hospitals and institutions for the disabled, have been taken over by counties and local communities during the last decades. In order to compensate for the differences in wealth between different counties and communities, a system of general state subsidies, as well as transfers between the local bodies, have been established.

Conclusions

The Danish health care system is financed primarily by taxes and is governed by county and local governments. The influence of the central government—the state—on the content of the services is fairly limited. Legislation states that the population is entitled to *care,* but does not state the kind of care and the level of care. *Preventive services* are also mainly the responsibility of the counties and local communities, but here more detailed specifications are defined by the central government. The health care sector's share of the GDP is close to the average of that of the European Union, when the nursing homes are included. Efforts at cost containment within the system have been successful during the last decades. It is not known, however, if efforts to increase efficiency have been as successful.

Among the strengths of the system should be mentioned the high degree of equity in access to it. For many decades equity has been a central theme of Danish health policy. One means of achieving equity in access is the very low degree of patient co-payment by Danish patients. Geographical equity has been achieved in the distribution of primary health care. The private sector is small, although out-of-pocket payments amount to a big share of dental care, drugs, and vision products. Private hospitals have been opposed because of their negative consequences for equity. Population surveys show a high degree of satisfaction with the health care system, especially with general practitioners.

Since the 1960s, the central government has sought to influence the health system by asking the counties to make plans for hospital development, and later for other health services. Although legislation in 1970 placed nearly all responsibility for health care with the counties, the Danish Parliament and the Ministry of Health have increasingly focused on health issues and have intervened several times. In the 1980s productivity of the public sector was the big issue. In the 1990s the introduction of market mechanisms into the health care sector became a major political theme.

So far reforms have been less radical in Denmark than in many other European countries, but changes are gradually taking place. Most changes are decided locally, such as the purchaser/provider split where counties establish separate bodies responsible for running the hospitals and others for purchasing patient services from the hospitals, contracting, and organizing the health care in company form. The most radical reform has been the introduction of free choice of hospital, which aimed at increasing the freedom of choice for patients, improving efficiency of the hospitals, and reducing waiting times for admission. Until now the effects of this reform have been small. Legislation in 1994 contains an obligation for the counties and municipalities to elaborate on their coordinated plans to include more on preventive measures and on quality assurance as well.

Despite recent legislation, negotiations with counties, along with financial and expert support, are the means mostly used by the state to influence the content of the health services. Reports from expert commissions have focused on the content and organization of health services. Topics have included priorities, coordination between hospitals and the primary health care, cost containment and productivity, and—lately—planning of highly specialized services and reduction of waiting times. A law in 1994 authorizes the Minister of Health to intervene in order to prevent excessive establishment of expensive procedures. So far this option has not been used.

During the last fifteen years innovative local initiatives have been an important tool to obtain changes in health care. Local health authorities and health workers have used this tool when economic constraints have created barriers to general changes and improvements. Defining an innovation as a local experiment has often been more acceptable to the state than a more costly general change. An example is the development of 24-hour domiciliary nursing care which was first introduced as a local experiment and later developed nationwide in primary health care. Similar examples are preventive visits to the elderly by home nurses, preventive health educational consultations in general practice, and establishment of community mental health centers. National health authorities have supported this development through conferences, guidelines encouraging local experiments, and a national health fund providing economic resources for local initiatives and evaluation activities.

The World Health Organization's "Health for All" has been adopted by the Danish government as a basis for Danish health policy. However, it has only very slowly become visible in policy, and some resistance has been demonstrated by the medical profession. Lately the WHO policy has become an important inspiration for the Danish health promotion program and for local health plans such as the "Healthy City Plan for Copenhagen." Two cities in Denmark have joined the WHO "Healthy City" network: Copenhagen and Horsens. Both cities have established a number of health promotion and prevention programs. On the basis of health profiles related to local districts, Copenhagen's comprehensive healthy city plan supports the strengthening of social networks in the local districts of the city as a platform for prevention and health promotion.

As compared to many other European countries reforms in the Danish health services have been few and moderate. Changes do, however, take place in different ways both in the counties and in the municipalities, and changes are in many ways directed toward the introduction of different market mechanisms and incentives aimed at increasing productivity and efficiency. However, differences in performance and organization of health care between the regions remain fairly persistent. Since the organizational changes and reforms have been limited in Denmark as compared to many other Western countries, one can assume that Danish health services will differ even more from those of other countries in the future.

NOTES

1. Vallgårda, S. 1991. The Danish health care sector in a historical perspective. In 1991. *Welfare administration in Denmark,* ed. T. Knudsen. Copenhagen: Institute of Political Science, University of Copenhagen.

2. Vallgårda, S. 1989. Hospitals and the poor in Denmark. *Scandinavian Journal of History* 13:95–105.

3. Steensen, J. P., and K. Juel. *Sygehusindlæggelser og sociale forhold.* Copenhagen: Dansk Sygehusinstitut.

4. Levetiden, I. 1994. *Danmark. Middellevetidsudvalget.* Copenhagen: Sundhedsministeriet.

5. Andersen, F. 1994. Flere Midaldrende læger. *Ugeskr læger* 156:6910–21.

6. Vallgårda, S. 1992. *Sygehuse of sygehuspolitik I Danmark. Et bidrag til det specialiserede sygehusvæsens historie 1930–1987.* Copenhagen: DJØFs Forlag.

7. Andersen, T. F., M. Madsen, and A. Loft. 1987. Regionale variationer I anvendelse af hysterektomi. *Ugeskrift for læger* 149:2415–19.

8. *Kvalitetsudvikling, hvorfor og hvordan?* 1992. Copenhagen: Sundhedsstyrelsen. *Kvalitetssikring og referenceprogrammer. Idékatalog.* 1991. Copenhagen: Sundhedstyrelsen.

9. Lov om ændring af lov om sygehusvæsenet og lov om offentlig sygesikring mv. 19. december 1992 (Danish legislation).

10. Schneider, M. Health Care in the EC Member States. 1992. *Health Policy* (special issue).

11. *Statistisk Årbog.* 1993. Copenhagen: Statistics Denmark. *Tal og data.* Copenhagen: MEFA, 1993.

Table 1 Population by Age, Sex, and Citizenship, 1994

Number of inhabitants		5,196,642	
Number of males		2,563,442	
Number of females		2,633,200	
Age distribution			
Age	0–16	17–59	60–
Males	520,158	1,598,027	445,257
Females	495,913	1,543,545	593,742
Total	1,016,071	3,141,572	1,038,999
Foreign citizens			
Other Nordic countries		24,192	
European Union		31,245	
Other European countries		56,824	
Non-European countries		76,753	
Total		3.6%	

Table 2 Live Births, Birth Rate, Fertility Rate, Infant and Perinatal Mortality Rates

	1960	1970	1980	1990	1993
Live births	76.077	70.802	57.293	63.433	67.442
Birth rate	16.6	14.4	11.2	12.3	13.0
Total period fertility rate	2543	1950	1546	1668	1764 (1992)
Infant mortality	21.5	14.2	8.4	7.5	6.5 (1992)
Perinatal mortality	26.2	17.9	8.9	8.2	8.2

Table 3 Infant Mortality Rate (%) by Six Most Common Causes, 1992

Diseases among newborns	0.24
Other congenital malformations	0.13
Symptoms and badly defined conditions	0.13
Malformations in heart and circulatory organs	0.11
Meningitis	0.04
Infectious diseases	0.02

Table 4 Estimated Death Rates per 100,000 Population for the Fifteen Leading Causes of Death, 1992

Ischemic heart disease	277.8
Coronary cerebral disease	109.4
Cancer in other organs	82.3
Cancer of the lung, larynx, and bronchi	63.7
Other heart diseases	57.5
Bronchitis, emphysema, asthma	50.1
Symptoms and badly defined conditions	47.2
Senility without informations or mental disorders	42.0
Diseases of the arteries	40.9
Other accidents	33.9
Pneumonia	31.7
Cancer of the colon	28.2
Breast cancer	27.0
Blood and lymph cancer	23.4
Suicide	22.0

Table 5 Selected Operative Surgical Procedures: Number per Thousand Population, 1992

Abrasio (per 1,000 women)	14.4
Hysterectomy (per 1,000 women)	2.4
Coronary bypass	0.7
Hip replacement	1.1
Cataract	1.9
Transurectal resection of prostata (per 1,000 males)	1.5
Caesarean sections (per 1,000 deliveries 1993)	12.5
Tonsillectomy	1.7

Table 6 Average Net Income before Personal Income Taxes of Doctors and Dentists

Profession	DKr	U.S. dollars*
Chief medical doctors,** hospitals, 1993	495,000	82,500
Residents,** hospitals, 1993	400,000	66,666
General practitioners*** (Family doctors, private practicing specialists), 1993	640,000	106,666
Private practicing dentists,**** 1991	480,000	80,000

*1 U.S. dollar = 6.00 DKr.
**Fixed public salary, the same for all specialties.
***Net income; office and professional expenses excluded. No information available by specialties.
****Net income; office and professional expenses excluded.

Table 7   Number of Acute Care General Hospitals Broken Down by the Number of Beds

Beds	Number
0–100	18
101–200	17
201–300	4
301–400	15
above 400	16

Table 8   Number of Acute Care Hospital Admissions Per Year (per 1,000 inhabitants), and the Overall Length of Stay in Acute Care Hospitals

	Number of admissions	Number of admissions—patients without symptoms	Number of admitted persons	Average length of stay in days
1930	189,245 (53)	—	—	31.0
1945	409,381 (101)	—	—	21.0
1960	521,541 (114)	518,108 (112)	—	16.1
1975	872,820 (173)	808,939 (159)	—	10.6
1991	1,068,615 (207)	961,514 (186)	676,000 (129)	6.9

During the 1970s a practice developed where persons admitted to hospital without symptoms such as healthy newborns and parents accompanying their sick children were registered as patients. The number of admissions are increasing more than the number of admitted individuals, due to movements of patients between departments and readmissions. Both these changes contribute to the lowering of the average length of stay. The first because the nonsick patients have a short length of stay, the second because moving a patient from one department to another gives two shorter instead of one longer stay.

Table 9   Number and Type of Nursing Homes and Related Types of Facilities and the Average Number of Beds per Facility, 1991

Nursing homes	1,055
Beds	42,285
Day centers	475

40 beds per nursing home as an average.

Table 10   National health expenditures by type of expenditure and source of funds for each category 1993, in million DKr*

Type of expenditure	Total	Local tax	County	State
Hospitals	34,667		31,776	2,891
Physician services	4,227		4,227	
Dental care	871		871	
Other professionals	300		300	
Drugs	1,773		1,773	
Vision products			3	
Nursing home	10,100	10,100		
Program administration				
Government public health	346			346
Research**	1,100		300	800
Construction	822		791***	31

*1 U.S. dollar = 6 DKr. There is no information on patient out-of-pocket payments or private insurance expenditures. They are estimated to 7,700 million DKr. No information is available on private health insurance, which covers some of the out-of-pocket payments for drugs, vision products, and dentists.
**Private funds and industry invest 2,000 million DKr.
***Includes a few private hospitals.

France's Health Policy Conundrum*

Marie-Pascal Pomey and Jean-Pierre Poullier

> *L'homme est bon par nature, c'est la société qui le corrompt.*
>
> (Man is good by nature, society corrupts him.)
>
> —Jean-Jacques Rousseau

In an only too rare poll on health systems, the French rated their delivery and financing setup higher than all other people except the Canadians and the Dutch, about on par with the Germans. All health insurance or public delivery systems, battered by external environmental constraints and internal contradictions, require mutations in order to ensure their long-run survival as equitable and performing institutions. Canada, Germany, and the Netherlands have since initiated preventive actions and/or reforms of their systems. France preferred a *médecine douce,* a soft therapy in which good practice should smoothly bring a new balance between multiple and evolving goals.

Second only to the United States in piling up blueprints of health systems reform, France's environment differs from that in North America. The European Treaties exempt social protection from a drive toward legislative harmonization, thereby safeguarding the wealth of multiple approaches to enhancing health status. They are also unambiguous about financial laxness, the sesame of European Monetary Union.

There is no single path to health, but unique experiences. Among those described in this volume, there have been over the years strong convergence features amid great institutional diversity. None were dictated by a single theoretical model or by an intergovernmental harmonization process. Shared problems and often also solutions are perceived through heterogeneous information infrastructures. No amount of goodwill can channel these analyses in a rigorously identical synopsis. The varying nature of the architectural designs and of the building materials leads to gradients in the description and in the critique of what decision-makers tend to consider the *best* health system in the world.

---

*The views expressed are the authors' own and do not necessarily reflect the opinions of the institutions employing them.

Geopolitical Considerations

Sire, faites-moi une bonne politique, je vous ferai de bonnes finances.

(May your Majesty adopt good policies, I shall produce good finances.)

—Louis Necker, finance minister, petitioning Louis XVI

Following the enlargement of the European Union from twelve to fifteen countries in 1995, a village in the center of France lost to a Belgian village just past the border on the north/northeast of France the honorific title of geographic center of the emerging Union. This anecdote—without strategic importance—translates a notion of size. France—a country sitting on the west/southwest of the European Union—is with 550,602 square kilometers (212,700 square miles) the Union's largest country. With 57,903 million inhabitants in 1994 compared with 81,410 million in the boundaries of the reunified Germany, 57,190 million in Italy, and 58,366 million in the United Kingdom, France is not Europe's most populous member state, but it is a fairly wealthy country. Its 1994 gross domestic product (GDP) per capita, measured at purchasing power parity (PPP), stood at $19,201 compared with $19,675 in reunified Germany, $17,830 in Italy, and $17,650 in the United Kingdom.

In many walks of life, the European Union (349,023 million inhabitants with an average $17,914 per capita GDP) may be viewed as a single entity. Healthwise, a strong informal convergence pervades but little formal harmonization has taken place. Institutions, incentive mechanisms, benefit baskets, finance are still largely country-specific. In the divide between an integrated finance cum delivery (Beveridgian) approach and a separate finance and delivery (Bismarckian) approach, Denmark, Finland, Greece, Ireland, Italy, Portugal, Spain, Sweden, and the United Kingdom opted for variants of a national health service; Austria, Belgium, France, Germany, Luxembourg, and the Netherlands maintained (and strengthened) a national health insurance path, which all European countries shared before World War II. Both approaches blend their base option with features more characteristic of the other model, contributing to an informal European convergence.

France's temperate climate does not lend itself to loss of life through heat waves, hurricanes, or long spells of deep cold. By European standards, France offers more topographic and landscape diversity than its neighbors. Several decades of strong gains in household income throughout the European Union and free trade have, however, erased the impact of many health-related bounties, starting with an affluent agriculture landed by nature on French soil. Malnutrition and nutrient deficiencies do not explain in any substantive way current intra–European Union differences in health status. France's relatively high standing in that league is accounted for more by gradients of cultural specificity (including perhaps wine and olive oil consumption) than by climate and soil. Geography and population settlements may not explain large differences in health status and in health systems between France and the four non-European countries in this volume, but they appear to be somewhat more significant determinants for comparing European countries.

A republic since 1795 (except for brief interludes during the nineteenth century), France enacted its fifth constitution in 1958. The basic law and its preamble extoll welfare principles laying the foundations of universal entitlement to medical benefits; the legal cornerstones of universal access are a 1945 ordinance; 1961, 1966, 1974, 1975, 1978, and 1988 laws; and a 1996 ordinance. A large part of medical delivery and financing regulation has not been enacted by a bicameral Parliament, no more than the National Assembly and the Senate vetted until 1996 the Social Budget (entitlement programs whose sum exceeds the expenditure on all other functions of government). Executive orders and implementing instructions by a technostructure constituted by labor unions (whose membership is less than a fifth of the labor force) and the largest employers' association determine the bulk of the rules applicable to medical and paramedical delivery and finance. Responsibility for public health is shared between the central government and local authorities (22 regions capping 96 metropolitan and 4 overseas *départements,* extended counties, with over 36,000 communes). Following the Devolution Act of March 2, 1982, and cost-shifting measures by a cash-hungry central government, regional and departmental authorities gained weight; since the beginning of 1995, regions exert discretionary authority in allocating hospital investments, while the *départements* manage various health promotion programs and part of social assistance. A number of cities and friendly societies *(mutuelles)* subsidize more than 2,200 outpatient clinics (dispensaries called "health centers") designed to remove access barriers (cultural and financial) for lower-income strata of the population and to congregate under one roof various medical and paramedical services. Although France opted for patient payment followed by reimbursement by social insurance, these institutions were innovative in requiring, notably, no advance payment. The bulk of the patient-physician/other health professionals contacts are monitored and regulated by quasi-nongovernmental agencies (quangos), national, regional, and local social security agencies (Caisse Nationale d'Assurance Maladie or CNAM, 16 CRAMs [regional], and 129 CPAMs [local]).

With each change of government, the ministry with the health portfolio has different attributions and a different name. Between May and November 1995, it combined responsibility for global health policy and for health insurance financing. It is concerned with the health professions, the medical establishments, the financial intermediaries (General Directorate of Health, Directorate of Hospitals, Directorate of Social Security), and it monitors the activities of 22 regional health planning–inspectorate bodies (DRASS) and, through the latter, similar bodies in the 100 *départements* (DDASS). The latter receive instructions from the government's regional or *département* overlords, the *préfets,* ensuring overall coordination of all central policies and their integration with the relevant local legislation. The Health Ministry's prestige is small, evidenced by the reluctance of the Ecole Nationale d'Administration (ENA) graduates (who hold the plum civil service jobs), to volunteer for a few years in health. Furthermore, the Health Ministry has little financial leverage. The spending authority is vested mainly in the CNAM technostructure already alluded to. Unlike the Health Care Financing Administration in the United States, CNAM is not a part of the central government and its decisions are taken by an "independent" council. Boards and councils that implement national policies are familiar in a number of countries reviewed in this volume. France has recently created several such institutions, notably a Medicine agency, a Blood agency, an Organ Transplant agency, and a Medical Evaluation agency.

The Social Security financing deficit on health insurance—distinct from the central government finances, unlike the Medicare Trust Fund in the United States—exceeded in 1995 35.5 billion francs (approximately U.S. $400 per capita) with a huge accumulated debt of 230 billion francs since 1992 to be repurchased over thirteen years through a special flat income tax of 0.5% starting in February. The new European aversion to deficit financing has already induced surgical cuts in economic and social legislation. In subsequent rounds toward financial respectability, health care systems are unlikely to be spared a major introspective questioning.

Environmental and risk avoidance legislation, coupled with scientific advances in areas such as occupational safety, product safety, hygiene, food additives, and other conerns of public health, have been a necessary companion to national health insurance.

The health benefit packages and the financial contribution scale are essentially determined by the government after consultation with a Commission des Comptes de la Sécurité Sociale. Revenue collection and benefit management are in the hands of the quango (quasi-governmental) agencies, managed respectively by the main employers' association and one of the labor unions. Charities play only a marginal role (albeit an essential one in specific settings). On the delivery side, patient-physician contacts in private practice dominate; private hospitals account for more than a third of the total bed complement with for-profit beds one in five; pharmacies are single retail outlets, privately owned. Friendly societies, called Mutuelles, and private insurance (virtually all with a labor-market connection) offer complementary coverage to that granted by Social Security reimbursements; they enroll around 87% of the population. Although health is a major citizen concern in opinion polls, it is typically a minor political issue.

Every seven years presidential elections select a leader embodying the nation's prospective legislative thrust. The National Assembly, elected every five years and the Senate, renewed by thirds for six-year mandates, enact laws. Differences in substance and wording are reconciled by a joint Commission before the last reading. Most laws require implementing decrees, frequently resulting in long delays before implementation. Most medical and health-enhancement statutes and regulations escape that process. Parliament, starting in 1996, will vote on a statement of prospective revenue and expenditure, an annual, nonbinding debate on the Social Budget.

The Social Security agencies are the Caisse Nationale des Travailleurs Salariés (CNAMTS) for the salaried employees, the Mutualité Sociale Agricole (MSA) for the farmers, CANAM for the nonfarm self-employed plus separate schemes for the miners, the railway workers, the nationalized power company workers, and a few other ''historical'' leftovers. These different schemes exhibit distinct cost-sharing features and administrative autonomy but, because they require cross-subsidization on account of their dwindling membership, they differ more in format than in substance. CNAMTS provides a number of operational tasks for all schemes and is thus frequently referred to as CNAM.

Users and patients are little empowered. Their overall satisfaction is explained by a perception of good ''performance'': life expectancy gains at birth exceed three months per year since 1945, measured healthy life expectancy (free of major disabilities) increased somewhat faster between 1981 and 1991, and a wide range of handicaps has vanished from the landscape. Rarely is any resident denied an operation or a costly treatment. Inequalities stem more from organizational inadequacies than any statutory omission. Queues are few and waiting times short. Furthermore, the average patient combines a primary and a complementary coverage, so that they do not have a major financial burden at the time of use. A vast modernization program following the 1970 Hospital Act endowed the country with an ample and well-equipped network of inpatient institutions. Health manpower is in abundant supply and is widely considered competent. Outcome inequities persist, which interest groups document. Homelessness is, for example, probably the largest source of inequity in that it both further weakens a population at risk and formidably complicates its access to medical facilities. The minorities exposed to inequity typically escape surveys and have little direct exposure to the media. Failure to achieve equity resides less in the supply potential or in social protection arrangements than in lack of will to manage the system and to establish priorities.

Medical Practice: A Patchwork of Different Concepts

*As if you would call a physician, that is thought good for the cure
of the disease you complain of but is unacquainted with your body,*

and therefore may put you in the way for a present cure but
overtroweth your health in some other kind, and so cure the
disease and kill the patient.

—Francis Bacon

While French medicine followed at close distance the world's exceptional advances in medical knowledge and contributed its share in the quest against diseases and impairments, the fundamental organizational principles remained: for the patient, *free choice of physician;* for medical practitioners, *freedom of prescription;* for both, a *socialization of the financial risks, fee-for-service payment* by the ambulatory care patient, and *confidentiality.*

Well-organized professional interest groups and loose patient representation formed a coalition to translate these principles as instant free choice, as a licence to consume regardless of proven efficacy, and no accountants to map health policy! Four-fifths of French patients visit practitioners near their place of residence or work; yet, no incentive payment method rewards that behavior. French patients are entitled to visit any number of self-employed practitioners on any day (or week, or month) for a single syndrome, a feature referred to as medical nomadism. The extent of nomadism is perhaps overstated in debates on the effectiveness of health institutions. Consumption of medicines averaged 52 boxes during 1993, suggesting that many patients purchase a box a week. The financial contribution required from the enrollees is high—a subject to be examined in a subsequent section. It is high too for the medical practitioners in terms of the rigor with which their professional incomes are regulated and in terms of a potential loss of clinical freedom.

In 1994, of an estimated 160,500 active physicians, 70% (112,586 doctors) were self-employed: 60,207 classified as general practitioners, 52,379 as specialists. An estimated 51,350 physicians had a salaried occupation, of which 43,108 (1992 figure) a full-time hospital job. Around 8,000 worked as program administrators, in pharmaceutical research, in occupational medicine, as school health physicians, and in the armed forces. There is some overlap in these figures, many holding part-time salaried positions in addition to near full-time self-employment schedules.

A watertight partition exists between ambulatory care (self-employed except in dispensaries) and both public and private nonprofit hospital care (salaried physicians). Under certain conditions, public hospital physicians can have a part-time private practice. Local hospitals that do not have a medical team of their own and that cater largely to long-term care patients allow general practitioners to take care of their own patients in that setting. Otherwise there are no visiting physician privileges in public hospitals. Separation of the general practitioner and other ambulatory care physicians from the hospital is not favored by the private hospitals, a sizable number of which are still owned by physicians. Patients in private hospitals pay physicians a fee-for-service. Between one-third and two-thirds of the self-employed physicians, as shown at the bottom of Table 6, have part-time salaried employment, notably in hospital outpatient wards and in preventive care settings, of which a number are located in health centers. The part-time commitments varied on average in 1991 between 2.1 hours per week for general practitioners to 4.5 for ophthalmologists, to 7.9 for cardiologists and 10.3 for psychiatrists. Few physicians are reported as unemployed but many young self-employed general practitioners are known to see very few patients; many longer established physicians have an overflow, "manageable" only with working weeks averaging in 1991 50.5 hours for ophthalmologists, 57.9 hours for general practitioners, and 61 hours for cardiologists.

The number of female physicians increases steadily (31% of all practicing physicians in 1994). Their practice styles differ slightly: greater propensity to take up salaried positions (only 24% among female physicians practice as self-employed), shorter working hours, slightly longer office calls, fewer night and weekend calls, fewer return visits. The share of women is highest in four specialties: dermatology (57% among the self-employed in 1991), gynecology-obstetrics (48%), pediatrics (41%), and ophthalmology (39%). The average age of female practitioners is lower than that of their male colleagues, except in anesthesiology. The deceleration in the inflow of physicians, generated by two decades of *numerus clausus,* causes a steady decrease in the number of young physicians and a concomitant increase in the number of physicians over 45 years of age.

Solo practice is still dominant. It varies according to specialties and gender. In general practice, 63% of the men and 67% of the females worked alone in 1991; in psychiatry, 73% of the men and 81% of the females; in ophthalmology, 45% of the men and 43% of the females. Specialists flock in greater numbers to the large cities, particularly in the vicinity of teaching hospitals. Health centers, some of which concluded a covenant with the sickness insurance bodies (CPAM) offer a setting for group practice that is attractive to physicians and medical auxiliaries: in exchange for adherence to the "conventional" fee schedule, CPAM pays their contributions to health insurance and to the pension schemes.

Patients have unrestricted access to the physician of their choice. No referral is required to access specialists. Surveys indicate that higher income patients and those with the highest schooling attainment tend to call more readily on specialists. General practitioners have mainly a diagnostic function and are paid a "conventional" fee (110 francs at the beginning of 1996, less than $20 at purchasing power parity rate), except for a small number with free(er) billing rights, labeled C on the bill. Small surgical interventions are paid the multiple of a K nomenclature (12 francs per K in money terms), a weighting system that is not frequently revised. Specialists (paid 150 francs in 1996) label the bulk of their services C's, except Z multiplied by a coefficient for radiologists. A large number of specialists in Paris and large cities have freer billing rights. In relative terms, a physician house call is billed at around a third of an average plumber's charge for a simple intervention on pipes. Emergencies aside, a strong separation between physicians and medical auxiliaries exists as well as among specialties in each group. Biological tests are a monopoly for laboratories, imaging diagnostics for radiologists and outpatient wards of hospitals. No integrated medical enterprises or retail chains are allowed, except hospitals and dispensaries. Physicians are not allowed to advertise, except indirectly through municipal bulletins and police precincts, which inform about general practitioners on weekend and summer vacation warding duty.

In 1994, an estimated 282.8 million services were performed by general practitioners, 4.9 per inhabitant, 4,697 per physician, a sizable increase since 1980 (3.5 consultations or visits per capita and 4,331 services per physician). The specialists billed 204.5 million services—3.5 per patient, 3,904 per specialist (a doubling since 1980). In 1993, in addition to 286.5 million visits by patients to their doctor's office, 82.2 million home visits were recorded. The overall steady increase in the demand for medical services, coupled with an increase in the number of professionals (e.g., the number of cardiologists, dermatologists, and ophthalmologists increased by a third between 1986 and 1992), worries health planners.

The right to physician unionization in France was granted in 1892 but membership in such groups is low: the three most vocal groups combined, the Confédération des Médecins Français (CSMF) representing both general practitioners and specialists, the Fédération des Médecins de France (FMF) with a larger number of specialists and the Syndicat des médecins généralistes de France (MG-France), have a combined membership of around 20,000. The physician unions bargain mainly for changes in fee schedules with three "social" insurers: CNAMTS for the wage earners, CANAM for the self-employed, MSA for the farmers; the smaller insurance bodies stay on the sidelines. An unwritten understanding requires CNAMTS's agreement to any negotiation.

Physician fee schedules are *administered prices,* assigning the self-employed profession to three main tiers. A self-employed physician opts between adherence or not to the *convention.* Regardless of the number of applicants or quality of services delivered, a physician cannot (unlike in Germany and the Netherlands) be denied accreditation to treat patients under the *convention,* which applies to around 99.6% of the population. Physicians are required to apply the fee schedule (but without limitation of volume), subject to a disciplinary exclusion clause in case of abuse. Physician incomes vary according to the number of services performed, fee schedule applied, professional expenses, and social contributions. Though self-employed, these physicians charge their patients according to the established fee schedule. The physicians contribute the "employee" share to their salaried pension and sickness insurance scheme; CNAMTS contributes the "employer's" share. This is not an insignificant "subsidy" in a country in which indirect wages exceed a third of earned income; in 1994, that indirect income supplement amounted to 10,187 million francs. Less than 0.5% of the physicians (in 1994, 410 generalists and 85 specialists) opted out of the *convention.* Their patients are not entitled to reimbursement and they are free to bill what the market could bear. These physicians have free billing with limitations, a Gallic way to introduce over-billing as a "safety valve."

Disparities in the distribution of aggregate physician earnings are an issue. In 1980, a "convention" allowed physicians to choose between adherence to the fee schedule or a free billing procedure, provided that at least a quarter of their patients be charged no more than the fee schedule and that they assume the full cost of their own social protection as self-employed. Given a wide shift toward this practice, it was subsequently tightened to apply to physicians who had spent two years at least as head or deputy head of a public hospital *(chefs de clinique):* without free billing opportunities their lifetime practice income would be lower. The design was to facilitate an increase in physician income without burdening the public funding arrangements. On average, over-billing is estimated to reach 50% of the contractual fee schedule and total over-billing to reach 10% of the self-employed physicians' aggregate income. The principle of noninterference with respect to the quality of the service and the fame of the physician underlying the single fee schedule was thus impaired because of the discretion of individual doctors and their judgment on what their "catchment" area would bear.

Used sparingly in the early 1980s, this "escape" valve rapidly became a favorite (about 29% of the self-employed physicians chose it in 1989). Another *convention* capped the free billing to around a quarter of the self-employed physicians. In the late 1980s and early 1990s there were geographical imbalances: in the distribution of physicians, central metropolitan areas were largely deprived of real choice between fee-schedule physicians and free-billing doctors, generating a risk of local exclusion for those patients not able to afford the extra-billing. For the country as a whole in 1994, an estimated 49,041 generalists and 31,759 specialists adhered to the fee schedule; 10,551 generalists and 17,700 specialists chose free billing. To square the picture, in addition to 495 self-employed physicians outside the *convention,* 205 generalists and 2,835 specialists were allowed to charge above schedule but with restrictions. They are the dwindling number of physicians allowed by an earlier *convention* to shift onto their patients and their insurers underpaid part-time hospital or public health work.

The signatories of the 1993 *convention* introduced quality norms, the Références Médicales Opposables (RMO), based on a professional consensus of science-based criteria related to medically useful therapies and prescriptions. ANDEM (Agency for the Development of Medical Technology Assessment), with a private nonprofit status, created in 1990, validates the proposed guidelines. History will determine the success or failure of the guidelines. They resulted during the first eight months of 1994 in a sizable slowdown in the pace of ambulatory care services and goods billings. Since then expenditures have increased. Most countries that adopted guidelines started with hospitals and only cautiously approached the ambulatory sector, and guidelines (as well as other innovations) were first adopted after experimentation. France opted for the seemingly more difficult path and for immediate implementation without a learning curve.

In March 1995, a decree created a *dossier de suivi médical,* providing for the maintenance of a medical file by a general practitioner for persons over seventy years of age with a diagnosis of two pathologies requiring at least six months of continuous care. The purported cost-benefit gain (an extra fee is paid to the general practitioner) is the prevention of drug interaction risks and the elimination of redundant medical services and prescriptions that will flow from a consolidation of clinical data, prescriptions, and other relevant information communicated by the medical practitioners consulted by the patient. The *carnet medical* (personal medical record, and the patient's property) must be exhibited for contacts with physicians and for reimbursement purposes. The government proposed in November 1995 the extension of this recordkeeping for the entire population without, however, an extra fee for the physicians.

The Medical Order, created in October 1940, amended in 1948, registers all physicians in its catchment area and serves as a peer disciplinary board at the departmental, regional, or national level. In addition to its role in mediating complaints, it is also the guardian of ethical orthodoxy. Composed mainly of older physicians, it is viewed by the younger ones as a body that slows down the adaptation of the profession's ethical and organizational standards.

Physicians are also represented by a myriad of learned societies, whose role to propel scientific advances intermingles with a lobbying role. The French Society of Anesthesia was thus instrumental in the early 1990s in expanding the number of postoperative wake surveillance rooms. As a consequence of that schizophrenia, the physician unions moved into the expert territory of the learned societies, co-determining for instance the contents of the medical guidelines adopted since 1994.

Estimates of professional incomes of the self-employed physicians in 1991 are found in Table 6. On average, they are not sizable relative to other professions requiring a long investment in education and/or atypical working hours. They are not high compared to those in the other nations contained in this volume. The distribution of earnings is fairly wide within each specialty and among them. The radiologists' turnover averaging 2.5 million francs in 1991 (after deduction of professional expenses, claimed to be 70%) yields at purchasing power parity a gross income somewhat over $100,000. In 1993, the combined salary of public hospital–based physicians with teaching responsibilities ranged from 232,600 to 488,500 francs, senior professors from 385,800 to 710,750 francs. In addition to a plurality of incomes from the Education Ministry and the Health Ministry, the medical university professors have an almost limitless control over the organization of their units *(services),* including the promotion potential of their medical staff, which has contributed to their reputation as "mandarins." Movements along the hospital earning scales are, however, based on seniority and there is no bonus for quality of service or fame. The hospital salary of high-ranking professors in 1995 ranged from 191,000 to 317,000 francs after twelve years, those of junior physicians with a teaching function from 128,000 to 251,000 francs after twenty-four years, those of unit heads *(chefs de clinique)* and assistants from 95,000 to 111,000 francs after two years, those of hospital-based physicians without a university appointment from 241,000 to 506,000 francs after thirteen years. For night duties, hospital-based physicians receive a supplement of 1,300 francs per shift. The incomes of hospital-based physicians have been assessed as comparable to that of senior teachers at secondary school level, those of professors as similar to those of upper-rank executives *(cadres supérieurs).* At the grassroots level, there appears to be a widespread attraction (particularly among general practitioners) in favor of different modes of remuneration. MG-France advocates a form of capitation. The issue is not yet on the political agenda.

The *numerus clausus* on the intake of second-year medical students from 1977 slowed the growth in numbers but did not stop it. The Medical Order registers six times more physicians than forty years ago. Their geographical dispersion remains uneven: 277 physicians per 100,000 population for the country as a whole. In some areas there are less than 188 per 100,000 inhabitants and in some more than 312. Paris is mushrooming at around 700. More than seven physicians in ten practice in the region where they completed their education. As a consequence of the large increase in the number of specialists (more than 65% between 1980 and 1994 in ambulatory care) and in the absence of gatekeeping, general practitioners and specialists compete directly in pediatrics, gynecology, dermatology, and cardiology.

The French residents have a quasi-direct access to the hospitals of their choice, many of which also have outpatient wards. For emergencies, aside from direct call on a hospital, patients have a wide array of facilities: general practitioners, dispensaries (health centers), fire brigades, and a national telephone system for emergencies. Manned by physicians, they assess the type of assistance most appropriate to the kind of emergency described during the phone call. Equipped ambulances attached to a local Emergency Medical Assistance center (SAMU) or to a regional Emergency Medical Assistance (SMUR) may be dispatched rapidly but, in nonemergency cases, advice is provided over the phone and people are directed toward a nearby general practitioner. Mechanisms are being explored to reduce the misuse of emergency facilities.

Continuing medical education is not compulsory, neither for the self-employed nor for hospital-based physicians, although the *code de déontologie* ruling the ethical standards of the profession specifies that "medical doctors are compelled to maintain and improve their knowledge." According to a 1992 survey of 300 physicians, 90.6% among the self-employed general practitioners and 92.7% among the self-employed specialists followed a recurrent education program, but it is thought the actual numbers are much lower. The largest annual medical event, Les Entretiens de Bichat, has around 6,000 physicians attending for a week. France's professional press—one of the most successful in the world—comprises several dozen titles in medicine, mostly subsidized by pharmaceutical advertisements. *Le Quotidien du Médecin* (a readership of 82,000), *Panorama du Médecin* (70,000 subscribers), *Impact du Médecin* (60,000 subscribers) provide an order of magnitude of the number exposed daily to digests on medical advances, therapeutic problems, and solutions. There is also an active pharmaceutical industry with over 16,600 detailmen, and manufacturers who subject physicians to a deluge of information on their new products. To remedy a too limited exposure to knowledge updating, the 1990 *convention* introduced a specific recurrent education provision, backed up since 1991 by an additional tax on the self-employed to finance it. The implementation appears to date to have been only modest.

Unshackling the Hospitals

> *The whole earth is our hospital*
> *Endowed by the ruined millionaire,*
> *Wherein, if we do well, we shall*
> *Die of the absolute paternal care*
> *That will not leave us,*
> *but prevents us everywhere.*
>
> —T. S. Eliot

With 4.3% of total employment in 1992 in inpatient care, hospital reform is not viewed with equanimity by unemployment figure watchers, particularly in small towns, where these establishments are often the largest local employer.

France's 3,810 hospitals in 1993 comprised 1,072 publicly owned establishments, 1,206 private nonprofit ones, and some 1,515 for-profit units (usually referred to as *cliniques*). The public establishments are larger: 478,815 beds in 1993, of which 348,301 for acute and convalescence care, 105,748 for long-term care, and 24,702 for day or night cases (4,476,947 patients recorded in ambulatory surgery, chemotherapy, dialysis, and so forth, for 11,484 bed equivalents and 320,791 patients "accommodated" at night in 13,218 psychiatric institution beds). Home care was supplied by hospital staff to 112,578 patients. The 2,753 private hospitals also obey a kind of certification of need principle, embodied by the *carte sanitaire*. Their bed count was 191,773 for acute and convalescence care, 1,393 for long-term care, 8,971 for day cases or night internment, which in 1992 serviced 509,378 sessions of chemotherapy, 1,769,451 dialysis sessions, a million ambulatory surgical procedures and other day cases and 131,750 "night" patients.

The *carte sanitaire* (the 22 regions divided into 147 sectors or catchment areas of at least 200,000 inhabitants) rests less on detailed epidemiological maps or on elaborate population-based registries and surveys than on expert opinion related to perceived needs, demographic factors, medical progress, and a quantitative-qualitative analysis of supply, the mix of which is translated into ratios. These, in turn, find their way into the *Journal Officiel*. The French hospital bed complement became large and is generally considered oversized because of the patient's free choice of establishment, and because of a social insurance scheme that acted through 1983 as a mere cash register, blindly paying the bills submitted without questions and still no questions about appropriateness. The Commissariat Général au Plan, an agency sketching the medium-term horizon of the government, proposed in 1993 a downsizing by 60,000 in-patient care beds. The then-government shifted part of the responsibility for this to regional authorities. Eighteen months of regional mapping, enshrined in 22 regional plans, identified less than half as many beds to be eased out over an undetermined period. Several regions supplied no aggregate target but vowed to "rationalize" surgical departments and obstetrical departments, and/or to convert short-stay into longer-term bed facilities. The Ile de France (Paris and surrounding *départements*) listed 13,000 beds to dispense with; the Provence-Côte d'Azur region with Marseille as the largest city listed 9,000 but offered to eliminate only half as many; Burgundy expressed an unwillingness to cut any excess beds.

A High Council on Hospital Reform issued in November 1995 confusing proposals to further cap inpatient care, instill new behavioral rules (including clinical guidelines), and add to the regulatory apparatus; the government vowed to enact these in 1996. Meanwhile, occupancy in short-stay hospitals declined from 80.1% in 1975 to 76.5% in 1993, mainly in private short-stay hospitals. In 1992, CNAM's chief medical inspector for the largest health insurance institution had denounced 120 billion francs of abuses, waste, and fraud in the health system at large, a fifth of total outlays, part of which is in hospitals. For inpatient care institutions, adjustments are not easy, even when the will exists; a gamut of financial and other incentives are notionally attached to "beds" whose clinical significance has faded. Symptomatic of that irrelevance: 52.7% of public in-patient investments in 1991 went into construction, down from 61% in 1980. Administrative planning and monitoring has barely changed in half a century.

The landmarks of France's post–World War II hospital story are the December 31, 1970 Act establishing a framework within which the hospital stock would be rationalized on the basis of perceived needs and defined norms—the chief instrument would be a *carte sanitaire* or physical plant adequacy approach—and the July 31, 1991 Act specifying rules of control designed to adapt the public and private stock to the medical and technical trends observed during the preceding two decades, as well as devolving to the regions a planning function. Comment has already been offered with respect to the regions' willingness to deal with excess capacity. The Languedoc-Roussillon region seized the opportunity to project alternative structures, home care, and day surgery, and the

Ile de France anticipates notably to ease out ineffective emergency wards. By and large, however, little forward-looking strategy emerged from the first planning exercise under the 1991 Act.

There appears to have been more success in the initial stages of implementation of another objective of that Act: a concurrence of medical and public health objectives for both private and public hospitals. Frictions between the two sectors had grown, particularly after the introduction in 1984 and 1985 of global budgeting for public hospitals. The private clinics had then shifted more resources towards gynecology, ophthalmology, elective surgery, long-term care, and interventions not requiring the most sophisticated technology, creating (in the opinion of public hospital spokesmen) an unfair competitive situation as the public sector had to deal with the complex and expensive cases, had to maintain emergency wards, and was capped by a global budget limiting the purchase of selected equipment. The fee-for-service operating theater billing and variable room rating procedures applied to the private establishments were seen as less constraining and "inflationary." In 1995, the Alsace regional health map stressed the complementarity between the two sectors; several other regions appear also determined to reduce duplication.

Public hospitals are deemed to be managerially and financially autonomous establishments. Their boards until 1996 were presided over by the mayor of the city where each is located and their managing directors are designated by the minister with the health portfolio. In April 1995, mayors of villages surrounding a local hospital whose maternity beds were to be consolidated with those of a local hospital in a neighboring city, successfully demonstrated that a hospital board should not display an "immoderate" zeal in rationalization matters. The difficulties of the transition process should not be blown up as total immobility. During the past decade, the number of short-stay acute beds in public hospitals declined by 34,000, that of medium- and long-stay beds, particularly in psychiatry, declined by 6,000 (that capacity adjustment went along with a program to increase the comfort and privacy of patients, namely, the total elimination of large wards, leaving only rooms with 1 to 4 beds).

The public sector comprises twenty-four teaching hospitals (CHU) with at least 600 beds each, affiliated with a university, and five regional hospitals (CHR), distributed over the entire territory. The 29 CHU-CHR offer a wide but not universal range of specialties linked to the sophistication of their equipment in nuclear magnetic resonance imagers, lithotriptors, cobalt therapy units, and so forth. They account for the bulk of complex interventions. The 489 hospital centers (of which 163 are general hospitals) with half of the total public beds are generally not equipped with the very sophisticated diagnostic and interventional equipment. These hospital centers undertake a large range of medical procedures including orthopedic, pediatric, and gynecologic interventions. Three-fifths of the long-term patients are mainly catered to in 314 local hospitals. Some 125 medium-term to long-term establishments cater to convalescent and other longer-term patients. 98 specialized hospital centers concentrate on mentally disturbed and psychiatric patients (141 of the 163 general hospitals have, however, psychiatric units as well). Local hospitals, averaging 160 beds, do not have their own medical team and may be open to self-employed general practitioners who are authorized for a period of five years to provide inpatient care. The general practitioners are paid out of the hospital budget on the basis of fee-for-service minus a 15% refund to the local hospital for use of facilities. The local hospitals establish formal agreements with hospitals that have a permanent medical staff. These agreements stipulate the conditions of access to intensive care and to medical technology in the hospital centers when required for patient treatment, and spell out the conditions under which physicians from these hospitals can intervene in the local hospital, as well as their remuneration. Self-employed specialists may be called on to intervene as well and are also paid out of the local hospital budget.

Since 1991 private hospitals have had to adhere to the same general principles as public hospitals, including certification of need, emergencies and, on an experimental basis in the Languedoc-

Roussillon region, prospective budgets. By 1993, all private hospitals agreed to change their charge system (fee-for-service, depending on the procedures performed plus operating room charge and a per diem for overnight stay) and to phase in a prospective budget system based on case-mix. These budgets are calculated not on historical costs as in the public sector, but on a case-mix basis. There have not been major problems in the first years of implementation. The nonprofit private hospitals deal more with medium-stay and long-term care. The for-profit hospitals (ranging from 50 beds to more than 250 beds) deal more with elective surgery, obstetrics, and other medical specialties. Surgical and specialized medical units in these private hospitals were prompt in detecting the opportunities offered, even by seemingly restrictive financing constraints, to cream a sizable share of day cases (in 1992, 63% of renal dialysis, 74% of chemotherapy, 66% of day surgery). In 1993, 37.9% of private sector surgical activity was day surgery, with a 37% increase that year in more complicated surgery. One of the large private hospital associations posts annual productivity increases among its members in the 7–8% range, contrasting with the average 1.8% increase in the public sector hospitals (admittedly different case mixes, nonetheless opposite trends).

Public hospitals for a decade balked at attempts to measure hospital activity by case-mix. France had been the first European country to experiment with Diagnosis Related Groups (DRGs), calling them *Groupes Homogènes de Malades* (GHM). In the 1990s, France lags behind other European countries in the monitoring of hospital activity; for instance, it has as yet no comprehensive statistics on discharge rates or average length of stay by disease categories or by case-mix. A large-scale experiment in the Languedoc-Roussillon region confirms that case-mix measurement is reliable not only with respect to throughput and output measurement but also with respect to prospective budgeting. This indicates what had long been suspected: global budgets, based on estimated 1982 throughputs, updated annually by the same amount for all hospitals except some very marginal adjustments, overallocated resources to some hospitals by as much as a fifth of their revenue, whereas other hospitals had to do with a shortfall. The analysis of that regional experiment further pointed to the need for an improved regional allocation of resources. It revealed, among other things, the patchwork nature of the current delivery apparatus (inside and outside hospitals), the lack of a public health culture (notable also in the resources allocated to prevention and promotion), the prevalence of repressive tools compared with incentives, and the absence of user empowerment at the delivery level. Designed for an accounting purpose, the experiment yielded a thorough X-ray of the entire health system.

Nine-tenths of hospital financing comes from social protection agencies. Since 1984–85 the bulk of public hospital funding originates in an operating budget paid in three monthly installments. The operating budget is calculated after deduction of a catering charge of around $10–12 per patient-day daily, raised to $14 from 1996 (which most users ask a complementary insurer to pay) and of cost-sharing dues. The global budgets are adjusted by a percentage determined annually by the government (in 1994, on average 2.7% or 1.5 percentage points above inflation to take account of population growth, aging, advances in medical knowledge, relative wage increases) plus a local adjustment determined at *département* level for special circumstances. Notwithstanding the principle of prospective budgets, public hospitals spent 4.66% above the previous year's level; overspending has been a chronic disease. Public hospitals are entitled to some revenue in addition to global budgets, but that increases total revenue by only 8.5%. Public hospitals charge patients a co-payment *(ticket modérateur)* for the first four weeks, from which thirty-one diseases (or clusters of diseases) are exempted and a number of insurees (e.g., war victims) are also exempted. Nearly nine patients in ten have, however, a complementary insurance which, depending on the contract, pays the full or a large share of the co-payment. Patient payments for hospitals in 1994 amounted to 6.2% of the total hospital bill, including the catering fee referred to. In 1980, before the "breakfast" charge was tagged on, patients paid 7% of the national hospital bill. Hospital policies, contrary to ambulatory care policies, are framed by the government, which is ill-equipped to monitor private hospitals.

The plethora of emergency wards is largely the product of the legislators' will in the December 1970 Act, stipulating that round-the-clock service should be available in all public hospitals. Eventually, 566 were strengthened or created, generating a major imbalance and a waste of resources. Six percent of them handle—according to a recent survey—fewer than 2,000 cases, 20% handle less than 5,000, and 44% less than 10,000. Slightly more than one hundred emergency wards deal with half of all cases. The ratio of hospitals with an emergency ward to population reached 1 to 141,000. If one includes emergency units other than those in public hospitals, the ratio is 1 to 105,000. An analysis of the reasons for admission reveals that well over two-thirds of these admissions could have been dealt with outside a hospital setting: patients turned to emergency wards instead of consulting a family practitioner. To reduce the waste as well as to increase their effectiveness, reports commissioned by the government recommended that local hospitals only deal with the demands of patients presenting a minor emergency, rerouting those with a severe distress syndrome toward specialized units in regional and teaching hospitals and large clinics. To prevent mere burden-shifting, a network linking hospitals and general practitioners through a national emergency telephone number would redirect much of the flow toward a prehospital setting. With respect to cases requiring emergency transportation, the former wild competition between public and private ambulances has been coordinated through the national telephone system with specialized doctors who dispatch ambulances to take patients to the nearest authorized public or private hospital that has spare capacity to deal with the emergency.

Once on the *carte sanitaire* and provided they obey myriads of regulations concerning the facilities, the materials purchased, the disposal of waste and other hygienic concerns, and the statutes governing staff training and promotions, inpatient care institutions are not subject to a formal accreditation process. Neither are most health personnel. There has, however, been a professional ethic so that quality assurance (specifically referred to in the July 31, 1991 Act) is regularly strengthened. This is more at the initiative of establishments since, for example, indicators related to outbreaks of microbial infections are not subject to central monitoring.

Seen from Sirius or some distant planet, France's public hospitals appear as interrelated webs of distinct creations, not a highly integrated network. In the aggregate, there is no shortage of physical plant, though it is in relative terms less endowed than in other countries if imaging equipment were a representative sample. With 9.5 CT scanners per million, it is less equipped than Belgium, Germany, Italy; the number of magnetic resonance imaging scanners per million (2.4) is among Europe's lowest but the number of radiologists is among the highest and their throughput rose rapidly during the 1980s. The potential performance of the human and medical capital is, however, not tapped optimally because of a global budget formula based on recorded 1982 observed activity. Cross-subsidization of insolvent demand, inappropriate use of facilities, and hoarding of staff are frequent bedfellows; evaluation remains a substandard priority. Hospitals combine high levels of excellence with huge baronies impeded by statutes to allocate resources more rationally. While the health systems of the United Kingdom, the Netherlands, Germany, Sweden, and Switzerland underwent radical surgery, France rehearsed a Jacobinist or centralized pull.

Public Health: Which Way?

The essential consists not in piercing through the target but in reaching its central point.

—Kong Fu Zi (Confucius)

Raising the health status of the population and better distributing the amenities by which this status is raised has meant in France, as in other countries, addressing selected diseases commonly held as social scourges as well as preventing the emergence of much avoidable dysfunctioning. Mental care, respiratory, and infectious diseases (France is Europe's country with the highest incidence/prevalence rates of AIDS) fall in the first group of actions, which is classified under the personal care expenditure categories just reviewed. Enhanced maternal and neonatal care, the eradication of nosocomial (hospital-acquired) infection illustrate the second group, which is accountingwise minute, yet essential to the acceleration of the health enhancement process.

Mental care is supplied in an institutional setting by 98 specialized psychiatric centers, 22 private hospitals, and 141 units in general hospitals, together some 80,000 conventional beds plus a capacity to deal with 30,000 day or night patients. That specialty employs 97,000 persons, of which 60,000 are nurses and 5,300 psychiatrists. With 17% of total inpatient capacity, 21% of admissions, 20% of bed days, 26% of the patients hospitalized according to a 1992 survey, mental care ranks as a petitioner for resources on par with surgery, well above gynecology (29,960 beds) and specialized units for cancer therapy (4,232 beds). It is the first cause of admission, well ahead of cardiovascular disorders (8% of admissions and 11% of patients) and of accidents and poisonings (8% of admissions and 11% of patients). There has been a drastic fall in average length of stay, from 290 days in 1965 to 57 in 1991, and a corresponding halving of the original bed stock. This is expected to continue but none of the new 1995 regional health "maps" singled this out as a strong potential. The annual demand for a psychiatric follow-up affects around a million persons with 8 to 10% requiring a hospital setting and the remainder organized around a community network. The catchment areas for day mental care therapy are 1 for 60,000 adults and 1 for 200,000 youths. Within the catchments, medico-social teams organize prevention, early diagnosis procedures, therapeutic sessions or internment, as well as posttherapeutic surveillance. Wide disparities can be found between the 100 *départements* with respect to the availability of beds and staff inputs. The mental care area is not the subject of a wide introspection, though there is a concern that, with an expected rise in old-age dementias, the organization and the effectiveness of mental care is in need of a review. France's leadership in the consumption of psychotropic drugs (11% of all adults in 1991 were regular consumers of tranquilizers, sleeping pills, antidepressants) led the country into a short-lived national public health debate.

The incidence of tuberculosis had experienced a steady decline, being efficaciously dealt with through a good pharmacopeia. The sanatoria, except one, have vanished from the landscape. However, in the late 1980s, and early 1990s, there has been a steep rise in new cases, from 15.9 to 17.1 per 100,000 population in 1992 and 1993, affecting elderly people, migrants, AIDS sufferers, and particularly those in economic hardship. In 1994, anti-TB dispensaries around the teaching and regional hospitals were strengthened, including the direct delivery of the appropriate pharmaceutical therapy. Vaccination of youths has long been compulsory; the monitoring of persons at risk and prevention of contamination in hospitals has been reinforced. In 1995, hepatitis B became a major public health target, the vaccination costs of which accounted for a sizable share of that year's recorded expenditure increase.

Specialized cancer therapy units were created in 1923 and operated as nonprofit autonomous institutions since 1945, and with global budgets since 1984. A sizable part of public research funds is allocated for cancer research and for AIDS. The prevalence rate of tumors rises steadily: from 2.8% of the population in 1980 to 4.6% in 1991 (in part due to the steady decline in avoidable premature death from other causes).

Blood banks—now monitored by a national agency—operate through a national nonprofit collecting and transfusion center, as well as through hospitals and a network of voluntary associations. The blood gift is in most of Europe altruistic and the donor cannot be paid. Following contamination problems mainly due to imported blood products inadequately controlled, the budgetary and the ethical surveillance of this network has been strengthened, including the closure of centers not offering the required quality standards.

The bulk of resources dealing with public health originates in social insurance, which pays for mental patient care, and also allocates a modest amount to finance specific prevention actions (e.g., flu vaccinations for the elderly and campaigns to fight home accidents, which are responsible for three times more victims than traffic and work accidents). Since 1983, legislation requires the *départements* to monitor maternal and child protection through a network of specialized dispensaries. That action is supplemented by specific national perinatal programs, one in the early 1970s designed to catch up with the best nations in terms of neonatal death rates. France moved up the ladder spectacularly. Further legislation was required in 1994 as the country had slid to thirteenth in the ranking of OECD countries for perinatal death. Within five years, maternal mortality should decrease by 30%, perinatal deaths by a fifth, low birth weights to below 4% (a 25% reduction), and unmonitored pregnancies/infant growth problems should be slashed by half. Obstetric safety has begun to be tightened, leading to the closure of many small maternity centers and pregnancy monitoring procedures have been enhanced. No incentives exist for births in the home. Parental leave, not on par with that found in several other European countries, is handled outside the insurance framework. Aside from vaccinations in childhood (diphtheria, tetanus, polio, tuberculosis and, for teenage girls, rubella), a *carnet de santé* revised in 1995 promotes throughout childhood and adolescence the monitoring of sensorial and overweight problems, tooth decay, and the prevention of accidents in the home. Prevention of disease is also backed by environmental legislation concerning air, water, and the disposal of solid waste, and by transport regulations (seat-belt wearing and drunk driving), with a special note for a late but relatively strong legislation to discourage smoking (forbidden, except in specially designated areas in establishments open to the public). Implementation is often not on par with the wording of legislation, but it has made an observable impact, particularly on the male population.

Although hospitals are not compelled to produce co-morbidity and complication indicators, hospital-acquired infections have, like perinatal deaths, become a sensitive issue. They are responsible for 0.25% of deaths in hospitals, an estimated 5% of bed days in short-stay hospitals and an excess cost per case between 4,000 and 10,000 francs. A national target to reduce the prevalence by 30% within five years was launched in November 1994. This action belongs to a spirit of revival of public health actions perceptible in all health care reform movements of Europe.

Medical Education

Est-ce qu'un homme comme vous ignore quelque chose?

Can anything be beyond the knowledge of a man like you?

—Beaumarchais, *Le barbier de Séville*

Medical students enter one of forty-one medical schools after completion of high school—among the most demanding secondary education in Europe, though veering somewhat toward a head full of facts than on critical reasoning. There is no selection at entrance, but after the first year a *numerus clausus* restricts entry into second year to 3,750 in 1995 (down from 8,588 students in

1972). The costs of medical education teaching are essentially borne by the taxpayers; a token fee of 1,000 francs per year, around $200 at exchange rate, is paid by the students or their parents. The curriculum is similar in most schools and only modifiable at the margin. Medical studies last six years.

During the first year, the main courses deal with physics, statistics, experimental sciences, behavioral and social sciences, and such fundamental biological disciplines as anatomy and physiology. Ethics, the history of medicine, and humanities are on the rise. Since 1993, 120 hours of English during the first three years is compulsory. The clinical education of the student starts from the fourth year, half at the bedside of patients, half in traditional theoretical classes and in tutoring. After validation of the first six years, students enter into a second cycle devoted either to general medicine or to a specialty, the latter accessed through an examination opening to a residency with 2,050 openings in 1995. Failure to apply for the entrance examination to the *internat* or failure to get accepted restricts students to general medicine, an additional two-year education period.

The choice of a specialty does not rest on ability or preferences, but on ranking in the entrance examination. Six branches are accessible: medicine, surgery, biology, psychiatry, public health, occupational medicine. A joint decree by the health and education ministries determines the number of openings for each branch. The students select in their ranking order their branch and specialty, and the hospital where to train among the twenty-four teaching hospital centers with vacancies. Future surgeons are residents for five years, other future specialists for four years. During these years the future physicians are full-time staff of their hospital with responsibilities similar to those of practicing physicians, benefiting from the latter's experience and guidance and some formal teaching, but paid at the level of a beginning nurse (between 82,900 and 129,500 francs in the mid-1990s). After eight to eleven years, medical students may defend a doctoral thesis.

Future dentists enroll as medical students in their first year and, following their rank in the examination, opt to continue in medicine or enroll in dentistry, which has also a *numerus clausus* and a five-year curriculum during which students practice in dental centers. The normal practice pattern is self-employment, but hospitals and health centers have a few openings in salaried positions. Fee-for-service is the dominant mode of payment. The fees are set at a low level but fees for services not included in the reimbursable list can be set freely; this generated a considerable demand for personal dental insurance.

Nurses are trained in schools attached to hospitals. Since 1992, the national curriculum extends over 37½ months leading to a national degree, but considerable local teaching freedom. The cost of the studies (30,000 francs per year) is fully subsidized by the Ministry of Health. The intake of students was 48,165 in 1992. The number of openings, around 19,000 a year, is rising as there is a shortage. There is a modest potential for promotion, requiring at least two additional years of study. Nurses working in self-employment—38,921 in 1991—are paid a fee-for-service determined through a bargaining process similar to that of physicians but with less visibility in the media.

Health Costs and Health Insurance

> *Ich will mit ihm gehen, den ich liebe,*
> *Ich will nicht ausrechnen, was es kostet.*
> *Ich will nicht nachdenken, ob es gut ist.*
> *Ich will nicht wissen*

It is my will to go with the one I love,
I do not wish to count the cost.
I do not wish to consider whether it is good.
I do not wish to know

—Bertold Brecht, *Der Gute Mensch von Sezuan*

Why so large cost, having so short a lease
Dost thou upon thy fading mansion spend?

—William Shakespeare, Sonnet 146

In 1994, France spent 9.7% of its GDP on health, using the OECD definition. A provisional estimate raises that ratio to 10% in 1995. In 1970, the expenditure ratio stood at 5.8%, in 1980 at 7.6%, and in 1990 at 8.9%. Only the United States and Switzerland overtake France.

Price increases are the single most important explanation for increases in expenditure on health. Between 1970 and 1980, the average annual increase in health spending was 16.5%, the national price level rose annually by 9.9%, population by 0.6%; benefit growth (number of services, their quality, their intensity) accounted thus for an annual gain of 5.4 percentage points. Between 1980 and 1990, health expenditure grew at an annual rate of 10.4%, of which 5.2 percentage points reflected national price increases, 0.5 point population growth and 4.5 points real benefit growth. Between 1990 and 1994, the measured annual rate of health spending growth was 5.6%, the overall rate of price inflation slowed to 3.8% per year, population still grew by 0.5%; real benefit increases slowed to 1.2 percentage points per year. Measurement vagaries in the underlying national accounting series and statistical interaction effect aside, prices explain 60% of the rate of increase in medical expenditure during the 1970s, 53% during the 1980s, 68% in the early 1990s. Using estimates from OECD *Health Systems: Facts and Trends,* updated through 1994 with OECD *Health Data 96* and with projections for 1995, France topped the twenty-six OECD nations for real benefit growth during the past quarter-century. The high real benefit growth exhibited is consistent with the fast expansion in average physician consultations, medicines consumed, and hospital throughput.

However, with more than three million recorded unemployed and many people without lasting labor market connections, there is a fair presumption that, in recent years, fairness in the distribution of real benefits deteriorated somewhat at the tail end. This contrasts with indirect evidence for earlier periods during which the take-up of benefits by the underprivileged had made advances, complemented by modest, but targeted, public health programs. While distribution problems are undeniable, and the correlation between high consumption of medical services and real health status gains is not straightforward, the gains in the health status of the French population are not insignificant.

For several decades, France recorded one of the highest increases in life expectancy at age 60 for both genders. Between 1981 and 1991, females gained 2.6 years in healthy life expectancy at birth, males 3 years; during the same period, measured at age 65, females gained 2.3 years of disability-free life, males 1.3 years. The record of potential life-years lost prematurely remains disheartening but, in the OECD tables alluded to, a number of partial indicators point to France as a middle-rank health status achiever and/or a middle rank health status gainer, with better results for the older age strata than for the younger age strata. Thus, it is a positive picture, albeit a mitigated one, in relation to the questions Where did the money go? On whom was it spent? For what benefit?

The annual growth rates of personal health care since 1970 are shown in Table A, as are the

Table A   Trends (%) in Costs and Utilization, Average per Year

	1970–75	1975–80	1980–85	1985–90	1990–94
Value of personal health care—growth rates	17.3	15.9	13.7	7.7	5.5
Value of preventive services—growth rates	18.5	15.6	9.5	4.8	4
Inpatient volume increases	8.9	6.9	3.6	2.5	3
Value of physician services—growth rates	15	13.7	14.6	9.2	4.1
Value of physician services—growth rates in constant prices	5.3	4.2	6.1	5.8	1.9
Dental care volume increases	5.6	6	5.3	5.7	3.4
Volume increases in pharmaceutical sales	10.7	4.3	8.3	8.1	3.7
Volume increases in optical lenses	—	—	4.9	5.2	3.4

trends of identified preventive services (which absorb only about 2% of total health expenditure on health). The slower growth rate experienced by preventive services reflects a societal preference for the private consultations between patients and their physicians, as well as an impoverishment of general government and a lack of a vision cast in terms of national priorities during these years. A recent advisory report by the Public Health Commission, *La Santé en France* sets out to correct that gap. Highlighting the relative size of premature death in France, that occurring before age 65, compared to that in the other European Union countries, and contrasting it to the high life expectancy of the elderly French population, the Commission focused on inequalities in health status according to socioeconomic class and, in line with the spirit of the World Health Organization strategy *Health for All by the year 2000,* mapped out specific targets. Whether these will become a burning national duty is an object of speculation. At the least, the publication of the report marks a break in an approach that had been largely confined to paying the health bill without an apparent overall health strategy.

Table A also shows the utilization (volume) increases per year since 1970. During the period 1980–94, the billing in private hospitals exceeded that of the public sector by 0.8% per annum, but following a contractual agreement between the private hospitals and CNAM, the two sectors have recently moved in parallel: 6.3% and 6.2% respectively in 1994, 3.9% and 4.8% in 1995 (eleven months). However, there are large differences in output and output per unit of input between the two sectors. Hospital output is not homogeneous between the sectors, but productivity gains seem to be more prevalent in the private units, reflecting perhaps too administrative an approach in public hospitals and a more flexible allocative efficiency in private hospitals. The annual increase in the value of physician services also appears in Table A. Cost shifting occurred in the 1990s from public funding to complementary insurance and, for the least well off, to households directly.

Dental care experienced annual volume increases for the same subperiods. Cost shifting occurred as well, but was greater toward households as the complementary insurance schemes typically reimburse less generously than for outlays on physician services and other professional services. In 1994, households paid 19,165 million francs in out-of-pocket expenses for physicians (22.5% of total expenditures), but 16,892 million francs for dentists (41% of dental expenditures). These are two of Europe's largest cost-sharing ratios and a matter of concern; France shares in the industrialized world's improved dental status, but a more recent survey on social protection is worrisome in terms of dental care postponed by patients declaring these outlays to be unaffordable.

Pharmaceutical sales reached 2,052 francs per person in 1994, at an average purchasing power parity of $314. Price trends differ, depending on registration status: nonreimbursable products are now virtually uncontrolled and experienced an annual average increase of 6.9% during the 1970s, 7.6% during the 1980s, 9.1% since 1990 while reimbursable products (a list that was slimmed down) are held on a leash: 3.7% increase during the 1970s, 1.8% during the 1980s and a decrease averaging 0.5% since 1990 (increases well below average inflation rates). Households pay dearly for low prescription pharmaceutical prices. There is only a marginal restraint on the number of items prescribed. Table A displays volume increases in pharmaceutical sales. Cross-subsidization between nonreimbursable and reimbursable medicines is large. Innovation in the French pharmaceutical industry has not been on par with that of the United Kingdom and several other economic partners. Cost-shifting between social security and complementary insurance has been high, inducing higher premiums, since the latter had little or no leverage on consumer and prescriber behavior. However modest the pharmaceutical bill is compared to the hospital one, it contributes to a sizable public finance deficit. None of these impeded household out-of-pocket outlays from rising to 19.9% of total purchases with a heavier burden falling on chronic patients. Optical prostheses (lenses) experienced similar trends (Table A). The patient's out-of-pocket share, together with audio- and other orthopedic prostheses, reached 26.7%, that of complementary insurers 31.4%.

Expenditure on ambulatory care price and volume increases appear in Table B. A slowdown in price increases explains much of the deceleration. Ambulatory care billings have since resumed their upward spiral: 6.4% during the first eleven months of 1995, with a strong increase in outlays on general practitioners office calls (3.5% in volume terms, whereas house calls declined by 1.3%).

Is the crux of the financial problem in health care an insatiable demand for medical services, unchecked by a *ticket modérateur* (co-payment), which complementary insurance for over four-fifths of the population renders controls otherwise ineffective? Is it instead inadequately restrained supply, facilitated by an open-ended solvency guarantee? Is it a bicycle syndrome applied to open-ended demand and pay-as-you-go revenue based on a labor market connection: in equilibrium as long as there is movement, unstable when still? Droves of long-term unemployed are pointed to as the culprit. "If a million people were put back to work," the refrain goes, "the deficit would melt overnight." "If the government paid the dues for noncontributors," the tune goes on, "the health insurance equilibrium would be safe." That melody postulates *inter alia* that medical consumption, whose growth rates slowed during the leaner post–Gulf War years, will not resume and that there is no backlog of inequities generated during the crisis years. It assumes huge productivity growth, including increased revenue to pay for the noncontributors. Otherwise the insurees are bound to pay in taxes what they now pay in higher than warranted contributions. It rests on a conviction that higher employment ratios will suffice to erase the accumulated public debt. It resolves without debate the structural soundness of the parameters on which the French model of social protection is grounded—an unquestionable model during the Golden Thirties (the first three post–World War II decades).

The French health system has grown into a cluster of institutions and mechanisms whereby entitlement to benefits has become quasi-universal, and payment is based on labor market affiliation (6.8% of total wages for salaried employees, 12.15% for employers, plus a variable levy averaging 2.5% for complementary insurance). Retirees pay contributions at a reduced rate. The farmers' scheme, as well as other schemes with dwindling enrollment and a large share of retired pensioners benefit from "demographic" compensation mainly transferred from the wage earners' scheme. The proceeds from specific duties on alcoholic beverages and tobacco do not compensate the

Table B   Ambulatory Care Increases (%) Average per Year

	1980–90	1990–94
Ambulatory care price increases	11.9	4.4
Ambulatory care volume increases	6.9	2.9

"demographic" subsidy. A cash-strapped government has shifted, in addition, costs formerly paid out of general revenue (e.g., some psychiatric costs) onto health insurance.

Not constrained in terms of accessibility to benefits (as the Netherlands recently did in removing entitlement to dental care at public expenses for able-bodied adults with adequate incomes), the French health care system has become a maze of cross-subsidization. The central government with only a minimal financial stake (in 1994, together with the local authorities, it paid 3.9% of total outlays), has satisfied itself over the years in raising health insurance contributions, and tackling benefit packages only marginally. In the early 1970s, the employee share of the costs was 2.5% of wages up to a ceiling, less than a third of the present burden. Complementary insurance bodies, which in 1994 funded 11.5% of the national health bill, do not manage their liability: they pay part or the total difference between 100% and what Social Security pays for goods and services purchased at the patients' discretion or on the recommendation of a patient. In 1994, households paid 13% of the total health bill.

Complementary insurance bodies have no voice in the determination of entitlement baskets or on behavior. They owe their growth to a small retrenchment of Social Security (68.8% of the outlays in 1994, down from 70.3% in 1980 and 69.2% in 1990) and to the tax advantage attached to fringe benefits. In 1993, employer contributions to Social Security and to private pension and welfare plans added 37.3% to the wages paid, exempting from immediate taxation 28.1% of the national wage bill. The main Social Security agency, CNAMTS, has little incentive to reform from within and is subject only to gentle persuasion. Low union membership (8% of the labor force) is not commensurate with its power to disrupt economic activity and to intervene as in December 1995 with *Touche pas à ma Sécu!* (Do not threaten my health and pension benefits!).

The European Treaties do not require a harmonization of the social protection arrangements. France's choice for generous health benefits, costing 0.7–0.8 GDP percentage points above European average in the 1970s, created little pressure to change. The 1.3 percentage point differential of the early 1990s (projected to climb to around 2 points from 1995) has been sending a signal to decision-makers long convinced that the best health system in the world was generating few competitive disadvantages. Different mixes in direct and indirect wages are compatible with the fabric of a European Union, but there is already an awakening of public opinion that perhaps France's social protection system is not the most generous, and that it is an expensive system relative to the benefits. With European nations committed to drastically lowering their public deficits during the second half of the 1990s, can France be spared a major overhaul of its health care financing arrangements or will an experience with expedients prevail, experience, which—Confucius warned—to be "similar to a lantern carried on one's back; it only sheds light on the path already covered"?

Averting drastic choices is a political favorite. On the health-financing scene, France developed a culture in which an accounting control of medical goods and services is objectionable, but rationalization based on the respect of medical guidelines and elimination of waste should be promoted. This concept underlies the case-mix measurement experiment of the early 1980s, still not generalized. It was present in the negotiations between the public health insurance bodies and various professional groups (laboratories, self-employed nurses, pharmaceutical manufacturers, etc.) culminating in 1993 in a *convention* with the physicians. One hardly perceives a major difference with self-policing expenditure restraint strategies in other countries, since after successful medically based restraint episodes the pressure was relaxed and the inflationary spiral started anew. Furthermore, the medical and allied professions remain by and large the guardians of the new orthodoxy. There is only a very limited capability within the social insurance institutions and the government regulatory bodies to promote guidelines since the relevant epidemiologic and consumption data to monitor levels and trends are not yet collated. From mid-1996, the employee health insurance payroll taxes will gradually yield to a flat-rate income tax, a generalized social contribution, designed to ensure more equity in funding, universal coverage regardless of contributory status and a more homogeneous benefit package for all. The previous social partners' confusion between social insurance benefits (which they are managing) and social assistance benefits (which are nominally general revenue–funded) should fade away for lack of being clarified. From 1997, following precedents in Germany and other European countries, a dependency insurance will finance medico-social benefits—a possible source of confusion, for what is social? Beyond outright capping of medical incomes and those of the pharmaceutical industry, no major structural reform has been announced designed to enhance the overall effectiveness of the system, to prune excess capacity, to ensure that money follows the patient, to massively expand managerial principles analogous to those being implemented elsewhere. Failing structural changes, France is at risk of lagging behind her partners which, during the first half of the 1990s, introduced sizable measures of microeconomic efficiency and better overall resource allocation of their health delivery system.

Can Adjustment Be Painless? Is There a Will to Change?

Les vrais hommes de progrès sont ceux qui ont pour point de départ un respect profond du passé.

The true movers of progress are men whose starting point was a deep respect for the past.

—Ernest Renan

No country has yet developed a fully equitable, efficient, effective, empowered health system, affordable to its citizens that obeys competitive market principles (or alternatively respects rational criteria accepted by most) without doing excessive violence to consumer preferences or the public purse.

Virtually second to the United States in spending on health, France opted in favor of a series of complex constructions. A Rothschild was fond of saying, "there are three ways to financial ruin: women, gambling, engineers; the first two are the most pleasant ones, the latter the most certain." Was he also thinking of health systems? In France, as in Australasia, Canada, and most European countries, the public sector has taken the responsibility to channel the largest part of the health care financing. The delivery of health care has largely remained outside its scope, even though two-fifths of the expenditures occurs in establishments it directly controls (e.g., public hospitals). Funding for the delivery of care is channeled through an offbudget technostructure under the control of unrepresentative unions that have no direct financial stake in the viability of the system. While in an awkward arm's-length position regarding financing, the government inherited centuries of centralized bureaucratic traditions without incentives for attracting the best talent to positions of command in the health arena. Many highly competent people are not even left the minutiae of management because of governing national rules that do not adequately deal with unique local conditions. Both publicly and privately supplied services are considered of high standards but, in an open-ended financing system, where are the incentives to avoid an excess supply reaching gigantic proportions?

France opted altogether for large clinical freedom and unrewarding remuneration modes. Within each professional category, fees are uniform regardless of ability and quality of service, thus stifling innovations in delivery and financing, except for the safety valve provided free-billing physicians. The free-billing safety valve, however, is destructive of the integrity of the system; it fails to accommodate needed flexibility and does not prevent abuses, waste, and fraud. The inherent persistence of deficits incurred by the health system threatens the timeliness or the attainment of European Monetary Union targets. A system that fails to bring its benefits in line with what has been determined to be affordable is at the mercy of emergency surgery that is likely to be more painful than where the will to remedy structural imbalances has been more prevalent, the blueprint for action has been more comprehensive, and a pilot to steer the ship in the straits has been more welcome.

A health system deals largely with the aches and pains of everyday life and dysfunctions. France's does too. It anticipates the emergence of risks and projects goals raising the average health status and lowering future liabilities. However, the structures are no longer relevant to the ambitious goals set and the environmental constraints because of the inefficiencies and distortions of a conflicting management system in which the division of responsibility between the actors is at best unclear, an oversupply of actors, and a belief in homeopathic administrative and managerial therapies. In October 1995, France recently celebrated the fiftieth anniversary of a Social Security system that, during three decades, propelled the country among the most equitable and among the relatively efficacious ones in health status terms. Visions of leadership seem to have since long faded, not only those related to the distant future of Social Security, even those related to a closer horizon: *Santé 2010* [Health 2010], the Planning Commision's last blueprint, moves but a decade too slowly.

REFERENCES

Beresniak, A., and G. Duru. 1995. *Economie de la santé* (Health economics). Paris: Masson.

50 ans de Sécurité Sociale—L'Oeuvre collective. 1995. (50 years of social protection). Paris: Espace social européen.

Duriez, M., and S. Sandier. 1994. *Le système de santé en France* (The health system in France). Paris: CREDES and Ministère des Affaires Sociales.

Les Francais et leur santé, Solidarité Santé (January–March 1994).

Johannet, G. 1995. *Dépenser sans compter, des pensées sans conter* (Spending without accountability, thoughts without parsimony). Paris: Espace social européen.

Lachaud, C., and L. Rochaix. 1993. *France.* In *Equity in the Finance and Delivery of Health Care—an International Perspective,* edited by E. Van Doorslaer, A. Wagstaff, and F. Rutten. Oxford: Oxford University Press.

New Directions in Health Care Policy. 1995. Paris: OECD, Health Policy Studies, no. 7.

OECD Health Data 96/Eco-Santé OECD 96. 1996. (A software on health systems: activities, performance and expenditure comparisons). Paris: OECD.

OECD Health Systems: Facts and Trends. 1993. Paris: OECD, Health Policy Studies, no. 3.

The Reform of the Health System in France. 1992. In *The Reform of Health Care.* Paris: OECD, Health Policy Studies, no. 2.

Soubie, R., J-L. Portos, and C. Prieur. 1994. *Livre Blanc sur le système de santé et l'assurance maladie* (White Paper on the health system and on health insurance). Paris: Commissariat au Plan.

Table 1 Population by Age and Sex, 1993
(in Thousands—Mid-Year Estimates)

	Total	Female	Male
0–4	3,708.7	1,811.0	1,897.7
5–9	3,817.0	1,864.9	1,952.1
10–14	3,919.8	1,913.1	2,006.6
15–19	3,882.5	1,899.0	1,983.5
20–24	4,347.5	2,148.1	2,199.3
25–29	4,321.5	2,153.5	2,168.0
30–34	4,341.0	2,176.1	2,164.8
35–39	4,274.7	2,147.6	2,127.2
40–44	4,335.6	2,159.3	2,175.4
45–49	3,674.6	1,818.7	1,855.9
50–54	2,772.8	1,382.1	1,390.7
55–59	2,882.3	1,473.2	1,409.1
60–64	2,936.6	1,546.7	1,389.8
65–69	2,683.7	1,472.8	1,210.9
70–74	2,184.0	1,249.4	934.5
75–79	1,261.2	771.0	490.2
80–84	1,261.2	849.2	449.5
85 +	1,012.6	739.8	272.8
Total	57,654.5	29,575.4	28,079.1
Mean age	37.4		
Median age	35.4		

SOURCE: INSEE, *Annuaire Statistique de la France*, Paris, 1995.

Table 2 Live Births, Birth Rate, Fertility
Rate, Infant Mortality Rate, 1993

Live births	710,340
Birth rate	12.3
Fertility rate	1.73
Infant mortality rate	6.2

SOURCE: INSEE, *Annuaire Statistique de la France*, Paris, 1995.

Table 3 Infant Mortality by the Six Most Common Causes, 1992

	Total	Girls	Boys
Syndrome instant death	1,291	463	828
Congenital anomalies, circulatory system	520	209	311
Syndrome of respiratory distress	225	88	137
Other respiratory disorders of newborn	220	85	135
Intrauterine hypoxy and asphyxy at birth	202	83	119
Respiratory tract obstruction due to ingestion of food	153	70	83
Unknown causes	613	292	321
All causes	5,075	2,063	3,012

SOURCE: INSERM, *Causes médicales des décès*, Paris, 1995.
NOTE: Metropolitan territory only.

Table 4   The Fifteen Leading Causes of Death, 1992 (Rate per 100,000 Female or Male Population)

	Female	Male
Cerebrovascular disorders	71.4	94.8
Ischemic disorders	58.4	121.1
Respiratory tract disorders	46.1	101.6
Symptoms of ill-defined conditions	44.2	66.0
Breast cancer	31.7	0.4
Prostate cancer	—	45.8
Malignant neoplasm of the intestine	22.2	38.2
Malignant neoplasm of the digestive tract	11.9	30.3
Suicides	10.5	32.3
Diabetes	9.8	11.4
Malignant neoplasm of the uterus	9.2	—
Malignant neoplasm of trachea, bronchus, lungs	9.2	79.7
Genitourinary disorders	8.8	18.6
Liver cirrhosis	8.4	23.1
Road traffic accidents	7.9	23.5
Malignant neoplasm of the digestive tract	7.3	16.8
Leukemia	6.1	11.1

SOURCE: INSERM, *Causes médicales des décès*, Paris, 1995.
NOTE: Metropolitan territory only.

Table 5   Selected Operative (Surgical) Procedures, Number per Thousand Population, and Average Length of Stay in Hospital for Each Type of Operation

Not Available

Table 6   Average Physician Net 1991 Pre-Tax Professional Income (In Thousand Francs, Except Where Indicated)

	General practice	Cardiology	Surgery	Ophthalmology	Psychiatry
Total income					
Average	322	500	748	467	313
Median	308	470	695	410	291
9th decile	562	844	1,237	842	498
3d quartile	418	631	948	636	402
1st quartile	201	323	479	261	200
1st decile	114	202	302	117	122
Average					
males	341	517	758	551	344
female	177	—	—	303	234
Average					
rural	357	—	—	—	—
small town	319	532	—	478	330
city center	277	488	—	478	298
suburban	298	373	—	378	325
Self-employment income					
Average	309	441	700	444	246
Median	300	404	639	388	219
9th decile	534	804	1,225	800	438
3d quartile	405	591	916	617	337
1st decile	96	132	225	98	49
Salaried income	13	59	48	23	67
(% perceiving)	(36)	(74)	(46)	(53)	(67)
Average turnover (pre-tax, pre-professional expenditure deductions receipts)	528	936	1,151	832	—

SOURCE: Ministère des Affaires Sociales, de la Santé et de la Ville, *Les revenus des médecins libéraux et ses déterminants*, Paris, 1995 (based on a CERC survey) and, for turnover, CNAMTS.

NOTES: The French franc—U.S. dollar exchange rate for 1991 was 5.41; the (more relevant) average purchasing power parity was 6.53. By that score, average G.P. income reached $49,300 and surgeon income nearly $115,000.

Salaried employment compensation (indirect wages included) was estimated as 180 thousand francs, a 1.8 ratio for general practitioners, a 2.8 ratio for cardiologists, a 5.7 ratio for surgeons.

The above-average estimates for general practitioners are close to the 1991 level in *OECD HEALTH DATA 95* (336 thousand francs), but the latter source for all physicians (368 thousand francs) is substantially lower than the above-weighted income for all physicians.

City center and close suburban refers to the very large towns only. Dashes indicates data statistically not significant or not applicable.

The 1991 average turnover or professional income revenue was 709 thousand francs; anesthesists (993) were preceded by radiologists (2,485), surgeons (1,151), followed by cardiologists (936), ophthalmologists (832), gynecologists-obstetricians (765) with pediatricians (515) well below the average.

Table 7   Number of Acute Care General Hospitals

Not Available

Table 8   Acute Hospital Care Admissions and Average Length of Stay (Actual Number, Rates and Days)

	1987	1992	% population
Admissions			
Total short stay	10,756,523	12,180,382	21.2
public hospitals	6,427,474	7,080,668	12.3
private hospitals	4,329,049	5,099,714	8.9
medical specialties	4,313,991	4,962,195	8.6
public hospitals	3,503,268	3,952,218	6.9
private hospitals	810,723	1,009,977	1.7
surgical specialties	5,175,500	5,922,371	10.3
public hospitals	2,187,089	2,370,611	4.1
private hospitals	2,988,411	3,551,760	6.2
gynecology, obstetrics	1,258,032	1,295,816	
public hospitals	737,117	785,839	
private hospitals	520,915	537,977	
Average length of stay			
Total short stay		6.2	
public hospitals	8.2	6.5	
private hospitals	7.2	5.7	
medical specialties		7.6	
public hospitals	9.1	7.2	
private hospitals	13.0	9.0	
surgical specialties		5.2	
public hospitals	7.4	5.9	
private hospitals	6.2	4.8	
gynecology, obstetrics		5.4	
public hospitals	6.0	5.2	
private hospitals	6.5	5.8	

SOURCE: Ministère des Affaires Sociales, de la Santé et de la Ville, *Annaire des statistiques sanitaires et sociales 1995.*

Table 9   Number and Type of Nursing Homes and Related Types of Facilities, Average Number of Beds per Facility, 1994

Number of establishments	4,181
Number of beds	54,470
Share of hospices	6 %
Share of retirement homes	76.1%
Share of residential-nursing	17.9%

SOURCE: Ministère des Affaires Sociales, de la Santé et de la Ville, *Annaire des statistiques sanitaires et sociales 1995.*

Table 10   National Health Expenditure by Main Sources of Funds, 1994 (Millions of Francs, Current Prices)

| | Total | Private funds | | | Public |
		Insurance	Friendly societies	Households	
National health expenditures	718,100	21,500	43,350	93,226	560,024
Medical services and supplies					
Personal medical care	652,764	21,500	43,350	93,226	485,820
In-patient care	321,477	2,990	6,596	20,011	290,805
nursing homes	—	—	—	—	8,276
psychiatric	25,120				
night cases	322				
day cases	4,675				
dialysis	1,116				
chemotherapy	201				
home care					
Physician services	85,145	4,850	8,485	19,165	50,606
Dental services	41,229	4,340	5,511	16,892	13,108
Medical auxiliaries	24,927	890	1,862	356	21,580
nurses	14,285				
physiotherapy	12,580				
speech therapy	2,142				
Dispensary/outpatient clinics	9,378	—	959	406	8,013
Laboratory tests/biology	17,184	1,030	1,844	3,248	10,715
Transportation	9,954	—	155	55	9,744
Spas	6,352	60	355	4,539	1,325
Pharmaceutical products	118,825	5,480	14,652	23,666	72,531
Therapeutic appliances	18,293	1,860	2,931	4,888	7,393
vision products	11,341				
orthopedic equipment	6,952				
Program administration	11,107	915	8,967	—	1,225
Government public health	17,557	—	—	—	17,557
school health	2,578	—	—		2,578
maternal/child	2,055				2,055
Occupational health	5,766	—	—	—	—
Research and fixed capital					
Research	24,187				9,360
Fixed capital formation	21,950				21,950

SOURCE: Ministère de la Santé Publique et de l'Assurance Maladie, *Comptes Nationaux de la Santé 1992–1993–1994*, Paris, 1995.

NOTES: National Health Accounts (NHA) monitor country-specific institutions. This table is an approximation using the United States NHA expenditure matrix and accessible French data; the French approach relies on a consumption-based NHA. The figures provide estimates for 1994, or trends through 1994, similar to those found in *OECD Health Data 95* without methodological update. In their present status the French NHA level appears to be understated by about 6 percentage points. No correction was introduced as details to adjust the time series used in the analysis are not readily available; the adjustment required, according to the authors, is somewhat stronger for past periods than in 1994 and does not allow a constant. The details exceed 100%, indicating that the table could not be fully squared on account of double counting. The orders of magnitude supplied appear, however, correct to a tenth of a percentage point.

The inpatient care entry combines hospitals, nursing homes, and a range of alternatives to conventional hospital care, including home care (164,541 patients in 1992), for which the private-public breakdown was not readily accessible.

Other professional services in France are broken down in medical auxiliaries (office-based and home care services by nurses, physiotherapists, speech therapists), pathology tests, ambulance services, spa cures. Dispensaries provide physician, dental, and other professional services.

Program administration excludes the management and revenue collection costs of the medical branch of Social Security schemes (a 30 billion franc underestimate).

Occupational health, fully funded by private employers, is accountingwise an intermediate consumption (cost of doing business), which is here converted into a final outlay as it is a service contributing to enhancement of the population's health status.

Private investment in health facilities, not included, may be estimated around 9 million francs in 1993 of which a quarter is funded by general government capital transfers (2,358 million francs in 1992). Public fixed capital formation, as reported, appears to overstate that entry.

Private insurance (total outlays: 21,500 million francs) and private provident institutions (8,594 million francs) have been aggregated; as have Social Security (276,974 million francs, including global budget transfers) and state and local government (27,127 million plus 21,250 million for capital formation).

The Health System of Germany

Wolfgang Greiner and J.-Matthias Graf v.d. Schulenburg*

Introduction

After the reunification of Germany in 1990, the East German health care system had to be integrated into the sickness fund–based system established by Chancellor von Bismarck in 1883. This process of transition affected health care services that had totally different methods of financing and providing service. This transition period lasted less than five years. The sickness fund system has now been established in the East German states, thousands of office-based physicians have founded new practices, and many pharmacies have been opened since the end of the socialist era. Market structures very similar to those in the Western part of the country can now be encountered in what was East Germany. The regulatory and economic conditions in both parts of Germany today are virtually the same.

The peaceful revolution in East Germany was thus not the occasion for reform in the structure of the German health care system, whose principles have stayed the same throughout the last century. These principles are:

1. social solidarity,
2. insurance premiums as a proportional payroll tax,
3. freedom of choice for the patient, benefits in kind and nearly full coverage for all services,
4. obligatory insurance for all employees with an income lower than a certain level,
5. divisional organizational structure of the sickness funds,
6. self-governing of the sickness funds.

*The authors would like to thank Rachel Gray for valuable comments on an earlier draft.

As a result of rising costs in the health care sector, the federal government has tried to influence expenditure with several reform acts since the 1970s. It has never been the aim of these reforms to change the structure and the principles of the health care system. The social and political environment in pre-reunification Germany had, however, already undergone certain changes before the introduction of these reforms, which mainly focused "on cost containment strategies on both the supply and the demand side."[1] The rise of the expenditure of the sickness funds slowed as a result of public debate about new health care reform acts. The effects of proposing the reform were clearly greater than the economic effects of the reform itself. Therefore the debate on reform can be seen as an instrument of the federal government to influence the global system.

According to the German constitution *(Grundgesetz)* the federal state and the sixteen single states have responsibilities for the health care sector. The most important actor for health policy in Germany is the federal minister of health. It is up to the state governments to initiate public health programs and to conduct hospital planning. Traditionally the German states *(Bundesländer)* have had very strong views regarding their rights and privileges. This is one reason for the decentralized structure of the German health care system. Since 1871, when the German federal state was founded, the states have been politically independent. In the process of reunification in 1990 five new states were established in the area of the former German Democratic Republic (GDR), because the people in East Germany continued to have strong feelings about their home area (like the Saxons, who are often compared to Bavarians with regard to their self-confidence). The five states had existed in the first years of the GDR but had later lost their autonomy.

Private provision of health services is especially important for ambulatory care. Office-based physicians in all fields of the profession run their practices at their own financial risk. In 1994 109,300 physicians worked in their own practices and the proportion of community physician teams, who use costly medical capacities more efficiently, was on the increase. For inpatient care some private hospitals have been founded in recent years, including eleven from 1991 to 1992,[2] which often specialize in certain treatments (e.g., ophthalmology). Both local communities and nonprofit making organizations (e.g., Red Cross, *Arbeiterwohlfahrt,* and churches) also run hospitals, but the investment costs are covered by government funds, if the hospital is listed in the hospital plan. The number of privately owned nursing homes is currently rising, because the new statutory nursing insurance introduced in 1995 is expected to increase the demand for nursing facilities. Private companies regard this development as the arrival of a new market due to the growing number of elderly people and the additional benefits of the statutory nursing insurance.

In the next sections some aspects of the German health system will be highlighted. First, health costs trends and the system of financing these costs are described. Some important changes after the recent reforms of the health system are also discussed. Medical practice in the ambulatory and inpatient sector, as well as the principles of medical education in Germany are explained. Finally the new nursing insurance run by the health insurers will be discussed as the starting point for a new market and for new challenges to the German social security system in view of demographic development. Some conclusions will be drawn about the current situation and future problems facing the German health system.

Financing the Costs of Health Care

Health Costs

Total health care expenditure amounted to 429.1 billion DM in 1992 (Figs. 1 and 2). The per capita expenditure at 5,299 DM, was relatively high in comparison with other European Union member

Figure 1 Expenditure on Health Care by Source (1992)

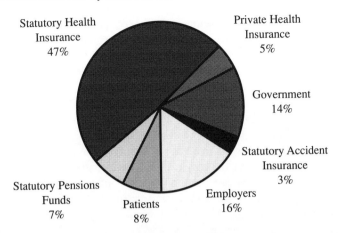

Statutory Health
Insurance
47%

Private Health
Insurance
5%

Government
14%

Statutory Accident
Insurance
3%

Statutory Pensions
Funds
7%

Patients
8%

Employers
16%

SOURCE: W. Müller, Ausgaben für Gesundheit 1992, *Wirtschaft und Statistik,* no. 10 (1994), 824.

Figure 2 Expenditure on Health Care by Sector (1992)

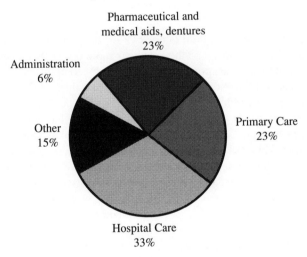

Pharmaceutical and
medical aids, dentures
23%

Administration
6%

Other
15%

Primary Care
23%

Hospital Care
33%

SOURCE: W. Müller, Ausgaben für Gesundheit 1992, *Wirtschaft und Statistik,* no. 10 (1994), 826.

states. But compared to health systems that contain more competitive elements (e.g., the United States) and also in comparison with health systems that are organized as national health services (e.g., Great Britain or Italy), health care expenditure as a percentage of the gross domestic product (GDP) has been relatively stable at about 8% since 1975. As in other countries nursing home care and care for the elderly are not included in this percentage of the GDP, but the costs of public health services are included. The percentages for different countries are comparable if the data are taken from OECD statistics. Obviously the German system has been relatively effective in cost containment.[3] But in Germany there is still a broad consensus on the need for reform of the health care system. The government and the social democrats, who hold the majority in the second legislative chamber, the Bundesrat, as well as doctors and hospital associations, support changes in the financing and delivering of health services, but naturally with different emphases. We shall come back to this point in more detail later.

It is not possible to describe the development of expenditure for the united Germany from a long-term perspective, as the new states in former East Germany have had a backlog of demand for health services during the first years since reunification. The increase in health expenditure in West Germany after 1991 was thus significantly lower than in East Germany. The expenditure in the West German states for ambulatory care (dentists, physicians, medication, and other outpatient medical resources) increased between 1970 and 1992 by 651%, while the costs of inpatient treatment increased in the same period by 948%. Therefore hospital costs are one of the major topics in the public discussion about cost containment in Germany, and the most important changes after the last health care reforms concerned methods of financing the hospital sector. The reasons for this development are manifold. First, the hospitals had few incentives to contain their costs, because they were paid on a per diem basis calculated on the basis of reported cost. Second, two-thirds of hospital costs are those related to personnel (physicians, nurses, technicians, administration), which rise more rapidly than other costs. Third, it was hardly possible to close hospitals in times of recession because they are one of the largest employers.

Sickness Funds and Private Health Insurers

The German system can be seen as a third alternative for financing health care, falling between a governmental system (like the British and the Swedish) and a primarily market-based system (like the United States). About 90% of the population is insured by compulsory social insurance against the costs of disease, that is, by one of the sickness funds; one-third of these people are insured as family members for free (unemployed spouses and children younger than 18 years are insured without their own premiums). At the present time only white-collar workers can choose the fund to which they want to belong. Beginning January 1997 blue-collar workers will also have free choice of sickness fund. This will lead to more competition between the sickness funds. Workers and employees whose gross income does not exceed a certain level (1995: DM 5,850.00 per month in the Western states and DM 4,515.00 in the Eastern states) have to join a sickness fund; people who earn more have the choice to stay voluntarily within the social security health system or to opt out and join a private health insurer. The deciding income level is adjusted each year to match salary development.

Half the premium for the sickness fund is paid by the employer, the other half by the insured person. Up to the above-mentioned income level the payments are calculated as a percentage of the gross income, and above this level a maximum premium in DM has to be paid (calculated as a percentage of the income level). The payment to the sickness fund depends not only on income but also on the sickness fund itself as each fund calculates its own percentage. This may range from 8.5% to 16.8%, with an average of 13.4% (Western states) in 1993. Most of the insured pay premiums in the range of 13% to 14% of their salaries. The average premium percentage for the different types of sickness funds increased over the last few decades from 8% to more than 13% (Table A).

As the premiums are not calculated according to risk, social insurance practices a system of redistribution and social transfers to the poor, to families, and to older people. The rationale of these transfer payments is the principle of solidarity within the health care system. The Social Security Act *(Sozialgesetzbuch V)* demands a stability of contributions and an increase in health care expenditure only in accordance with wage increases. These demands are justified by the particular characteristics of a market with full insurance protection such as the health care service market.

Table A   Premium for Different Types of West German Sickness Funds as a Percentage of Gross Income[4]

Year	Total	Local sickness funds	Industrial funds	Crafts' funds	Sailors' fund	Miners' fund	White-collar funds	Blue-collar funds
1970	8.20	8.15	7.51	7.82	6.60	9.60	8.07	8.89
1975	10.47	10.64	9.43	10.38	9.00	11.90	10.17	10.70
1980	11.38	11.70	10.49	11.21	9.90	12.60	11.01	11.22
1985	11.80	12.09	10.29	11.26	10.50	11.60	11.33	12.10
1986	12.20	12.69	10.76	12.01	11.70	11.60	11.49	12.10
1987	12.62	13.16	11.18	12.66	12.30	12.36	11.62	12.42
1988	12.90	13.46	11.45	12.79	12.80	13.13	11.96	12.69
1989	12.90	13.48	11.47	12.74	12.80	13.30	11.96	12.68
1990	12.53	13.13	11.10	12.28	12.52	13.30	11.23	12.32
1991	12.20	12.74	10.85	11.94	11.90	12.70	11.01	12.04
1992	12.74	13.46	11.33	12.54	11.90	13.90	11.10	12.37
1993	13.41	14.05	11.86	13.27	13.10	13.90	12.39	13.18

As there is no rationing of the direct demand for health services through market price, cost containment by the government is necessary. Otherwise price and volume of services would explode.

In 1993, social health insurance was organized into 1,221 sickness funds *(Krankenkassen)*, which work all over Germany *(Ersatzkassen)*, each fund in a specific region *(Ortskrankenkassen)*, or for a specific industry *(Betriebskrankenkassen, Innungskrankenkassen, Landwirtschaftliche Kassen)*. The number of sickness funds is decreasing due to the merger of local funds. There is no direct funding from federal, regional, or local government except for hospital investment costs, which are paid by the German states. This "dual financing" leaves the operating costs of the hospitals to the sickness funds, while long-term investments (for example, for building and for costly equipment) are paid for by the states.

The total expenditure of all sickness funds was 207.6 billion DM in 1992, which was 47% of the whole expenditure on Health Care (Fig. 2). Some 4.9% of the sickness funds' expenditure was needed for administration, although the sickness funds in the Eastern states spent a little higher percentage of their expenditures for administration—6.4% in 1993.[5] Sixteen percent was spent on office-based physicians, 11% on dental care, 16% on drugs, 31% on hospital care, and 2% on maternity care. The remainder was mainly spent on sick leave compensation. Sick leave compensation is granted after the employer has paid the wage or salary for the first six weeks; if the patient is still not able to work, the statutory health insurance pays 80% of the net income lost, up to 78 weeks within a period of three years. These transfer payments are not counted as health expenditures in the official statistics.

Co-payments are required for drugs, bandages, remedies, dentures, stays in hospital and in rehabilitation facilities. In case of hardship the insured can obtain complete or partial exemption from these obligatory payments. Some specified groups of people (for example, students and recipients of social assistance) and people whose income falls below a certain level (which is index-linked), are entitled to file an application to escape the additional payments.

To avoid adverse selection, and to equalize the competitive position of the sickness funds, a risk-structure pool was established in 1994. The aim of this pool is to remove contribution-rate differences between the sickness funds caused by factors outside their control, for example, low income or increased risk of disease due to advanced age. It is expected that this compensation pool will strengthen competition on quality of service and on reduction of administrative costs, and that it will avoid cream-skimming (picking of the best applicants) between the funds. The compensation is calculated by a simple computation of the average contribution of the members of a certain sickness fund (to determine its financial strength) and by calculating the standard expenditures of a fund, taking into account the age and sex distribution of the fund's membership. The subsidies to funds with an unfavorable risk-structure are paid prospectively, without regard to "the real cost and ex-post financial status of the fund."[6]

Employees who are above a certain income level and self-employed persons have the choice to opt out of the sickness fund system and to insure their health with private insurance companies. This decision is usually irreversible. In 1992 the 65 private health insurance companies paid 5% (21.5 billion DM) of the total health expenditure in Germany and insured 9% of the population (7.1 million persons). 6% of sickness fund members (4.5 million) have additional insurance with private companies. In contrast to the statutory health insurance system, private health insurers calculate their premiums on a risk-related basis. The premiums are dependent on age (at the time of admission to the insurance scheme), gender, and medical history. In contrast to the sickness funds, private health insurers do not have to accept all applicants for insurance; in particular, high-risk persons with chronic illnesses will not have the chance to obtain protection under a private health insurance scheme. As the companies are not allowed to insure persons with less than a certain income, and as they can select their clients, the risk of picking only the best applicants (cream-skimming) is particularly high among private health insurers. Young people with an above-average income find it particularly favorable to opt out of the statutory health system and to take out private insurance. Sickness funds retain merely those who are older, have more children, or a lower income. The effects of such adverse selection are partly compensated by higher costs per patient in the private health insurance companies due to more extensive benefit schemes, and higher charges for physician services. The expenditure per insured of private insurers is shown in Figure 3.

Over the last few years, private health insurers have had to increase the premiums for older insurees due to unexpected inflation in the health care sector. The reserves for older age groups

Figure 3   Expenditure* per insured

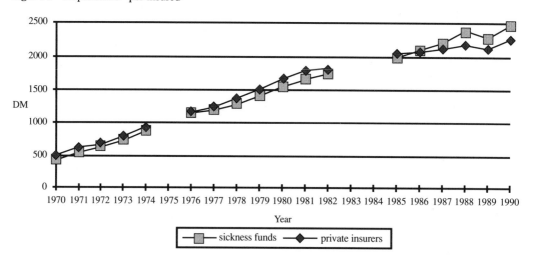

*Subtracted by payouts on premiums; data for 1975, 1983, and 1984 not available.

Source: Advisory Council for the Concerted Action in Health Care, 1992, *Jahresgutachten 1992, Ausbau in Deutschland und Aufbruch nach Europa,* Baden-Baden, 215 and 269.

were no longer sufficient, and the premiums of the pensioners had to be increased. At this age a change of insurance company is virtually impossible for the privately insured, because the reserves for older age-groups cannot be transferred to competitors and so, after a change, premiums would be extremely high. The provision allowing aged, privately insured persons to reenter the sickness funds has been abolished, as it was considered to be unfair: the privately insured have not contributed to the intergenerational transfer system of the sickness funds and should therefore not profit from this solidarity when they become older. It would have demanded that the premiums for younger insurees be raised to strengthen the reserves for older ages to avoid increasing insurance premiums for the elderly.

Private health insurers also supplement the benefit scheme of the statutory health insurance by offering coverage against co-payments and gaps in the coverage of the public system (e.g., for dentists' services or eyeglasses). The most important supplementary health insurance in Germany is against the costs of single and double rooms in hospitals, which many patients prefer. It is also common to be supplementarily insured against the additional cost of treatment by chief hospital physicians, or the cost of health services abroad (which is not included in the sickness funds' benefit scheme). Sickness funds are not allowed to offer such supplementary health insurance. To avoid the insured exploiting the system (moral hazard), private health insurance companies pay part of the premium back to their clients if they have not called on the services of the insurer during the previous year. This method of co-payment is designed to avoid trifle payments, which cause high administrative expenditure.

In contrast to the public health insurance scheme, it is quite difficult for private insurers to set incentives to the providers of health care to avoid unnecessary costs. For example, due to their small market share of about 10%, and due to the competition between private insurance companies, they are not able to pursue cost-containment policies such as global budgeting for particular sectors like hospitals or drugs. This is why the insurers often demand that prices be cut by law, especially for ambulatory services. But after the last health care reforms of the statutory insurance, in which cost containment was a major topic, office-based physicians who are paid on a fee-for-service basis increased the number of services to privately insured patients as a reaction to the budgeting of the public health insurance (cost-shifting). It is obvious that reforms of the sickness funds also affect the private insurers.

Providers of Medical Services

In Germany, development within the physicians' profession over the last few decades can be characterized by three major trends:[7] (1) the total number of physicians has been increasing; (2) the percentage of hospital physicians has been growing; and (3) the percentage of specialized physicians has been increasing. In 1960 only 79,350 physicians were employed; by 1992 this number had risen by more than 250% to 209,255 (Fig. 4). The public feared a flood of doctors *(Ärzteschwemme)*, and access regulations for the study of medicine were made more restrictive. The number of inhabitants per physician fell from 705 in 1960 to 310 in 1992. This figure was higher in East Germany, where on average there was one physician to every 369 inhabitants.

In the 1960s most physicians were office-based (1960: 62%), but in 1992 only 38% (East Germany: 41%) had their own practice. In Germany as a whole 267,100 physicians were employed in 1994 (129,100 working in hospitals, 109,300 office-based, and 10,500 employed at administration).

Figure 4   Number of physicians, 1960–1992 (West Germany)

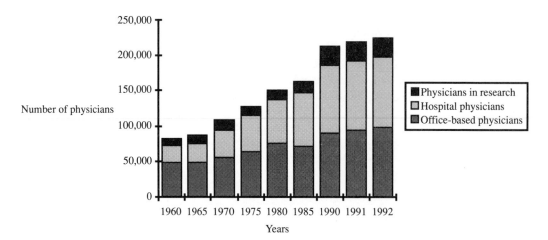

SOURCE: Bundesministerium für Gesundheit, *Daten des Gesundheitswesens 1993*, 220.

In 1992, exactly 18,477 physicians worked in group practices (9%), whereas in the mid-eighties only 6% worked in this type of practice (Fig. 5). A major reason for this development is that the equipment necessary for a new, modern practice is virtually unaffordable for one physician alone.

Ambulatory Care

Private health insurance companies allow the patients to seek treatment from any office-based physician. Sickness fund members have to choose a physician who has been accredited by the funds. This, however, is not a severe restriction, as 95% of all office-based physicians are accredited (Fig. 6). Sickness fund members receive ambulatory health care by presenting their *Versichertenkarte,* which proves the membership of the patient, to an office-based physician of their own choice. The physicians do not bill the patients, but are directly reimbursed by the sickness funds via regional insurance doctors' organizations *(Kassenärztliche Vereinigungen).* The charges for ambulatory care are fixed and regulated by a point-based charge system, which determines a number of points for a list of health care services *(Gebührenordnung Ärzte [GOÄ]; Einheitlicher Bewertungsmaßstab [EBM]).* The value of a point in this fee-for-service system depends on the total number of services to be settled, as the total budget available for expenditure on ambulatory care is restricted. The point value is calculated ex post by the budget and the total number of points billed by all physicians. If the total amount of charges exceeds the budget, the value of a point will be reduced for all physicians. The relative value fee schedules were introduced in 1980 in Germany, initially in Bavaria. The budget is adjusted each year according to the general increase in wages,

Figure 5 Physicians in Group Practices (West Germany)

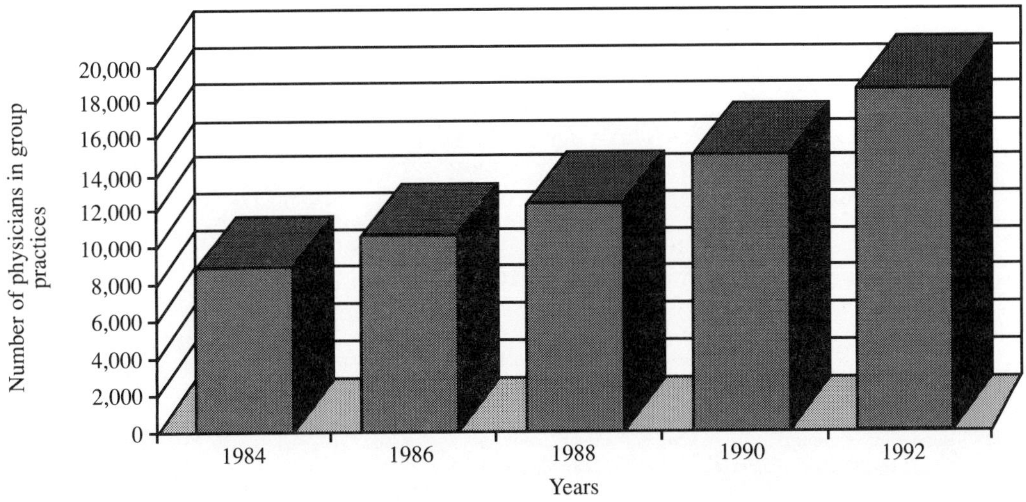

SOURCE: Bundesministerium für Gesundheit, *Daten des Gesundheitswesens 1993*, 244.

and is negotiated by the doctors' and sickness funds' associations. The total amount and the kind of services provided by each physician is monitored by the physician's association. The physician will be asked to explain any variations if the amount charged exceeds that physician's proportion of the budget.

The physicians are organized into various associations, which can be divided into three groups: compulsory organizations; scientific, specialist associations; and unionlike professional associations. Physicians are required to be members of the *Ärztekammern*, which are organized in regional and federal associations, and which supervise the actions of their members with regard to ethical standards and further education. Physicians who want to treat sickness fund members have also to join the *Kassenärztliche Vereinigungen*, which negotiate contracts with the sickness funds and distribute the total amount allocated for services to the ambulatory care physicians. The scientific, specialist associations represent the interests of the different branches of health care (such as gynecology, orthopedics, and so forth). Membership in these associations is voluntary.

The most important professional associations are the *Hartmannbund* (for all physicians), the *Marburger Bund* (for physicians who are employed in hospitals and by the state) and the *Verband der leitenden Krankenhausärzte Deutschlands* (for chief physicians in hospitals). All organizations are members of the *Deutsche Ärztetag*. The number of doctors organized within these voluntary associations is less than 50%. Due to conflicts of interest between the various doctors' associations, their influence on the official health policy has declined in recent years during the debate over the various health reform proposals.

In 1992, 33,601 general practitioners were accredited in Germany, which equates to 42% of all physicians with their own practice. The number of general practitioners has increased over the last decade, but due to rising numbers of other specialized doctors the proportion of general practitioners has decreased (1980: 44.5%). In Germany, patient demand for each group of physicians

Figure 6   Office-Based Physicians (1990)

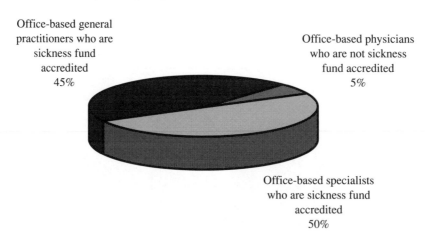

Office-based general
practitioners who are
sickness fund
accredited
45%

Office-based physicians
who are not sickness
fund accredited
5%

Office-based specialists
who are sickness fund
accredited
50%

SOURCE: Bundesministerium für Gesundheit, *Daten des Gesundheitswesens 1993,* 187, and Advisory Council for the Concerted Action in Health Care, *Expert Report 1992,* Baden-Baden, 223.

(specialized doctors and general practitioners) who are allowed to reimburse themselves with the sickness funds has been set since 1976 by the federal association of the *Kassenärztliche Vereinigungen* and the sickness funds. For example, the figure for general practitioners in 1992 was 2,450 inhabitants per doctor (which equates to 41.7 doctors per 100,000 inhabitants). Thanks to this normative measure, it is possible to establish for each physician group and each region whether the supply is too great or too small.

Beginning in 1994, sickness fund accreditations were awarded much more strictly in accord with the calculated demand on the regional markets. Just prior to this there was a large increase in the number of doctors accredited by the sickness funds, about 10,000 just in 1992. Cost containment and a higher number of doctors inevitably limit the income of ambulatory care physicians. With respect to this technique, an excess supply is to be identified in almost every region and specialization, except in the new *Bundesländer,* where the organizational structure of general practitioners and specialized doctors still differs from the Western part of the country. In Brandenburg, Mecklenburg-Vorpommern, Saxony, Saxony-Anhalt, and Thuringia (the area of the former German Democratic Republic), the supply of general practitioners is much higher than the official demand figure. Therefore a shortage of specialized doctors can be identified. It is expected that in the next few years the normal fluctuation will assimilate the physicians' structure of East Germany into that of the West. In addition, the regional distribution of physicians in Germany as a whole is uneven, as the physician-population ratio is much lower in some rural areas than in urban areas. This is particularly true for specialists, who mainly settle down in urban regions.[8]

Patients are not obliged to go to a general practitioner first if they need medical aid. Instead, they can choose to consult a specialized doctor directly without referral from a GP. This system is often criticized as certain diagnostic procedures may be repeated if the patient consults more than one physician for a particular medical problem. For this reason, some sickness funds are currently planning to offer their members an alternative scale of contribution, with lower payments for those members who always contact a general practitioner first if they need medical services. Field studies have examined whether this system will save the sickness funds money due to lower costs for diagnosis services. Up to now the results of these studies have not been available.

Only a few physicians involved in ambulatory care also work in hospitals, as office-based and hospital-based patient care are strictly separated in Germany. "The separation of outpatient and inpatient sectors invariably leads to preventable loss of effectiveness and efficiency."[9] Hence it is planned to improve the coordination between ambulatory and hospital care. According to the Health Care Reform Act of 1993, hospitals are allowed to provide outpatient surgery, as well as inpatient treatments, which are coordinated with the referring ambulatory care physicians. These doctors can also treat their own patients in hospital.

All ambulatory care services are paid on a fee-for-service basis. The average net income before personal income tax (returns minus costs) of physicians declined in the 1990s from 170,000 DM to 159,000 DM per year as a result of the recent health care reforms and the cost containment policies (Table 6a). The average net income of radiologists in particular decreased by 36% from 275,000 to 175,000 DM per year. The fee-for-service system particularly favors specialized doctors, and places GPs at a disadvantage, because specialized examinations are better paid than verbal consultations. As a result, GPs are at the bottom of the income list (before tax, cost deducted) with 135,000 DM per year on average. The average working hours per week of ambulatory care givers are not known.

The average net income before personal taxes of dentists in West Germany decreased from 230,000 DM in 1982 to 179,000 DM in 1993 (Table 6b), which is still more than the average of all physicians. The number of dentists was quite stable in the 1970s. In the 1980s, the number increased from 33,240 in 1980 to 47,745 in 1993. Due to this development, the accreditation of dentists has been restricted in a growing number of areas.

Quality Assurance

The social security act (*SGB V*) calls for quality and efficiency of medical services according to current medical knowledge and research. It also calls for the economical use of resources, which can be achieved by evaluating medical procedures and products. By way of contrast, the quality of physicians' ambulatory care is not permanently monitored. The doctors' associations and the sickness funds have agreed on some guidelines for medical care. These guidelines especially regulate the educational prerequisites for medical services, but are not very precise about the care-giving itself. Programs for cancer prevention and pregnancy care for example have already been launched, but in most other areas it has not yet been possible to establish diagnostic and therapeutic standards to prevent the patient from being treated with inappropriate or unnecessary treatments.

Whether quality of inpatient care should be controlled by outside bodies and which criteria the hospitals should meet is not yet decided. These decisions depend upon current negotiations between sickness funds and hospitals. As Germany has a decentralized health care system with decision-making at the lowest level, it is not possible to make general statements about new procedures for assessing and assuring quality of care. The only decisions taken by top decision-making bodies are the following: (1) the social security law defining benefits, premium calculation, and organization of sickness funds; (2) overall expenditure caps for major group of services; and (3) guidelines for local negotiations between suppliers and purchasers.

Inpatient Care

In 1992, 2,013 general hospitals were situated in West Germany and 368 in the former GDR (Tables 7a and b). This was slightly less than in previous years, as in 1990 exactly 2,029 general hospitals were operating in the Western part of the country and 389 in the East. In addition there were 1,209 medical institutions for rehabilitation and prophylactics and 210 special hospitals for neurologic and/or psychiatric care.

Hospitals are owned by either the state *(Bundesländer)* or town councils, nonprofit organizations (like the Red Cross or the churches), or private companies. The total number of hospitals is distributed almost equally among these three groups, but half the beds are provided by the state-owned hospitals. However, their share is decreasing and the private owners' share of the market (mainly doctor-owned hospitals) is growing. Special hospitals are mainly owned by private entrepreneurs (especially rehabilitation institutions).

Hospital-based doctors are paid by salary, although the chief physicians may supplement their salaries by charging patients who specifically seek them out for treatment. The role of chief physician and the top administrative personnel of the hospital varies from hospital to hospital. Large institutions in particular employ specially trained administrative personnel with no medical background. As there has been no great pressure to keep the costs low until now, conflicts between administration and medical staff have been quite rare. This might change in the future due to the introduction of new payment systems like Diagnosis Related Groups (DRGs).

Patients are admitted to the hospitals by ambulatory care physicians. Patients have free choice of hospital, but they generally follow the advice of their doctor in choosing a certain hospital. Without the referral of an ambulatory care physician, admission to hospital is only possible in the case of an emergency, or for patients who are privately insured. It is believed that some general practitioners send their patients to hospital rather than to a specialized doctor because they fear the patients will not come back once treated by a specialist. This might cause a percentage of unnecessary hospital stays large enough to be worth mentioning. Patients are usually referred to special hospitals by general hospitals, and only very rarely by ambulatory care physicians. In the case of an emergency, referral from an ambulatory care giver is not necessary. Emergency rooms are available in almost all general hospitals in Germany while trauma centers are not common. Emergency rooms are usually staffed by junior doctors and (in hospitals with a higher number of beds) some specialized physicians.

The hospitals are financed according to the *Krankenhausfinanzierungsgesetz* (KHG) and the *Bundespflegesatzverordnung* (BPflV). Long-term investments, short-term assets, and smaller building repairs are financed by the states *(Bundesländer);* current operating and treatment expenses are financed by the patients and their insurers (dual financing). Due to this financing system, hospital policy is highly dependent on decisions made by the sickness funds (for example, hiring of staff) and the states (for example, number of beds). The new DRG system of financing will enlarge the autonomy of the hospitals, giving them more freedom.

Up until 1995 operating and treatment expenses were paid on a cost-price basis *(Selbstkostendeckungsprinzip)*. According to this system, prospective budgets were fixed for each hospital each year. The hospitals still had to observe the order of efficiency and the principle of stable contributions to the sickness funds (i.e., the percentage of income to be paid to the sickness funds would not be raised), both of which limit payment on a cost-price basis. The budgeting was flexible; that is, if the number of hospital services given were to differ from the amount foreseen, overheads would be paid (in the case of less than the foreseen services being performed) or the variable costs of any exceeding services would be paid (in the case of more than foreseen services being performed). The hospitals were generally paid on a per diem basis for all services regardless of the disease, the severity, or the length of stay. However, it was possible to negotiate prices for certain procedures like transplants *(Sonderentgelte)* or to obtain special per diems for the treatment of particular patient groups (for example, dialysis or treatment of very costly diseases like cystic fibrosis). More than 90% of hospital expenses were paid by general per diems.[10]

One advantage of this old system from a medical point of view was that the treatment of patients and the relationship between the patient and doctor in the hospital were not influenced by economic considerations, as all expenses were paid by the sickness funds. From an economic point of view further advantages were the very simple calculation of hospital financing and the absence of any incentive to provide more services than necessary. On the other hand the system also offered no incentives to save resources, as all diagnostic and therapeutic procedures could be carried out regardless of their cost-efficiency. The accounting system in the hospitals was quite outdated; no cost-center accounting or calculations for unit costs were made as the hospitals were compensated for all costs anyway.

The old system also offered an incentive to extend the length of stay in hospital, because the last days of a hospital stay are in general cheaper than the first. (This is supposedly one of the main reasons why the average length of stay is significantly longer in German hospitals than in other countries). Experiments with DRGs and patient management groups in clinics in Kiel, Mannhagen (near Hamburg), and Bad Neuenahr have shown an important influence of the payment system on the length of stay in hospital.

In addition, the total days of hospitalization (which were calculated for the budget in advance) had to be reached at the end of the year; otherwise the hospital received only the fixed costs (about 25% of the general per diem) for any unused days. Finally, sickness funds were burdened with very costly services if a hospital with high-tech equipment for expensive diseases was situated in their regional area. If this equipment was used for patients from other areas who were insured by other regional sickness funds, their treatment was subsidized by the lump sums of the per diems.

As the old system had no incentives for the providers of hospital care to limit the costs of treatment, the system was changed to a diagnosis related group–based scheme. Since 1995, hospitals have had the opportunity to negotiate prices for the treatment of certain diseases *(Fallpauschalen)* and of certain procedures *(Sonderentgelte)*. Moreover, specific department per diems and a basic per diem for accommodation costs may be granted. Beginning in 1996, this new system must be established in every hospital in Germany.

As a first step, a catalogue of 40 DRGs, and prices for 160 certain procedures were drawn up. It is planned to extend this list in the coming years. A calculation of the costs was carried out in about one hundred model hospitals as a basis for weighted prices; that is, the actual prices are fixed for each state *(Bundesland)* in negotiations between the hospitals' and the sickness funds' associations. With the introduction of this pricing system, it will be possible for hospitals to make a profit or loss. Therefore, hospitals will have an incentive to save resources and to specialize in certain procedures. It is suspected that one disadvantage of the system may lie in the maintenance of the quality of service in German hospitals, because lower costs could be reached by lower quality. Therefore a quality control system will be established by the sickness funds to guarantee the quality of care and to avoid the upgrading of a patient to better paid disease categories or adverse patient selection by the hospitals. Another problem of DRGs is the present lack of experience in Germany with such systems. In particular, the accounting methods of the hospitals must be adjusted to the new payment system. This might increase the administrative costs of the hospitals as they seek to categorize patients.

Another risk that arises with this system is that health care providers might try to compensate for the low fees they receive for the treatment of sickness fund members by setting higher fees for privately insured persons or for special benefits such as a single room. Co-payments by the patients are of only minor importance for hospital financing. For each day of inpatient care, the patient has to pay 12 DM, which does not even cover the cost of accommodation.

A typical hospital is state-financed and has 300 to 400 beds. Most operations can be carried out except very sophisticated ones such as transplants, which are done by university hospitals. Nevertheless, a typical hospital would own a computer-tomograph (CT), for example, and other expensive technological equipment. In 1993, there was on average one CT per 72,000 West German inhabitants (in East Germany, one per 100,000). A normal hospital room is equipped with three or four beds, although in older hospitals even six bed rooms are not rare. In most of the hospitals it is also possible to take a single or a double room for an extra charge (DM 165 on average for a single room per day). The extra costs for this service are not covered by the sickness funds, but are covered by most of the private insurers. It is also possible for sickness fund members to insure against the costs of single or double rooms with private additional insurance.

The competition between hospitals is quite low as many of them still have a regional monopoly, especially in rural areas. Competition on price is especially unusual, as the sickness funds only have a limited chance of denying reimbursement to general hospitals. Only highly qualified hospitals are allowed to practice sophisticated and high-cost procedures like transplants. Therefore, university-based hospitals compete for leading medical staff as the reputation of the institution depends on its staff.

In future, the competition between hospitals and ambulatory care givers, now almost absent, will increase substantially. The hospitals will provide more facilities for ambulatory care and physicians with their own practices will enjoy the benefits of working in hospitals. Until now cooperation between these two sectors of the health care system has been unsatisfactory, because ambulatory care physicians are not allowed to treat hospitalized patients and hospitals are forced to limit their outpatient services to a very low level. It is intended that the next health care reforms will diminish this strict separation. The dovetailing of inpatient and outpatient care will improve the quality of service and efficiency and may decrease costs, if double examinations and laboratory tests can be avoided.

Surgical waiting lists are not common in German hospitals except for procedures not solely dependent on the number of hospital facilities. For example, transplants are highly limited by the organ supply. Due to there being fewer accident victims and more patients who are physically in good enough condition to be transplanted (especially older patients), the gap between the number of those who reach the transplant waiting list and those who are actually transplanted increases each year. The willingness of relatives to agree to an organ transplant decreased between 1989 and 1992 from more than 90% to less than 70%. This development intensifies the problems in the field of transplantation, and is mainly a result of rising mistrust among the population of transplant medicine. It is expected that the federal government will present a new law to improve confidence in this field. A first attempt to launch a transplantation act which was undertaken by the *Bundesland* Rheinland-Pfalz in 1993 was not successful, as public opinion was not convinced that the so-called contradiction model would prevent misuse of potential organ donors. This model is quite similar to the transplant regulations in Austria and Belgium, where each corpse can be used as an organ donor, unless the person had stated a prior unwillingness to be a donor. Opponents of this system argue that nobody should be forced to make a statement about his attitude to organ donation, because personal freedom also includes the freedom not to decide. Therefore the "information model" was developed, which is quite similar to previous common practice in Germany before a transplant was carried out. The closest relatives of the deceased are asked whether the organ may be transplanted. If they do not offer objection within a fixed period of time, this is taken as an assent.

In 1994, only 1,894 kidneys were transplanted while 8,996 patients were still on waiting lists at the end of the year. These people receive full dialysis care regardless of age or social position. Most of the patients are treated with hospital dialysis, which is more expensive on average than ambulatory dialysis, but physician incentives obviously do not support a change in this treatment structure. Other waiting lists are only to be found for specialized physicians who have a high reputation and therefore enjoy excess demand for their services.

Medical Education

Physicians

The total number of medical students decreased before 1991, but increased in 1992 to more than 105,000 (1991: 94,710). The number of medical graduates has been stable since the mid-eighties (1991: 9,439). As studying medicine is quite expensive and an excess supply of physicians seems to be apparent in Germany, a reduction in the number of medical students was perceived as a major aim of health politics. Therefore admission to medical universities is strictly regulated and limited. University admission usually takes place after secondary school, between the ages of eighteen and twenty.

Study programs for medicine are regulated by law *(Approbationsordnung für Ärzte [AppOÄ])* as far as examination requirements are concerned. Studies last at least five years with verbal and written exams. A practical year *(Praktisches Jahr)* is required afterward in which the students work in hospitals under supervision. Finally a last set of oral examinations complete the studies. Most students start work on their doctoral thesis just before or after the practical year. During the first eighteen months after passing the last exams, the young physicians are only allowed to work under the supervision of an experienced doctor *(Arzt-im-Praktikum)*. Subsequently they may work independently and on their own responsibility. No student fees are charged, but admission to the university is highly regulated and depends on final high school grades *(Abitur)*, on the current waiting time, and on entrance tests. The medical schools are financed by the German states.

Exams are carried out using multiple-choice tests, which are controversial as they cannot fully reflect detailed medical knowledge. But the strain on medical faculties due to the huge number of students makes the use of this standardized method necessary. Another criticism is that medical studies bear too little relation to the practical work of physicians. For example, geriatric treatment should be integrated into medical curricula due to the demographic changes. Furthermore, medical studies tend to focus on high-tech medicine, which is more curative than preventive. Preventive medicine becomes even more important in an aging society.

Dentists

Dental studies focus initially on biological knowledge. Later, more emphasis is placed on technical skills for the treatment of dental problems. A particular problem in the training of dentists is that it is very difficult for the universities to motivate junior professors to stay for a longer period, as they can earn much more money outside the university. The average dentist earned 179,000 DM (net income before personal income taxes) in 1993, which is, as the result of the recent health care reforms, less than in previous years (Table 6b). Dentists, like other ambulatory doctors, are paid on a fee-for-service basis. The sickness funds cover all costs of the care they provide. The patients have to make significant contributions toward materials needed for the treatment (for example, gold or inlays).

Nurses

Nurses' training is not university-based. Instead, nurses are educated in one of about 1,000 medical care schools, which are run by the owners of the hospitals and hospital chains. After either one year (for nurse assistants, *Krankenpflegehelfer*) or after three years the nurses receive a diploma. Due to the particular burdens of the profession the mean period for staying in the job is only ten years. This is one of the reasons why in some regions the hospitals complain about a shortage of nurses. An attempt was made to change the conditions by increasing the wages of nurses to attract more to this profession. Apart from their core tasks such as washing, feeding, taking temperatures, and distributing drugs, nurses today often act as assistants to the physicians, especially in intensive care units and, for example, for endoscopy. Their duties also include documentation, coordination of the treatments, and information management.

Care for the Elderly

Since the mid-1970s the risk of becoming dependent on nursing care in old age has been widely recognized among the general public. Changes in family structures and in the demographic situation of the population have increased the demand for professional care. In 1982, the federal government had already announced its intention to introduce social insurance covering the risk of needing care. The broad discussion of possible alternatives in covering this risk, and the political and administrative efforts of the German reunification, led to delays in the realization of this plan.

Since 1973 the sickness funds have paid for ambulatory care in very severe cases. These benefits have never been of great significance, only 3.4% of the total budget. The majority of the costs of caring were not covered by the sickness funds but by public social assistance. This is funded mainly by the local authorities, who thus emphasized the need for a general nursing insurance scheme. The patients had to deplete all savings they had accumulated before they were eligible for public social assistance.

Caring for the elderly is carried out in various different institutions. Only a few patients (in 1991 only 744) stay in part-time nursing homes, in which they receive only day care (or care during temporary absence of their relatives). It is planned to increase the number of these institutions as they contribute to the amount of self-determination patients retain over their own lives, and as this kind of care is relatively cheap. The nursing homes are paid on a daily or monthly basis.

Ambulatory care is mainly provided by church organizations and state-financed institutions *(Soz-*

ialstationen). It is also financed by the sickness funds and by patient contributions. Nursing homes are mainly run by nonprofit organizations (1993: 991 institutions with 80,343 beds). Private nursing homes are usually smaller (980 institutions with 44,922 beds) and their number is increasing. State-owned nursing homes are primarily run by local government authorities and play only a minor role in the overall care of the elderly (1993: 300 institutions with 31,227 beds).

Mentally ill persons are treated in various institutions that provide out-patient and in-patient care. A special program of the federal government supported smaller units to avoid long-term care in large-scale hospitals. Special departments for mentally ill patients in general hospitals were reduced and specialized ambulatory care units were founded. The provision of these facilities is not guaranteed for all areas of Germany. Therefore the concept of regional integrated care for the mentally ill is not yet fully realized.

Patients needing care are often treated in general hospitals for a short time until a nursing home place is found for them. The number of these patients is not known, but it is estimated to be about 35,000. Before the introduction of the new social nursing insurance it was advantageous for the patient to be treated in a general hospital, because it was fully paid for by the sickness funds, while nursing homes had to be paid for by the patient.[11] This incentive will be abolished by the new nursing insurance. Patients in general hospitals receive treatment to improve the status of their health (treatment for disease or injury), whilst patients in nursing homes need care for their most basic needs (condition does not respond to medical treatment). Most of the patients stay in the nursing home until the end of their life; only a few come just for day care. The regional lack of qualified institutions for rehabilitation and home care for older people still leads to misuse of general hospitals.

At the time being 1.1 million patients receive ambulatory care and 450,000 persons are treated in inpatient institutions. Most of these patients are female (more than 75%) and older than seventy. One of the most important factors in the increase of the number of patients needing care is demographic progression, as older people have a much higher risk of needing care. As in other countries the number of very old people has increased in Germany during the last decades. It is expected that in the year 2030 more than 18 million people over sixty will live in West Germany (1990: 12 million). Their proportion of the total population will grow from 20% to more than 37%.

The ratio of patients to potential caregivers will also deteriorate in the coming decades. It is principally women of 45 to 60 who care for their relatives, the so-called caring-reserve *(Fürsorgereserve).* The proportion of these women to people older than 65 will be halved in the period up to 2030. This will further increase the problems of caring for the elderly. On the other hand, more and more men and people older than 65 will care for their relatives in the future.[12]

Ten years ago there were no private insurance companies in Germany that offered insurance against the cost of nursing, either in nursing homes or in the patient's home. This was mainly a consequence of the fact that the state paid social assistance for those who had no money to pay for the care they needed. This behavior decreased private provision and increased the burden of social transfers of the state. Therefore the possibility of obliging each inhabitant in Germany to take out nursing insurance with a private company is being discussed. While social insurance programs use a pay-as-you-go financing system, private insurers work with a fully funded system, that is, accumulate age reserves. Among the disadvantages of this model, which is quite similar to the obligation for car owners to have a liability insurance, are the high administrative expenditures required (for example, to check that everyone pays the premiums on time), the high premiums for older people, and the problem that people who already need care still have to be financed by the active generation. This would lead to a double burden for the employed, who would have to pay for patients currently needing care and additionally for their own insurance.

Therefore, a fifth social insurance (apart from sickness funds, accident insurance, pension funds, and unemployment insurance) was introduced in 1995. Under the administration and control of the sickness funds, patients who need care can obtain money either for ambulatory or inpatient care. Home care should have priority over hospital or nursing home care. The sickness funds provide facilities for ambulatory care. This is also offered by private and nonprofit organizations. Relatives of the patient are also able to provide care. They have the opportunity of being trained in nursing and may be offered financial support dependent upon the level of care needed.

Three such levels of need were set. The financial support ranges between DM 400 per month for level 1 to DM 1,300 for level 3 (level 2: DM 800). The patients have the choice of receiving benefits in kind or a combination of benefits in kind and in cash. The maximum equivalent for the benefits in kind is DM 750 for level 1, DM 1,800 for level 2, and DM 2,800 for level 3. The patients are categorized by the medical service of the sickness funds. Relatives who care for patients may take a short course on nursing if they so wish and they receive an extra pension in their old age. In addition, it is possible for the relatives to take one month's holiday per year as nursing insurance covers the cost of relief care.

Full nursing care with meals costs about DM 4,500 to DM 6,000 per month. Even with the benefits of the new nursing insurance it will not be possible for many patients with small pensions to afford this. Social insurance pays a maximum of DM 3,300 in very severe cases; for other patients whose need is less it is even more likely that they will have to exhaust their pensions and demand additional public social assistance. Therefore a major reason for introducing nursing insurance may not be fully resolved, as many patients will still be dependent on public social assistance.

Public Health

In Germany there are no official public health agencies that perform treatment or care activities other than those already described. Only the health offices (Gesundheitsämter), which are run by local government and which are tax financed, have a role similar to that of public health agencies (vaccinating, fighting epidemic diseases, and advising pregnant women). However, their role is predominantly supervisory: control of nutrition, drinking water, and compiling health statistics. Prevention services are mainly provided by ambulatory care physicians. The sickness funds pay for these examinations as for other treatments. The programs to fight against cancer and infant diseases in particular can be utilized by sickness fund members.

Public health has now been constituted as a university research field in Germany. The federal government is supporting this development by financing several projects with public health emphases. Finally, an increasing number of students are interested in public health topics, which are often taught as supplementary studies.

Conclusion

Recent Reforms in Health Care Financing

In recent years the health care sector in Germany has been on the way to becoming a regulated system in which much is predetermined by law, and political influence plays a major role. In particular the system of drug budgeting, the limitation in the accreditation of doctors, budgets for hospitals, and the reference price system for drugs are indications that the health authorities and politicians mistrust a system with a free market allocation in this sector.

Based on the 1991 expenditure for prescribed drugs, a drug budget was brought into effect in 1993. The physicians must pay a proportion of any amounts that exceed this budget. Their ambulatory services and hospital expenditures are also budgeted and index-linked to wages. After the introduction of the drug budget, sales of generic drug firms increased by 40%, whilst the sales of research-based pharmaceutical companies in Germany decreased by 10 to 20%. Another consequence in the first budgeted year was that physicians did not know exactly how many drugs they could prescribe without finding themselves responsible for exceeding amounts. This uncertainty led doctors to reduce the amount of drugs prescribed to lower than that covered by the budget. In addition the number of referrals to specialized physicians increased by 9% and to hospitals by 10%. For drug-intensive diseases like Parkinson's, asthma, ulcers, and cancer the increase in referrals was even higher.[13]

For more than 50% of the drugs, reference prices have been set since the health care reform act of 1989. Drugs with the same ingredients, the same pharmaceutical principle, or the same intended effect are classified and a reference price is set for each group on a daily dosage basis. If the price of a particular drug is higher than this reference price, the patient has to pay the difference out of pocket or has to choose an equivalent drug that is fully covered by the sickness funds. This system is quite attractive for health systems in other countries as it avoids regulating the price of each particular drug separately. The result of the reference price system was a quasi-fixed price for each group, as higher prices could not be maintained due to market conditions.

The most important modifications of the next decade will be to the hospitals. The systems of finance in particular are heading for change. Forty DRGs have now been established and it is planned to increase the number of them. Each DRG covers all hospital and professional services needed by the patient regardless of how long the patient is in hospital. Germany also has another system—*Sonderentgelte*—used to pay for special procedures such as transplants. There are 104 *Sonderentgelte*. The *Sonderentgelte* cases consist of lump-sum payments for the operations but not for the general hospital care; the general hospital care component is financed on a special per diem basis. The per diem payments for the *Sonderentgelte* cases consist of two components: one part is for accommodation and hospital administration; the other part is for the clinical department. For services not currently financed by DRGs or *Sonderentgelte* the costs are budgeted; that is, the total amount paid by per diem is limited by the budget. The *Sonderentgelte* system was introduced during the 1980s: rather than adjust all per diems for all hospital admissions, which some thought would be inflationary, it was thought more desirable to establish the *Sonderentgelte* system.

Before the DRG system was introduced, the experiences of the United States and other countries were studied. It is expected that the new system will decrease the average length of stay by 30%. It will also contribute to the development of specialized controlling departments in hospitals—not necessary in the old per diem system, because all costs arising were simply divided by the number of in-patient days for the relevant period. On the other hand, the new system will give rise to more administrative expenses, as much more data is necessary to establish the current costs of a procedure. DRGs are also an incentive to specialize in certain treatments that can be carried out at relatively low cost by a particular hospital. The system has to ensure that quality of care and a sufficient supply of hospital services is guaranteed in rural areas, too. In the future, hospital investment will not be funded by the state (dual financing); instead it is planned to hand over responsibility for investment and operating costs to the hospital management. This will decrease political influence on hospital planning and financing.

Outlook

The German health care system has demonstrated great ability in providing the services needed by patients. There are hardly any waiting lists within the inpatient sector, and patients have a choice of various ambulatory care physicians. Nearly 100% of all citizens have comprehensive insurance coverage and the share of the health sector from the gross national product has been stable for the last decades. On the other hand, among industrialized countries Germany is ranked thirteenth with respect to infant mortality and only fifteenth for life expectancy. There have been reforms to the financing system every three or four years over the last few decades, which may indicate that the system is not so good as the above description would suggest.

One of the most significant problems in the coming years will be the demographic change in the German population. The revenues of the sickness funds are determined in the first instance by the number of employed people and the development of wages. The rising level of long-term unemployment and the increasing number of people opting out of the statutory health insurance aggravate the problems of financing the system, particularly as there are at present very few incentives for the supplier to save the sickness fund members' money.

Another important question will be whether all benefits offered at present by the sickness funds are necessary, sufficient, cost-effective, and affordable. There is controversy about whether it is possible to define core benefits, the provision of which is (from a medical point of view) a basic necessity. Different models for the future development of the health care system in Germany are being discussed. The Advisory Council of the Ministry of Health has proposed various models for the restructuring of the sickness funds' benefit scheme. The basic principle of these models is to differentiate between core and optional benefits, with the opportunity for the insured to opt out of certain benefits that may be covered by private insurance companies.

Sickness funds prefer models that resemble U.S. health maintenance organizations (HMOs) and preferred provider organizations (PPOs). According to these models the sickness funds would reduce the freedom of the insured to choose their physician and would negotiate individual contracts with office-based physicians and hospitals. The patient would have the choice of different sickness funds offering varying services and different choices of physicians. As a first step the sickness funds will start with models in which the insurees have the choice of visiting specialized doctors without the referral of a general practitioner, or of agreeing always to see a GP first. It is expected that the second alternative will lower costs by reducing the number of visits to and examinations by specialists (which are generally more costly). The insured will therefore pay a lower premium for the second alternative (with general practitioners as gatekeepers) than for the first alternative.

The German health care system is in a transition period whose clear priority is the development of cost containment. At present it is equivocal as to whether Germany is on the way toward a system of managed competition with various offers of health care provision and choice of health insurer, or whether it will become a uniform, highly regulated public sickness fund system. The second option may be more attractive for politicians, enabling them to maintain their influence on the key issues of health politics, which is a very sensitive area for voters.

NOTES

1. Henke, K.-D. May–June 1994. The German Health Care System: Structure and Changes. *Journal for Clinical Anesthesia* 6:252–62.

2. Statistisches Bundesamt. 1994. *Statistisches Jahrbuch 1994*, Bonn, 466f.

3. Schulenburg, J.-M. Graf v. d. 1983. Report from Germany—Current conditions and controversies in the health care system. *Journal of Politics, Policy and Law* 8:320–51.

4. Bundesminister für Gesundheit. 1991. *Daten des Gesundheitswesens 1991*. 1993. Baden-Baden, 177, 220, 244, 254, 282, 302, and 333.

5. Kieselbach, K. 1995. Buhlen um Mitglieder—Selbständige fordern rigoroses Werbeverbot für Krankenkassen. *Die Welt* 2(1):11.

6. Schulenburg, J.-M. Graf v.d. 1994. The German Health Care System at the Crossroads. *Health Economics* 3:301–3.

7. Alber, J. 1992. *Das Gesundheitswesen der Bundesrepublik Deutschland—Entwicklung, Struktur und Funktionsweise.* Frankfurt, 69ff.

8. Henke, K. D. und Ade, C. Administrative Modernization: Health Care Reforms. Discussion Paper No. 177. University of Hanover, Department of Economics, 28.

9. Advisory Council for the Concerted Action in Health Care: Health Care and Health Insurance 2000, Individual-responsibility, subsidiarity and solidarity in a changing environment, expert opinion report 1994. Abbreviated version. 1994. Bonn, 34ff.

10. Advisory Council for the Concerted Action in Health Care. 1990. *Jahresgutachten 1990—Herausforderungen und Perspektiven der Gesundheitsversorgung.* Baden-Baden, 109ff. and 146.

11. Thiede, R. F. 1990. *Die gestaffelte Pflegeversicherung—Sozialpolitische und ökonomische Aspekte eines neuen Modells.* Frankfurt am Main, 60.

12. Bundesministerium der Finanzen. 1990. *Stellungsnahme des wissenschaftlichen Beirates beim Bundesministerium der Finanzen zur Finanzierung von Pflegekosten.* Bonn, 2.

13. Schulenburg, J.-M., and O. Schöffski. Transformation des Gesundheitswesens im Spannungsfeld zwischen Kostendämpfung und Freiheit: Eine ökonomische Analyse des veränderten Überweisungs- und Einweisungsverhaltens nach den Arzneimittelregulierungen des GSG. 1994. In *Probleme der Transformation im Gesundheitswesen,* edited by P. Oberender. Baden-Baden.

Table 1   Total Population by Age and Sex (per 1,000)

	1990			1991			1992		
	M	F	Total	M	F	Total	M	F	Total
0–9	4,508	4,279	8,787	4,532	4,300	8,832	4,547	4,315	8,862
10–19	4,373	4,146	8,519	4,343	4,119	8,462	4,388	4,153	8,541
20–29	6,856	6,468	13,324	6,794	6,382	13,176	6,718	6,257	12,975
30–39	6,093	5,807	11,901	6,289	5,962	12,251	6,521	6,127	12,648
40–49	5,181	4,976	10,157	5,118	4,921	10,039	5,189	4,993	10,182
50–59	5,432	5,370	10,802	5,599	5,531	11,130	5,669	5,599	11,268
60–69	3,506	4,687	8,192	3,565	4,584	8,149	3,624	4,502	8,126
70–79	1,712	3,348	5,060	1,749	3,407	5,156	1,770	3,422	5,192
≥ 80	839	2,172	3,011	851	2,230	3,081	874	2,307	3,181
Total	38,500	41,253	79,753	38,840	41,436	80,276	39,300	41,675	80,975

SOURCE: *Statistisches Jahrbuch für die Bundesrepublik Deutschland 1992,* 64, *1993,* 66, *1994,* 66.

Table 2a   Live Births

	1990			1991			1992		
	M	F	Total	M	F	Total	M	F	Total
West Germany	373,727	353,472	727,199	371,056	351,194	722,250	369,499	351,295	720,794
Former East Germany	91,652	86,824	178,476	55,042	52,727	107,769	45,308	43,012	88,320
Total	465,379	440,296	905,675	426,098	403,921	830,019	414,807	394,307	809,114

SOURCE: *Statistisches Jahrbuch 1994 für die Bundesrepublik Deutschland,* 74–75.

Table 2b   Birth Rate*

	1980	1989	1990	1991
West Germany	46.7	51.6	53.9	52.9
Former East Germany	67.4	58.2		33.1

SOURCE: *Statistisches Jahrbuch für die Bundesrepublik Deutschland 1991,* 79, *1994,* 79.

*Birth Rate = number of live births per 1,000 women aged between 15 and 45.

Table 2c-1   Fertility Rate* by age (West Germany)

Age	1980	1989	1991
<15	0.0	0.0	0.0
15	0.7	0.8	0.8
16	3.6	3.3	3.3
17	10.7	7.8	8.6
18	22.6	14.7	18.2
19	39.1	25.7	29.1
20	55.9	34.4	39.4
21	69.5	42.3	47.8
22	81.7	51.0	54.5
23	93.6	64.6	62.4
24	104.7	79.6	72.8
25	111.1	93.8	87.3
26	112.5	106.8	101.2
27	109.8	111.1	109.4
28	105.0	111.7	112.0
29	94.7	108.0	108.6
30	85.8	99.9	103.0
31	72.7	88.9	91.8
32	60.8	75.8	79.8
33	48.9	65.0	67.6
34	39.4	52.6	55.6
35	32.6	42.3	45.4
36	24.7	33.8	35.6
37	19.1	25.8	27.5
38	14.7	18.8	19.9
39	10.1	12.9	14.4
40	7.5	9.4	9.9
41	5.0	6.1	6.9
42	3.5	3.6	4.0
43	2.2	2.3	2.4
44	1.3	1.3	1.3
<44	1,443.4	1,394.2	1,420.6

*Fertility rate = live births per 1,000 women of a certain age group.
SOURCE: *Statistisches Jahrbuch für die Bundesrepublik Deutschland 1991*, 79, *1994*, 79.

Table 2c-2   Fertility Rate* by Age (Former East Germany)

Age	1980	1989	1991
<16	0.8	0.8	1.1
16	4.5	3.2	3.9
17	17.0	9.5	10.3
18	52.4	27.8	22.3
19	115.2	63.8	51.0
20	169.2	103.9	75.0
21	191.5	128.6	90.1
22	195.1	142.3	94.6
23	187.9	149.7	93.9
24	172.9	151.6	92.1
25	155.8	143.4	83.6
26	134.7	125.5	72.9
27	111.9	105.8	58.4
28	92.2	87.2	45.6
29	75.0	69.4	36.5
30	59.7	56.8	29.3
31	47.8	45.8	24.5
32	38.7	37.6	19.6
33	29.9	28.9	16.2
34	23.8	23.4	12.4
35	17.9	19.1	10.5
36	13.6	14.5	8.8
37	9.9	10.9	6.9
38	7.9	8.1	5.4
39	5.5	5.7	4.1
40	3.8	3.8	3.1
41	2.9	2.3	2.2
42	2.0	1.4	1.3
43	1.2	1.1	0.7
44	0.7	0.4	0.5
45	0.4	0.1	0.3
<45	1,941.8	1,572.3	976.7

*Fertility rate = live births per 1,000 women of a certain age group.
SOURCE: *Statistisches Jahrbuch für die Bundesrepublik Deutschland 1991*, 79, *1994*, 79.

Table 2d-1   Infant Mortality Rate by Age (West Germany)

Age	1990		1991	
	M	F	M	F
0–1	8.1	6.1	7.4	5.9
1–5	0.4	0.4	0.4	0.3
5–10	0.2	0.2	0.2	0.2
10–15	0.2	0.1	0.2	0.1

SOURCE: *Statistisches Jahrbuch für die Bundesrepublik Deutschland 1994*, 83.

Table 2d-2   Infant Mortality Rate by Age (Former East Germany)

Age	1989 M	1989 F	1991 M	1991 F
0–1	8.5	5.9	7.0	4.9
1–5	0.4	0.4	0.5	0.4
5–10	0.3	0.2	0.3	0.2
10–15	0.3	0.1	0.3	0.2

SOURCE: *Statistisches Jahrbuch für die Bundesrepublik Deutschland 1994*, 84.

Table 3   Infant Mortality Rate by the Six Most Common Causes (per 100,000 Live Births)

	Causes	1991 M	1991 F	1992 M	1992 F
1	Certain affections that go back to perinatal period	279.0	208.5	259.6	200.4
2	Congenital anomaly	202.5	177.0	217.2	176.5
3	Sudden death through an unknown cause	182.1	129.2	132.1	99.4
4	Delayed fetal growth and fetal malnutrition, affections of shortened period of gestation and underweight	115.7	85.2	113.8	95.1
5	Respiratory affections	78.4	55.0	66.3	46.4
6	Infectious and parasitic disease	13.1	12.1	8.2	6.1

SOURCE: *Statistisches Jahrbuch für die Bundesrepublik Deutschland 1993*, 467, *1994*, 456.

Table 4   Estimated Death Rate per 100,000 Population for the 15 Leading Causes of Death

	Causes	1990			1991			1992		
		Total	M	F	Total	M	F	Total	M	F
1	Diseases of cerebrovascular system	127.6	97.4	155.4	132.7	101.6	161.3	126.1	97.1	152.7
2	Ischemic heart diseases	105.1	95.0	114.5	108.2	96.2	119.2	108.1	95.7	119.4
3	Cardiac insufficiency	77.3	56.3	96.6	70.7	51.8	88.0	65.2	47.1	81.9
4	Injuries and toxipathies	57.0	71.8	43.4	57.3	72.4	43.3	54.5	69.8	40.4
5	Malign neoformation of trachea, bronchial tubes, and lungs	42.5	70.7	16.5	42.9	70.6	17.5	42.5	69.4	17.7
6	Symptoms and bad specified affections	33.2	33.0	33.3	27.0	27.2	26.9	24.2	24.2	24.1
7	Psychiatric diseases, diseases of nervous system and sense organs	27.8	30.7	25.0	28.7	32.3	25.3	29.2	32.8	25.9
8	Malign neoformation of colon	24.6	20.9	28.0	25.1	21.5	28.4	26.2	22.6	29.6
9	Pneumonia	24.2	22.2	26.0	20.3	18.7	21.7	18.9	18.1	19.7
10	Diabetes mellitus	24.0	16.2	31.1	24.0	16.3	31.1	23.8	16.1	30.8
11	Chronic liver diseases and cirrhosis	22.4	29.7	15.6	23.9	32.2	16.4	23.3	31.3	16.0
12	Malign neoformation of uterus	22.1	0.3	42.2	22.8	0.3	43.5	22.8	0.3	43.4
13	Malign neoformation of stomach	21.4	22.8	20.0	21.2	22.2	20.2	20.3	21.6	19.0
14	Bronchitis	19.0	26.7	12.0	18.3	25.2	11.9	15.6	21.7	10.1
15	Malign neoformation of lymphatic and hematopoietic tissue	17.8	18.0	17.5	18.0	18.3	17.6	17.9	18.0	17.8

SOURCE: *Statistisches Jahrbuch für die Bundesrepublik Deutschland 1994*, 458–59.

Table 5   Data in Germany not available (due to the decentralized character of the German health care system)

Table 6a   Average Net Income before Personal Income Taxes* of Doctors Broken Down by Specialty (per 1,000)

	1991	1992	1993
Radiologists	267	275	175
Orthopedists	226	239	226
Urologists	188	193	192
ENT-Doctors	219	226	222
Gynecologists	193	198	188
Internists	168	170	163
Dermatologists	193	195	186
Oculists	191	204	185
Surgeons	159	160	137
Pediatricians	160	163	156
Neurologists	155	154	166
Generalists	143	169	135
All specialists	166	170	159

*Income before taxes = Returns minus costs.
SOURCE: *Angaben der Kassenärztlichen Vereinigung.*

Table 6b   Average Net Income before Personal Income Taxes* of Dentists

	1991	1992	1993
West Germany	196,502	204,015	179,060
Former East Germany	75,700	154,272	142,660

*Income before taxes = Returns minus costs.
SOURCE: *Erhebung der Kassenzahnärztlichen Vereinigung für 1976, Erhebungen GEBERA für 1977–1980, Erhebungen für Kassenzahnärztlichen Vereinigung für 1981–1993 (1993: Auswertung auf der Basis des Rücklaufs bis 15.10.1994).*

Table 7a   Number of Acute Care General Hospitals (West Germany)

No. of beds	<100	100–149	150–199	200–299	300–399	>400	Total
1990	585	262	236	340	216	390	2,029
1991	592	259	227	342	215	387	2,022
1992	584	258	230	340	216	385	2,013

SOURCE: *Sachverständigenrat für die Konzertierte Aktion im Gesundheitswesen 1994, 369.*

Table 7b   Number of Acute Care General Hospitals (Former East Germany)

No. of beds	<100	100–149	150–199	200–299	300–399	>400	Total
1991	55	57	44	68	50	115	389
1992	53	50	38	78	42	107	368

SOURCE: *Sachverständigenrat für die Konzertierte Aktion im Gesundheitswesen 1994, 369.*

Table 8   Number of General Hospital Admissions per Year, and the Average Length of Stay

	Nursing days	Admissions	Internal obstruction	Discharges	Internal obstruction	Number of persons died	Number of cases	Average length of stay
1991	174,650,879	14,172,064	1,034,904	13,728,607	1,037,707	439,856	13,529,603	12.9
1992	172,026,151	14,536,185	1,067,229	14,131,253	1,070,931	432,250	13,820,308	12.4

SOURCE: *Statistisches Jahrbuch für die Bundesrepublik Deutschland 1993, 479, 1994, 468.*

Table 9   Number and Type of Nursing Homes and the Average Number of Beds per Facility in 1993

	Old people's home (flats without nursing and board) (1)	Old people's home (flats/ rooms, care and full board included) (2)	Geriatric nursing home (3)	(1)–(3) in one facility (Mehrgliedrige Einrichtungen)	All facilities for old people	Facilities for handicapped
number	664	2,033	2,271	3,331	8,299	2,325
beds	51,839	127,213	156,492	338,469	674,013	115,648

SOURCE: *Angaben des Bundesministeriums für Familie, Senioren, Frauen und Jugend, Stand: 30.06.1993.*

Table 10   National Health Expenditures by Type of Expenditure and Source of Funds for Each Category in 1992 (per million DM)

Type of expenditure	Total	Public funds	Statutory Health Insurance System	Social Insurance Pension Fund	Social Accident Insurance	Private Health Insurance	Employer	Private households
Preventive and care measures	31,071	17,984	9,155	230	999	—	2,703	—
Health Services	7,649	4,082	637	230	—	—	2,700	—
Disease prevention and early detection (insofar as not health services)	3,558	78	2,478	—	999	—	3	—
maternity help	2,758	25	2,733	—	—	—	—	—
measures of nursing	17,106	13,799	3,307	—	—	—	—	—
Treatment	254,825	16,938	170,761	5,836	3,167	14,924	10,905	32,294
ambulatory treatment	75,205	2,856	50,714	4	1,209	5,000	3,820	11,602
stationary treatment and stationary cure treatment	103,967	13,899	69,041	5,832	1,929	6,576	4,767	1,923
drugs, curative, devices, denture	75,653	183	51,006	—	29	3,348	2,318	18,769
epinosic services	116,138	16,723	16,060	21,959	6,122	2,047	53,227	—
Professional and social rehabilitation	15,913	14,487	443	581	402	—	—	—
Sick leave compensation	48,430	—	—	—	—	—	48,430	—
other income service in case of illness	20,010	1,234	13,908	1,068	1,213	2,047	540	—
disability pension	29,781	903	—	20,144	4,497	—	4,237	—
Other epinosic services	2,004	99	1,709	166	10	—	20	—
education and research	6,966	6,966	—	—	—	—	—	—
expenditures which can not be divided up	20,083	—	11,578	960	2,987	4,558	—	—
Total	429,083	58,611	207,554	28,985	13,275	21,529	66,835	32,294

SOURCE: C. Gräb, and C. Kühnen, *Wirtschaft und Statistik*, no. 10 (1994), 670.

The Health System of Japan

Toshitaka Nakahara*

Introduction

General Description

Japan consists of four main islands covering an area of 377,435 square kilometers, and some 3,000 kilometers long, slightly smaller than the state of California. More than 67% of the land is covered by mountains and forests; the remainder is divided into residential and industrial areas, and cultivated land. The population is about 125 million. As a result, the country is heavily overpopulated. Distinct seasonal climatic changes are observed in all parts of the country. The people are ethnically homogeneous and speak one language, Japanese. Illiteracy presents no problem.

Japan has been called the most rapidly changing society in the world. In the health field, for example, during the five decades after World War II, the nation's health scene changed drastically, beginning with the challenge of nationwide epidemics such as typhus, smallpox, and cholera, through the battle against tuberculosis, and then on to the problems of environmental pollution episodes and chronic degenerative diseases. Currently, it is facing and adapting to its aging society. Japan, however, has been also called a dynamic society without change, and this seems true, too. For example, the delivery of medical services depends heavily on private medical practitioners along with a nationwide social health insurance scheme.

To understand the health system, it is essential to note the character of the social, cultural, and political contexts within which the system evolved. The modern health system in Japan evolved

*The author wishes to acknowledge Professor Masami Hashimoto, whose earlier work appeared in *Comparative Health Systems* (ed. M. Raffel, Penn State Press, 1984) from which this account is drawn.

during the past 120 years in response to the country's pressing social needs and demands of each period. It bears many similarities to its original models in the Western countries, but there are also many differences. Mainly due to the natural milieu and geographical setting—an insularity in the Far East—Japan's culture has been highly self-centered and closed off from the rest of the world, especially from the West, for some 2,000 years since Japan's unification. However, situated at a meeting point of East and West, the people of Japan have shown a unique aptitude for learning foreign cultures and ideas, and for adapting them to their own cultural milieu. A history of the modern health care system started from the official adoption of Western medicine in 1870, but it should be noted that Chinese medicine had been known in Japan for more than 1,000 years.

A Short History of the Health System

In 1867 there was a short civil war known as the Meiji Restoration: an alliance of powerful land-owners, young samurai, and mercantile capitalists overthrew the feudal system. The Meiji Era (1868–1912) represents a most brilliant period in the history of Japan: within only a few decades, a modern nation with up-to-date industries, political institutions, and social patterns was established. Leaders of the new government eagerly sought to adopt the institutions of Western countries, which then seemed best suited to the modernization of the country. The government decided in 1870 to adopt the German medical system, which was then considered the most advanced in Europe; this remained a strong influence until the end of World War II. Meiji leaders also selected the Prussian political system as a model because of its strong central government based upon well-developed industries. In 1874 a medical code (ISEI), which heralded the start of modern medical and public health administration, was enacted. The ISEI covered medical, public health, and pharmaceutical administrations as well as medical education, a licensing system for medical practice, and other areas. During the succeeding decade, a transfer from traditional medical methods to Western methods (substantially German) was completed. Adoption of the German system as Japan's official medical policy lasted as a strong influence in every field of medicine, including medical education and research, and social health insurance.

During the 1870s and 1880s, many German physicians came to Japan to teach medicine, and many younger Japanese medical scholars went to Germany to study. In 1875, on the occasion of the medical practice examination, the government required that all physicians should study Western medicine. Traditional Chinese medicine was not prohibited, though it was allowed only for physicians trained in Western medicine. Chinese medical practitioners then constituted a majority of physicians, but, under strict governmental policy, Chinese medicine quickly lost its official position.

In 1889 a constitution was promulgated that set up a constitutional monarchy; a highly centralized nation was established, aspiring to be both ''a wealthy nation and strong army.'' Japan soon became involved in the Sino-Japanese War (1894–95) and the Russo-Japanese War (1904–5), which were accompanied by an industrial revolution. By the end of World War I, which Japan joined under the provisions of the Anglo-Japanese Alliance of 1902, Japan was recognized as one of the world's major powers. After the war, however, the country underwent a series of depressions, sustaining serious damage especially from the Great Depression; the resulting social tension was exploited by extremists, and the political parties lost power steadily, being replaced by a military clique. After the outbreak of the China Incident in 1937, Japan became ever more deeply involved in war, leading finally to surrender in 1945. Thus, only eighty years after the Meiji Restoration, with its attendant great hopes of modernization and democratization, Japan had to start again.

World War II brought almost complete destruction of the old system, with the loss of nearly two million people and about one-half of the land area.

After World War II, Japan was occupied by foreign forces for the first time in its history. During the occupation period, which lasted until April 1952, the country carried out a democratic social reform with strong guidance and support from the U.S. occupation authority. The postwar period may properly be called a period of American influence. The new constitution, which was effective on May 3, 1947, became the cornerstone of its new era.

The Current Government System

The new constitution differs in three essential points from the Meiji Constitution: (1) the emperor is only the symbol of the state and of the unity of the people. Sovereign power now rests with the people; (2) Japan renounces war as a sovereign right; and (3) fundamental human rights are guaranteed as eternal and inviolable. As a basis of the nation's health, Article 25 of the constitution declares that the promotion and improvement of public health, together with social welfare, are the responsibilities of the nation. The Diet is the highest organ of state power and the sole lawmaking body. Executive power is vested in the cabinet, which consists of the prime minister and not more than twenty ministers of state. The cabinet is collectively responsible to the Diet. The judiciary is completely independent from the executive and legislative bodies.

The Ministry of Health and Welfare has prime responsibility for health administration and for the actual services provided for people living in a community. The Ministry of Labor is responsible for health and safety in workplaces. The Ministry of Education is responsible for school health. The environmental agency is responsible for the supervision of rivers and lakes, outdoor air, and conservation of nature.

Decentralization is a basic principle underlying national policies. The country is divided into forty-seven prefectures, including the metropolis of Tokyo. Local administration is conducted at the levels of prefectural governments, and municipal (city, town, and village) governments, each level with its respective assemblies. The prefectural governors and city, town, and village mayors, as well as the members of the local assemblies, are elected by the registered voters of the districts. The power of these units are specified by the Local Autonomy Law (1947).

In principle, preventive health services are provided by the government as a public service, and are financed by the governments at central level and local levels. Medical care, however, is largely supplied by hospitals and clinics belonging to the private sector, though national and some local governments operate their own hospitals and clinics that are financed by the respective governments. The medical care provided by both the private sector and the public sector is financed by the social health insurance scheme.

Medical Practice

Physicians and Their Distribution

The ratio of physicians to population grew steadily after a national policy to increase the number of medical schools and physicians (1970). At the end of 1992 there were 219,704 physicians (176.5

physicians per 100,000 population). The number increased 7,907 (3.7%) from the end of 1990. Of these physicians, 211,498 (96.3%) were in medical practice, 3,904 (1.8%) in nonclinical teaching or research, and 2,315 (1.1%) in public health administration. Of the physicians in clinical practice, 56,731 (26.8%) were owners of medical care facilities (for example, hospitals or clinics) and 154,767 (73.2%) were employed in medical care facilities. The geographical distribution of physicians is uneven. For example, several prefectures showed about 220 physicians per 100,000 population and other several prefectures showed as low as 100. The specialty distribution is also uneven. The shortage of physicians in the fields of public health, as well as in the basic medical sciences, has been serious.

From the beginning of the 1970s, three medical schools were established to cope with the shortage of physicians in rural or remote areas, mining and other industries, and the Defense Agency: the Local Autonomy Medical College, the Industrial Medical College, and the Defense Medical College. As the annual number of students at the entrance to the medical schools was 8,360 in 1981, a future excess of physicians has become of concern. The number of physicians per 100,000 population was estimated to be 220 in 2000 and 300 in 2025, if the present annual graduation from the medical schools lasts until the twenty-first century. The Ministry of Health and Welfare and the Ministry of Education have decided upon a 10% reduction of annual new enrollments in the medical schools by 1995. Some 7,710 new medical students entered the eighty medical schools in 1994.

Private Practitioners

Throughout the history of medical practice in Japan, the role played by private practitioners has been significant. Even today, despite the establishment of a nationwide social health insurance scheme in 1961 which led to a form of socialization of the medical services, the delivery of services still depends heavily on the private sector.

The private practitioner in Japan is not a general practitioner. Typically, a private practitioner spends four years in a medical science course, or five years or more in medical school teaching hospitals (after the completion of six-year medical education at the undergraduate level) to get the higher academic degree of Doctor of Medical Science. This degree is also a valuable status symbol for private practitioners. Despite a long-standing debate, there is no nationally recognized or formal system of specialty training and registration. Therefore, the private practitioner in Japan may properly be called an expert. However, a new trend has emerged from the 1970s: academic societies in medical science have established their own system of specialty training and registration. Currently, there are thirteen academic societies that have this system, including internal medicine, medical radiology, general surgery, dermatology, neurology, and clinical pathology.

The Japan Medical Association (JMA) started a lifelong education system for medical practitioners in 1987, and has been conducting various programs of continuing education through television, radio, meetings of various academic societies, training seminars, and similar methods. Centers for the continuing education of community medicine have established twenty-five teaching hospitals by the support of the Ministry of Health and Welfare. However, such continuing education is not mandated, and currently there is no formal reexamination required for medical practitioners to continue in practice.

Solo practice is overwhelmingly prevalent among private practitioners; group practice is still in the experimental stage, appearing sometimes, for example, in new towns. Meanwhile, hospitals are predominantly closed systems; that is, staffed by full-time salaried medical staffs and almost always closed to private practitioners in the district. However, the JMA has been encouraging the establishment of local medical association hospitals; that is, hospitals established and utilized by a local medical association, aimed at the promotion of effective community medicine. Currently, the Ministry of Health and Welfare has given a special advantage in the payment system of the social health insurance to the hospitals of "open system", that is staffed by full-time salaried medical staffs but open to private practitioners in the district. In 1994, there were 102 open-system hospitals including local medical association hospitals authorized by the Ministry of Health and Welfare.

Local medical associations, which are composed mostly of private practitioners, form the JMA, which currently includes about 110,000 active practitioners. The JMA was founded at the beginning of this century, and has been the most powerful medical group. Many voluntary professional organizations (not trade unions) organized at the national, prefectural, and local levels exert considerable influence on national medical policies, and also pursue various professional as well as academic activities.

Currently there are no formal data as regards the working hours and incomes of the various medical specialties. Generally speaking, private practitioners are working hard, and their income in general is high, compared to that of other professionals. According to a nationwide sampling of private practitioner clinics conducted by the JMA in 1978, the average working hours (including participation in community health programs by a practicing private practitioner) are 216 hours per month, that is, 54 hours per week. According to the survey conducted by the national personnel authority in 1994, a monthly salary figure regularly paid by a private hospital for the director-general showed 1,439,785 yen at the average age of 59.4; for the chief of the section, 1,031,698 yen at the average age of 44.6; and for the medical practitioner, 799,029 yen at the average age of 36.6; for the pharmacist, 312,213 yen at the average age of 33.3; and for the nurse, 316,031 yen at the average age of 33.2.

Patient Access to Care

For most of the Japanese people, accessibility and availability of medical care are fairly well assured. A person who wants to receive medical care is free to go to any clinic or hospital and simply present the health insurance membership card; practically all medical care facilities are under the health insurance program. The most common route is to call their "home doctor's" office, but there is no restriction on choosing another doctor or facility. Needless to say, this pattern is very convenient for patients, but it is an expensive system and easily results in abuse of medical care. Currently, people tend not to have their own "home doctor" and go easily to a bigger hospital. It is the same even in the university hospitals. Under the amendment to the Medical Service Law in 1993, however, people who want to consult specific high-level function hospitals, including the university hospitals, without a letter of reference from a physician now have to pay an extra charge under the social health insurance system.

There were 83,394 general clinics in 1992, an average of 67.0 clinics per 100,000 population. Some 60,243 clinics (72.2%) were practitioner's offices with examining rooms; 23,151 clinics (27.8%) had 19 or fewer patient beds, for a total of 270,618 beds. It should be noted that private clinics are equipped with fairly elaborate equipment for diagnosis and treatment and, as mentioned before, most of the private practitioners have become expert in some area of clinical medicine.

It should be also noted that in Japan the pattern of dispensing drugs is quite different from the prevailing one in the Western countries with their separation of medical and pharmaceutical practices. Efforts had been made by the government since the beginning of the Meiji Era for a separation; finally, in 1951 the Diet passed a new law amending the related laws for this purpose. However, the traditional pattern has remained prevalent, mainly because a large part of a physician's income has come from prescriptions under the present payment system by health insurance. At the same time, there is an expectation among Japanese people that all drugs should be prescribed and supplied by the physician. The Ministry of Health and Welfare introduced to the social health insurance system in 1974 an advantageous payment program: health insurance would pay the extra money for the issuance of prescriptions to pharmacists outside the hospital, thus promoting the diffusion of the "separation."

Private practitioners in modern Japan have played an essential role in the delivery of medical care services. At their clinics, they have provided primary medical care to the patients in their communities. However, as there has been no obvious difference between the roles of the clinics and the general hospitals, hospitals have also provided primary medical care. In general, medical school teaching hospitals and large public hospitals have highly specialized full-time medical staffs, but in the outpatient departments of these hospitals primary medical care has also been provided.

Recently, emergency medical care has drawn considerable citizen attention, and prefectural and municipal governments are making efforts, with the support of the Ministry of Health and Welfare, to establish an emergency medical care system including medical care on holidays and at night.

HOSPITALS

Historical Overview

Hospitals and related systems in Japan have notable peculiarities compared with the systems in the Western countries, mainly due to their historical and cultural background. The first Western-style hospital was established in Japan in 1557 by Portuguese doctor and Jesuit Louis Almeida. However, because of the Japanese policy of isolation for a period of more than two hundred years, the study of Western ideas, including medicine and medical practice, was possible only through a small window in Nagasaki by a Dutchman: in 1861, the Dutch naval medical officer, J. L. Pompe van Meerdervoort, established a hospital in Nagasaki that heralded the start of a first modern Western-style hospital. Subsequently, a great interest in studying Dutch spread among the young Japanese generation.

At the time the Meiji government decided to adopt Western medicine officially, the only Western medical care facilities were public hospitals attached to medical schools. It was from these hospitals that physicians were sent out to national and prefectural hospitals, which were then the only medical care facilities in those communities. It should be noted that the Japanese traditionally regard public institutions as superior to private ones, and this has been responsible for the development of private clinics mainly staffed by graduates of private medical schools rather than public medical schools. As noted already, public hospitals were operated on the basis of a "closed system," having very little contact with private practitioners.

Hospitalization

The concept of hospitalization in Japan has traditionally been different from the Western concept. Specifically, there are no "acute" hospitals at the present time, and, traditionally, the patients with chronic illnesses, who would be in nursing homes in the Western societies, have always been treated as inpatients in Japanese hospitals and clinics. This has resulted in a much longer average length of stay in general hospitals (36.2 days in 1992) as compared with the Western countries. Another peculiarity in the hospital system is the lack of a formal referral system between clinics and hospitals, and there has been strong competition between clinics and hospitals, particularly small hospitals. The Ministry of Health and Welfare has decided to promote the referral system from the economic viewpoint, and has started the advantageous payment in the health insurance system for the referral of patient information between hospitals and clinics, between hospitals, and between clinics. As of October 1992, some 91.9% of clinics referred their patients to hospitals or other clinics.

Medical Service Planning and Hospitals

In 1985 the Medical Service Law was amended, and medical service planning was legalized. Prefectures had to determine the "medical service zones," and the necessary number of hospital beds in each zone. In principle, prefectures have to reject the establishment of hospital beds exceeding this necessary number. This amendment was based on the understanding that, in contrast to the trend in the Western countries, the number of general hospitals and their beds had been increasing steadily despite the already high bed to population ratio. In 1994, there are 342 medical service zones, in 149 of which the present hospital beds are in excess of the limit.

Hospitals are classified into five groups: general hospitals, tuberculosis sanatoria, mental hospitals, communicable disease hospitals, and leprosy sanatoria. In 1992, there were 8,877 general hospitals, 11 tuberculosis sanatoria, 1,052 mental hospitals, 7 communicable disease hospitals, and 16 leprosy sanatoria. The total was 9,963 hospitals. In 1985 there were 9,608 hospitals. Thus, during the last seven years the number of hospitals has grown by 3.7%. The hospitals were also classified by sponsorship into 398 national hospitals, 308 prefectural governmental hospitals, 770 municipal governmental hospitals, 294 hospitals of public service corporatives, 136 hospitals of health insurance associations, 4,459 hospitals of private medical service corporations, 2,738 individual hospitals, and so on. Among the mental hospitals, 686 hospitals were owned by private medical service corporations and 229 hospitals were individually owned; among leprosy sanatoria 13 were owned by the Ministry of Health and Welfare and 3 were owned privately; and all communicable disease hospitals are sponsored by municipal governments.

In 1992, there were 1,686,696 hospital beds. The hospital bed ratio per 100,000 population was 1,355.3. Hospital beds are classified into five categories. The first is general beds, which were 1,264,719 in 1992; the second is tuberculosis beds, which were 39,570; the third is mental beds, which were 361,982; the fourth is communicable disease beds, which were 11,285; and the fifth is leprosy beds, which were 9,140. In 1985, there were 1,495,328 hospital beds. Thus, during the last seven years the numbers have grown by 12.8%. In recent years tuberculosis beds have decreased notably, and general and mental beds have greatly increased, reflecting the changing disease patterns. The ratio of general beds per 100,000 population was 1,016.2 in 1992; however, adding the clinic beds of 270,618, it would be some 1,234.

In 1993, an amendment to the Medical Service Law was enacted, the main purpose of which was the systematization of functions of medical service facilities. The systematization of new types of hospitals such as "specific high-leveled function hospitals" of hospitals of "care type sickbed group" and the incorporation of "health facilities for the aged" into the medical service system were introduced. The category of the "specific high-leveled function hospitals," which means the university hospitals and the national center hospitals, was separated from the category of the general hospital. This amendment was basically a countermeasure against the increase in recent medical expenditures. It was thought to be the result of the growth of the population of the aged, the advancement of medicine, and the development of medical services; this concept recognizes that the medical service system should be changed so as to fit the times. This could be understood as a move to convert the medical service system from centering around the acute diseases after World War II into centering around the chronic diseases of the aged, as well as to put a high-level medical service into a special frame and formulate a suitable system.

General Hospitals

In 1992, 8,877 general hospitals in Japan had a total of 1,411,751 general hospital beds, the average number of beds per one hospital being 159.0. Of these hospitals, 1,848 (20.8%) had 20 to 49 beds; 2,446 (27.6%) had 50 to 99 beds; 2,285 (25.7%) had 100 to 199 beds. Thus, 6,579 (74.1%) of the general hospitals had fewer than 200 beds. Individuals and private medical service corporations sponsored 70.7% of all general hospitals; the remaining group was publicly sponsored. The number of full-time personnel per 100 beds was 10.4 medical doctors, 0.6 dental doctors, 2.4 pharmacists, 39.7 nurses, 7.7 laboratory technicians, and 29.6 others. Thus, for every 100 beds there were 90.4 personnel. As regards the technological services, for example, 733 hospitals had 756 MRIs (0.61 per 100,000 population); 286 hospitals had 307 lithotripters (0.25 per 100,000 population); 648 hospitals had 648 digital radiography apparatuses (0.52 per 100,000 population); 1,393 hospitals had 2,675 microsurgery apparatuses (2.1 per 100,000 population); and 5,603 (5,001 hospitals and 602 clinics) had 5,939 X-ray CTs for whole body scan (5,337 and 602, respectively, 4.8 per 100,000 population).

General hospital beds are typically classified into three categories: (1) private room for one patient or two (additional charge required for this type of accommodation); (2) semiprivate rooms, which usually have three to six beds; and (3) ward beds, that is, large rooms with many beds. This last type is a carryover from the old charity hospitals, and is rapidly on the decline.

As regards the emergency services, 4,404 hospitals in 1992 accepted emergency admissions and performed emergency operations, and 6,994 hospitals accepted outpatients on holidays and/or at night. In these areas, the private sector plays a significant role, and these activities are usually supported by junior doctors. The transportation of emergency patients is handled by the fire stations in the district concerned.

Special Hospitals

There are traditionally four types of special hospitals in Japan as mentioned above. In addition to the traditional special hospitals, since the 1960s there has been a trend to establish high-level medical centers for special diseases or categorical areas by the Ministry of Health and Welfare and by prefectural and large municipal governments. At the national level, for example, there are the National Cancer Center, the National Cardiovascular Center, the National Center of Neurology and Psychiatry, and the National Center for International Health. Meanwhile, many prefectures established prefectural cancer centers, cardiovascular disease centers, or chronic degenerative disease centers, and several large prefectures and municipalities established child medical centers or maternal and child medical centers. With regard to the emergency services, since 1992 the Ministry of Health and Welfare has facilitated the establishment of emergency and trauma centers in each population area of 300,000. In 1994, there were 122 centers, which had specialists in emergency medicine, the facilities including the CCU, and, if necessary, the "doctor's car"; that is, a transportation vehicle with a medical doctor. Since 1992 the ministry has also established four trauma centers, which have more advanced functions and facilities for trauma and poison treatment.

Hospital Licensure and Inspection

The Medical Service Law (1948) at present provides detailed licensing regulations for hospitals, which must have twenty or more beds. Although clinics can have up to nineteen beds, the law specifies that their managers shall endeavor not to accommodate any patient for more than forty-eight hours, except in cases where there is an unavoidable necessity in medical consultation. Consequently, there is almost no essential difference between clinics and small hospitals in the services they provide.

Based on this law, permission to establish a hospital has to be secured from the prefectural governor, except, of course, for national hospitals. The law sets the standards for a hospital as regards the structure, the equipment, and the number of staff. These standards have to be met not only in order to open a hospital but also to ensure that the levels for appropriate medical services are met by hospitals already in operation. Medical care inspectors from the prefectural government periodically inspect the hospitals.

During the two decades following the establishment of a nationwide social health insurance scheme (1961), national medical policy had emphasized the quantitative strengthening of medical care facilities and medical manpower. In recent years, however, where these quantitative requirements have been met, the quality aspects of medical care have drawn the attention of citizens as well as of the medical profession. There has been no formal quality-check system of medical care such as peer review or the PRO (professional review organization) system in the United States except the assessment, guidance, and auditing system from social health insurance administration. There remains the traditional emphasis among the medical profession for professional freedom and individual professional independence.

Hospital Finance and Policy

Medical care services are financially supported by the social health insurance scheme. As will be described in more detail later, payment for medical practice is based on a "fee-for-service" pattern as is calculated by a "point system," which is based on the monthly bills submitted to the authorities. Here even university hospitals are no exception.

Investment expenditure of nationally owned hospitals is financed by the national government, while maintenance and current expenditure for medical care is paid by the social health insurance with partial liability for patients. Conditions for publicly owned hospitals are similar to the nationally owned hospitals, with substitution of the prefectural or municipal governments for the national government. Among privately owned hospitals, most of which are proprietary, there are public loan schemes for capital investment: the Social Welfare and Medical Care Facilities Financing Corporation finances private medical facilities by long-term loans at low interest. The corporation chooses and screens the recipients of loans on a priority basis according to policy guidelines set up by the national government. Maintenance and current expenditures of private hospitals are also financed by the social insurance carriers and the patients.

Generally speaking, the sponsoring body has considerable influence over hospital policy. However, the legal requirements already mentioned and the "self-paying financial rule" basically limit the activities of a hospital. This rule provides that the whole expenditure of a hospital should be covered by the medical service income of the hospital. For private hospitals, the investment cost is included. Competition between hospitals is considerable, particularly after the application of this rule to the local governmental hospitals in 1966—which resulted in a decreased number of public hospitals due to serious financial deficit.

Hospital abuse is very complicated and a difficult problem to judge mainly because of the peculiarities of the hospital system. A basic issue relating to hospital abuse would be unusually long general hospital stays, 36.2 days in 1992. This is three to four times longer than stays in Western countries, and results from the peculiar pattern of hospitalization in Japan, as already mentioned. There have been discussions of these long average lengths of stay as a problem mainly from the financial side of the health insurance system. The fee schedule of health insurance maintains that the fee paid by the health insurance to the hospital would be reduced gradually depending on the length of the stay, and the extent of the reduction has been stepped up again and again with revisions in the fee schedule.

At present the patients tend to consult the famous and prestigious hospitals; in those hospitals there are complaints about the waiting time for surgical operations. However, even in these hospitals, the order of the operations is decided by medical judgment. When the operation is urgent and cannot be done for some reason or other in one hospital, the patient would be referred to another hospital by that hospital on the responsibility of the hospital. Therefore the patients' complaints are in general thought to be only the expression of their anxiety; generally speaking, there is no problem about the surgical waiting time. There is no available information as regards surgical waiting lists.

Medical Education

Historical Overview

After World War II, based upon the new constitution and under the powerful guidance of the U.S. occupation forces, the national health system was reorganized as a part of the overall social reform. Medical education was no exception. In 1947 the Fundamental Law of Education and the School Education Law were enacted as the basic structure and principle for the educational system of the new era. Thus, based on the so-called six-three-three education system (that is, twelve years of general education), six-year medical and dental education and four-year education for other disciplines in university or college were set. Furthermore, in line with the U.S. pattern, a system of internship and national medical examination was introduced in 1946. The national medical examination initially came after completion of a one-year rotating internship; however, the internship system produced many problems, particularly related to the social and financial status of the medical graduates. The internship system was finally abolished in 1968. In the same year the Medical Practitioners Law was amended to recommend that graduates of medical schools undergo graduate residency training for more than two years immediately after acquiring the license to practice.

Medical Education

An applicant for medical education must graduate from high school and pass an entrance examination for medical school. Afterward, the medical student has to take two years of premedical course work, followed by four years of medical education. Then, to achieve a license to practice medicine, the student has to pass the national medical examination, which is administered by the Ministry of Health and Welfare.

In 1994 there were 80 medical schools in Japan with a total yearly enrollment of 7,710 students. Sponsorship of these schools is as follows: 43 national schools (4,165 students), 8 public schools sponsored by prefectural or large municipal governments (660 students), 29 private schools (2,885 students). Among the national schools is one Defense Agency medical school with 65 entering students. The national and public medical schools are financed by each government, but their medical students have to pay a fee equal to that of other university disciplines. The private medical schools are in principle financed by the student fees and the revenues of their hospitals, although the Ministry of Education gives a subsidy to them.

Graduate Education

The residency training is carried out in the hospitals attached to a medical school and in hospitals designated by the Ministry of Health and Welfare. The trainees get a salary from these hospitals that is subsidized by the national government. In 1992, some 86.1% of newly licensed physicians (15,341 physicians), who were recommended by the Medical Practitioners Law to take this residency training, received it, and 79.5% of them were trained in the medical school teaching hospitals.

In 1957 a new program, a doctoral course in medical science, was introduced in the medical schools as an integral part of advanced graduate education in universities and colleges. This course lasts four years, and graduates can obtain the higher academic degree of Doctor of Medical Science, which roughly corresponds to a Ph.D. in the Western system, if the doctoral thesis is accepted by the faculty. For graduates of medical school, there is an entrance examination and a knowledge of two foreign languages is required. As regards public health, the Institute of Public Health conducts graduate education programs together with continuing education programs for the various health professions.

Medical School Teaching Hospitals

The original structure and character of medical school teaching hospitals were established by teaching hospitals attached to medical schools earlier in the Meiji Era. At that time, due to the official adoption of German medicine as a substitute for long-standing Chinese medicine, the urgent task of these teaching hospitals was the education and training of Western-style physicians at a quick pace. Consequently, physician-centered treatment and medical services became dominant instead of patient-centered ones. At the same time, these teaching hospitals were strongly influenced by the German hospitals, particularly the German university hospitals, as evidenced by the great power and freedom enjoyed by the directors or chiefs of each therapeutic unit. This resulted in a lack of cooperation and coordination among various clinical and specialty units in a hospital, which we now recognize as essential for effective hospital care. It might be noted that this milieu of the early university teaching hospitals remains to some degree in the teaching hospitals of national university medical schools and other large-scale public hospitals even today, despite the change of medical policy from the German system to the American system after World War II.

There are 80 teaching hospitals attached to universities or medical colleges: 43 national, 8 public, and 29 private teaching hospitals. Sponsorship of the national medical school teaching hospitals is by the Ministry of Education. Generally, teaching hospitals of medical schools are large facilities with highly advanced, sophisticated equipment for diagnosis and treatment. These hospitals are primarily aimed at medical education, the training of undergraduate as well as graduate medical students. In addition to the medical school teaching hospitals, the Ministry of Health and Welfare designated 268 teaching hospitals in 1994 for the residency training of newly qualified physicians. This total was made up of 253 general hospitals and 15 mental hospitals: 55 hospitals at the national level, 130 hospitals of prefectural and other public hospitals, and 68 hospitals in the private sector.

Dentists, Nurses, Physicians' Assistants, Physical Therapists, and Other Health Practitioners

Dentists

It is necessary to undergo a six-year education to become a dentist, and all of 29 dental schools belong to a university or college. In 1992, there were 77,416 dentists and the ratio was 60.8 to 100,000 population. Some 75,628 dentists were in clinical practice, 60.4% of whom had their own clinics. The health insurance scheme is applied to dental care in the same way as medical care. The cost for dental care except special denture material is paid by the health insurance on fee-for-service basis.

Nurses, Midwives, and Public Health Nurses

It was not until 1899 that the national government provided the first Midwives Regulation, and regulations for clinical and public health nurses did not arrive until 1916 and 1941, respectively. After World War II, the professional education system for nursing improved significantly. The Public Health Nurses, Midwives, and Nurses Law (1948) dictated that the nursing education system be based on a three-year course with recruitment of students from among high school graduates. This basic course has been modified: it takes the form of a nursing college or university (a four-year session), a junior college (a three-year session), or a nursing school (a three-year session with a four-year part-time school version). This basic course can be followed by the public health nursing or midwifery training, each running at least six months (the majority are one-year schools at present). An assistant nurse training course (a two-year session) and an upgrading course exist, whereby assistant nurses may be raised to the status of nurses. Assistant nurses are licensed by the prefectural governors, whereas nurses, midwives, and public health nurses are licensed by the minister of health and welfare. This 1948 version of the nursing education curriculum was revised in 1968, and new curricula for the preparation of public health nurses and midwives followed in 1971.

Currently, problems in nursing education include: (1) the coexistence of various types of nursing educational institutions, which tend to generate a gap between them; (2) the establishment of nursing schools that depend heavily on private medical care facilities, leading to severe financial limitations; and (3) no special standards for nursing instructors other than possession of a nursing license and clinical experience. In recent years, due to the changes in disease patterns, the increase of the aged population, and the advancement of medical science and technology, the actual shortage of nursing personnel and the growing need for them have been recognized. In 1992 the Law for Securing Nursing Personnel was enacted, and nursing universities or junior colleges have been established very rapidly.

Physical Therapists and Other Health Practitioners

After World War II, such various nonmedical, health practitioners as dental hygienists, radiology technicians, clinical laboratory technicians, occupational therapists, physical therapists, clinical engineers, and so forth emerged as a result of progress in medical science and advances in technology. (Prewar occupations include dental technicians, X-ray technicians, dieticians, and so forth.) A basic common problem among these nonmedical health practitioners is that their education and training systems still depend on special training schools apart from the formal education system based upon the School Education Law. The resulting shortage of facilities, poor staffing, and financial provisions (when compared with formal schools under the School Education Law) is noteworthy. Currently, there are no health occupations such as the physicians' assistants or nurse practitioners as in the United States.

Nursing Homes, Care Homes, Community Ambulatory Care Programs, Mental Health Facilities, and Other Community Health Agencies

Care Facilities and Community Ambulatory Care Programs for the Aged

Mainly due to the traditional hospitalization pattern, nursing homes are not well developed. At present, there is one kind of intermediate facility for the aged ("health facility for the aged"), based on the Health Service for the Aged Law and the Medical Service Law, and four kinds of residential facilities for the aged, based on the Welfare Law for the Aged ("home for the aged," "home for the aged with a moderate fee," "home for the aged with a full charge," and "nursing home"). Of these, the "home for the aged" has a fairly long history from the prewar periods, but the others are postwar institutions.

"Health Facilities for the Aged" were introduced in 1987, and provide not intensive care, but moderate medical and nursing care, along with rehabilitation to prepare the individual to return home, or to enter a nursing home after receiving medical care at a hospital. The cost of medical care is paid by the health insurance scheme on a per capita basis, but the costs of meals and daily necessities are paid by the clients. In 1994, there are 893 facilities with total capacity of 75,862 beds. Of these, 49 facilities are publicly sponsored, and 844 are privately sponsored.

"Homes for the aged" are for those sixty-five and older who have difficulty in being cared for in their homes because of their physical or mental conditions as well as for environmental or economic reasons. "Homes with moderate fees" are divided into three types. In type A the meals are provided; in type B the residents have to cook for themselves; in "care-house" type, meals, bathing, and other services are provided. "Nursing homes" accommodate bedridden aged who are terminal. Although a national subsidy is given for the costs of construction and administration of these homes, the majority of the homes are owned and operated by the private sector. The municipal governments supervise administration of the homes, and are responsible for placement of the clients. The clients of "homes with moderate fees" are required to pay a fixed, small amount of money. The clients of "nursing homes" who can afford to pay are requested to meet the cost, the amount of which is decided according to the economic status of the client. They need not turn over their pensions, nor deplete any savings they may have acquired. The medical care for "nursing home" clients is, in principle, provided by a part-time doctor. "Homes for the aged with a full charge" are quite new facilities and all of them are owned and operated privately. The Welfare Law for the Aged requires notification of such homes' establishment to the prefectures by the owner. The Ministry of Health and Welfare provides guidelines for the facility and its operation, and homes that meet these guidelines are authorized by the public agency established by the ministry. In 1993, the number of these homes and total capacities were 902 homes for the aged with 64,929 beds, 2,770 nursing homes with 194,091 beds; 368 homes with a moderate fee with 20,842 beds; and 261 homes for the aged with a full charge with 26,120 beds.

In 1989, a "10-year strategy for promotion of health and welfare for the aged" (so-called Gold Plan) was published by the ministers of finance, health and welfare, and home affairs. According to this plan, the number of beds in "health facilities for the aged," "nursing homes," and "homes with a moderate fee (care-house type)" would be expanded to 280,000; 290,000; and 100,000 respectively by the end of fiscal year 1999.

In 1991 the home-visiting nursing care system for the frail aged was introduced by the amendment to the Health Service for the Aged Law. Its core concept is that the aged people should be able to carry out their daily activities and receive nursing care at home and in communities in which they have been used to living, with the support of family members. Home-visiting care is provided by nurses, occupational therapists, and physical therapists who visit the frail aged by the order of their "home doctors." In 1994, there are 389 stations of home-visiting nursing care. According to the above-mentioned Gold Plan, the stations would be expanded to 5,000 by the end of fiscal year 1999.

Mental Health Facilities

It was not until the enactment of the Mental Hygiene Law in 1950 that mental health became an important element of national public health policy. The law was revised in 1987 after domestic and international criticism relating to the human rights of mentally ill persons. The aim of the new law, called the Mental Health Law, was to further enhance the protection of the human rights of the mentally ill, and to facilitate their social rehabilitation. Based on this law, in 1992 there were 46 "supported dormitories" for those who could not carry out daily living on their own; 64 "welfare homes" for those who could carry out daily living on their own but had no place to live; 50 "group homes" for those who could live in the community; 51 units of "sheltered workshops" subsidized by the Ministry of Health and Welfare for those who could work well but had no place to live; and 252 "small workshops" subsidized by the Ministry of Health and Welfare for work training.

Psychiatric day-care facilities have rapidly increased in number; there were 246 centers in 1992. There are 300 residential facilities and 217 ambulatory facilities for the mentally retarded in 1993 based on the Welfare Law for the Mentally Retarded.

Other Community Health Agencies

The welfare office is the comprehensive, first-line organ for social welfare administration and services; it carries out not only various aid programs for the needy, activities of care, and fostering and rehabilitation as stipulated by the relevant laws, but also other overall activities related to social welfare. The total number of welfare offices was 1,190 in 1992, some 338 of which were established by prefectures, 849 by cities and metropolitan Tokyo wards, and 3 by towns and villages. There also were child guidance centers, providing a number of child welfare services, established in 174 prefectures and large municipalities in 1992.

Public Health

Historical Overview

The modern public health administration of Japan has evolved during the last 120 years in response to the pressing social needs and demands of each period. The pattern of public administration was introduced from Western countries and evolved on the basis of the Meiji Constitution of 1889. Consequently, its long-standing pattern of strict legislative character was based on relevant administrative laws and stressed ''line'' organization much more than ''staff'' organization. The public health administration, started by the enactment of the ISEI in 1874 and oriented by the Meiji Constitution, was solely the responsibility of government agencies up to the end of World War II—in contrast to the medical care delivery scheme, which was heavily dependent on the private sector.

During the first half of the Meiji Era, the pressing health problems were outbreaks of acute infectious diseases such as cholera and smallpox. The public health administration became highly centralized and oriented toward legal control. In the latter half of the Meiji Era, Japan underwent its industrial revolution, and environmental sanitation became an urgent task of the government. However, because of financial difficulties and repeated wars during the period, the provision of basic sanitary facilities was delayed for a long time. The Taisho Era (1912–26) was marked by growing social tension under a series of economic and natural disasters. This period saw a change of disease pattern, from acute infectious diseases to socially rooted chronic infectious diseases, such as tuberculosis. Although there were continuing wars and increasing pressure from the military clique, various health laws were nonetheless enacted to cope with the changing disease pattern.

In 1938, in response to the social situation, the Ministry of Health and Welfare was established. As regards public health, it should be noted that the first Health Center Law as enacted in 1937; also, the Institute of Public Health and rural and urban health training centers were established by a grant from the Rockefeller Foundation in 1938. Immediately after World War II, based upon the new constitution, the national health system was reorganized. This was done with powerful support from the U.S. occupation authority under an extremely depressed economy accompanied by inflation, shortage of food, and nationwide epidemics. The government made all efforts to reorganize and strengthen the national health system by legislation and by establishing the nationwide health center network in particular. At that time when urbanization and industrialization were hardly noticeable due to the destruction of the war, and health activity of the municipalities was very weak, health centers contributed remarkably to the improvement of community health, especially in communicable disease control, maternal and child health, nutrition improvement, tuberculosis control, food and sanitary inspection, public health nursing, health education, and so on. A most notable change in the demographic pattern, "from high birth-death to low birth-death," occurred during the first postwar decade. From the beginning of the second decade, urbanization and industrialization were accelerated, and an improvement of the social health insurance scheme for the whole population was achieved in 1961. Since the 1960s, the country has undergone a drastic socioeconomic change accompanied by rapid growth in the GNP, heavy chemical industries, information technology, and so forth. The improvement of life expectancy at birth and the decrease in the birth rate resulted in an aging of the population and changing disease patterns. The third decade was marked by serious environmental pollution episodes and a great awakening of the people to the importance of environmental and community health. The environmental agency was established in 1971. After the energy crisis in 1973, public health administration faced financial difficulties due to the low economic growth. The aging of the population has been acknowledged as a very serious social problem. Correspondingly, the fourth and fifth decades have been marked by the restructuring of the public health system.

In the latter half of the 1970s, the Ministry of Health and Welfare decided to establish a subsidy system for the health activities performed by the primary local governments. It started with an 18-month-old child health examination in 1977. In 1978, the ministry began a national health promotion program, encouraging the establishment of municipal health centers and the strengthening of manpower resources such as public health nurses. The Health Service for the Aged Law was enacted in 1983. This law put the measures for health and medical services for the aged unitarily under the control of the primary local governments, and caused them to implement health measures such as health examinations, health education and health consultation for chronic degenerative disease prevention (for example, cancer, circulatory disease, and diabetes). Services were to be provided by this law for the middle-aged and the aged in order to strive for the gradual reduction in medical care expenses on a long-term basis by promoting people's good health. The health center became an organ supporting the primary local governments. The position of the health center in the entire health business was highlighted.

In 1989, the "10-year strategy for promotion of health and welfare for the aged" was published. The objectives regarding home welfare of the aged were set in the primary local governments. Furthermore, in 1993, all of the primary local governments and the prefectures were mandated to formulate a health and welfare program for the aged that would set target values of future health and welfare services.

In 1993, on the other hand, the Council on Public Health, located in the Ministry of Health and Welfare, presented a written opinion to the minister of health and welfare. It urged the necessity of transferring the power concerning public health services from the prefectures to the primary local governments, the entities that were closer to the residents. At the same time, the need to promote both decentralization of power by attaching importance to the role of the primary local governments in public health services, and cooperation among the health, medical, and welfare services was stressed. The establishment of municipal health centers was recommended to all primary local governments. These situations elicited the amendment to the Health Center Law, and the Community Health Law of 1994 (to be enforced totally in 1997).

Present Status

Under the central government, there are 47 prefectures including metropolitan Tokyo, and some 3,200 primary local governments (municipalities; that is, cities, towns, and villages), each with local government units and elected assemblies. These local governments conduct local public administration with the local autonomy power designated by the Local Autonomy Law of 1947.

There are usually four levels of general health administration in the country: central government, prefectural government, prefectural health center, and primary local governments. Currently, thirty-two large primary local governments designated by the Health Center Law of 1947 (designated by the Community Health Law of 1994 after 1997) are required to establish their own health centers in place of prefectural governments.

Public health administration is principally divided into three categories: general health administration, school health administration, and industrial health administration. Of these, school health administration is highly decentralized in contrast to the highly centralized industrial health administration; general health administration falls somewhere between these two extremes. There are at present more than one hundred national laws relating to medical and health matters. Many of them were enacted after World War II, and some were enacted by amendments to prewar legislation. Some are very old; for example, the Infectious Disease Prevention Law (1897) and the Leprosy Prevention Law (1907). There are many orders and regulations for implementation of these national laws, made by the cabinet or a related ministry. Within the above-mentioned legal framework at the national level, local regulations or rules are made by the local governments under the terms of the Local Autonomy Law (1947).

The fiscal year begins on April 1 and ends on March 31 in the following year. At the national government level, the annual general account budget for each ministry or agency is designated in the standard budget, which includes the national subsidy rate that is based in turn on the relevant national law. In fiscal year 1994, the national general account budget amounted to 73,082 billion yen, of which general expenditure without the payment of national bonds and equalization grants to the local government amounted to 40,855 billion yen. The social security scheme amounted to some 13,482 billion yen under the jurisdiction of the Ministry of Health and Welfare. The total general budget of the local government budget has been some 30% larger than the national government general account budget in recent years. Local government income consists mainly of local taxes (about 30% of the total revenue), equalization grants from the national government, national subsidies, and local government bonds.

Ministry of Health and Welfare

The Ministry of Health and Welfare has various missions to serve the people of Japan in protecting their health and promoting welfare. The ministry is composed of nine bureaus (health policy, health service, environmental health, pharmaceutical affairs, social welfare and war victims' relief, health and welfare for the aged, children and families, health insurance, and pension), two departments (statistics and information, and water supply and environmental sanitation), and one separate agency (social insurance agency). The principal roles of the ministry are: (1) health and medical service—taking measures for the prevention and treatment of various diseases, improvement of environmental health, adequate provision for medical care facilities, training of health and medical manpower, quality control over pharmaceutical preparations, and control of narcotics; (2) social welfare service—taking measures to provide a minimum standard of living for indigent people, giving aid to disabled people and widowed families for facilitating their eventual self-support status, helping to provide adequate care and protection of children, and taking measures for the serious problems of the aged population; (3) social insurance—administration and implementation of various health insurance and pension schemes to relieve the economic burden on individuals in the case of sickness, old age, invalidism, and so forth.

In addition to the above, the ministry is giving aid to war-bereaved families as well as atomic bomb sufferers. It also directly administers its own national hospitals and sanatoria including highly specialized institutions such as the National Cancer Center, National Cardiovascular Center, National Center of Neurology and Psychiatry, and National Center for International Health. The ministry also has some affiliated research institutes: the Institute of Population Problems, Institute of Public Health, National Institute of Health and Nutrition, National Institute of Health, National Institute of Health Services Management, National Institute of Hygienic Sciences, and National Institute of Leprosy Research. The ministry conducts as well the research necessary to carry on its work by the distribution of research grants to universities and research institutions. In fiscal year 1994, research grants amounted to 1.2 billion yen. The ministry regularly conducts a number of health statistical analyses and nationwide health-related surveys. The results are published annually by the ministry.

Prefectural Government and Health Centers

The organizational structures of prefectural government is designated by the Local Autonomy Law. The number of health-related divisions are four to eleven, according to the population size of prefectures. Each prefectural government has a department or bureau responsible for health administration in order to carry out its own health programs and the programs in compliance with the national policies directed by the Ministry of Health and Welfare.

All prefectural governments and large municipalities have a local health laboratory that assists their health centers by performing various laboratory tests and investigations on diseases. There are seventy-three local health laboratories in 1994. Forty-six prefectural governments also have a mental health center that both assists mental health consultation in the usual district health centers and provides counseling services for complicated and difficult cases.

As mentioned before, based upon the Health Center Law (1947), all prefectural and the thirty-two large primary local governments have to establish health centers for the improvement of public health in each district. The health center is financed by local and national governments. In 1994, there are 848 health centers throughout the country; of these, 631 are prefectural, 164 are municipal, and 53 are in metropolitan Tokyo. The health centers serve the community health service agencies as well as the district health administration units. In 1993 these were staffed by 34,463 persons, including 1,288 physicians, 856 veterinarians, 8,408 public health nurses, 1,257 X-ray technicians, 1,533 laboratory technicians, 1,303 nutritionists, 756 health statisticians, 565 health educators, 5,280 food and sanitary inspectors, and 4,420 administrative service personnel. The functions and programs of the health center as provided by the Health Center Law of 1947 are dissemination and improvement of hygienic thought; vital statistics; nutrition improvement; environmental sanitation (sanitary control of food and drink, water supply, waste disposal and so on); public health nursing; medical social work; maternal and child health; health of the aged; dental hygiene; mental health; infectious and contagious disease prevention (including tuberculosis); and hygienic tests and inspection.

As regard to the prefectural health planning, almost all prefectures conduct health and medical service planning instead of a mere medical service planning, as based on the Medical Service Law amended in 1985. In 1993, all prefectures formulated the "health and welfare program for the aged" as mentioned above. Regarding the planning of health centers, in 1990 the Ministry of Health and Welfare encouraged the leading health center in each of the medical service zones to establish a health service plan for each zone. This was the forerunner to the idea of Community Health Law as mentioned below.

City, Town, and Village Governments

At the primary local governments (the city, town, and village governments, the municipalities), there is a division or section responsible for health; usually public health nurses are employed. In addition to the basic environmental services such as water supply, waste disposal, night soil treatment, and so forth, the primary local governments carry out various community health programs based on the relevant laws (for example, preventive vaccination, health screening against tuberculosis, and health examinations for people over forty years of age), and community health programs not based at present on the laws (for example, nutrition improvement activities, and health guidance for babies and infants). The functions and programs of the primary local governments after the enactment of the Community Health Law are as mentioned below. There are 1,215 municipal health centers in 1994 at the primary local government level.

All primary local governments are required by law to establish and run a national health insurance program; in many cases, medical care facilities, including hospitals, are established by the local national health insurance association and provide medical services directly to the residents. Health planning by primary local governments had been encouraged by the Ministry of Health and Welfare since 1960; however, mainly due to the traditional public administrative milieu of the country, categorical health planning by respective administrative units (for example, tuberculosis control and maternal and child health) had been predominant at all levels of government for a long time. In 1969 the local governments were requested by the Local Autonomy Law Amendment to develop a "principal vision" or long-range goals as the guideline for a socioeconomic development plan for each local authority. Afterward, medium-term development plans were formulated at the primary local government level, with a health sector plan as a part of these plans. A popular pattern of the planning at this level is to organize advisory committees composed of members of the local medical association, health-related professionals, and members of voluntary organizations, and often representatives of schools, social welfare agencies, and health centers concerned. In 1994, all of the primary local governments completed the formulation of their plan for the health and welfare program for the aged.

Community Health Law

When the Community Health Law of 1994 is totally in force in 1997, the functions and programs of the primary local governments will be as follows: maternal and child health (home visit guidance to expectant mothers, nursing mothers, and newborn babies; health examination of expectant mothers, nursing mothers, and infants; and health examination of 18-month-old children, and 3-year-old children); preventive vaccination; general nutritive guidance; and health services for the middle-aged and the aged (health examinations, health counseling, health education, home visit guidance, and so on). The functions and programs of the health center established by the prefecture will be medical and pharmaceutical affairs; measures against intractable diseases; collection of community health information, investigation and research; technical assistance to the primary local governments; and the activities of the present health center listed above in the absence of activities by the primary local governments. The activities of the health centers of the large primary local governments designated by the Community Health Law will consist of all of the functions and programs of the health center and the primary local government.

This new policy is based on the idea that the primary local government should deal with common personal health services of high frequency and the health center should deal with personal health services of low frequency, which require more special knowledge in a wider area than an average area of the primary local government (for which the "medical service zone" is suitable). Thus, some health centers should merge and one health center in one medical service zone is suitable on average for the new functions and programs of the health center.

Grassroots Organizations and Community Participation

The traditional grassroots organizations are popular both in rural and urban communities, for they are helpful in contributing to daily community life. In addition to these multipurpose citizen organizations, there are commonly diversified organizations, groups, and circles such as women's associations, clubs for the aged, children's associations, PTAs, and so on.

After World War II, people actively participated in various community primary health care programs. This community health action was based at first in the field of environmental sanitation, particularly with vector control campaigns against serious outbreaks of epidemics in the 1950s. This pattern of citizen participation then grew steadily in various community health programs, for example, in maternal and child health, family planning, tuberculosis control, parasite control, and nutrition. From the end of the 1950s through the 1960s interested citizens received technical guidance from their health centers. At present, many primary local governments nominate voluntary health leaders or communicators for the promotion of community health. Under these conditions, many different kinds of volunteer associations have been organized, aimed at the improvement of the community's health. Every prefecture now has some kind of federation of the voluntary health associations in the cities, towns, and villages of its area.

Health Costs and Health Insurance

Social Health Insurance Scheme

Background

In 1922 the Health Insurance Law, the first social insurance program in the Asian region, was enacted to cover laborers working in places covered by the Factory Law or the Mining Law. Enforcement of the law was delayed until 1927 because of a series of socioeconomic and natural disasters. Following this law, in 1938 the National Health Insurance Law was enacted, covering farm, forestry, and fishing people. Since then, efforts have been continuously made by all levels of the government to improve and promote health insurance programs; finally in 1961 the national goal of universal coverage had been achieved by an entirely revised National Health Insurance Law.

Meanwhile, in 1973 medical care expenses for the aged were made free of charge in order to improve the welfare of the aged. The medical care expenses of the aged accelerated in line with the advancement of medicine and the diffusion of medical services, as a measure against which the Health Service for the Aged Law was enacted in 1983.

There are now three major schemes for medical care security, and they are an integral component of the social security scheme. The first, and the core of the system, is the social health insurance scheme covering the whole population of the country. The second is the medical assistance scheme based on the Daily Life Security Law (1950). This law provides for public assistance, subject to a means test, to all needy persons. This scheme consists of aid for livelihood, education, housing, medical care, maternity, occupation, and funeral expenses. All aid, except medical care, is provided in cash. The third major scheme is the public medical care scheme for selected diseases or disorders. There are at present thirteen such programs based on the laws, for example, the Tuberculosis Control Law (1950), the Mental Health Law (1950), the Maternal and Child Health Law (1965), and so forth. And there are two such programs based on the budgetary support of the Ministry of Health and Welfare without specific laws: financial aid for the medical care of selected intractable diseases, and selected chronic diseases of children.

Classification of the Programs

Medical services are supported, for the most part, by health insurance. The health insurance programs can principally be divided into two categories: health insurance for employees and their dependents, and the national health insurance program for others. The former category is subdivided into several programs. One is the government-managed health insurance, the insurance carrier being the national government. Another is the association-managed health insurance, which is established for large enterprises through a special health insurance association for the employees. There are also such insurance programs for specific groups of workers such as the seamen's insurance program and the mutual aid association insurance programs for civil servants of the national and local governments, and employees of the private schools.

The national health insurance programs for other citizens are managed by the primary local governments throughout the country. These programs also include specific national health insurance associations that are organized exclusively for a profession or trade such as medical practitioners, dentists, and construction workers.

As regards the medical costs of the aged, a special program is provided by the Health Service for the Aged Law of 1983. This program is operated by the primary local governments, and seeks financial adjustment regarding medical care expenses for the aged among respective health insurance associations.

Benefits

Any insured persons who wish medical care are free to go to any hospital or clinic and present their membership card. Practically all medical facilities are under health insurance programs. Generally, the benefits include physician and dentist services in the hospitals and clinics for diagnostic procedures, treatments including medication, surgical operations, and hospital care and services. Preventive examinations, normal delivery, and expenses for a private room, for special denture material, or for meals in hospital are excluded from the benefits. There are also cash benefits for normal delivery and for absences from work due to sickness or injury from the fourth day of disablement for at most six months, providing allowances equal to 60% of their standard remuneration.

Because of the differences in financial conditions, the degree of partial liability borne by the beneficiaries varies between the programs. The benefit rate for beneficiaries in the employees' health insurance programs is 90%. The benefit rate for dependents covered by the employees' health insurance program is 70% for outpatient care and 80% for inpatient care. With the national health insurance program, the benefit rate is 70% for both householders and dependents for outpatient and inpatient care. Many health insurance associations provide such fringe benefits as a partial liability benefit for dependents, in addition to the legal benefits. Under the special health insurance program for the aged, the aged of seventy years old and over and those between sixty-five and seventy with disabilities designated by the national government can take outpatient care with cost-sharing of 1,000 yen per month and inpatient care with cost-sharing of 700 yen per day, if they are covered by any social health insurance program.

There has been a maximum-amount cap on the amount of money an individual patient might have to pay since 1973, when partial payment by the patient and dependent in employees' health insurance was subsidized by the national government as "special payment for expensive medical care." This became a benefit to members of the national health insurance program in 1975. If the payment of the patient exceeds 63,000 yen a month, at present, he or she is entitled to reimbursement matching the amount in excess of 63,000 yen.

Finances and Contributions

Health insurance is supported by contributions and subsidies from national or local governments. As a rule, the employees' health insurance premium is shared on a 50-50 basis by employee and employer, and the amount is determined by multiplying the wage of the insured by a fixed rate. In the government-managed health insurance, the rate is 8.2% of a standard remuneration, at present. The rate of the association-managed insurance varies among associations, but it is generally low as compared to the government-managed health insurance.

In the national health insurance, most insurers collect premiums from their members as an object tax under the Local Tax Law. Since 1959 the liability of the national treasury in connection with the medical care benefit of the national health insurance has been provided for in law. The national subsidy is at present between about 32% and 52% of the medical care benefits, varying according to the financial conditions of each association. In the government-managed health insurance, because of continuing deficits, the liability of the national treasury has also been provided for since 1973. The national subsidy rate is now 13% of the medical care.

In the special health insurance program for the aged, the national government contributes 20% to the medical cost of the aged, the prefectures and the primary local governments contribute 5% each, and the remaining 70% is provided jointly by the health insurance associations. The national government's share is more than 30% of the total medical care cost of the aged when the contributions and subsidies to the health insurance and national health insurance mentioned above are taken into consideration.

Payment Method and Cost Control System

In the early stage of health insurance in Japan, a contract was made between the insurers and a medical association determining a yearly sum per capita, but in 1943 the present fee-for-service payment system was adopted. The fee schedule is called the "point system"; each act of medical practice is given a certain point score determined by the minister of health and welfare, and a fee is computed by multiplying the point score by the unit cost. The unit cost at present is 10 yen. Under the Health Service for the Aged Law of 1983, a special fee schedule for the medical care of the aged was introduced, which was essentially based on the ordinary "fee schedule," but which reflected the characteristics of the chronic state of the diseases of the aged. Each participating hospital or clinic makes, at the end of each month, a monthly bill for the services rendered based on the fee schedules. The bill relating to the health insurance is submitted to the prefectural office of the Social Insurance Medical Care Fee Payment Fund, which pools the money from each program, and the bill relating to the national health insurance is submitted to the Federation of National Health Insurance Associations in each prefecture. The bill is, before payment, checked by the committees of medical consultants organized by the Fund or the Federation. Unnecessary treatment is sometimes checked here and deleted, which often brings complaints from participating hospitals and clinics.

In order to determine the fee schedules, the minister of health and welfare requests the recommendation of the Central Social Insurance Medical Council, which consists of six representatives of insurers, six representatives of providers (physicians, dentists, and pharmacists), and three representatives of the public interest. Today, there are no restrictions by the government relating to the examination and treatment under social health insurance, and practically no drugs, clinical tests, or surgical operations are excluded from use if effective. For example, renal dialysis, kidney transplant, pacemaker implant, CT scan, and MRI scan are approved under social health insurance. However, there is continuous tension between the Ministry of Health and Welfare and the Japan Medical Association focusing on the fee schedules. The major complaints are that the point system is too low, that there are restrictions on the use of some new drugs and technologies that physicians wish to administer but are regarded still as experimental, and that all physicians receive the same payment regardless of qualification or experience. These complaints have been continuously urged by the JMA and seem to be valid to a considerable extent, but it might be very difficult for the Central Social Insurance Medical Council and for the Ministry of Health and Welfare to solve or accept them because they are issues relating to the essence—the principles—of the current fee schedule.

National Medical Care Expenditure

The figure of medical care expenditure announced by the Ministry of Health and Welfare includes the costs covered by social health insurance, accident insurance, public medical care, and the sum of the partial payment by the patient. Therefore, this figure excludes expenses for health examinations, normal delivery, vaccination, corrective eyeglasses, artificial limbs, and treatments by a massage therapist, acupuncturist, or moxibustioner. There is no all-inclusive health expenditure figure in Japan, as distinct from medical care. The amounts of the items such as public health, casual medical supply purchases, medical research, are very small compared to the national medical care expenditure. In this account I use the figure of medical care expenditure as announced by the ministry and which is different from the figure announced by the OECD.

Since 1955 national medical care expenditures have increased more rapidly than growth in the GNP (Fig. 1). The ratio of national medical care expenditure to GNP rose from 2.77% in 1955 to

Table A   Medical Care—GNP Trends

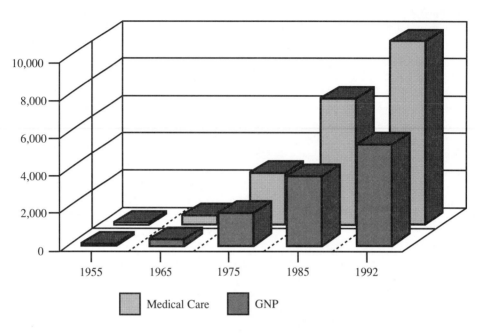

3.33% in 1965, responding to the attainment of a nationwide social health insurance scheme; it continued to increase up to 1973. In 1973, a revision of the point system was made due to the increase in wages and prices after the energy crisis, and was accompanied by a new medical care policy of free medical care for the aged. All of these factors contributed to the unprecedented annual increase of national medical care expenditure by 36.2% in 1974, or 3.89% of the GNP.

The GNP growth was abruptly slowed after the energy crisis, but the trend of increasing medical care expenditure did not change. Such a situation led to arguments in favor of limiting free medical care for the aged and increasing the share of the cost to be borne by the patients; in 1983, the Health Service for the Aged Law was adopted. The Ministry of Health and Welfare proposed to the Diet such countermeasures as the reduction of benefit rate for beneficiaries in the employees' health insurance programs from 100% to 90% in 1984; and to the Central Social Insurance Medical Council the reduction of medical remuneration through the many revisions of the fee schedules. As these measures were essentially adverse to patients and hospitals and physicians, there was much debate in the Diet and the Central Social Insurance Medical Council. However, due to the recognition of the critical financial conditions of the health insurance system and to increased personal income, these measures were eventually accepted.

From 1983 to 1990, the annual increase rate of medical care expenditure had been less than that of national income, except in 1986 and 1987; it had been less than the annual increase of the GNP from 1984 to 1985 and from 1988 to 1990. In 1991 and 1992, due to a depression of the economic growth, the increase rates of medical care expenditure were 5.9% and 7.6% respectively, which were higher than the annual increase of national income (4.7% and 0.3%, respectively) and the GNP (5.4% and 2.4%, respectively). In 1992 national medical care expenditure was 4.99% of GNP.

In 1992, the national medical care expenditure was about 23,478 billion yen, increasing 7.6% from the previous year. Contributing factors were the increase of population (0.3%), the aging of population (1.6%), the political increase due to the revision of the point system (2.5%), and the advances in medical care (3.0%). Some 23.8% of the national medical care expenditure in 1992 was paid by the national government, and 6.6% was paid by the prefectural and primary local governments. The proportion covered by the premium was 57.6%, and the rest, 12.0%, was borne by the patients. On the other hand, 49.6% of the national medical care expenditure was used for the salaries of medical and paramedical staffs, 20.5% was for drugs, 5.9% was for medical and food stuffs, 3.6% was for depreciation, and 20.4% was for the lease of equipment, expenses for water, light, and fuel, and other miscellaneous expenses.

Recently complaints of hospitals and physicians about the financial difficulty of medical management have risen so much that the Central Social Insurance Medical Council has started an examination of the health insurance system including the fee schedule. However, no results have been announced yet from either the Central Social Insurance Medical Council or the Ministry of Health and Welfare.

Conclusion

Japan's health and medical care system is complex. It bears many similarities to Western systems but, at the same time, many peculiarities due to its sociocultural background. It is now at a turning point, especially as concerns the aging of the population and the trend for decentralization of power. The Ministry of Health and Welfare has investigated reforms in Western countries including the DRG payment system, the PRO system, and other countermeasures useful for the reduction of medical care expenditure in the United States. These measures have been reviewed by the ministry because they have been widely accepted all over the United States, where medical care is highly advanced. There has been a trial of the fixed amount payment system per patient for complete care of the patient on hospital admission, with a special fee schedule for the aged. This approach is now gradually being accepted by some hospitals. This trial is obviously influenced by the DRG system, but it is not based on the diagnosis. Rather, the fixed amount paid to the hospital is per inpatient day. As there are differences between the systems of medical care and health insurance in the United States and Japan, the American DRG system is not likely to be introduced. Currently the Ministry of Health and Welfare and the Social Security Council of the prime minister are studying the "care insurance" system in Germany. In the near future a similar insurance system for the care of the aged might be introduced in Japan; the health insurance system in Japan was originally based on the German system and both Germany and Japan have been facing similar severe problems in care for the aged. However, it is felt by the Japanese government and the people concerned with health issues that Japan has now to perform its own reform without models from foreign countries due to the peculiarities of the Japanese health and medical system.

Essentially, the medical service system has a goal that anybody can be readily provided with the best medical service, anytime, and anywhere. In Japan, such a goal has been that all of the people join one of the social health insurance programs, and all of the expenses are paid by social health insurance except for a small co-payment borne by the patient. The goal has also been to enhance accessibility to medical care under the physician's "free commencement of practice" and the free choice of medical facilities by the patients. It has resulted in a good level of health and medical services, as shown in high average life span and low infant mortality despite relatively low sums of medical care expenditures as compared with foreign countries. However, it should be pointed out that (1) there is uneven distribution of medical facilities and manpower, (2) health and medical service resources have not been utilized effectively and efficiently, (3) there has been a tendency for medical services to revolve around treatment while prevention and health promotion have been neglected, (4) cooperation among health services, medical services, and welfare services has not been sufficient, and (5) administrative structural reorganization of medical facilities has been delayed.

The Ministry of Health and Welfare is now preparing the next amendment to the Medical Service Law to accomplish the administrative reorganization of medical facilities making the organization more suitable for the aging society. The amendment may include the establishment of new categories in the hospital system that may be related to the fee schedule in social health insurance, the expansion of ''medical service planning'' to the whole medical service system, and the strengthening of the system for home care. The objective of the amendment would be the reorganization of the medical service system to fit an aging society, but its precise contents have not been announced. The Community Health Law shows only the framework of a new administration system relating to health services. The local governments have yet to establish the new public health system.

It could be said that the measures taken by the Ministry of Health and Welfare in the reforms of the health and medical service systems since World War II have been at last accepted, willingly or unwillingly, by the Japanese people and in particular by the people concerned with the health and medical services, only because there have been no other better choices at each juncture, and their results were on the whole adequate. However, the basic principle of the Community Health Law is local autonomy and, due to the substantial centralization of power based on the strong subsidy system and due to the success of the measures taken by the Ministry of Health and Welfare, we have to acknowledge that local autonomy in the field of health and medical services is still quite weak, especially in the municipalities. We should encourage and take active part in the local autonomy movement, because these services should be tailored at the municipal level to the needs of every resident.

References

Boshieisei-Kenkyukai. 1994. *Maternal and Child Health in Japan.*

Kokusai-Kosei-Jigyo-Dan. 1994. *Annual Report on Health and Welfare 1992–1993.*

Kosei-Tokei-Kyokai. (Trends in the nation's health). 1994a. *Kokumin Eisei no Doko.*

———. 1994b. *1994 Health and Welfare Statistics in Japan.*

Miyagishima, K., and T. Nakahara. 1994. Current Topics on Health Care Planning in Japan. *Bull. Inst. Public Health* 43(3):279–85.

Nakahara, T. 1994a. Japan's Health Reform: Historical Outline from the Viewpoint of Local Autonomy. *Bull. Inst. Public Health* 43(4):422–30.

———. 1994b. Policy Trends of Community Health in Japan. *Bull. Inst. Public Health* 43(3):263–69.

———. 1995. Philosophy and Issues of Japan's Medical Assessment and Guidance/Auditing System. *Bull. Inst. Public Health* 44(1).

Table 1 Japanese Population by Age and Sex, 1992

Age	Male (in thousands)	Female (in thousands)
All ages	60,597	62,879
Up to 4 years	3,163	3,002
5–9	3,647	3,470
10–14	4,073	3,871
15–19	4,906	4,656
20–24	4,837	4,636
25–29	4,104	4,007
30–34	3,881	3,803
35–39	4,100	4,039
40–44	5,411	5,368
45–49	4,445	4,464
50–54	4,179	4,261
55–59	3,881	4,038
60–64	3,406	3,651
65–69	2,574	3,123
70–74	1,614	2,420
75–79	1,231	1,894
80–84	747	1,305
85–89	300	616
90 and over	97	258

SOURCE: Ministry of Health and Welfare, *Vital Statistics of Japan (1992)*.

Table 2 Live Births, Birth Rate, Fertility Rate, and Infant Mortality Rate, 1992

Live births	1,188,317
Birth rate	9.6
Fertility rate	0.72
Infant mortality rate	4.3

SOURCE: Ministry of Health and Welfare, *Vital Statistics of Japan, 1992*.

Table 3 Infant Mortality Rate by the Six Most Common Causes, 1992

Congenital anomalies	91.7/100,000 live births
Birth trauma	76.0
Septicemia, including newborn	11.2
Premature babies of unknown details	4.7
Heart diseases	2.9
Other external causes	2.6

SOURCE: Ministry of Health and Welfare, *Vital Statistics of Japan, 1992*.

Table 4   Estimated Death Rates per 100,000 Population for the Ten Leading Causes of Death, 1992

Malignant neoplasms	187.8
Heart diseases	142.2
Cardiovascular diseases	95.6
Pneumonia and bronchitis	65.0
Accidents	28.1
Senility	18.9
Suicide	16.9
Nephritis	14.8
Liver cirrhosis	13.8
Diabetes mellitus	8.0

SOURCE: Ministry of Health and Welfare, *Vital Statistics of Japan, 1992.*

Table 5   Information not available

Table 6   Information not available

Table 7   Number of General Hospitals, by Number of Beds

No. of beds	
20–49	1,848
50–99	2,446
100–199	2,285
200–299	1,016
300+	1,282
Total	8,877

Table 8   Information not available.

Table 9   Number and Type of Nursing Homes and Related Types of Facilities and the Average Number of Beds per Facility, 1993

	Number of facilities	Average number of beds per facility
nursing home	2,770	70.1
health facility for the aged	893	85.0
home for the aged	902	72.0
home for the aged with a moderate fee		
type A	253	60.5
type B	38	47.6
care-house type	77	48.4
home for the aged with a full charge	261	100.1

SOURCE: Ministry of Health and Welfare, *Survey of Social Welfare Institutions.*

Table 10 National Health Expenditures (NHE) by Type of Expenditure in Billion Yen and Source of Funds, 1992

| | | Government | | Health insurance | Patient co-payment |
		National	Local		
NHE	23,478	5,592	1,556	13,521	2,810
Hospital	13,960				
Inpatient	9,123				
Outpatient	4,837		(Data not available)		
Clinic	6,357				
Inpatient	523				
Outpatient	5,834				
Dental	2,297				
Pharmaceutical service	713				
Health facility for the aged	152				

SOURCE: Ministry of Health and Welfare, National Medical Expenditure.

The Health System of the Netherlands

J. A. M. (Hans) Maarse

Introduction

The Netherlands is a small Western European country, located on the North Sea. With a total population of 15.7 million in 1994, it is one of the most densely populated areas in the world (452 inhabitants per square kilometer). In its present form it came into existence in 1839 when Belgium was separated from it. Since then, it has always been a constitutional monarchy. Until the 1960s, the political and social structure of society was to a great extent dominated by five political parties, three of which had religious (Catholic and Protestant) roots. The two others are the Socialist Party and the Liberal Party. Large parts of society were organized in separate segments or pillars (*verzuiling*) which ran their own schools, welfare organizations, broadcasting corporations, and had their own political representatives in Parliament. The pillars were also active in health care, where they established their own provider organizations. The prominent role for private initiative in the delivery of health services, still an important feature of the Dutch health care system, cannot be seen apart from the traditionally pillarized structure of the Dutch society. In the sixties, however, the traditional religious and sociopolitical boundaries began to erode (*ontzuiling*).

There has never been a single political party in a position to control the political scene, although it is fair to state that the Christian political parties have always played a leading role. Until 1994, Christian political parties intermittently formed a coalition cabinet with the Socialists or the Liberals. The new government that took office in 1994 was in fact the first postwar government without participation of the Christian political parties. In a sense, the new government symbolized the definite end of the process of *ontzuiling* in Dutch society.

The Netherlands has been described as a decentralized unified state. It consists of twelve provinces and 633 municipalities. Provincial and local governments operate in some areas as autonomous policy-makers and in others mainly as the implementing agency of national policy programs.

Their role in health care is rather limited. Whereas provincial government is involved in hospital planning, the activities of local government focus upon public health and health-related social work. Health care policy-making in the Netherlands has to a great extent been monopolized by the national government.

The gradual but steady growth of state intervention is an important aspect of the modernization of Dutch health care. In the nineteenth century, state action mainly concentrated upon the quality of medical care through the legal protection of the medical profession. According to the then prevailing political ideas about the proper role of the state in society, the state should only play a limited role in health care. This would be altered in the early twentieth century, however, when the political conception of the role of the state in society was gradually redefined into the direction of a leading role in society and the development of the welfare state. The prominent role of the state in health care was formalized in the revised Constitution of 1983. Article 22 reads that the state must take appropriate policy measures to protect the health of the general public.

The present health care system constitutes an important sector of the Dutch economy. In 1993 total expenditures amounted to 8.7% of the Gross Domestic Product. In 1990 health care employed 11.2% of the total workforce and the share of health care investments was 9.4% of total investments in building and construction works. Health care is financed through a mixture of social health insurance (67.8%), private health insurance (13.7%), taxes (10.3%), and out-of-pocket payments (8.2%).

The structure of Dutch health care cannot be properly understood without a brief sketch of three core values that have helped to shape it and that still enjoy much political support. The first value can be best described as equity. All citizens are entitled to receive all medical care they need. Health care is not seen as a market commodity, but instead as a social right. It is the political responsibility of the state to ensure that all citizens can really effectuate their right to health care. The equity principle also implies the rejection of any difference in medical treatment of patients with similar conditions. The medical treatment of sickness fund patients must be similar to the treatment of patients with private health insurance. Physicians are denied the option to refuse patients on the ground of their economic status.

A second core value is solidarity in health care finance. Solidarity is a key principle in social health insurance, which is financed by means of income-dependent contributions (payroll taxes). The principle of actuarial fairness does not apply under social health insurance. The solidarity principle states that any financial barrier to the consumption of necessary medical care is considered unacceptable. The introduction of a common risk pool in 1986 secures accessability under private health insurance.

The third value points to the public-private mix in the institutional structure of the health care system. As already spelled out before, there has traditionally been a high value placed upon the role of private initiative in health care. This value has shaped much of the present institutional structure of health care. Some 85% of the hospitals are private entities. Most general practitioners and the majority of medical specialists work as private entrepreneurs. Private institutions also play a prominent role in health care finance. Sickness funds are nongovernmental institutions that act under public law. The representative associations of all these institutions have acquired a strong position in the political and administrative structure of the Dutch health care system.

Medical Practitioners

A key feature of the Dutch health care system points to the prominent role of general practitioners (family doctors). Over the last decade the number of GPs has steadily grown from 3.7 per 10,000 population in 1980 to 4.3 in 1993. In 1992 the GP-to-population ratio was 2,315 inhabitants, which is relatively high in the European context (cf. Belgium, 725 in 1985; and France, 1,150). About 53 percent of all GPs operate as free entrepreneurs in a solo practice. The number of GPs working in a group practice has gradually increased from 25% in 1982 to 38% in 1992. The other 9% work in health centers together with other providers such as physiotherapists, dentists, social workers, and pharmacists. In contrast with the prewar period, GPs no longer work in a hospital setting. Hospitals have become the exclusive domain of medical specialists. The technical equipment in a GP practice is modest. Most GPs only employ an assistant for administrative and simple medical support. The presence of a nurse in a GP practice is still uncommon. In rural areas GPs may also operate a pharmacy for prescription drugs.

GPs have on average 142 patient consultations a week, 19% of which take place in the home setting of the patient. The volume of home visits is falling. Many GPs used to have separate appointment hours for private patients, but this has become rather uncommon. The average working hours per week were estimated at 50 hours in 1993 (availability service not included): 28 hours are spent in the office, 11 hours on home visits, and the rest on nonpatient related activities such as consultations with other providers, postgraduate training, and administration.

All citizens can choose their own GP. Because of the capitation payment system for sickness fund patients, sickness fund members need to register with a GP practice. When registered, they cannot consult another GP unless in case of emergency. If they are dissatisfied with their GP, they have the option to register with another. This does not frequently happen, however, the more so because GPs have an informal mutual agreement to abstain from active recruiting among each others' patients. The general pattern is that families stick to their GP and that a relationship of trust develops between the GP and the family. "GP shopping" is uncommon, even among persons with private health insurance who do not need a registration.

Until the mid-1980s local GP associations tried to regulate the number of GPs in their own area, but this self-regulatory strategy did not prove very effective. They could only use informal sanctions, mostly by not cooperating with the "wild practices" on the weekends and at night. The Association of General Practitioners (LHV) then asked the Ministry of Health for public regulation. The new regulation, introduced in 1986, required GPs to obtain a formal authorization of local government to start a practice. This arrangement did not last very long, however; GPs were unhappy with the interference of local authorities in their business. Under the current regulations, GPs must apply for a contract with the regional sickness fund, which has the formal opportunity to deny such a contract.

The prominent position of GPs in the health care system is to a large extent based upon their gatekeeping role. Except in case of emergency, sickness funds and most private health insurance plans require a referral from a GP when a patient wants to consult a medical specialist in the hospital. Their key role is further highlighted by the fact, that in 1992 the number of consultations with a GP averaged 3.9 per year, with a medical specialist 1.8, and with a dentist 1.9 consultations per year. About 75% of the population had at least one contact with a GP, whereas only 39% visited a medical specialist.

Yet, GPs are gradually losing portions of their former market. For instance, they no longer perform deliveries. Emergency medicine in the cities and psychiatric care have also largely been taken over by other professionals. A similar development can be observed in the area of preventive medicine and maternity care. In the near future, GPs may experience more competition from the Occupational Health Agencies, which contract with employers to improve health and working conditions and reduce sickness leave.

It is interesting to see how the role of GPs will develop in future. An important goal of the minister of health is to strengthen the position of GPs. The underlying belief here is that a key role for GPs will help to reduce health care expenditures. Unnecessary visits to medical specialists are seen as inefficient. The training program of GPs has recently been prolonged from two to three years after the completion of the basic physician training program, which takes six years. Being a GP is considered a medical specialty.

At present, much attention is given to the improvement of the quality of GP health care. Thirty standard protocols for frequent symptoms have already been implemented and another thirty are under preparation. These standards will be used in peer reviews. Another method to improve quality refers to the instrument of reregistration after each five-year period. GPs will only be reregistered if they participate in peer reviews and if a demonstrated lack of expertise has been corrected through postgraduate training.

When referring a patient to a specialist, the GP must write a referral letter stating the reason for the referral. The specialist is supposed to keep the referring GP informed about the patient. There are often complaints, however, that communication from the specialist to the GP fails, which may help to explain why their relationship has been described as "Working Apart Together." GPs and specialists also organize common meetings to discuss new developments in diagnostics and treatment of diseases or patient categories.

The growth in the number of medical specialists has outpaced the growth in the number of GPs over the last decade. The specialist-to-population rate grew from 4.2 per 10,000 population in 1980 to 6.0 in 1992. An overwhelming majority of medical specialists work as free entrepreneurs in only one hospital, mostly in a group practice (*maatschap*). Only a few specialists, such a psychiatrists, plastic surgeons, dermatologists, and ophthalmologists, may have (part-time) private practice outside the hospital. Specialist care in the Netherlands is still very much hospital-centered. As in all other countries, medical care is characterized by rapid specialization. The Royal Dutch Medical Association (KNMG) has now recognized twenty-nine different medical specialties. Each of the specialties has established its own scientific specialty board, which plays, as will be discussed later, a prominent role in the specialists' training programs.

Finally, it is important to mention new developments in the physician-patient relationship. Since 1995 the Law on the Codification of Patients' Rights is operative. This new law defines the patients' right to informed consent about their treatment, their right to access to information on their treatment and their right to privacy. In general, patients become more critical and the number of litigation procedures steadily increases.

Payment of Medical Practitioners

The payment of GPs depends upon the type of patient. GPs receive an annual capitation payment for each sickness fund patient who is registered in their practice. Patients with private health insurance pay a standard fee per visit, which may be partly reimbursed by the private insurer depending upon the content of the insurance policy. GPs are not allowed any form of extra-billing. The capitation rates and fees are uniform all over the country. In 1993 expenditures for GP care amounted to 3.8% of the national health care bill.

The National Association of General Practitioners (LHV) negotiates each year with the representative associations of health insurers about the capitation rate and the fees for private patients. The result of their negotiations, which is regulated by the Health Care Tariffs Act, must be approved by the Central Agency for Health Care Tariffs (COTG). If no agreement can be obtained, the COTG has formal authority to set fees unilaterally. In order to review the fee proposals, it must write guidelines, which are subject to approval of the minister of health. The minister can also unilaterally impose binding guidelines upon the COTG.

The payment of GPs may be altered in the near future. The so-called Biesheuvel Committee (Mr. Biesheuvel was a former prime minister) recently proposed a more differentiated payment scheme according to which GPs would receive on average 80% of their income through capitation payment. In contrast with the present situation, however, payment would depend upon the age of the patient: GPs would receive a higher capitation rate for older patients because they generate a higher workload. The committee also recommended higher capitation rates to physicians working in the big cities to compensate them for their higher workload. The remaining 20% would be paid on a fee-for-visit basis. Health insurers may agree to additional payments for more efficient GP referral, prescription, and diagnostic behavior.

In 1986 the share of medical specialists paid on a fee-for-service basis was estimated at approximately 63% of all registered specialists. Specialists who are salaried mainly work in academic and psychiatric hospitals (in academic hospitals the revenues from private patients are used to pay the specialists an additional income). Salaried specialists also concentrate among specific specialties in acute hospitals, for example, pediatrics, rheumatology, and rehabilitation. In 1993 the revenues of the specialists who were paid fee-for-service accounted for 3.9% of total health care expenditures (the revenues of salary-paid specialists and dental specialists are not included in this figure).

Fees for specialist care are negotiated between the National Association of Medical Specialists (LSV) and the representative associations of the health insurers. The negotiating process is regulated in a similar way for GPs by the Health Care Tariffs Law. There are about 8,000 different fees for medical services to sickness fund patients and 5,000 different fees for patients with private health insurance. Private insurers have always paid higher fees than sickness funds, but this form of cross-subsidization from the private to the social sector is coming to an end now that fees are being equalized. Extra-billing of patients by medical specialists is forbidden.

The fee-for-service payment scheme for specialist care has been one of the main targets in Dutch health care cost-containment policy in the eighties. As policy-makers considered it a source of inefficiency, various attempts were undertaken to reduce the growth in expenses for specialist care. All failed more or less. A remarkable event took place in 1989, when the representative association of the medical specialists negotiated an agreement with the representative associations of the health insurers and the hospitals. Part of this agreement was the introduction of a fixed budget (an expenditure target would perhaps be a better term) for specialist care over the period 1990–92, whereby the level of 1992 expenses was defined as the basis year. If this target were overrun, retrospective adjustments of the fees in subsequent years would follow to offset the difference between target and real expenditures. Another part of the agreement was a reshuffle of the fees to reduce the inequality of income among specialties (for cardiac surgery, a 30% fee cut; for cardiology, a 12.5% fee cut; for radiodiagnostics, a 15% fee cut; for pediatrics, a 10% fee increase; for rehabilitation, a 25% fee increase).

The expenditure target proved to be counterproductive. Average annual growth in the volume of inpatient treatments grew from 1.0% over the period 1982–88 to 2.1% over the period 1989–92 and for outpatient treatments from 2.4% to 4.2%. Aggregate expenditures for specialist care sharply increased from a 2.6% average over the period 1983–88 to 6.7% over the period 1989–92, whereas it should have been nil. This outcome gave rise to fierce conflicts between the specialists' association and the minister of health about the size of the overspendings, about the identification of the specialties who could be held mainly accountable for them, and about the appropriate fee cuts in subsequent years to offset the overspendings. Not surprisingly, these cuts caused much frustration among the specialists. The main reason for the increase in the annual growth rate of expenditures for specialist care must presumably be sought in the presence of a prisoner's dilemma in which every specialist is caught. Because the production of fellow physicians may eventually affect the specialist's own income, all feel a strong incentive to increase their own production to counteract a potential decrease in income. An institution that monitors the total expenditures for specialist care over the year and implements interim fee cuts to preclude overspendings does not exist.

It remains to be seen whether the fee-for-service payment system will survive in future. The Biesheuvel Report recommended banning it and replacing it by some form of differentiated salary payment that would be incorporated in the hospital budget. Specialists with longer residential training and with more inconveniences must be paid more. The new government has accepted the recommendations of the Biesheuvel Report on the payment of medical specialists. Many local initiatives are now under way to experiment with new forms of payments.

The Royal Dutch Medical Association

The Royal Dutch Medical Association (KNMG) was established in 1849. One of its first targets was to improve the quality of medical care and, in particular, to protect the medical profession against the obscure ''medical'' activities of various alternative practitioners. The Association was successful: in 1865 the national government adopted four health care laws, one of which gave the medical profession a professional monopoly. The current goals of the Association are described as follows: (a) to contribute to the advancement of the art of medical treatment; (b) to promote the application of scientific advances in medical practice; (c) promotion of good relationships between members of the organization and the improvement of the public image of medical practitioners.

Membership is not compulsory. Overall membership goes up to some 51% of all Dutch physicians. Particularly among medical specialists membership is declining because of dissatisfaction with the results of the negotiations on fees. The Association can be described as a mother organization (since 1991 it has the structure of a federation) with four different constituent daughters: the National Association of the General Practitioners (LHV), the National Association of Medical Specialists (LSV), the National Association of Salaried Physicians (LAD) and, since 1980, the National Association of Community Health Physicians (LVSG). This last association represents the interests of the physicians who work for companies, insurance organizations, and public health agencies.

The Royal Dutch Medical Association plays an important role in Dutch health care policy-making. It has its own representatives in a number of standing advisory bodies in health care and advises the government on a wide range of policy issues, such as medical ethical issues. The aggregation and representation of the material interests of the physicians are primarily handled by the four constituent associations.

Another important task of the Association lies in the area of accreditation and registration of medical practitioners. With respect to medical specialists, three different colleges exist. The Central College—consisting of professors of all medical facilities (each faculty appoints one representative), an equal number of medical specialists, and a number of advisers—defines the standards of the medical specialist training programs, the teachers, and the teaching hospitals. The scientific specialty boards play an important role in the formulation of the specific requirements of the specialty concerned. Second, there is a Specialist Registration Commission. Since 1991, each registration lasts five years. After that period the Commission evaluates whether reregistration is appropriate. The Commission also inspects teaching hospitals and the teachers to assess the quality of their performance. A new development is that also nonteaching hospitals are visited. Finally, there is an Appeal Committee. A similar three-committee structure has come into existence for the other constituent associations.

Hospitals

Hospital care in the Netherlands is to a very large extent rendered by private institutions. The share of the private sector in the number of hospital beds is significantly higher than in the United Kingdom, the Scandinavian countries, France, and Germany. Many hospitals originated from initiatives of churches, religious orders, charitable societies, and even individual philanthropists. During the last two decades, however, all of them have rapidly evolved into professional entities with only very loose ties to their original founders. This development cannot be seen apart from the erosion of the traditional religious and sociopolitical boundaries (*ontzuiling*) in Dutch society. Another group of hospitals was founded by local governments. Over time, these hospitals have also been transformed into entities with much independence from local government. The financial link between the hospital and local government has been cut.

Hospitals in the Netherlands are not-for-profit institutions. They are permitted to make excess revenue. For-profit hospitals have been prohibited by the Hospital Facilities Act, the Sickness Fund Act, and the Exceptional Medical Expenses Act. It is interesting to see whether this formal ban on for-profit hospital care will be dropped in future, the more so because the distinction between for-profit and not-for-profit care has become increasingly blurred.

The Netherlands has developed an elaborate network of acute care hospitals that can be divided into three groups: general acute care hospitals, special hospitals, and academic hospitals. In 1991 there were 113 general acute care hospitals with a total number of 51,599 beds; 9 academic hospitals with 7,576 beds; and 36 special hospitals with a total number of 4,569 beds. With 127 beds they are on average much smaller than general acute care hospitals (457 beds) or academic hospitals (842 beds). A typical hospital has only single, two- and four-bed rooms.

Since the 1970s general acute hospital care has become increasingly concentrated. Over the period 1981–91 the total number of general acute care hospitals dropped by 30% and the number of special hospitals by 25%. The total number of beds in general acute care hospitals fell by 12.7%, and in special hospitals by 23.7%. These reductions were the result of a number of bed reduction programs started by the Department of Health. The minister wanted to eliminate the presumed overcapacity in the hospital sector because "a built bed was a filled bed." The programs have resulted in a considerable drop of the bed-to-population ratio. Over the period 1980–91 the number of beds per 1,000 population was reduced from 4.2 beds in 1981 to 3.4 beds in 1993 for general acute care hospitals. Further reductions are planned for the near future.

These reductions in the hospital sector, however, form only one part of the general trend. They were accompanied by a substantial growth in the capacity for outpatient care as well as day surgery and in the number of medical specialists. The drop in the number of hospital beds and the concurrent growth in the number of special units reveal a deeper trend in hospital care; namely, that the hotel function of hospitals is rapidly losing importance, whereas the treatment of patients is gaining more emphasis than ever before. This general trend is also found in the production of services in general acute care hospitals. The figures in Table 8 not only suggest the changing face of hospital services (fewer admissions and patient days, sharp increase in outpatient care and day surgery), but also that hospital care has become more efficient over the last fifteen years. Yet, health care policy-makers still believe that more efficiency can be obtained, in particular by a further growth in day surgery and a further reduction in the number of unnecessary admissions.

In the context of tight hospital planning and a limited growth in hospital budgets, hospital managers and medical practitioners have expressed their concern about what they call unacceptable waiting lists. Waiting lists present a very complicated problem, however. Some lists can presumably be best considered no problem at all (say, in the case of elective surgery). The causes of waiting lists are also multiple: lack of personnel, lack of operating theaters, mistaken planning of medical services, regional scarcity, lack of donors, and so forth. Reliable and accurate data on the problem are still missing. Finally, it is fair to say that the problem of waiting lists is more acute in the sector of nursing homes, psychiatric care, homes for the mentally retarded, and home care than it is in the acute care sector.

The National Hospital Institute has collected some crude data about waiting lists for a selected number of specialties or treatments. Data refer to 1991 and are based upon information reported by hospitals. The waiting list of patients with urgency 1 for clinical treatment was measured for orthopedics 16.7 days, for ophthalmology 14.0 days, for plastic surgery 12.0 days, for surgery and gynecology 14.5 days, for urology 19.8 days, and for heart surgery less than a week. In the outpatient setting waiting lists are 23.3 days for orthopedics, 55.8 days for ophthalmology, 36.4 days for plastic surgery, 6.7 days for surgery, for gynecology 10.1 days, and for urology 11.2 days.

Over the last few years political discussion on waiting lists has been stimulated by the concept of indirect health costs. Waiting lists may not only harm patients but also generate high indirect health costs, because of lost working days and lost earnings. In order to reduce absenteeism some employers have begun to hire operating theater time over the weekend to get their employees treated as soon as possible. In border areas they may decide to send them abroad. Also, some health insurance companies have deliberately used the promise of a quick treatment in case of illness as a marketing instrument.

Hospital Planning

The hospital sector is a heavily government-regulated part of the health care system. The Hospital Facilities Act (WZV) regulates the number of hospital beds, the number of specialist units in the hospital, and all major investments and construction activities. Each hospital needs a formal authorization by the minister of health of all its beds, specialist units, high-tech facilities, and major building activities in order to be reimbursed through social health insurance. The minister of health has set government standards for the number of hospital beds, and specialist units.

The Hospital Facilities Act (1971 with major revision in 1979) was originally intended primarily as a planning act to help achieve a balanced growth of health care facilities from a regional and sectoral point of view. But the emergence of cost containment as a top priority in health care policy-making in the mid-1970s rapidly transformed it into a volume act that gave the minister of health some instruments to control the growth of health care facilities and health care expenditures.

The experiences with hospital planning as an instrument to reduce the number of beds has been rather disappointing. Hospital planning provides some instruments to reduce the growth of health care facilities but it fails as an instrument to reduce hospital capacity. For that reason, the minister of health used alternative instruments to reduce hospital capacity. For instance, when two or more hospitals merge and apply for government authorization to build a new hospital, the minister of health negotiates with the hospital boards on a substantial cut in their total bed volume in exchange for the authorization.

Hospital planning is generally considered a very bureaucratic process. Its complicated institutional framework gives all parties involved plenty of opportunity to delay the planning process. The determination of regional hospital plans appears very cumbersome and goes along with many and lengthy delays. This is also why the minister of health introduced an annual building ceiling in 1975 to put a limit to the expansion of the hospital sector. Through this ceiling he actually bypassed the Hospital Facilities Act. Political competition between the hospitals on who gets what, when, and how, also plays a prominent role. Hospital managers on their part complain about the lengthy procedures to get their requests approved. The minimum approval period for building a new hospital has been estimated at six years. It is generally felt that hospital planning must be simplified and deregulated. Yet, it is inconceivable to believe, even in spite of today's rhetoric to the contrary, that the minister of health will give up the instrument of planning of major investments in the hospital sector. It is still considered too important an instrument for cost containment.

Hospitals also need an authorization for a specific category of top-clinical facilities, if they are very expensive, if they require very specialized knowledge, or if they are controversial from an ethical point of view. The rationale for this arrangement is that the minister of health wants to concentrate facilities in order to improve the quality of care, reduce expenses, and prohibit their uncontrolled growth. In 1992 the following facilities were regulated under the Hospital Facilities Act (the numbers between parentheses refer to the number of hospitals with a certification): renal dialysis (48); kidney transplantation (8); radiotherapy (21); neurosurgery (main centers) (16); heart surgery (14); PTCA (percutaneous transluminal cardiac angioplasty) diagnostics (50); PTCA treatment (12); neonatology (11); clinical genetic research (9); in vitro fertilization (12). Bone marrow transplantation; liver, lung, and pancreas transplantation; and positon emission tomography (PET) have been added to the list in 1993. Computer tomography and nuclear medicine have been dropped from it.

Hospital Funding

Funding of hospital services was dramatically transformed in 1983 through the introduction of a system of prospective fixed budgets to reduce the escalating growth in hospital expenditures. Until 1983 hospitals were funded according to an open-ended, mainly per diem arrangement. Budget guidelines linked the allowable costs for personnel to the expected volume of medical care, but did not control the volume of medical care itself. This funding arrangement was a source of concern among health care policy-makers who felt it entirely inconsistent with the goal of cost containment. It gave hospitals in fact a strong financial interest in a high production of hospital services and did not stimulate them to control costs and improve efficiency.

The introduction of fixed hospital budgets in 1983 meant that the minister of health imposed a national budget for hospital care (one for general acute care and special hospitals and one for academic hospitals). This budget was fixed at the 1982 level of hospital expenses plus some adjustments (historical budgeting). Next, each hospital had imposed a prospective budget (the permissible revenues) by which most of its expenses had to be covered. This prospective budget can be considered a global budget. Case-based budgeting by using DRGs is not used in the Netherlands.

After the introduction of the new funding scheme, hospitals could no longer increase their budget by doing more. The traditional link between the volume of hospital services and revenues had been cut. Hospitals could add the full surplus to their reserves, but were also made responsible for their deficits. Budget adjustments to relieve financial problems were canceled.

The hospital budget did not include the revenues of the medical specialists who continued to operate on a fee-for-service basis in the hospital. The Dutch Association of Medical Specialists (LSV) successfully opposed the proposal to integrate the specialists' revenues into the hospital budget, because it saw in this proposal an unacceptable restriction to their professional autonomy. Of course, the specialists also feared its impact upon their personal income.

Functional budgeting was introduced in 1988. The essence of it was that hospitals were paid an equal budget when performing equal tasks. The new model distinguishes three major budget components. The availability component is measured as the size of the clinical catchment area of the hospital. The capacity component is measured as the number of authorized beds and medical specialist units that render outpatient care. The production component requires annual negotiations between hospital management and the health insurers about the volume of hospital care. Production (volume) contracts have to be made upon the number of hospital admissions, inpatient days, first-outpatient visits, and the volume of day surgery. Additional contracts are required for some specific high-cost treatments such as cardiac surgery or renal dialysis. In 1992 the availability component accounted for 15% of the national budget for hospital care, the capacity component for 34%, and the production component for 51%. The availability and capacity components are assumed to cover the fixed part of hospital expenses and the production component the variable part. Hospitals are paid additional budgets for interest payments, investments, salaried physicians, and a wide range of other items.

The determination of a hospital budget is separate from the payment by the health insurers to the hospital. Patient per diem rates have remained the most important payment method, but according to the latest revision, hospitals must charge health insurers separately for all surgery, expensive diagnostics and treatments, outpatient visits, and day surgery.

From a financial point of view, fixed budgets have been reasonably effective. In the period 1978–82 (pre-budgeting period) the annual growth rate of hospital expenditures was 8.7%. This rate was radically slowed down after the introduction of hospital budgeting: 1.3% over the period 1983–88. Since 1989 hospital expenses have begun to rise again, with an annual growth rate of 7.7% over the period 1989–92. There are many causes for this reemergence of growth, the most important presumably being that hospitals were forced to raise the salaries of their personnel in order to keep up with the market.

Another way of looking at the effects of hospital budgeting is the extent to which hospital expenditures have been kept within the fixed national budget for hospital care. The figures suggest a slight underspending over the period 1983–88 and growing overspendings after that period. In 1991, for example, the reported overspending was 2.9%, and 3.1% in 1992. These outcomes suggest that the instrument of hospital budgeting is now losing part of its former effectiveness.

It is hardly surprising that the policy of strict budgetary restraint has affected the financial position of hospitals. Many of them have not been able to keep their expenditures within their budget limit. According to a COTG study, the percentage of hospitals with a negative result in operating costs was 34% in 1992. This figure highlights how fixed budgets have put many hospitals under great financial pressure. It is no wonder that they have always associated fixed budgets with expenditure cuts.

Hospital Administration

Hospital administration has gone through a period of dramatic change over the last twenty years. Until the mid-1970s part-time medical superintendents, supported by a small administrative staff, administered the hospitals and simultaneously rendered care to their patients. But these times have gone. Modern hospitals are big and complex entities that require professional management. The enormous changes in the hospital environment (for example, the extension of regulations and the introduction of hospital budgeting) have also enhanced the need for professional management. Getting things done with the Department of Health or with the health insurers nowadays requires great political skill and determination. Strategic management has become indispensable.

The typical hospital is increasingly administered by two or three directors (general affairs, financial affairs, medical and nursing affairs), one of whom is appointed as CEO. There is also a hospital board with representatives from the local community that controls the activities of hospital management and appoints the hospital directors. The appointment of the members of the board usually occurs by co-optation. The heart of hospital administration has clearly shifted from the board to hospital management.

There is much variation in the internal structure of hospitals. All hospitals, however, have a medical staff committee. The general trend is that this committee not only articulates the specialists' interests within the hospital, but also closely participates in hospital administration through its head. Many hospitals are involved now in reorganization processes to renew the structure and culture of their organization. Division structures with a high degree of decentralization have gained much popularity, particularly in the bigger hospitals. Parallel to that, various forms of internal (departmental) budgeting are being put into practice. The cultural shift refers to the stronger emphasis upon client orientation within the hospital. The growing scarcity of financial and other resources in hospitals makes it hardly surprising that hospital administration has become a complex activity. One of the most conspicuous problems points to the difficult relationship between hospital administration and the medical specialists. Their relationship is characterized by mutual dependency. Specialists need beds, physical space, personnel, operating theaters, prescription drugs, medical equipment, junior staff support, which are all under the control of the hospital administrators. They have also become increasingly dependent upon the strategic and tactical skills of hospital administration to get things done with the Department of Health and the health insurers. Hospital administrators on their part are obviously strongly dependent upon the quality of their medical staff and upon the voluntary cooperation of the medical staff to achieve the strategic goals of the hospital.

At the same time, however, there exists a potential strategic conflict of interest between the staff and hospital administration. Most medical specialists operate principally as free entrepreneurs in the hospital, and hospital administrators lack the common instruments of a more hierarchical organization to control their behavior (firing a specialist is almost impossible). The existing fee-for-service payment system, which stimulates specialists to increase their production (or to keep it at a high level) for income reasons, may conflict with the goal of hospital administration to keep expenses within the limits of the hospital budget. Most hospital administrators still see a medical specialist primarily as a cost center, not as a revenue center!

A new development in hospital administration relates to a growing emphasis upon the management of the quality of care. Many hospitals have started new quality of care projects. Medical specialists are stimulated to improve the quality of hospital care. Experience shows that the attitude of the specialists toward quality management is crucial to its success. Internal and external peer reviews are becoming important tools in quality management.

Medical Education

The Netherlands has eight medical faculties where medical students receive their basic medical training program. The total annual number of new medical students is strictly regulated by the minister of education. Quantitative models are used to estimate the future demand for medical practitioners. The minister of education also determines for each medical faculty a ceiling to the number of admitted students (*numerus fixus*). Because the total number of students who want to enroll in a medical training program exceeds the number of places available, complex lottery systems have been developed to select among students. The Department of Education pays the academic hospitals for their involvement in the basic medical teaching programs.

The basic teaching program takes six years and is mainly paid by the Department of Education. Students only pay a small tuition. After the basic program has been successfully completed, a basic physician has several options. As a fully licensed physician he or she may start a career, for instance, as a medical adviser to a health insurance company or as a medical researcher. Another option is to apply for the program to become a general practitioner or a medical specialist. The GP training program lasts another three years and is only delivered by medical faculties that have set up a network of affiliated GP teaching practices for that purpose where the physician receives practical training. The total admittance of physicians to the general practitioner training program is limited by the Department of Health. The program is partly funded by government money; the bulk of the financial resources comes from the Exceptional Medical Expenses Fund. The content of the training program and the quality standards of the teachers and the teaching practices are regulated by a Committee for General Practitioner and Nursing Home Care.

The medical specialist training program requires an appointment as a junior physician in a teaching hospital. This may be an academic hospital but need not be. The hospital receives separate financial resources for the training of medical specialists. As spelled out earlier, the Central College defines the requirements of the training program, which specialists may teach, and which hospitals may serve as teaching hospitals. It also regularly visits each teaching hospital to assess the quality of the program. The average length of the training program varies by specialty. Finally, it is important to note that the scientific specialty boards are free to decide on the number of physicians who are admitted to the training programs. Thus, they regulate themselves the number of specialists in their specialty. This self-regulatory arrangement obviously strengthens their market power. The Department of Health on its part regulates the number of specialist units in the hospital.

Other Health Institutions and Health Professionals

Nursing homes nowadays play a key role in the delivery of care to the elderly for whom no acute treatment in the hospital is necessary or possible. In 1991 there were 325 nursing homes, most of which had less than 200 beds. Nursing homes can be categorized into three groups: homes that only provide somatic care, homes that only provide psychogeriatric care, and combined homes that deliver both types of care (Table 9). The total number of beds in nursing homes (52,075 in 1991) rapidly approaches the total number of acute care hospital beds. Because the acute sector will remain a target for further reductions and the psychogeriatric part of the nursing home sector is still growing (9.5% over the period 1987–92), it is plausible to expect that in the future the total bed capacity of nursing homes will exceed that of acute care hospitals. In 1992 there were 15.2 admissions per 1,000 population of 65 and older for somatic care and 6.1 admissions for psychogeriatric care. The occupancy rate in nursing homes is very high.

Another important aspect of nursing home care points to the delivery of day treatment to patients. These patients still live at home, but visit the nursing home to receive some care (for example, physiotherapy). The number of such units amounted to 3,354 in 1991. This number is expected to rise further because it fits perfectly into the overall policy of the government to have the elderly living in their home setting as long as possible.

The Exceptional Medical Expenses Act covers the major part of the total expenses for nursing home care. Patients pay the remainder by means of income-dependent user charges for hotel costs. Nursing homes are subject to the same planning arrangement as acute care hospitals. The Department of Health must approve the total number of beds and day-treatment units. A general government policy is to provide the nursing homes with more autonomy in spending their financial resources. Experiments to set up local substitution projects are stimulated. Some nursing homes have set up close affiliations with homes for the elderly or are even merging with them in order to organize a comprehensive local network for the delivery of care to the elderly.

Although the total capacity of nursing homes has significantly grown over the last two decades, there are still shortages resulting in long waiting lists. Patients who apply for a place in a nursing home are assessed by a local indication committee, which measures the capabilities of the applicant. Only the severest cases are admitted. The average waiting list for somatic nursing home care was 6 weeks in 1990 and for psychogeriatric care 23 weeks. In 1990 about 9% of the somatic patients and 15% of the psychogeriatric patients died before admittance.

The delivery structure of *psychiatric care* is quite differentiated. There are many different types of institutions, ranging from intra-mural to semi-mural to extra-mural facilities. In 1991 the number of psychiatric hospitals amounted to 85 with 24,849 beds (Table 9). The general trend is to treat patients in a non-intramural setting as much as possible. Some examples of principal psychiatric facilities are general psychiatric hospitals, which also operate part-time units; special psychiatric hospitals for children and adolescents; clinics for addicted people; psychiatric departments in academic and general acute care hospitals; sheltered housing; centers for ambulatory psychiatric care, which are intended as low-threshold facilities (no referral needed) for people with mental problems. The Exceptional Medical Expenses Act pays the bulk of the expenses of psychiatric care. There are user charges for hotel and living costs for patients who live in psychiatric hospitals or in sheltered housing units. Patients who attend a center for ambulatory psychiatric care must also pay a user charge.

Care for the mentally retarded is considered a full part of the Dutch health care system. Over the years a broad variety of facilities has been developed. Some examples are general institutions and special institutions for the retarded; day care centers; family-replacing group homes. The total number of institutions for the mentally retarded was 123 in 1991 with 31,674 beds. The bulk of the funding for the facilities comes through the Exceptional Medical Expenses Act. Clients usually pay for their hotel and living costs. Waiting lists for the mentally retarded are a continuing source of concern. Capacity problems inside the institutions are another source of concern. There are many complaints about the effects of the reductions in personnel upon the quality of care.

Dental care is an area in health care where maximum emphasis may be placed on prevention. Most of it is given by dentists who have a solo practice of their own. In 1990 there were 7,710 dentists registered. Dentists are paid a fee-for-service for both sickness fund patients and patients with private health insurance. Sickness fund patients need to register with a dentist of their own choice. The benefit package of sickness fund patients is fair but limited; crowns are not included. The package of patients with private health insurance is variable. Sickness fund patients are required to see their dentist every half-year. Recently, the government has substantially reduced the menu of dental care for sickness fund patients. Sickness funds still pay for a comprehensive package of services for children up to eighteen years, but the package for people over eighteen years has been drastically limited. The government argued that these people should buy a complementary health insurance plan to cover at least part of their expenses for dental care. The health insurance industry has offered a wide bunch of plans to take their portion of the complementary health insurance market. This market is expected to expand further in future as health care reform will go on.

The Netherlands has a good network of pharmacies all over the country. The total number of pharmacies amounted to 1,491 in 1993. In addition, 673 GPs operated their own pharmacy, especially in the rural areas where a nearby pharmacy is not always available. The Dutch are the lowest consumers of prescription drugs in the OECD countries. The number of over-the-counter drugs is limited. Most drugs require a prescription from a medical practitioner. As yet, pharmacists have been successful in obstructing the introduction of mail-ordered drugs.

A typical characteristic of Dutch health care points to the high percentage of home deliveries (35.4% in 1980 and 31.6% in 1993). This requires an extensive network of *midwives* (51.8 midwives for 10,000 deliveries in 1993).

Another aspect of health care relates to the growing need for *home care*, due to the shortening of the length of stay in the hospital, the general policy of the government and health professionals to keep patients as long as possible in their home setting, and in particular the increasing share of the elderly in the population. There was a period that health policy-makers thought that home care was cheaper than care in hospitals and other health care facilities, but this belief is seriously questioned now. At present, the need for home care is more than in the past based upon considerations of health care quality and the desire to bring the care to patients in line with their personal wishes. Let us consider the case of home care for the elderly more in detail.

The increasing share of the elderly in the population has changed the demand for health care because of a growing prevalence of chronic disorders and other age-related disorders such as dementia. The elderly usually suffer from multipathological problems that cannot be dealt with by a single provider or a single discipline. What they need is a coordinated delivery of health care and health-related social services in their home setting by a variety of health care professionals and social workers: medical specialists, GPs, district nurses, family help, physiotherapists, and social workers. Practice shows, however, that the coordinated delivery of care to the elderly is far from an easy enterprise. Coordination problems evolve from the fact that many different kinds of disciplines and institutions are involved in the delivery process, each of which has its own methods of working and its own professional culture. Deeply rooted professional values hinder cooperation between disciplines and often prove an effective barrier to consensus-building about comprehensive health care delivery arrangements in the home setting. Legal provisions and payment arrangements also frustrate the coordination process. Problems further arise because the financial resources for home care do not keep pace with the growing workload, in particular, of the district nursing and home help agencies. Finally, there are conflicts among the health professionals over the leadership. Who should act as the coordination center in the home care delivery process?

Public health is mainly a local government affair. The Law on Collective Prevention requires local governments to establish a public health agency. They may also collaborate and establish a district public health agency. The goals and activities of public health agencies are only loosely prescribed and give local government and the local agency much autonomy in public health policy-making. Common target groups are the young, the elderly, minority groups, and inhabitants of backward city quarters. Public health agencies are often engaged in health promotion and health education, vaccination, and public health research projects. They may also operate ambulance services.

Health Care Finance

The Netherlands is one of the countries in the European Union—the others are Germany, Belgium, and France—that strongly rely upon social health insurance in health care finance. In 1992 social health insurance covered 67.8% of total health care expenditure. The remainder came from private health insurance (13.7%), taxes (10.3%), and out-of-pocket payments (8.2%).

Social health insurance legislation started in the early twentieth century. Legislation was held necessary to improve the accessibility of health care to all citizens. Another goal was to regulate the labyrinth of hundreds of small insurance funds whose solvency was often highly questionable. Risks were also unevenly distributed over the funds. The passage of social health insurance legislation proved a difficult political exercise, however, mainly because of conflicting views among political parties, physicians, and operating insurance funds over the scope of a government-imposed health insurance scheme, the methods of finance, and the formal competence of the sickness funds. The financial crisis in the late 1920s also paralyzed the legislative process. Ironically, it would last until 1941 when German occupiers issued a decree that introduced a compulsory health insurance scheme for all employees with a limited income. The legislative process continued after the Second World War and finally resulted in the adoption of the Sickness Fund Act in 1964 and the Exceptional Medical Expenses Act in 1967. Both acts can be considered an example of social health insurance of the Bismarck type.

The sickness fund scheme offers statutory health insurance to all employees and their dependents whose income does not exceed a certain ceiling and to recipients of welfare assistance. Membership is compulsory. The income ceiling was a concession to the physicians who wanted to keep their profitable private patients. For those over the income ceiling, private health insurance is available. The health benefit package has been gradually expanded over time and provides now full coverage of a comprehensive list of medical services: consultations with general practitioners and medical specialists; inpatient and outpatient hospital care with a maximum duration of one year; limited dental care; childbirth allowances; and physiotherapy.

One of the hot issues in the current policy debate on health insurance is how the health care menu can be restricted and how to achieve a fair but modest package. The Dunning Report, released in 1991, proposed an analytical instrument for rational decision-making on this issue, consisting of four consecutive sieves: medical care must be necessary, effective, and efficient to justify inclusion in the benefit package. The forth sieve regards individual responsibility. As yet, the discussion on the benefit package has had several results. Homeopathic drugs were eliminated from the package in 1994. The standard package of dental care for persons over eighteen was considerably reduced in 1995.

The sickness fund scheme has no deductibles. User charges only apply for a limited range of services, for example, eyeglasses. In 1991 a reference price system was introduced for prescription drugs. Government efforts in the 1980s to introduce user charges for specialist care failed after a short period of time because of social resistance. The Dutch are still addicted to the idea that health care must be free.

The sickness fund scheme rests upon the principle of solidarity. Employers and employees together pay a fixed percentage (6.35% in 1994) of the employee's gross income (income solidarity). The principle of actuarial fairness does not apply (risk solidarity). Dependents are statutory-insured (family solidarity). The payroll tax, determined by the government, is calculated on a pay-as-you-go basis. Since 1989 sickness fund members must also pay a flat-rate premium (Dfl 198 per year in 1994).

The sickness fund scheme has a redistributive arrangement in the form of a Central Fund. All payroll taxes plus government transfer payments are collected in this fund. Sickness funds directly pay the providers and get all their payments reimbursed by the Central Fund. This arrangement is now in a process of radical change as part of the ongoing health care reform.

The institutional structure consists of three layers. At the bottom operate the authorized sickness funds (*ziekenfondsen*), which are private not-for-profit institutions under public law. In 1985 there were 53 operating funds, but this number has now been halved. They are regionally organized and, until recently, acted as a regional monopolist. At the middle level operates the Sickness Fund Council, which administers the Central Fund, supervises the activities of the sickness funds, and advises the minister of health on all health insurance–related policy issues. At the top operates the government, which is in charge of health insurance policy-making. It decides on the payroll tax rate, the employer-employee split, the composition of the health benefit package, and upon the income ceiling.

The Sickness Fund Act does not allow sickness funds to develop health care facilities of their own, to employ physicians, run hospitals, have Health Maintenance Organizations, and so forth. Until recently, they had to contract with all physicians and institutional providers. This formal ban on selective contracting can be seen as a victory of the providers in the legislative process. Since 1994, however, sickness funds have been given the option of selective contracting of medical practitioners.

The Exceptional Medical Expenses Act came into force in 1967. Originally, this scheme was intended as insurance for the entire population against catastrophic risks that were not covered by the sickness fund scheme and private health insurance (nursing home care, long-term psychiatric care, and care for the mentally handicapped). Over the years, however, a great variety of services have been brought under the scheme as well, including ambulatory psychiatric care and district nursing. Since 1992, all outpatient prescription drugs are also covered by the exceptional medical expenses scheme. A contrast with the sickness fund scheme is the use of co-payments. In 1993 about 5.5% of the payments came from user charges (mainly for hotel costs). For the rest, there is much resemblance to the sickness fund scheme. The scheme is administered by regional coordinating offices of sickness funds and private health insurers.

The Netherlands has not only developed statutory social health insurance, but also voluntary (private) health insurance. Under the Sickness Fund Act every person with an income higher than the income ceiling is not entitled to enroll in the sickness fund scheme and is expected to buy a private health insurance plan. This arrangement explains why the Netherlands has the highest percentage of privately insured persons (33%). Enrollment is not compulsory, but because of widespread risk-aversion almost everybody has voluntarily opted for private health insurance. Private health insurance plans typically offer a comprehensive package of basic health services that are not covered by the exceptional medical expenses scheme. Because the private health insurers do not operate under public health insurance law, they are more flexible in their benefit policies and premium strategies. They contrast with the sickness fund scheme in the frequent use of co-payment arrangements (user charges, deductibles). Subscribers also do not pay an income-dependent but a flat-rate risk-related premium that is determined at the point of enrollment. Private health insurers have waived the right to terminate a contract with high risks. Due to government regulation in 1986, private health insurers have a common risk-pool to which they transfer all their high-risks who are offered a standard policy for a fixed premium (policy and premium are determined by the government). The expenses of these high risks are borne by all persons with private health insurance for which they must pay an additional flat-rate premium of Dfl 440. This common risk-pool and internal cross-subsidization arrangement explain the nonexistence of an accessibility problem in private health insurance. There also exists a form of external cross-subsidization: due to government regulation in 1986 privately insured persons must pay a flat-rate premium to compensate the sickness funds for the overrepresentation of the elderly in the sickness funds.

In 1985 there were sixty-nine private health insurance companies. Most of them operate nationally and actively compete with each other for new subscribers who are lured by attractive plans. The private health insurance industry has a complicated structure. Part of it is not-for-profit and another part operates on a for-profit basis. Whereas some private health insurers see health insurance as their only or core business, other insurers offer a wide range of insurance services to their clients. Private health insurers are also active in the market of employer-based group contracts, which now cover approximately 40% of the privately insured. Private health insurers are subject by the Insurance Chamber, which controls their solvability.

Health Care Costs and Health Care Cost Containment

Table A depicts the rise of health care expenditures since 1972. The figures clearly demonstrate that health care expenditures were escalating in the 1970s, but their growth has been considerably slowed over the 1980s. According to the OECD statistics, the Netherlands spent 8.7% of their GDP on health in 1994. This percentage is only slightly higher than in the surrounding countries like Belgium and Germany and much lower than in Canada, the United States, and France. Disaggregation of the growth rates reveals that the bulk of the growth in health care expenditures over the period 1973–82 was caused by inflation. Nominal growth was much less over the period 1983–93. Interestingly the volume growth remains constant. This volume growth in health care expenditures can be mainly attributed to demography and the increase of treatment intensity in health care delivery.

Health care cost containment became a policy issue in the 1970s and has ever remained so. Cost-containment programs were launched at the end of the seventies. It is important to spell out here that until recently health care cost containment has always included both public and private health expenditures. Cost containment had to control the total volume of health expenditures, not only the volume of public health expenditures. This comprehensive approach partly rested upon the argument that private health expenditures have a similar effect upon employment, labor costs, and competitiveness as public expenditures. Furthermore, policy-makers often argue that a more limited approach to cost containment, focusing only upon the public part of health expenditures, would eventually result in a two-layer health care system with minimum facilities for the lower layer and

Table A   Average Annual Growth of GNP and Health Care Expenditures (%)

	1973–1982			1983–1993		
	total	volume	nominal	total	volume	nominal
health care	12.3	2.3	9.8	4.3	2.3	1.9
GNP	9.1	2.1	6.8	4.0	2.4	1.5
Real growth in health care*		5.2			2.8	

SOURCE: Department of Health, 1995.
*Defined as the growth in volume plus difference between nominal growth in health care expenditures and nominal growth in GNP

generous facilities for the upper layer. Such a system would violate the principle of equity that is traditionally highly valued in Dutch health care.

It is interesting to note, however, that an important policy shift is going on in the Netherlands. Greater parts of the private health expenditure may in future no longer be considered a target of cost-containment programs. A clear example of this is that the government has stated as its opinion that all expenses for supplementary health insurance (for example, dental care) are no longer under consideration in its cost-containment programs. Whether people spend their money on cars, CDs, or supplementary health services is now seen as their own personal responsibility.

Dutch health care policy-makers have relied more upon a supply than upon a demand approach in their cost-containment programs. User charges have always met much political and social resistance. Free access to health care for everybody is still a deeply rooted belief. This is not to say that there are no user charges or other forms of out-of-pocket payments, but that their share in health care finance has always been small.

Health care cost-containment programs have always been targeted mainly upon the supply and price of health care facilities. Some prominent examples are reduction of the number of acute care hospital beds; tight planning of hospital and other health care facilities; limiting the enrollment of students into medical schools; modest wage raises for medical personnel; reductions in the payments to medical specialists and abolition of the fee-for-service payment system (did not succeed); the introduction of hospital budgeting and other forms of fixed budgets all over the health care sector in conjunction with very tight fiscal policies (overspendings must be offset by expenditure cuts in subsequent years).

An important political effect of all these programs has been that the extent of state intervention in health care has been considerably expanded over the years. This is also true in the area of health insurance. The sickness fund scheme and the exceptional medical expenses scheme have always been subject to tight state control. The interesting thing, however, is that parts of the private health insurance have now also been brought under the jurisdiction of the national government. The internal and external forms of cross-subsidization and the introduction of a common risk pool under private health insurance are good examples of this centralization process in health care finance. The paradoxical effect of the ongoing reform of health care, which is trying to bring more market competition in health insurance, will probably be that the extent of state intervention in health care will increase in the future. This will be explained in the following section.

Health Care Reform: Toward Managed Competition

Dissatisfaction on the results of health care cost containment, the high degree of fragmentation in health care finance and the overbureaucratization of health care motivated the government in 1986 to set up an ad hoc committee under the chairmanship of Dekker (a former CEO of the Philips Company in Eindhoven). The Committee released its report *Bereidheid tot Verandering* (Willingness to change) in 1987. Initially, this report was well received and in 1988 the government officially accepted it as the cornerstone of health care reform. The new undersecretary for health, Hans Simons, published his modified version of the Dekker Plan in 1990.

The political attractiveness of the Dekker Report was probably to a great extent due to the fact that its underlying policy framework nicely harmonized with prevailing general political ideas about public policy and the role of government in society in general. For instance, the report saw market competition as a promising policy instrument to improve efficiency and client orientation in health care. Furthermore, it promoted a substantial deregulation of health care policy. And last but not least, it emphasized the merits of more freedom of choice and individual responsibility in health care. All these ideas were not typical at all for health care, but for public policy-making in general. In other words, the Dekker Report was not a coincidence, but a product of political thinking in the 1980s.

The essence of the Dekker Report was to introduce a system of managed competition in health care. The Committee proposed the development of a statutory comprehensive basic health insurance scheme for the entire population in conjunction with the development of a voluntary complementary health insurance for those benefits which would not be covered by the basic health insurance scheme. Figure 1 summarizes the key elements of managed competition in health insurance. Everybody must pay an income-dependent payroll tax for basic health insurance that is collected in a central fund (a). The payroll tax rate is determined by the government. The resources in the central fund flow to the health insurers according to a system of prospective risk-adjusted capitation payments (b). The insured also pay a flat-rate premium directly to their health insurer for the basic health insurance scheme (c). This premium is determined by each health insurer. Directly paid premiums must cover the difference between the total medical expenditures of an insurer and the revenues received from the central fund. The key idea here is, that a more efficiently operating health insurer can set lower premiums than an inefficiently operating health insurer. Finally, everybody can voluntarily enroll in a complementary health insurance plan for which another flat-rate premium must be paid (d). Competition between the health insurers concentrates on the premiums under (c) and (d).

The proposals of the Dekker Committee must be understood as a compromise between the values of solidarity and efficiency in health care. Solidarity is achieved through the introduction of an income-dependent payroll tax for basic health insurance (a). Efficiency is enhanced by the introduction of competitive flat-rate premiums for basic health insurance (c) and complementary health insurance (d). Competition and risk-adjusted capitation payments will also give health insurers a serious interest in effective cost containment.

The Dekker Committee saw market competition in health care as a promising instrument to improve efficiency in health care, both at the system level (macro-level) and at the institution level (micro-level). The key idea was that health care expenditure at the system level could be effectively controlled by enhancing efficiency at the institutional level. The Committee considered market

Figure 1

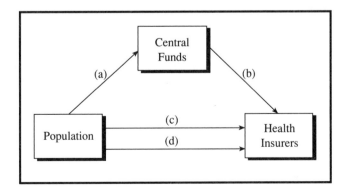

competition not as a policy goal per se, but only as a more effective instrument than government intervention to achieve effective cost control in health care. At the same time, however, the Committee was well aware of the necessity of public regulation to preclude market failures in health insurance that have been well documented in most textbooks on health economics. In view of the Committee, competition needed public management. The most important government-imposed constraint on market competition was that health insurers were forbidden to practice preferred risk selection (cream-skimming). Furthermore, the government kept its authority to regulate the standard benefit package of the basic health insurance scheme, to determine the payroll tax for basic health insurance, to plan clinical health care facilities, and to set maximum prices for health services. In fact, managed competition did not mean less rules, but only other rules.

Political decision-making on the implementation of the Dekker Plan and the later Simons Plan has always been dominated by conflicting interests, divergent points of view, and growing doubts about the cost-containment potential of managed competition in health care. In fact, there were five major issues. The first issue pointed to the fact that comprehensive health insurance reform would have significant income redistribution effects. Some categories will win, others will lose. These effects developed as a very sensitive political problem, not only for the labor unions but also for the employer associations which, not without reason, feared that the workers would seek compensation for their loss of net income. The composition of the standard health benefit package under the basic health insurance scheme proved a second difficult issue. The Dekker Committee recommended a package that would correspond to about 85% of total health care expenditures. The remainder of health services (prescription drugs, appliances, physiotherapy, abortion, plastic surgery) had to be covered by supplementary health insurance. Undersecretary Simons deviated from this proposal by considerably expanding the basic package service to 95% of total health expenditures. The third issue referred to the contributions for basic health insurance. The Dekker Committee had proposed that income-dependent contributions would cover 75% of expenditure for basic health insurance and flat-rate premiums the remaining 10%. In fact, this proposal meant that 25% of total health expenditure would be covered by flat-rate premiums. Simons wanted a 82-18 ratio between income-dependent contributions and flat-rate premiums in order to reduce the regressive effect of flat-rate premiums. The health insurers, in particular the private health insurers, requested a much lower portion for income-dependent contributions. In their view, competition would only work effectively if the portion of income-dependent contributions was limited to some 40% in health care expenditure. The risk-adjusted capitation payments from the central fund to the health insurers presented another critical issue. Which criteria were available to ensure that preferred risk selection would not be a profitable strategic option for the health insurers? Preferred risk selection could easily impair universal access to health care. It could even lead to a situation in which efficiently operating insurers would be driven out of the market by inefficiently operating health insurers who deliberately pursued a strategy of preferred risk selection. Preferred risk selection would be forbidden by law, of course, but would it really be completely eliminated? Health insurers could always initiate subtle risk selection strategies, for instance, through selective marketing, selective contracting, or through putting up administrative barriers. The final issue was simply a growing doubt whether market competition would be an effective approach toward cost containment in health care anyway. Competition, for instance, presupposed some excess capacity among the providers which in many areas of health care in fact did not exist after many years of strict government planning and bed reduction programs. Hospitals and nursing homes could easily act as local monopolists. To what extent would the health insurers be really interested in competition, when cartel formation was perhaps a more promising alternative?

The Future of Dutch Health Care Reform

At this moment the future of health care reform is confusing. Some politicians have argued that health care reform à la Dekker and Simons is politically dead. The new government that took office in 1994 says it prefers a less ideological and more pragmatic approach. If one, however, takes a closer look at its policy changes proposals for health care, one sees that it is too soon to argue that health care reform is dead. There is much more continuity in health care policy-making than is often suggested. The most important changes point to the general structure of health insurance.

According to the latest policy proposals, health insurance will not consist of two parts (basic health insurance and supplementary health insurance) but of three parts. The first part is the Exceptional Medical Expenses Act (AWBZ). The stepwise transformation of this scheme into a basic health insurance scheme for the entire population would be reversed. It will only cover long-term care and catastrophic risks for which market competition does not work. The scheme would be paid for through income-dependent contributions. Planning of long-term health facilities and price control are seen as a government responsibility.

The second part consists of compulsory health insurance for acute care (GPs, medical specialists, and hospital care). Here, the traditional dividing line between the sickness funds and the private health insurers would be maintained for the near future, but a further convergence between sickness funds and private health insurers is intended. Although the government is not clear on this point, it may be expected that compulsory health insurance for acute care will further develop as an area for market competition among health insurers, particularly among the sickness funds. Benefit package and income-dependent contributions would continue to be set by the government. New is the introduction of a compulsory Dfl 200 per year deductible for all insured (GP care will be exempted from this arrangement). Another important proposal points to the introduction of fixed budgets for the sickness funds.

The third part of the health insurance system proposal relates to supplementary health insurance plans. These plans cover those services not included in the benefit package of the exceptional medical expenses scheme or health insurance scheme for acute medical care. Enrollment is voluntary. The market for supplementary health insurance in competitive. The government only accepts responsibility for the quality of care; costs and accessibility are beyond its responsibility.

The government has also confirmed that it wants to screen the benefit package of the health insurance scheme with the Dunning method. This method identifies four different criteria in order to justify that a health service is covered by either the Exceptional Medical Expenses Act or the sickness fund scheme for acute care. A health service must be necessary, effective, and efficient. The fourth criterion points to co-responsibility. Services that do not meet each of these four criteria should no longer be covered by social health insurance, but health insurers may develop supplementary health insurance plans to provide coverage for them. Although the expectations are not very high, the screening procedure may result in a considerable shift of health services from the exceptional or acute scheme to supplementary health insurance.

In our view, health care reform is not only a top-down government initiated process of structural change of the health care system, but also a bottom-up process, consisting of changes in, for instance, health care finance or health care delivery, that gives the process of transformation some dynamics of its own. This second face of health care reform will be briefly clarified with some examples. It is evident that a process of cultural change is going on, both at the providers' and the insurers' side of the health care market. Many hospitals, for instance, are taking initiatives to improve their market profile and to strengthen their client orientation. All sickness funds have started a process of cultural transformation from a strong rule-oriented bureaucratic organization into an open client-oriented organization. Another aspect of cultural change points to the new policy debates in health care. Good examples are the discussion on the limits to solidarity and government responsibility in health care.

It is also evident that the scope of market competition in health care is expanding. An essential change here is that the sickness funds may now operate on a nationwide basis. The establishment of some new sickness funds will certainly stimulate further competition in the near future. The market for employer-based health insurance contracts has become more competitive than ever before. Competition is also expanding among health care providers in the acute and long-term care sector. The decline in the average length of stay opens new possibilities for small-scale organizations to enter the new markets for home care and to provide health and social services that meet the demand of their clients. District nursing agencies on a commercial basis have already become common. On the other hand, it is less plausible to expect that the scope for the market competition among the big institutional providers (hospitals, nursing homes, psychiatric hospitals) will rapidly grow in the near future. Another aspect of health insurance relates to the ongoing process of concentration. By 1993 the total number of sickness funds (26) was halved compared with 1985 (53). Over the same period the number of private health insurers dropped from 69 to 52. Various kinds of strategic alliances have been developed, not only among the sickness funds and among private health insurers but also between these two categories of health insurers. Although the process of concentration is not new in health insurance, it is evident that the developments since 1985 are linked to the expanding scope of market competition in health care. All parties want to strengthen their strategic position in order to cope with the new market challenges they face. It is inconceivable that the new insurance agencies will accept a return to the structure of the old health insurance market. Rather, they will push for change for health insurance reform. There are also processes of integration under way. Health insurance may be increasingly expected to become part of large-scale financial conglomerations offering a vast array of financial and insurance services and operating on an international scale. Another tendency is to offer employer-integrated packages for social insurance of which health insurance only forms a part. Health care providers are increasingly establishing integrated networks for the delivery of health services.

This brief overview of some developments demonstrates that health care reform is a much more complicated process than a simple top-down implementation of government plans to rearrange the structure of the health care system. Rather, it is a continuous process of interrelated top-down and bottom-up processes. Assessing the success of health care reform solely on the basis of what parts of the Dekker and Simons plan have been put into practice would neglect the continuity and complexity of health care reform. Health care reform must be seen as a long-term process in seeking new balances between efficiency, equity, and individual responsibility.

References

Central Office of Statistics. 1995. *Vademecum of Health Statistics 1994*. The Hague.

Commissie Structuur en Financiering Gezondheidszorg (Commissie Dekker). 1987. *Willingness to Change*. The Hague.

Commissie Keuzen in de Zorg (Commissie Dunning). 1991. *Strategic Choices in Health Care*. The Hague.

Grünwald, C. A., and A. F. Mantel. 1991. The Netherlands. In *European Health Services Handbook*, 104–15.

Hurst, J. 1992. *The Reform of Health Care: A Comparative Analysis of Seven OECD Countries*. Paris: OECD.

Lieverdink, H., and J. A. M. Maarse. 1995. Negotiating fees for medical specialists in the Netherlands. *Health Policy*, 81–101.

Maarse, J. A. M. 1995. Hospital Financing in the Netherlands. In *Hospital Financing in Seven Countries*, 95–119. Office of Technology Assessment, U.S. Congress, Washington, D.C.

———. Health care finance in the Netherlands. *Revue d'E-conomie Financière*. Forthcoming.

Maarse, J. A. M., A. van der Horst, and E. J. E. Molin. 1993. Hospital budgeting in the Netherlands: effects upon hospital services. *European Journal of Public Health*, 181–87.

Mur-Veeman, I. M., A. van Raak, and J. A. M. Maarse. 1994. Dutch home care: towards a new organization? *Health Policy* 141–56.

Schut, F. T. 1995. *Competition in the Dutch Health Care Sector*. Rotterdam.

Ven, W. P. M. M. van de. 1991. Perestrojka in the Dutch health care system. *European Economic Review*, 430–40.

Ven, W. P. M. M. van de, and F. T. Schut. 1994. Should catastrophic risks be included in a regulated competitive health insurance market? *Social Science & Medicine*, 1459–72.

Table 1   Demographic Aspects of the Dutch Population

	1994
Male	7,586,000
Female	7,756,000
Total	15,342,000
0–19	24.5%
20–39	32.7%
40–64	10.1%
65–79	10.1%
80+	3.0%
unmarried	6,689
married	7,075
widowed	877
divorced	700

Source: *Statistical Yearbook 1995.*

Table 2   Life Expectancy, 1990

	men	women
0 years	73.8	80.1
15 years	59.7	65.8
25 years	50.0	56.0
45 years	31.0	36.7
65 years	14.4	19.0
75 years	8.6	11.4

Source: *Vademecum of Health Statistics 1994.*

Tables 2 and 3   Births, Infant Mortality, and Abortions

	1993
Live births (in thousands)	196
Birth rate per 1,000 population	12.8
Birth rate per 1,000 women 15–44 years	56.5
Fertility rate	1.6
Infant mortality rate per 1,000 births	6.3
Perinatal mortality rate per 1,000 births	9.1
Place of birth	
home	31.6%
hospital	68.1%
other places	0.3%
Abortions (in thousands)	29.5
Ratio of abortions to 1,000 live births (1987)	98.9

Sources: *Statistical Yearbook 1995* and OECD.

Table 4 Death Rates per 100,000 Population: Ten Leading Causes of Death, 1990

	Male	Female
Coronary heart diseases	175.9	124.2
Cerebrovascular disease	66.7	98.7
Diseases of the respiratory system	57.4	23.9
Diabetes	17.8	31.3
Pneumonia	19.3	27.4
Malignant neoplasms		
Colon and rectum	24.0	28.2
Lung	94.9	16.3
Breast	—	43.5
Prostrate	28.9	—
Stomach	17.2	10.8

SOURCE: RIVM, *Volksgezondheid Toekomstverkenning 1993*, 51.

Table 5 Patient Discharges by Specialty, and Average Length of Patient Stay by Specialty

Specialty	Discharges per 100,000 population	Average length of stay in days
internal medicine	1,350	14.2
cardiology	909	8.6
disease of lung	363	15.2
gastroenterology	37	12.4
surgery	1,784	11.0
urology	442	8.7
orthopedics	696	11.2
neurosurgery	141	12.6
ob/gyn	1,674	5.8
pediatrics	653	9.9
neurology	650	15.1
psychiatry	118	39.7
ear, nose, throat	483	4.6

SOURCE: Central Office of Statistics, *Vademecum of Health Statistics of the Netherlands*, 1994.

Table 6 Not available

Table 7   Number of Beds of Acute Care Hospitals

	1991	
General hospitals		
less than 100 beds	1	
101–200	18	
201–300	19	
301–400	32	
more than 400	47	
Total number of hospitals	117	
Total number of beds	51,599	
Academic hospitals		
101–200	1	(children's hospital)
601–700	1	
701–800	2	
801–900	3	
more than 901	2	
Total number of hospitals	9	
Total number of hospital beds	7,576	
Specialized (categorical hospitals)		
less than 100 beds	20	
101–200	12	
201–300	3	
301–400	0	
more than 400	1	
Total number of hospitals	36	
Total number of hospital beds	4,569	

SOURCE: National Hospital Institute (NZi), *Intramural Health Care in Figures (January 1992)*.

Table 8   Performance of Acute Care General Hospitals

In thousands	1981	1993
Inpatient days	18,149	13,104
Admissions	1,392	1,338
Day surgery	—	491
First outpatient visits	3,364	4,490
Outpatient visits	16,276	19,098
Occupancy rate (%)	82.8	71.0
Length of stay (days)	13.0	9.8

SOURCE: *Financial Report on Health, 1995*.

Table 9 Nursing Homes, Psychiatric Hospitals, and Institutions
for the Mentally Retarded

	1991
Nursing Homes	
Number of institutions	
somatic	95
psycho-geriatric	69
combined	161
Number of beds	
somatic	27,209
psycho-geriatric	24,866
Beds per 100 population 65 +	
somatic	1.39
psycho-geriatric	1.27
Day care units	
somatic	1,747
psycho-geriatric	1,607
Psychiatric Hospitals	
Number of institutions	
general	46
academic	4
special	35
Number of beds	
general	22,544
academic	265
special	2,030
Beds per 1,000 population	1.64
Part-time treatment	2,230
Institutions for the Mentally Retarded	
Number of institutions	
general	91
special	32
Number of beds	
general	28,395
special	3,279
Beds per 1,000 population	2.09

SOURCE: National Hospital Institute (NZi), *Intramural Health Care in Figures (January 1992).*

Table 10   National Health Expenditures in Million Dfl by Type of Expenditure and Source of Funds, 1994

	Sickness fund	Except. Medical Expenses Act	Private health insurance	Government	Other
General and categorical hospitals	8,137	1,097	3,473	126	
Academic hospitals	1,744	—	797	940	106
Medical specialists	1,112	112	998	108	
Psychiatric hospitals	—	2,905	—	29	—
Ambulatory psychiatric care	—	640	—	109	26
Care for mentally handicapped	—	4,392	—	—	—
Nursing homes	—	5,317	—	—	—
General practitioners	1,197	—	574	—	474
Dentists	914	12	362	—	1,086
Pharmaceutical drugs	—	5,222	14	—	—
Administration	857	454	894	287	—

SOURCE: *Financial Report on Health, 1995.*

Reform of the Health System of New Zealand

Claudia D. Scott

Introduction

New Zealand is a small country in the western Pacific region, consisting of 3.5 million people who are concentrated on two main islands, the North (73%) and the South Island (27%). It is governed by a parliamentary political system which is modeled on that of the United Kingdom to which it was a colonial possession. While self-government began in 1907, constitutional independence did not occur until 1946. Though New Zealand's economic and political interests have become refocused from Britain and Europe toward the Asia-Pacific region in recent years, the link to the United Kingdom remains in that the British monarch is still official head of state of New Zealand.

The Maori, the indigenous people of New Zealand, migrated about one thousand years ago. In 1840 the Treaty of Waitangi was signed between the British Crown and Maori, which granted rights of governance to the Crown; in return, Maori were to be given the privileges of British subjects and protection of their lands, forests, fisheries, and cultural treasures.

While New Zealand was traditionally an economy relying heavily on the export of agriculture products to Britain, it currently exports a much wider range of goods and services to a growing number of diverse world markets.

Funding and Delivery Arrangements

Free inpatient treatment was introduced in 1938; by 1947 a predominantly tax-funded health care system was put into place which included government subsidies for GP services but allowed them the right to set fees for the services they provided. Since the late 1930s, the public sector has played a very dominant role in both the funding and the provision of hospital services in New Zealand. The funding for health care, not unlike other areas of social service and income maintenance expenditure, is derived predominantly from general taxation and there are no explicit social insurance arrangements. Morbidity and mortality patterns are generally similar to those in other Western countries. Though there were significant differentials between Maori and non-Maori forty years ago (14–17 years), they are now reduced to 4–5 years. Poorer health status for Maori is largely explained by lifestyle factors. Diabetes, cardiovascular diseases, and obesity are important health problems for both Maori and Pacific Islanders.

Health care expenditure as of the year ending June 30, 1994, was $6.19 billion, or 7.57% of its gross domestic product (GDP)—an amount which is equivalent to $1,698 health expenditure per head of population. The health sector employs about 4.5% of the labor force. The public sector's share of total health expenditure in 1994 was 76.7%, made up of 66.9% from the health vote, 3.7% from other government departments and city councils, and 6.2% from the Accident Rehabilitation and Compensation Insurance Corporation (ARCIC) scheme. ARCIC is a state-run compulsory insurance scheme providing care and income maintenance through earnings-related compensation in the case of accident. The private sector's share of total health expenditures in 1994 was 23.3% and made up of private household (out-of-pocket) 16.6%, health insurance 6.3%, and charitable organizations 0.3%.

Of the funding from *Vote: Health,* 55.1% was devoted to the funding of institutional care including public (47.9%) and private (7.2%) establishments; 39.4% was devoted to community care including general practitioner (10.5%), specialist services (7.7%), dental (3.7%), and medicaments (14.9%); 2.7% was devoted to public health services and 2.8% to teaching and research.

Although in 1994 more than half of New Zealanders held private insurance, this private insurance contributed only 6.2% to total expenditures on health care. Total private expenditures were 22.8% of all health expenditures, including private insurance, out-of-pocket payments (16.3%) and charitable and nonprofit organizations (0.31%). Private insurance covers reimbursement for patient part charges for services delivered by the public system and funds elective surgery in private hospitals.

Total health care spending as a percentage of GDP has grown little in real terms since the 1980s; however, there have been noticeable shifts in the sources of funding. Over the past decade there has been a downward trend in the share of funding from public sources. The growing impact of private funders, purchasers, and providers in health care is significant. Between 1980 and 1994 the share of public expenditure dropped from 88% to 76.7%, while the share of private sector expenditure grew from 12% to 22.8%. New Zealand's per capita health expenditure in real terms grew over this period at an annual rate of 1.4%; however, private sector spending increased by 6.2% and public expenditure by 0.4%.

Government health sector funding arrangements vary considerably between the primary and secondary care areas. This partly reflects that secondary care is provided by hospitals that are mostly owned by the government whereas primary care is funded on a fee-for-service basis to self-employed providers. The primary sector in New Zealand includes doctors in general practice (GPs), as well as other Independent Service Providers (ISPs), which may be fully funded by the state, partly funded, or completely private. Examples of some ISPs are independent nurse practitioners, midwives, and the Plunket Society, which provides maternal and child health care.

The total budget for health care is set within the context of the standard government budget cycle. Traditionally, provider subsidies for many primary care services have been open-ended, while expenditures for secondary care and public health services have been set centrally and distributed regionally to area health boards according to the Population Based Funding Formula (PBFF). The formula uses the age-gender composition of boards' populations, with adjustments being made for other population factors that have been identified as contributing to the health needs of a population. Special Health Needs (SHNs) factors are based upon a number of characteristics identified in the national census, including income, ethnicity, education, and home ownership.

Primary Care

General practitioners attract partial subsidies (called *health benefits*) from the government with the balance of funding met by individuals either through insurance or out-of-pocket payments. The government does not regulate the price of primary care but has some influence over its level through the amount of the subsidy paid. Government funds a set amount per consultation, but doctors' fees are often more than the subsidy.

Health benefits provide subsidies for consultations (which are commonly paid directly to the practitioner) and full or partial subsidies on pharmaceuticals, laboratory tests, and diagnostic imaging. The public sector funds free maternity care, and free dental care for people under age sixteen and those in school until the age of eighteen. Health benefits were $1.06 billion in 1993 with 28.1% of benefits devoted to primary services (including GP services) and 54.8% to pharmaceuticals. GPs act as gatekeepers to hospital services.

While there has always been broad public support for a health care system in which the public sector plays a dominant role in funding and provision, the 1980s brought increasing attention to the need for reform. Access to primary care—in particular the services of general practitioners—was threatened by the very substantial growth in part charges for services. While some attempts were made to increase subsidies, this was often done on an ad hoc basis and in a way which did not guarantee that public resources used in primary care provided good incentives for efficient care.

While there has always been both private funding and private provision of services, the private funding system serves more as a complement to the public sector rather than as a direct competitor. The main areas of private provision have been general practitioner services and rest home care for the elderly, though both areas have received subsidies in the form of health benefits to cover services. Other private hospitals have traditionally specialized in elective surgery and have expanded in response to increasing delays in people receiving treatment through the public system. It is common for surgeons working in the public hospital system also to provide services to private hospitals.

Medical Practice

In 1993 there were 6,872 members of the active New Zealand medical workforce, with significant representation from general practitioners (39%), specialists (31%), and house officers and registrars and medical officers (25%). Approximately 73% of the workforce is male, 50% is below 40 years of age, and 70% are graduates of New Zealand medical schools. Statistics for 1993 showed the following specialty fields for surgery: general (44.1%), orthopedic (33.3%), urology (8.1%), plastic surgery (6.6%), neurosurgery (2.9%), cardiothoracic (3.7%), and pediatric (1.3%).

The New Zealand Medical Association (NZMA) is the umbrella organization representing the interests of the medical profession in New Zealand. Membership in the NZMA is voluntary, and in 1995 approximately 65% of doctors were members. The NZMA acts as the representative of the profession in dealings with the government and statutory agencies such as the ARCIC. It provides a forum for the debate of issues, promotes improved health standards, and aims to establish and promulgate ethical standards for the profession. The NZMA has 22 geographically determined divisions across the country; under a recent reform each division will have an enhanced role in the Policy Council of the Medical Association. The Association maintains formal links with 21 affiliates, including several Royal Colleges and associations representing the specialities within medicine and 9 associate organizations.

The number and distribution of doctors among specialities and general practice has considerable effect on patient access. Financial incentives are provided for general practitioners to work in some rural areas. Shortages of specialists usually impact on waiting times at public hospitals. The effect of this is that some people opt to enter the private sector to gain faster access to services. The recent reforms have also enabled the public sector to purchase additional services, including operations, from the private sector. High technological services such as heart transplants are performed at only one center in New Zealand. Access to this service is subsidized by the local Crown Health Enterprise (CHE), with individuals having to meet considerable costs. Some of these individual costs are met by local public fund-raising ventures. As noted later, CHEs are publicly owned hospitals that replaced the area health boards as providers of hospital services and are to operate in a more businesslike manner.

General practitioners are generally the first point of contact and act as gatekeepers for specialist care. In only a few specialties is it common for patients to access specialists directly and without referral. While individuals can access specialists directly through private hospitals, their access to them in public hospitals is gained through referral by a general practitioner or by direct admission. Apart from maternity care, it is uncommon for general practitioners to operate from public hospitals. Maternity is also the one area where specialists provide primary care service.

Specialists are paid in different ways. They are commonly salaried in public hospitals but receive fee-for-service in private hospitals. The fees may be reimbursed by insurance, paid for by private households, or by the government's accident insurance fund in case of accidents. Specialists in ambulatory care are paid by many different means including out-of-pocket, insurance, and public sources.

General practitioners supply a range of nonspecialist services but many undertake extra training in order to qualify them to provide maternity care. Laboratory tests and other diagnostic services are usually undertaken at laboratories or special facilities. Pharmaceuticals are dispensed from pharmacies that are usually separate from doctors' rooms. In some countries diagnostic technologies such as MRI have diffused into nonhospital settings, but in New Zealand general practice services do not generally provide access to sophisticated technologies.

The estimated average income of self-employed doctors and dentists is comparable to that earned by other professionals, with average income of doctors roughly equivalent to that of solicitors. Over the 1985–90 period average income of dentists was approximately 80–85% of that of doctors and comparable to the average income of accountants. In 1990 average income of self-employed doctors was 3.5 times that of an average worker.

An important factor affecting health care delivery is the way the small population is dispersed throughout a large geographical area. This dispersion creates difficulties in ensuring services are accessible. The health services are organized according to four regions, each of comparable size in terms of population: Northern, Midland, Central, and Southern. General practitioner and specialist distribution varies. The ratio of general practitioners to the population within the four regions varies from 1:1,452 to 1:1,187. Lower ratios of GPs to the population are often found in rural and less affluent areas. Specialist ratios vary from 1:1,529 to 1:2,019; within the four regions there are marked variations and the ratios range from as low as 1:999 and as high as 1:2,793. Where there are serious shortages of primary care providers, the government has sometimes responded by employing general practitioners or other primary care providers under contract. In recent years there has been active recruitment of trained medical specialists from overseas to fill vacancies in public hospitals.

While doctors are largely self-regulated, there are policies under development that will require them to maintain their skills and their ability to practice competently. Such regulations are likely to become mandatory and to be administered by the Medical Council, which has, by law, disciplinary powers and deals with matters concerning the registration and training of medical practitioners. Greater emphasis is being placed on the use of accreditation as a part of a number of measures designed to improve the quality of service. The government is at present reviewing safety of health services and it is likely that measures governing their safety will be introduced.

Hospitals

Patient access to public hospital for acute or chronic care is gained by two means. In the case of accident or emergency, patients can be taken by ambulance or they can present themselves to the nearest hospital. Other cases are referred by general practitioners to specialists at hospitals. With a small number of hospitals in any one geographical area, patients are likely to be referred to their nearest hospital, so long as that hospital provides the service that is required. Some hospitals specialize in particular services and services at rural hospitals are more limited.

Admission to continuing care facilities for the elderly varies according to whether the care is financed by the individual or the government. Admissions to public hospitals are controlled by local Geriatric Assessment Services that refer patients to appropriate care. Individuals who are funding their own care may be admitted without reference to this service. In the case of public psychiatric hospital care, the Mental Health (Compulsory Assessment and Treatment) Act of 1992 defines criteria for the admission and discharge of patients with mental disorders.

As of March 31, 1991, there was a total of 19,619 public hospital beds and 6,963 private beds, with more than 79% of the private beds in the geriatric and long-stay medical sector. There were a total of 5.6 public beds per 1,000 population of which 3.4 per thousand were general, 1.7 per thousand were psychiatric and intellectually handicapped, and 0.5 per thousand were maternity. The average length of stay for long-stay public hospital patients over the ten-year period 1983–92 was 13.5 months (417 days). There was a progressive decrease in average length of stay for general, acute care over the decade reducing from 10.6 days in 1982–83 to 8.7 days in 1991–92.

Private hospitals in New Zealand are owned and administered by a large variety of nonprofit and for-profit organizations. There are two types of private hospitals: those providing elective surgery and those providing long-stay geriatric care. The presence of private hospitals in areas such as maternity and mental health is limited. Private hospitals charge on a per procedure basis, with separate charges for room and other services, and costs are met either by individuals or by private insurers. Under the new health reforms it will be possible for public purchasers to contract with private hospitals to provide services, though experience of this to date is very limited.

The National Government's 1991 Health Reforms

A program of wide-ranging reforms to the health sector was unveiled in July 1991 in a so-called Green and White Paper entitled "Your Health and the Public Health." The health reform proposals emerged from the work of a Health Services taskforce appointed by the minister of health and from earlier work, but were strongly influenced by the National Government's overall strategy of reforming economic and social policy.

It is helpful to view the design of the health reforms within the context of economic and public sector reforms that occurred over the 1984-90 period. Deregulation in part or in full was undertaken across many sectors including banking, finance, transport, energy, telecommunications, and broadcasting. Economic reforms included the lowering of fiscal assistance to industry and border protection as well as initiatives in the direction of establishing a common market with Australia. Public sector reforms included extensive corporatization and privatization through the selling of state assets, which resulted in a very dramatic reduction in the size of the public sector. The State-Owned Enterprises Act of 1986 involved the transformation of several government organizations into successful business or commercial enterprises. Important in this regard were measures that streamlined and clarified the role of government as owner of each organization from the management of each organization. The reforms emphasized greater clarity and transparency regarding the roles of purchasing and service delivery and the merits of competition and contestability (how easy it is for new service providers to challenge existing ones) among private and public purchasers and providers.

Figure 1 provides an overview of the structural changes surrounding the health reforms.

Basic features of the reform included:

- integration of primary and secondary care funding as well as some movement to integrate funding for ACC and continuing care;
- separation of the purchasing and providing of care through the establishment of four Regional Health Authorities (RHAs) to act as purchasers of health care;
- abolition of fourteen area health boards and reorganization of public providers of hospital services into Crown Health Enterprises (which would operate according to commercial objectives) or community trusts;
- public health services to be purchased and coordinated by a separate agency called the Public Health Commission;
- individuals to have the opportunity to opt out of their RHA and choose an alternative Health Care Plan as their purchasing agency. They would take an entitlement of government funding to the Health Care Plan;
- A National Advisory Committee on Core Health Services (Core Services Committee) to be established to advise the Minister of Health on what personal health services should be provided on a reasonably accessible and affordable basis to all New Zealanders;
- introduction of a regime for the targeting of user charges for health services and the introduction of a kiwi card (to be later renamed a community service card).

There were two main mechanisms designed to protect access under the Interim Targeting Regime: service stop-losses and the High Use Health Card. The service stop-losses were family-based, the stop-loss consisting of a service threshold beyond which families pay either no charge

Figure 1   Proposed Health Care Structures (1991)

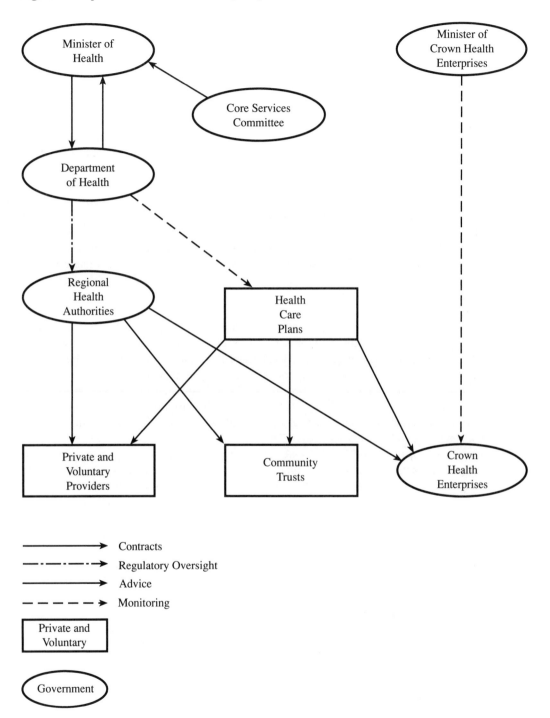

or a reduced charge. For example, the stop-loss family threshold was 15 prescription items per year in the case of pharmaceuticals and 10 charged services in the case of public hospital inpatient services. The High Use Health Card was granted to individuals who have an ongoing condition or conditions and who use GP services, public hospital services, and approved private specialist services in excess of a threshold of 6 services in 6 months or 12 services in 12 months. The recipient of such a card pays no charge for public hospital services, has reduced prescription charges, and an increased GP subsidy.

The reforms suggested that the government would maintain a key role as funder of health care; however, it signaled that it did not expect to maintain its monopoly position as the owner of provider units such as hospitals. Furthermore, the reforms envisaged the possibility of competing private and public purchasers and the ability of individuals to supplement coverage of publicly funded core services with the purchase of supplementary insurance to fund care outside of the core. As part of the reform package, the government sought public consultation on core services and on whether to maintain tax funding or alternatively to move to a system of health premiums. The public consultation revealed widespread support for the continuation of health funding from general taxation.

The health service reforms followed the design of other economic and social policy changes. The split between the functions of purchaser and provider made clear the separate interests of the government as a purchaser of health care from its ownership interest in hospitals. CHEs were designed to operate as successful businesses and this was reflected in the business emphasis of members appointed to the CHE establishment boards. As in the case of the reform of state-owned enterprises, there was a preference for separating commercial from social objectives. However, following widespread concern about the government's proposals to make CHEs motivated by profitability, modifications were made to the Health and Disabilities Services Bill. The final Act (1993) calls for CHEs both to exhibit a sense of social responsibility and to "be as successful and efficient as comparable businesses not owned by the Crown" (Section 11). As well as their need to exhibit a sense of social responsibility, CHEs also differed from private profit and nonprofit service delivery agencies in that they must serve as providers of last resort—though with provision for explicit compensation for such services.

A controversial part of the 1991 health care reforms was the extension of patient co-payments for outpatient and inpatient services in hospitals. The government modified its subsidy measures to link the subsidies more tightly to health care for low-income groups. The extension of part charges supported the government's objective that, in the future, a larger share of health care expenditure would be met by individuals.

When the reforms were introduced efforts were still ongoing to try to integrate the funding of health care arising from accident and illness. Subsequent to the release of the original documents, the RHAs assumed responsibility for both health and disability support services—though there is some partitioning of disability support expenditure to preserve historical levels of expenditure. As a result of these changes the brief of the Core Services Committee was extended in June 1992 to include advice on disability support services. Figure 2 shows the structures as modified for these changes. (The Public Health Commission [PHC] in this figure was an agency established to purchase and coordinate public health services. It was abolished at the end of 1995.)

Implementing the Reforms

Because of the three-year parliamentary term, the timetable for implementation was extremely tight. Only two years were allowed from announcement to implementation of both a system of

Figure 2   Advisory and Contracting Relationships in the Health Care System (1993)

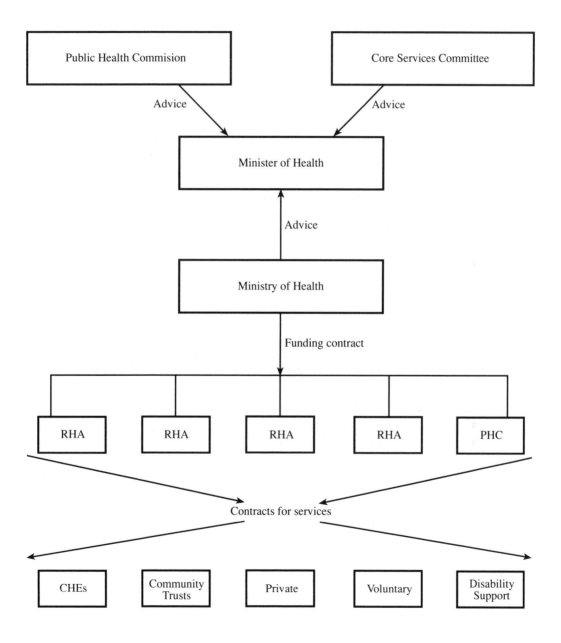

competitive provision of health care and the introduction of competitive purchasing through the health care plans. This schedule was extremely ambitious in that the public purchasers had limited experience engaging in formal contracting arrangements with private providers, and much work would be needed to define the nature of "core services" to allowing competitive purchasing. Existing insurers were largely filling a gap, rather than providing comprehensive health insurance.

Progress in terms of defining a package of core services was much slower than expected and technical and information problems limited the feasibility of risk-rating individuals (so that they might move from the Regional Health Authority to a Health Care Plan). As structural changes and greater competition between public and private providers evolved, it was expected that historical relationships as regards costs and differentials between public and private provider would alter. Thus historical information appeared particularly limited as the basis for estimating risk and the amount individuals would require to secure a comprehensive package of core services from a health care plan. Despite extraordinary efforts by officials, the ambitious timetables for reform were unable to be met. The financial position of CHEs was much worse than originally envisaged and there has been a need to make several further cash injections to improve their balance sheets.

The detailed analysis required to implement the policy and structural reforms was much greater than originally estimated and difficult to deliver on the required time frames. Progress was slower than expected in terms of defining a package of core services, and technical and information problems limited the feasibility of risk-rating individuals (so that they might move from the Regional Health Authority to a Health Care Plan). Structural changes and greater competition between public and private providers meant that historical costs had limitations as the basis of estimating prices and future funding requirements.

In early 1992, following extensive consultation, the government decided to retain a tax-based funding and to no longer pursue the option of funding health care through premiums. The premium approach would have eased the way for the government to target its own subsidies to high-risk and/or low-income individuals. Once health premiums were abandoned, so was the prospect of making very substantial fiscal savings by a greater targeting of funding for health care. Hospital charges were extremely unpopular and difficult to sustain. Outpatient charges were retained for those without community services cards. Community services cards were exempt from fees for low-income groups and reduced the fees of ambulatory care services.

The new structures were established with various limitations and transitional arrangements governing their operation. While the Health and Disability Services Act (1993) makes provision for health care plans (HCPs), the government has announced it has no immediate intention to move in this direction. Some serious problems were envisaged in the transition to HCPs. Experts expressed concern about the ability of the system to assess this risk accurately. The changing structures in the health care system suggested that historical costs were a poor basis on which to estimate levels of funding. Were HCPs for Maori to be allowed, this would result in the pooling of a group with poor health status into a single insurance fund—raising doubts about their financial viability.

Progress in defining an individual's entitlement to core services has been slow. In the first year of the reformed system (July 1993–June 1994), purchasers and CHEs were constrained by requirements to provide the same range and level of services, with the same terms of access as were available on June 30, 1993. Service entitlements for some disability support consumers were protected or "grandparented" until July 1996. RHAs agreed to retain fee-for-service payments until December 1995 for general practitioners and private specialists, unless other forms of contracting were adopted. This meant that despite the integration of funding there were elements of the RHA budgets that remain open-ended.

While such policies were aimed at protecting people's access to services during the transition, and giving new agencies time to settle in, the provisions have limited purchasers and providers in their efforts to define a more appropriate and efficient level and mix of services. Provisions that allow GPs to be subsidized on the basis of fee-for-service, with no limits on service utilization, have thwarted the efforts of the RHAs to get demand-driven expenditure under control. The achievement of overall efficiency gains will require technical service innovation and shifts in resources among services which are difficult, in some cases, to implement.

Service Delivery in the Post-Reform Era

Table A offers information on public hospital inpatient discharges by major diagnostic category (MDC) for 1992. Data presented in the 1994 Core Health and Disability Support Services Committee Report shows that public hospital volumes of service increased over the 1991–93 period with corresponding reductions in both average length of stay and average cost per discharge. Day surgery counted for approximately 30% of total public hospital surgery in 1992. Inpatient admissions by service category in 1991 shows the four major categories to be surgical (39.1%), medical (23.9%), maternity/obstetrics (18.1%), and pediatric (11.5%). The contribution of services to total costs in 1991–92 is shown in Table B.

Over the period 1982–83 to 1991–92, there has not been a significant change in the private sector's share of the short-stay care market. The private sector's market share was 16.6% in 1982–83, rose to 17.2% in the following year, and has oscillated around 15% thereafter. This result is somewhat counterintuitive in light of increased expenditure on private hospital care and by private insurers, the increased marketing by both health insurers and private hospitals, and the presence and growth of public hospital waiting lists. Table C compares the share of high-volume private sector operations over two periods.

The private hospital's share of short-stay patients has not changed significantly over the decade. The share of patient days in 1991–92 involving stays of less than 92 days was 91.6% public and 8.4% private and has been virtually unchanged over the past ten years. The private share of long-

Table A Hospital Inpatient Discharges by Major Diagnostic Category, 1992

	(% of total)
Nervous System	6.4
Eye	1.9
Ear, nose, mouth, and throat	4.8
Respiratory	8.0
Circulatory	10.4
Digestive	9.3
Liver, Pancreas	1.7
Musculoskeletal system	10.5
Skin, breast	3.8
Kidney, urinary	2.8
Reproductive system	4.7
Pregnancy, birth, newborns	22.0
Mental health	2.1
Injury, poisoning	2.5
Other contacts	9.0

Table B Individual Service's Contribution to
Total Cost of Services, 1991–92 (%)

Surgical	26.6
Medical	19.0
Older people	15.1
Mental health	10.5
Pregnancy/childbirth	8.5
Primary care	5.8
Intellectual handicap	5.3
Child health	5.2
Dental	1.8
Health promotion	1.4
Health Protection	.9

Table C Market Share (%) of High-Volume Private Sector Operations,
1983–83 and 1991–92

Operation	1982–83	1991–92
Tonsillectomy	47.9	55.8
Insertion of prosthetic lens	60.1	51.1
Excision of semilunar cartilage of knee	73.5	87.7
Hernia operations	38.4	44.9
Myringotomy	60.0	48.1
Hysterectomy	50.9	66.2
Dilation and curettage of uterus	20.4	21.7
Ligation and stripping of varicose veins	40.3	51.6
Prostate operations	33.4	49.1

stay patients has increased however from 45.2% in 1982–83 to 50.8% in 1991–92. One category that has caused significant growth in private long-stay care is continuing care for the elderly. Here, the share of private subsidized geriatric patients grew from 53.2% in 1983 to 69.2% in 1992.

Publicly owned hospital policies are influenced by decisions at regional and central level. Under the Health and Disability Services Act of 1993 publicly owned hospitals (Crown Health Enterprises) are expected to make a profit and manage themselves like efficient businesses not owned by the Crown. However they are not completely autonomous and their management and policies are influenced by government either as shareholder or as purchaser. Ultimately hospitals owned by the government are accountable to Parliament.

Levels of hospital care are determined by the extent to which purchasers (usually the regional health authorities) are prepared to buy the services. Other constraints on hospitals by government are exercised through the monitoring of hospital performance and profitability by the Crown Company Monitoring Unit and the Minister for Crown Health Enterprises, who is also responsible to Parliament. Crown Health Enterprises' freedom to expand their services and enlarge their capacity is therefore limited by whether there will be a market for those services and whether the government, as owner, considers this to be a prudent investment. Private hospital policies are subject to little government control outside licensing and safety requirements.

Public hospitals provide emergency rooms and some specialize in being centers for major trauma cases. Emergency rooms are staffed by junior doctors under supervision. In recent years there has been less tendency to use emergency services to deliver primary care. There has also been a growth in 24-hour private emergency services. In most hospitals individuals are cared for in rooms that accommodate four individuals though there are sometimes private rooms that are assigned according to the severity of the medical condition.

The area of consumer safety is one that has been given increasing attention over recent time. In April 1994 the government released a discussion document on this topic and has suggested that reform will bring both new legislation and modifications to existing legislation. The primary purpose of the reforms to existing provisions is to achieve greater consistency of standards across health care providers and institutions that deliver health care. The existing approach to consumer safety in the health and disability support services puts emphasis on the licensing or registration of institutions, such as hospitals, rest homes, and homes for people with intellectual, physical, or psychiatric disability. These requirements are specified primarily in the Hospitals Act of 1957 and the Hospital Regulations of 1993, the Health Act of 1956, the Old Peoples' Homes Regulations of 1987, and the Obstetrics Regulations of 1986. Other relevant legislation includes the Disabled Persons Community Welfare Act of 1975, the Intellectually Handicapped Persons' Homes Regulations of 1955 and in the Alcoholism and Drug Addiction Act of 1966 as well as general legal measures such as the Building Act of 1991 and the Health and Safety in Employment Act of 1992. In addition a number of other mechanisms are used, including occupational regulation by doctors and nurses, accreditation processes and codes of practice, professional ethics and training, the regulation of therapeutic products, external ethical reviews, monitoring systems by providers, and consumer participation through advocacy and complaints systems.

While the above mechanisms make a significant contribution to safety in treatment and care, several limitations and criticism have been levied and form the basis for reform proposals currently under discussion. Criticisms of the existing regime include the fact that the regulatory requirements do not provide adequate coverage within services where there are recognized safety risks. Some regulatory requirements do not apply to all providers who cover a service and others tend to focus on institutions rather than on the safety with which services are provided. This results in similar risks being treated differently in different settings. The government has recently appointed a commissioner of health and disability services who has the job of dealing with consumer complaints in the health services. Medical and nursing disciplinary complaint procedures are also in place as is greater emphasis on quality assurance and auditing within professional groupings.

While the exact nature of the reforms is still under discussion, its broad thrust will be to put emphasis on principles that focus on safety in the provision of services to consumers rather than on the safety standards of the institution providing care. They will require both new legislation and the repeal or amendment of some existing legislation. It is likely that the changes will result in a more active role for the government in the setting of safety standards, an increase in the level of consultation, an increased focus on compliance and more developed processes and procedures for registering service complaints. (Consumer Safety in Health and Disability Support Services, Ministry of Health, Wellington, Ministry of Health 1994).

Since public hospitals are funded from a fixed budget, there are reduced tendencies to allow unnecessary admissions, prolonged stays, and unnecessary medical, surgical, and diagnostic procedures. Tight budget constraints in public hospitals raise, if anything, concerns about the possibility of underservicing rather than overservicing. Lengths of stay have been falling and the combining of funding for primary and secondary care under Regional Health Authorities under the new reforms now provides expanded opportunities to fund care that was traditionally carried out in hospitals in the community.

On June 30, 1992, there were 65,240 people on public hospital surgical waiting lists (see Table D). Even allowing for large margin of error, it is clear that this number represents a growth in waiting lists over the period 1982–83. In its 1993 report to the government the Core Committee on Health and Disability Support Services recommended the introduction of a booking system for

Table D   Public Hospital Surgical Waiting Lists (June 30, 1992) and Estimated Average Waiting Times (1991)

Specialty	Waiting List (Number)	Average Waiting Time to Clear List (months)
Dental	523	2.2
Cardiothoracic	1,111	4.7
Ear, Nose, and Throat	9,037	7.8
General surgery	12,849	4.8
Gynecology	6,531	5.0
Neurosurgery	451	2.5
Ophthalmology	8,045	12.5
Orthopedic	16,663	10.3
Plastic	3,991	15.3
Urology	5,605	10.0
Other surgical departments	10	1.0
Total	65,240	7.0

SOURCE: C. G. McKendry et al., *New Zealand Hospital Sector Performance, 1983–92,* 59 and 61.

nonurgent surgery and medical procedures so that those on public hospital waiting lists have a definite date for their operation. Also in progress is work that would specify maximum acceptable waiting times for health and disability support services. This work would aim to establish maximum waits for a range of services; for example, cataract surgery, coronary artery bypass and angioplasty, hip and knee joint replacement, and prostrate surgery. It is envisaged that within each service a set of priority rankings would be established related to the severity of the condition and the likely responsiveness and effectiveness of treatment, and that maximum waits would be established for each of five levels of priority.

There was a progressive decrease in average length of stay over the decade, from 10.6 days in 1982–83 to 8.7 days in 1991–92. The average length of short-stay inpatient care was 6.2 days and the most common length of stay was one day (overnight). The reduction in average length of stay can usefully be related to the decline in the annual number of patient days and a relatively constant number of annual discharges from public hospitals. This shows that public hospitals are now seeing approximately the same number of inpatients but for a shorter average time. It can be demonstrated that the decline in average length of stay has not occurred as a result of changing the case mix toward cases with shorter stays. This trend has not, however, led to major resource savings in that average costs per day for inpatient visits have risen. In an attempt to get a measure of improvements in technical efficiency an estimate of public hospital aggregated output was derived as a weighted sum of outpatient, day patient, and inpatient volumes. Using this approach, it is estimated that aggregated outputs increased at an annual average rate of 0.3%.

There is significant competition between public and private hospitals for patients and medical staff. Private hospitals provide for choice of specialist and the timing of operations and are commonly sought to access more immediate access to care. Most private hospitals provide elective surgery, leaving accident and emergency care to the public hospital. Many specialist consultants split their time between the public and private hospitals.

The issue of quality is receiving considerable attention in the reformed health sector. Dimensions of quality have become the concern of various health care professional organizations and are taken up in the context of specifying contracts between the funder, purchasers, and providers of health care. Monitoring of quality is to some degree taken up by purchasers, funders, and monitoring agencies. Greater attention is being focused on the way in which the interaction of the service environment and the service provider will affect service quality. A recent review of tertiary services addressed the problem of establishing a quality framework for tertiary services. It is anticipated that over time, RHAs will develop effective input, process, output, and outcome measures of quality—including the establishment of minimum volume thresholds for providers of tertiary services.

Medical Education

There are two medical schools in New Zealand based at the Universities of Auckland and Otago. Otago University in Dunedin has three clinical schools based in Christchurch, Dunedin, and Wellington. The clinical schools deal with the education needs of fourth-year students and beyond. They are also centers for specialist training.

New Zealand provides training for a full range of specialties. These result in membership in either the New Zealand College or in an Australian College, which overseas the training in both Australia and New Zealand. Many New Zealanders also obtain some of their experience overseas, generally in Britain, and in some cases it is possible to train in New Zealand for membership in a British Royal College.

Through its education policies the government can determine the number of places it wishes to fund in university medical schools while various Royal Colleges are given responsibility for training and for establishing professional standards for specialists who are able to practice. The education of doctors and other health professionals is carried out in state-funded universities and polytechnics.

In July 1993 there were 1,965 dentists on the register. Access to the register is given by the Dental Council, which examines and approves the qualification of applicants and provides administrative services for the Dentists Disciplinary Tribunal. Most dentists operate on a fee-for-service system. The government provides free dental care to children under eighteen, by dental nurses in the case of primary school children and through dentists under contract in the case of secondary school students.

In July 1993 there were 3,478 pharmacists on the register, the bulk of whom operate in community pharmacies and the balance in hospitals, government departments, and the pharmaceutical industry.

In 1992 there were 27,970 registered nurses and 7,294 enrolled nurses. Basic nursing training is a three-year degree or diploma course at a polytechnic. Postbasic training is provided at polytechnics and university, as well as through hospital inservice. Nurses are accountable for their care and are not able to prescribe medication or authorize treatment without the authority of a medical practitioner. The exception to this is in midwifery. Here, nurses who have received advanced training can register as an independent practitioner and can fully manage a normal labor and birth. In public health and in some rural areas of New Zealand nurses are also able to give immunizations without a doctor's authority. Nurse income, with the exception of some midwives, is generally about half that of medical practitioners.

Care for the Elderly

A major area of health care expenditure is on long-term for the elderly. About 63% of all expenditure on disability support services is directed to older people with disabilities and approximately

90% of this is used to provide full or partial subsidies to 26,300 who are in residential rest home care. While prior to July 1, 1993, the majority of these individuals were fully subsidized, individuals are now income- and asset-tested. The overall proportion of women in rest homes is 54:1,000 population over 65 years, which is more than twice the rate of men. The rate of women in private hospital is 21:1,000 and men are 12:1,000. More than 80% of spouses of private hospital residents and 53% of spouses of rest home residents continued to live in their own homes. There is increasing interest in supporting individuals to allow greater reliance on home care to institutional care.

Long-term care for the elderly is provided in public and private hospitals, nursing homes, and in the home. Nursing homes and hospitals are inspected annually, and elderly are classified as to the level of care required. Nursing homes are contracted to provide care to people at the different levels. The cost of care until recently has been organized between the Departments of Social Welfare and Health. However it is now to be coordinated and purchased by the regional health authorities. Elderly people in public hospitals for long-term care turn over their pension (less a small allowance) for their care. Those in private nursing homes and hospitals must pay for their care until their income including assets is below a certain level (currently $6,000). This requires many elderly to sell their homes. Once their income is at this level they are able to obtain a government subsidy for their care. The cost of many nursing homes and hospitals exceeds this subsidy and sometimes when people meet this threshold they have to change premises. Private nursing homes and hospitals are run by church groups, and not-for-profit and for-profit organizations. Medical input to the nursing homes and hospitals is generally provided by a local general practitioner.

Care in the home is provided in the form of home help, nursing care, and meals on wheels. Home help and meals on wheels are organized and subsidized by the local CHE. Generally, nursing services are provided free. There has been some concern expressed that this is financially advantageous to those living within the community. The concern is an equity issue: those who remain in the community are able to receive highly subsidized services without their assets and incomes being touched whereas those who require inpatient services are asset- and income-tested.

Care for the Mentally Ill and Impaired

Historically the mentally ill were cared for in specialized psychiatric institutions. Now their acute care is in general public hospitals. Few patients have access to private inpatient care. Those with chronic mental illness are steadily being returned to live in the community. Here their care is coordinated by either the local CHE or community-based trusts—a recent development in the care of the mentally ill. The trusts contract with the regional health authorities to care for the mentally ill on discharge. Providing adequate housing is the main problem these services have to address. Currently mental health services in some areas have major staff shortages, particularly in nursing and medical staff.

Unlike other outpatient services, there is no charge for people to attend psychiatric outpatients. This is seen as creating a disincentive for people to have their care managed in the primary care setting where they would have to pay for a consultation. The fee-for-service payment in general practice also acts as a disincentive for general practitioners to care for the mentally ill.

The mentally handicapped have also moved from specialized hospital settings to the community. In the main their community care is coordinated by the Intellectually Handicapped Corporation (IHC). The recent reforms have posed particular problems for organizations like the HIC, which have traditionally provided a national service. Under the reforms, they now have to negotiate with four regional authorities and it is possible that this will provide different levels of service regionally. Community groups working with both the mentally ill and mentally impaired are also dependent on annual public charitable appeals to subsidize the services they provide.

Care of Infants

The Plunket Society of New Zealand contracts to provide a standardized service of infant welfare to all babies born in New Zealand. Plunket is a voluntary organization that works independent of other primary providers, although in most situations a complementary relationship exists with local general practitioners. Public health services have contracts to provide infant welfare in some rural settings and for high-risk families in some urban settings.

Public Health

Public health services consist of population-based strategies designed to prevent disease, prolong life, and promote health. It includes strategies such as programs to encourage healthy lifestyles, to ensure the provision of safe food and water, and to control epidemics of disease. Under the 1993 health reforms the government created the Public Health Commission as a Crown entity, at arm's length from the government, with a brief to monitor the state of public health and to identify public health needs, to advise the minister of health on matters relating to public health and to purchase or arrange for the purchase of public health services. The Public Health Commission purchases services—rather than providing them directly—by entering into contracts with providers such as Crown Health Enterprises (CHEs) and other private and public sector agencies. The PHC also serves as the agent of the director-general of health by purchasing the services of designated officers who are responsible for public health regulation and its enforcement.

Following a review in late 1994, a decision was made to abolish the PHC as a separate entity and to integrate its functions and staff into the Ministry of Health, leaving responsibility for purchasing with the Regional Health Authorities. Responsibility for advising on public health priorities has been added to the existing responsibilities of the Core Services Committee allowing issues of priority setting to now span the areas of both public and personal health services.

Local authorities also provide some health services. In particular they cater to the hygiene of premises, and the disposal of waste. The Department of Labour has the role of ensuring occupational health and safety. This role extends to public health where there is a role with the management, use, and storage of many chemicals used in industry.

Analysis of the Reforms

New Zealand's health reforms consisted of a set of structural changes aimed to promote greater efficiency, limit the government's resource commitment to the sector, and provide opportunities for individuals to supplement access to a basic core with supplementary private spending. Public understanding concerning the rationale and nature of the reforms has been poor, with attention focused primarily on structural rather than functional issues. Limited appreciation exists of the wider economic, social, and public sector reform context within which the health reforms were developed, and considerable skepticism exists among the public concerning the magnitude of gains that the reforms will deliver.

Much effort to date has been spent in establishing new structures and contracting arrangements among funders, purchasers, and providers of health care. These processes have taken far more time and resources than was originally anticipated. In the short term, the RHAs rolled over existing services and aspects of the former open-ended health benefits system that will remain for some time. The CHEs have only experienced limited competition from private providers. The government has been required to making further injections of funds to assist CHEs in trying to address their financial difficulties. The decisions to roll over various aspects of funding, purchasing, and service delivery was a political and pragmatic response to a sector undergoing turbulence and structural change. At the same time, limited changes to the level and mix of services and service providers has led critics of the reforms to argue that resources needed for health care services are being diverted to higher administrative and management expenditures.

Efficiency

Of all the policy goals, the pursuit of efficiency, particularly through greater competition in provision and purchasing, must be seen as a major strategy of the reform proposals. The most important achievement of the reforms to date has been their ability to integrate the funding for primary and secondary care, including disability support services, under a single public purchaser. This integration of funding, together with greater competition and ease of entry into the market for service provision, has the potential to enable major shifts in resources among service categories, and to foster innovation in the way services are provided.

In the health reform proposals, choice was to be enhanced on a number of separate fronts. The introduction of greater competition in service provision was expected to facilitate individuals being able to access services more suited to their needs. Moreover, the potential for the entry of several competing purchasers and for supplementation allowed greater scope for individual preferences to be addressed than did the previous system with its emphasis on monopoly funding, purchasing, and provision. Competition was deemed to be a major force in driving greater efficiency into the health care system. While some providers will compete on the basis of price, in other cases competition will occur along other dimensions such as quality and technology. Evidence already exists of providers introducing new technologies to increase market share. While technological advances may bring about service enhancements and greater efficiency in resource use, they may alternatively increase service costs with limited associated health gains.

The health service reforms were designed to reduce the government's exposure to fiscal risk and to provide some opportunities to shift and share risk to individuals, employers, and providers of health care. Fiscal pressures have and will continue to offer potential for health policy strategies to become fixed on short term goals of cost-containment and cost-shifting over strategies for improving allocative and technical efficiency.

Equity

The equity goal implicit in the reformed health care system is to provide all citizens with reasonable access to agreed core health services according to their health need. Emphasis is placed on equal access to core services rather than equal outcomes or expenditure. An element of the strategy has been the goals of directing the government's limited resources to those who have poor health status and limited private resources. Clarification and uniformity of public entitlement has been considered an important ingredient in producing a fairer system, one that allows individuals greater certainty as to the nature and limits of state support and the capacity to supplement public expenditure with private resources.

While issues surrounding access to health care are often debated in financial terms, consideration should also be given to socioeconomic, locational, and cultural dimensions. Cultural barriers and low socioeconomic status contribute to the poor access of Maori to appropriate health care. Health indicators for Maori while improving are still consistently lower than those for the New Zealand population as a whole. Separate delivery systems in some areas for Maori are seen as a necessary part of a strategy to encourage more appropriate delivery. Support among some Maori for the concept of health care plans stems from the belief that this would empower them and enhance their control over resources.

Implicit in the design of the reforms is the view that fairness will be promoted by clarifying the rights of individuals to basic health care funded by the government while not interfering with the ability of individuals to supplement this with private resources.

Choice and the Role of Core Services

The National Advisory on Core Health and Disability Support Services has proposed four criteria to determine the circumstances when the services should be publicly funded for an individual: (1) benefit or effectiveness of the service; (2) value for money or cost-effectiveness; (3) fairness in access and use of the resource; and (4) consistency with community values. The baseline or "implicit core" of services includes broad general areas of primary care, secondary and tertiary medical and surgical services, mental health services, and disability support services. Within this baseline, by mid-1995, more than twenty areas of health care or disability support services have been systematically evaluated.

In concept, core services should be closely related to that of "cost-effective interventions" and does not sit comfortably alongside the concept of a list of services universally available "as of right." Core services link patient characteristics, health care conditions, and statements of likely benefits from the health care intervention. Increasingly the concept is being operationalized through practice guidelines and protocols. Practice guidelines and protocols are being developed by consensus conferences made up of a range of experts in a given field. These have been held in areas of high total costs, where there is public concern about an issue, where there is information available, and where there is a chance of reaching a consensus. To date, more than twenty areas have been reviewed (Edgar 1995).

Concepts of core are also difficult to relate to the identification of the ''priority areas'' of child, Maori, mental, and physical environmental health, as defined in the purchasing agreements of RHAs. Concepts of priority areas within the purchase agreements do not serve to link health care outputs effectively to outcomes (in terms of improvements in or lack of deterioration in health status). Priority areas merely identify particular groups or services. They do not make effective linkages between the attributes of individuals receiving services, the characteristics of the services, and the health outcomes attributable to such services. They do not provide guidance as to where the best value for money can be obtained from marginal health care dollars. Moreover, it appears that the funder's requirements upon RHAs to give attention to priority areas is subject to the availability of resources. To hold purchasers accountable for the delivery of services, it will be necessary to specify service outputs as opposed to outcomes. It is clearly impossible to hold purchasers accountable for improvements in the health status of particular groups in light of the multitudinous health and nonhealth factors that may impinge on health status.

In seeking moves to improve results in the areas of efficiency and effectiveness, the role and activities of the Core Services Committee on Health and Disability Support Services seems somewhat problematical. The Committee has played a useful facilitative role in engaging provider, purchasers, and the public in debate about the concepts of core services. However, its role is merely that of an adviser to the minister and to RHAs. Its recommendations are not binding on RHAs, nor are they costed to ensure affordability to the government.

Inability to clarify the core has contributed to a lack of policy clarity concerning the ideal interfaces between the public and private sectors in the areas of funding, purchasing, and providing. Greater recognition is required of the complex interrelationships between health outputs and outcomes, and policy clarity is needed so as to see the separate and collective responsibilities and accountabilities for health outputs and outcomes. Many of the processes established to obtain public input on priority-setting are taking place in an expenditure vacuum. There has been too much attention given to identifying where additional resources are needed and too little to the identification of resources that should be shifted from other areas of health care. There is a risk that such exercises primarily serve to raise expectations concerning access and provide a poor basis for making decisions on how to shift limited resources between services. Of particular concern is the preoccupation of various groups with total needs assessment. Greater emphasis should be placed on weighing up the merit of shifting resources between services to the point where, for the last dollar spent on each service, the marginal benefit gained is equalized.

Variation in service entitlements across different parts of the country provided a major impetus for the policy guidelines that underpin the contracts between the Ministry of Health and the RHAs as purchasers. Yet the Core Services Committee and the Ministry of Health have adopted, in general, a conservative stance concerning the feasibility and desirability of adopting a well-defined core. Further research, discussion, and debate about priorities and priority-setting techniques are required as is a clearer concept of core services. Explicitness regarding entitlement to public funding is required whether or not competitive purchasers are introduced into the health care system. The job of determining a basic public entitlement to health care and managing a process for addressing competing claims for services are key tasks for the Ministry of Health, which carries primary responsibility for policy advice.

While the reforms are designed to provide greater explicitness in the concept of an individual's entitlement to core services, progress to date has been slow in delineating the boundary between core and noncore services. Such delineations will require new approaches for setting priorities across services and the design of strategies that ensure that all dollars spent on health care are put to best use. Lack of explicitness as regards service and expenditure priorities will limit opportunities to make the government and RHAs more accountable for their performance as purchasers.

Conclusion

The New Zealand reforms were ambitious in their design and in their timing. In terms of international precedents, while the basic system shares many features in common with that in the United Kingdom, the 1991 reforms drew their inspiration from the Dekker reforms in the Netherlands with their provision for competition in purchasing and opportunities for individuals to supplement the core health entitlement. New Zealand currently has deferred consideration of any moves to competitive purchasing and to this extent resemble the U.K. reforms. While there are unlikely to be competitive purchasers of a comprehensive core in the near future, there has been considerable growth in the degree of subpurchasing of services. One example is that of Independent Practice Associations, groups of general practitioners who contract with purchasers to deliver a comprehensive primary care service. The largest of these in operation is the Pegasus Group, based in Christchurch, which consists of 190 practitioners.

The current hold on proposals for competitive purchasing has now made the New Zealand reforms resemble those in the United Kingdom to a greater degree, though substantial differences exist. GP fund-holding, while growing substantially in the United Kingdom, is still in its early stages in New Zealand. In part this reflects the absence of a history of contracting between GPs and the government, the absence of a tradition of individual enrollment with general practitioners and an unwillingness of general practitioners to be funded by a formula based on capitation.

Implementation of the health reforms when viewed as "implementation as a process" is clearly under way, though more could be done to evaluate the process and learn about how to undertake efficient implementation. Implementation of the health reforms in terms of the second concept—"the accomplishment of a set of achievements which can be demonstrated"—needs further attention, including care in ensuring that the policy does not "drift" or become diverted in terms of its original goals.

There is little available by way of a comprehensive evaluation of the impacts of the reforms. Moreover, information on the details of purchasing agreements and performance is difficult to uncover within the public domain. Careful independent evaluation of reforms would form a useful part of any strategy to guarantee achievements and results. In the case of the health reforms, successful policy implementation defined as "the achievement of results" requires the objective demonstration of significant gains from the health reforms when evaluated against set criteria such as equity, efficiency, a greater role for the individual, quality, and accountability.

With the structures now in place, it is time to address issues surrounding expenditure priorities across services, and modifications to and innovation in service delivery. While the government has wished to encourage private sector purchasers and providers to spur the competition which it sees as a major strategy for greater efficiency, there is need for a regulatory environment to shape this more competitive market for purchasers and providers. Higher levels of servicing and expenditure by some groups may contribute to rising expectations as to the level of public sector resources that should be made available.

The health reforms introduced greater separation in the roles of funding, purchasing, and providing as part of a strategy to promote greater efficiency, enhanced accountability, and improved transparency. Key to the design was the ability to deliver greater uniformity and transparency of entitlement to publicly funded core health services. This clarity would allow individuals the opportunity to extend coverage beyond the core through the purchase of efficient private supplementary insurance coverage.

A clearer delineation of the operational meaning of the "government's guarantee of access to core health services on fair terms" is urgently required. While contracts and service conditions that are specified too precisely run the risk of locking in technology and stifling both innovation and efficiency, there are problems with a publicly funded core that is poorly defined. Lack of clarity in the definition of core limits opportunities for promoting efficiency and equity of access, delays a move to competition among purchasers, and thwarts the efforts of individuals to buy efficient supplementary care from competing private insurers. More recently, growing support for regional variation of the core within a national specification serves to change the concept of universal and uniform national entitlement. Dual accountability has resulted as purchasers seek to serve both funders and their communities.

Greater contestability in purchasing has limited the capacity of RHAs to demonstrate themselves to be "smart purchasers." Without pressures from competitors, they have had reduced scope to demonstrate their contribution to efficiency and effectiveness. The more the system becomes constrained and unable to shift care from hospitals to the community and to challenge old ways of delivering care, the less chance there will be that the additional administrative costs associated with the separation of purchasing and providing will be translated into efficiency gains. Because community care has been less subsidized than hospital care, these shifts have important impacts on the requirements for public funding or alternatively a more substantial element of part-charging. Also, there is little guarantee that the amount of resource which a government is willing to commit to health care will necessarily ensure a level of resource that will fund all cost-effective interventions. Existing contracts between the Ministry of Health and the RHAs indicate that future levels of funding will only grow in response to population changes. This suggests that despite growing resources being devoted to the search for cost efficiency and effectiveness, there is limited potential for further resources—even if they could be justified in terms of efficiency—to come from the public purse.

Problems with implementing the move to contestable purchasing, if not public reform pressures themselves, have led to neglect of the important public-private interface in the reforms. The public policy goals of efficiency, effectiveness, and choice have become transformed to a more modest objective of getting better value from limited public sector resources. In some cases, attention and concern to issues of efficiency and effectiveness appears to have become relegated to a position of lesser importance relative to policy goals concerning public sector cost containment, greater targeting of public dollars, and improved risk-sharing arrangements. The nature of the public entitlement and a clarification of the regulatory environment in which competition in funding, purchasing, and providing will take place is imperative if the policy clarity, transparency, and accountability that inspired the reforms is to become a reality. Given fiscal constraints, this search for the nature of the public entitlement must be effectively linked to the budget constraint. This task is beyond the reach of an advisory committee and must be seen as the single most important task of the Ministry of Health, as key adviser to the government on health policy matters.

The New Zealand reforms have occurred in an environment that is severely cost-constrained. Ambiguity remains as to whether the reformed health care system aims to confer universal entitlement to public funding of a core or whether policies are in fact moving toward a much greater targeting of government assistance to those unable to access care through their own resources. Whichever of these strategies is to prevail, the slow progress in getting clarity and transparency in the core and an appropriate regulatory environment for the development of private sector funding and purchasing is limiting the full potential for gains across those policy goals—such as efficiency, equity, and choice—that were the very inspiration for the reforms.

REFERENCES

Edgar, Wendy. 18–19 May 1995. Publicly funded health and disability services. Paper presented to the International Seminar on Health Care Priority Setting, Birmingham, Alabama.

Gibbs, A., et al. 1987. *Unshackling the Hospitals: Report of the Task Force on Hospitals and Related Services.* Wellington.

Health Benefits Review. 1986. *Choices for Health Care.* Wellington, Government Printer, 129.

McKendry, C. G., and D. Mutumala. 1995. *Health Expendi-*ture Trends in New Zealand: 1980–1994. Wellington, Performance and Monitoring Unit, Ministry of Health.

Minister of Health. July 1991. *Green and White Paper, Your Health and the Public Health.* Wellington.

Ministry of Health. 1993. *Post Election Briefing Ministry of Health.* Vols. 1 and 2. Wellington.

N/e/r/a (National Economic Research Associates). May 1993. *The Health Care System: New Zealand.* 64pp.

Salmond, G., and G. Mooney, eds. 1994. *Health Policy.* Special Issue on New Zealand Health Reforms, vol. 29.

Table 1 Total Population by Age, Race, Sex, and National Origin

Age	Female	Male	Total	Maori	Non-Maori
0–4	135,654	141,492	277,146	62,004	215,142
5–14	247,521	258,975	506,496	101,043	405,453
15–44	796,902	788,007	1,584,909	213,084	1,371,825
45–64	311,961	313,635	625,596	47,757	577,839
65 +	219,333	160,443	379,776	10,959	368,817
Total	1,711,371	1,662,552	3,373,923	434,847	2,939,076

SOURCE: 1991 New Zealand Census data as published in *New Zealand Hospital Sector Performance* 1983–92.

Table 2 Live Births, Birth Rate, Fertility Rate, and Infant Mortality

Year	Total live births	Birth rate*	Fertility rate	Infant Mortality**
1991	60,001	17.62	2.61	8.4

*Per 1,000 mean population
**For 1990
SOURCE: Yearbooks 1993 and 1994.

Table 3 Infant Mortality Rate by the Six Most Common Causes

Cause of Death	Rate per 1,000 live births
1. Perinatal causes	2.57
2. Sudden Infant Death Syndrome	2.45
3. Congenital Abnormalities	2.35
4. Accidents, Poisonings, Violence	.32
5. Diseases of Respiratory System	.28
6. Diseases of the Nervous System	.20

SOURCE: Yearbook 1994.

Table 4 Estimated Death Rates per 100,000 Population for the Fifteen Leading Causes of Death

Cause of death	Rates per 100,000 of mean population 1991
1. Malignant neoplasm	201.1
2. Ischemic heart disease	199.7
3. Cerebrovascular disease	78.8
4. Other forms of heart disease	33.5
5. Pneumonia	32.4
6. Other diseases of respiratory system	28.5
7. Motor vehicle accidents	20.2
8. Diseases of arteries, arterioles, and capillaries	19.2
9. All other accidents	14.0
10. Suicide and self-inflicted injury	14.0
11. Bronchitis, emphysema, and asthma	12.6
12. Diabetes mellitus	11.9
13. Hypertensive disease	7.3
14. Congenital abnormalities	6.0
15. Birth injury, difficult labor, and other causes of perinatal death	4.7

SOURCE: Yearbook 1994.

Table 5 Selected Operative (Surgical) Procedures: Number per Thousand Population, and Average Length of Stay in Hospital for Each Type of Operation

Number per thousand population	Average Length of Stay in Public Hospital	
	1982–83	1991–92
Appendectomy	5.5	4.5
Cholecystectomy	12.8	8.5
Extracapsular extraction of lens	6.2	2.6
Mastectomy (simple)	14.1	8.3
Partial excision large intestine	20.9	16.5
Repair inguinal hernia	5.6	2.9
Total hip replacement	21.1	18.0
Transurethral resection prostate	24.2	14.2

Table 6 Income from Work of Medical Workforce* by Gender, 1991, in NZ dollars

	Median Income	Average	Proportion Self-Employed
General Practitioner			
male	70,002	61,692	68.4
female	56,304	53,001	56.8
Medical officer			
male	47,616	46,668	2.0
female	34,863	35,043	1.0
Surgeon			
male	70,002	66,627	24.2
female	45,834	47,502	—
Physician			
male	70,002	64,128	15.5
female	55,002	50,589	6.1
Gynecologists and obstetricians			
male	70,002	67,632	.30
female	69,999	61,665	.33

*Statistics on income include full-time employees only whereas those on employment status include both full- and part-time.
SOURCE: Statistics from the 1991 New Zealand Census of Population and Dwellings.

Table 7   Number of Acute Care General Hospitals by Number of Beds (Public Only)

under 100	12
101–200	12
201–300	8
301–400	5
over 400	11

SOURCE: Appendix 12, *Core Services for 1995/ 96.*

Table 8   Not available.

Table 9   Number of Licensed Old People's Homes and Number of Beds per Facility in New Zealand

Region	Licensed Homes	No. of Beds
Auckland	248	7,485
Hamilton	144	4,476
Wellington	199	5,257
Christchurch	140	4,285
Dunedin	78	2,034
Total	809	23,537

Table 10 National Health Expenditures in NZ dollars by Type of Expenditure, Year ending June 30, 1994: $(000)

Expenditure	Public*	ACC	Local Govt.	Total Public	Out of Pocket	Health insurance	Charitable organs	Total private	Total
Institutional Care									
Public institutions									
Surgical and medical	1,631,434	138,866		1,770,300	11,349	4,517	1,352	17,218	1,787,518
Care of older people	284,391			284,391					284,391
Mental health	178,418			178,418					178,418
Dental	31,497			31,497					31,497
Maternity	233,976			233,976					233,976
Disability Support	254,499			254,499					254,499
Other	10,850			10,850		712	4	716	11,566
Private institutions									
Surgical and medical	5,112	23,498		28,610	94,967	178,301		273,268	301,878
Care of older people	292,829			292,829	246	513	1,030	1,788	294,617
Mental health	2,343			2,343	2,307		1,029	3,336	5,678
Disability Support	66,971			66,971		69		69	67,040
Other	2,573			2,573	4,002	210		4,212	6,785

Table 10 *(continued)*

Expenditure	Public*	ACC	Local Govt.	Total Public	Out of Pocket	Health insurance	Charitable organs	Total private	Total
Community Care									
General practitioner services	243,737	96,769		340,506	183,073	62,115		245,188	585,693
Midwife	62,362			62,362					62,362
Specialist	10,949			10,949	69,566	28,398		97,964	108,913
Referral services									
Diagnostic	11,423	47,398		58,821	13,490	19,680		33,170	91,991
Physiotherapy		49,081		49,081	35,149	5,730		40,879	89,960
Laboratory	135,774			135,774	691	140		831	136,605
Other	5,532	8,774		14,306	79,035	32		79,067	93,373
Dental	24,540	10,477		35,017	212,035	23,170		235,205	270,222
Medicaments	655,647	1,543		657,190	295,734	40,437	106	336,277	993,467
Disability Support	76,004			76,004					76,004
Other	56,988			56,988	6,888	16,581	8	23,478	80,466
Public Health Services									
Health protection	22,184		33,891	56,075			1,526	1,526	57,601
Health promotion	24,028			24,028		34	6,100	6,134	30,162
Teaching and Research									
Teaching	89,383			89,383	2,000		1,961	3,961	93,344
Research	54,004			54,004			6,194	6,194	60,198
Total Health Care	4,520,712	376,406	33,891	5,119,500	1,010,531	382,179	19,310	1,412,019	6,531,520
Total as a % of GDP	5.625	.67	.07	6.37	1.26	.48	.20	1.76	8.12

*Includes Vote Health and other government departments.
SOURCE: *Health Expenditure Trends in New Zealand, 1980–1994.*

The Health System of Sweden

STEFAN HÅKANSSON AND SARA NORDLING

Introduction

Health care is regarded as an important part of the Swedish welfare system. A fundamental principle being that all citizens have the right to good health and of care on equal terms, regardless of where they live and their economic circumstances. The following conditions are especially characteristic for the Swedish health care system:

- It is mainly a public responsibility.
- This public responsibility belongs to regional political authorities—the county councils—whose members are elected every fourth year concurrent with the general and municipal elections.
- The county councils levy taxes directly on the population, other sources of income are national government grants and dues charges by the county councils for certain services.
- The health care system is supported by a national health insurance system and other social welfare services.

Sweden is a constitutional monarchy with a parliamentary form of government. Since 1974 the king has only ceremonial functions. The highest decision-making body is the Swedish Parliament (Riksdagen), which is directly elected every fourth year. The country is sparsely populated, but in land area, Sweden is the fourth largest country in Europe. The population of 8.8 million is mainly concentrated in the coastal regions and in the south. About 18% of the population is over 65 years of age. Average life expectancy is 75.5 years for males and 80.8 years for females (1993).

For many centuries, Sweden was ethnically very homogenous. Previously most immigrants came from the other Nordic countries. Today refugees and relatives of already immigrated people domi-nate the picture. More than one million of the population of 8.8 million are immigrants or have at least one immigrant parent. About 80% of the Swedish population belong to the Lutheran State Church. The many immigrants who have settled in Sweden have also brought their religions with them.

By international standards, health in Sweden is relatively good. Infant mortality rate is the lowest in the OECD countries, about 4.8 deaths per 1,000 in the first year of life (1993). The birthrate has varied greatly during the last decades. In the 1950s the birth rate was 16.4 per 1,000 population. Toward the end of the 1970s the birthrate was reduced to 11.7. Later on the trend changed and in the beginning of the 1990s the rate was 14.5 (see Table 2).

Full employment has always had priority in Swedish labor market policy. Until now that policy has been relatively successful, especially in comparison with other countries. Of Sweden's 8.8 million inhabitants, 4.3 million are in the labor force, of whom almost 50% are women. In the beginning of 1995 about 7.5% of the labor force were unemployed; if we include the people within labor market programs (hidden unemployment) the unemployment rate was about 13%.

The Nordic countries—Denmark, Finland, Iceland, Norway, and Sweden—are closely linked by the common background of their languages, culture, and their common historical roots and development. They have a long traditions of cooperation, for example, the Nordic Council, which is an advisory body to the Nordic parliaments and governments. The Council deals with questions concerning cooperation between the Nordic countries in economic, legislative, social, and cultural fields and regarding environmental protection and communications. An agreement established in 1954 enables Nordic nationals to work and to settle in another Nordic country without permit or permanent residence permit.

That Sweden has not been involved in any war, invaded, or bombed since 1809 makes the country quite unique. One of the most important foreign policies for Sweden is its neutrality. Even though Sweden joined the European Union January 1, 1995, the policy of nonparticipation in military alliances continues.

The National Level of Health Care

The Swedish Government has the responsibility for ensuring that the health care system develops efficiently according to its overall objectives, based on the goals and the constraints of social welfare policy and macroeconomic factors. As noted later, the dominance of the central government is compromised by the autonomous position of the counties and municipalities. The measures that the government has at its disposal for controlling development within health and medical care are primarily financial control measures, legislation, supervision, the granting of permits, and sanc-tions. The government is also responsible for the majority of research and significant parts of training.

Unlike most other countries Swedish ministries are relatively small units. The ministries are mainly concerned with preparing different bills regarding budget, new laws and regulations and also drawing up general guidelines in such fields as health care, social welfare services, and health insurance. The actual work of implementing and administering the government's decisions is en-trusted to a number of central administrative agencies. It is their work to follow up and evaluate what is going on in their respective sectors, to function as professional expert agencies and to carry through different government programs.

Under the Ministry of Health and Social Affairs (Socialdepartementet) come the National Board of Health and Welfare (Socialstyrelsen), the Medical Products Agency (Läkemedelsverket), the National Social Insurance Board (Riksförsäkringsverket), the National Institute of Public Health (Folkhälsoinstitutet), The Swedish Council of Technology Assessment in Health Care (Statens Beredning för Utvärdering av Medicinsk Metodik, SBU), and certain other smaller agencies.

The National Board of Health and Welfare, which is the central administrative agency for matters concerning health care and social welfare services, is one of the most important organizations within the health care sector. Its tasks include: (1) supervising, following up, and evaluating developments in all areas of social policy, including health care, and the quality thereof; (2) being a center of knowledge in the field of health and social policy; and (3) being the government's expert body in this field.

The Federation of County Councils (Landstingsförbundet), which is a joint interest organization representing the county councils, handles negotiations with the national government on political and economic questions affecting the relations between national and regional levels and trade unions regarding salaries and working conditions of health care personnel. The Federation is not subordinate to the national government or any of their administrative agencies (see Fig. A). In recent decades the Federation has increased its influence on health care development, not in any formal way, but depending on the political strength of its guidelines and recommendations. Political representatives of the county councils (the executive committee) meet monthly to discuss health policy issues and important economic questions. Like the county councils, the municipalities have formed a joint organization on the national level: the *Swedish Association for Local Authorities.*

Figure A   The Organization of Health Care Services in Sweden

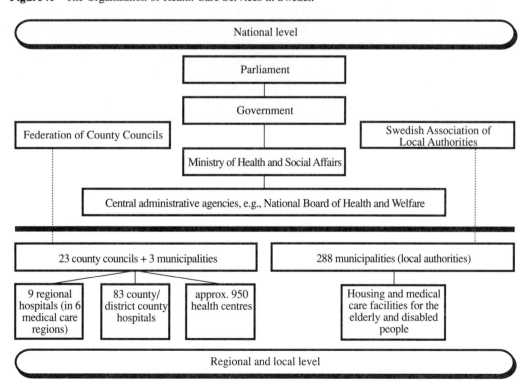

The Regional and Local Levels of Health Care

Responsibility for health care in Sweden, both inpatient and ambulatory services, belongs to twenty-three county councils and three large municipalities, which are not part of the county councils' areas. These units, with populations ranging from some 60,000 to 1,700,000, are also responsible for the care of the physically and mentally disabled, and for dental care through the Public Dental Service. Each county is governed by a local council, which is elected every fourth year. The main source of revenue for the counties is the direct local income tax, which the residents have to pay. The county councils were established in the 1860s, mainly to operate hospitals for somatic illnesses. Over the years their health care tasks have expanded. In the mid-1960s they took over from central government the responsibility for outpatient services (which includes all general practitioners) and psychiatric care. *The Health and Medical Services Act* of 1983 (Hälso- och sjukvårdslagen) extended still further the areas of responsibility of the county councils. Health care now accounts for approximately three-fourths of the total expenditure of most county councils. Responsibility for social welfare services and for environmental hygiene, as well as for schools and housing, rests primarily with the municipalities. These are 288 in number with populations ranging from about 5,000 to 700,000. Like the counties, the municipalities are governed by a locally elected council.

The work of both the municipalities and the county councils is regulated by legislation. The Social Service Act emphasizes the right of the individual to receive municipal services at all stages of life. The Health and Medical Services Act states that health care shall be available to all members of society, thus ensuring a high standard of general health and care for everyone on equal terms. The Act requires county councils to plan the development and organization of the health care system with reference to the aggregate need of the county population. This planning must also include the health care provided by private practitioners, industrial health physicians, and so forth.

Local self-government has a long tradition in Sweden. The municipalities and county councils enjoy a considerable degree of autonomy vis-à-vis the state, compared with most other countries. Important to note is that the municipalities are not subordinate or accountable to the county councils (see Fig. A). The laws on social services and on health care allow the municipalities and the county councils great freedom to plan and organize their own services and impose taxes in order to finance them. In some respects you can say that Sweden has twenty-six different health care systems.

The Health Care System

Primary care is the basic level of care in the Swedish health care system. The function of primary care is to improve and maintain the health of the population and to treat illness and injuries which do not require hospitalization. The County Medical Services operate central county and district county hospitals for illness which requires hospital treatment. Rare and complicated illnesses are handled by the Regional Medical Services. Psychiatric care is also the responsibility of the County Medical Services. Today, it is becoming increasingly common for patients to continue living at home and visit psychiatric care centers or hospitals for preventive and treatment services.

Primary Care

The outpatient care is organized into primary care districts. Their task is to assume primary responsibility for the health of the population in their area. Each district has one or more local health care centers, about 950 in the whole country. At the health centers, district physicians, normally general practitioners but sometimes also specialists, provide medical treatment, advisory services and preventive care. Primary care is also provided by private doctors, physiotherapists, nurses, midwives; at district nurse clinics; and at clinics for child and maternity health care.

During recent years there has been a structural change in the work of the doctors in primary care—today all may choose a doctor, who has qualified as a general practitioner, as their own family doctor. The family doctor is responsible for providing the health services and medical care needed by persons listed with him or her. Efforts are being made to allow the sick and disabled to be cared for at home as much as possible. Nursing staff of the primary care services and municipally employed social welfare personnel work together in teams. They visit the sick or disabled in their homes and provide necessary services twenty-four hours a day.

Hospital Care

Sweden has about ninety acute hospitals, which are divided, according to their size and degree of specialization, into regional hospitals, central county hospitals and distrct county hospitals (size distribution is given in Table 7). County-level health care covers patients with critical conditions or other illnesses requiring access to resources that are concentrated in one or a few hospitals within each county. These county hospitals are divided into:

- *Central county hospitals* ($n = 28$) with fifteen to twenty specialties, usually one hospital for each county council area. These hospitals also serve as district hospitals for their neighborhood. The average number of short-term beds are 460 per hospital.
- *District county hospitals* ($n = 56$) with at least four specialties (internal medicine, surgery, radiology, and anesthesiology). The average number of short-term beds is 148 per hospital.

The regional medical care system is responsible for those patients whose problems require the collaboration of a large number of specialists. For such purposes, for example, there are neurosurgery, thoracic surgery, pediatric surgery, plastic surgery, and highly specialized laboratories. Sweden is divided into six medical care regions, each serving a population averaging more than one million. Their activities are regulated by agreements between the county councils within each region. In these six regions there are nine *regional hospitals,* which are highly specialized hospitals, affiliated with a medical school and also functioning as a research and teaching hospital. These hospitals are administered by its local county council and have an average number of 936 short-term beds per hospital, which is relatively large, compared to hospitals in other countries.

The top administrative structure of a Swedish hospital may differ somewhat between counties but the following description is very common. Every hospital has a chief executive officer (CEO) who has the total responsibility for all hospital activities, including balancing income and expenditures. In staff positions there are chief physicians who assist in planning and managing the hospital. The board of the hospital consists of about ten politicians, who are appointed for a period that corresponds to the term of general elections (since 1994, four years). During recent years there has been a slight increase in the percentage of CEOs who are physicians. Every medical department, both clinically and ancillary, has a chief physician or a head of department. The head of a department is, almost without exception, a doctor with the overall responsibility for the management of the clinic. This includes responsibility for both medical services and administration, finance, and personnel. The head of department has also in his management team a head nurse, a controller, and other chiefs within the department.

A relatively large proportion of the resources available for medical services have been allocated to the provision of care and treatment at the hospitals. This can be seen, for example, in the low number of visits to doctors per person and year (see Table A). The number of general practitioners is also low in relation to the total number of doctors, approximately 20%.

Extensive changes have been made in the area of psychiatric care during the last ten years. People with mental handicaps have, to a great extent, left the institutions and now live in the community. At the same time as reductions have been made in inpatient care, more outpatient and so-called alternative forms of care have been established.

The total domination of the county councils in the provision of the health services enables the county councils to make decisions on structural issues in the health services. During recent years considerable changes have taken place in this area, particularly the reduction in number of beds but also where other hospital activities are concerned, for example the reduction in the number of casualty wards open twenty-four hours a day. The reduction in the number of beds has been made possible by increases in productivity generated by new medical technology, shrinking financial resources, and incentives resulting from the development of financial management systems. The number of beds in short-term care has been reduced from 4.4 per 1,000 inhabitants in 1985 to 3.1 per 1,000 inhabitants in 1993. The corresponding figures for psychiatric care are 2.5 in 1985 and 1.2 in 1993 (see Table 8).

One example in the management of medical services is the introduction of a guarantee for patients that has been in force since 1992. This guarantee was the result of an agreement concluded on the national level by the minister of health and social affairs and the Federation of County Councils to reduce the waiting time for certain forms of treatment for which there were long waiting lists. The content of the guarantee is that, after an opinion has been given by a specialist, no patient needs to wait more than three months for treatment. If the waiting time is expected to be longer, the patient has right to secure treatment in another hospital be it in another county or even in a private hospital (see below).

Another recent significant change is the possibility for patients to choose where and by whom they wish to be given medical attention. Patients can choose the health center and/or family doctor and even which hospital they wish to use. If a patient wishes to have medical care at a hospital outside the county council in which he resides, a referral may be required, but freedom of choice covering the medical services of several county councils is available in several of the health care regions. Patients do not usually need a referral to obtain specialist hospital care; they can go directly to the hospital without going via the primary services. The primary level therefore does not always have a referral function. The method available to the county councils to influence the decisions of patients is, rather, to differentiate the fees patients have to pay.

Freedom of choice in some densely populated areas, (for example, in western Sweden) has resulted in considerable streams of patients to primary health centers and hospitals in other county councils. This has caused financial problems in some county councils as the money follows the patients. Many small and medium-size hospitals are trying to administer such care themselves that was earlier referred to larger hospitals. An explanation for this is that several county councils nowadays hold their health-care districts financially liable for all the health care, even specialist care at regional hospitals. The trend toward purchaser organizations which reimburse hospital treatment per case, also contributes to this development. Earlier, the incentives were rather the opposite. By a physician's referral to the central county or regional hospital, the cost for complicated cases could be transferred to somebody else.

As a supervisory authority, the National Board of Health and Welfare is responsible for monitoring the health and medical care services, regardless of whether these services or activities are under county council, local authority, or private management. The Board is specifically required to fulfill its responsibility in this respect through an active follow-up program.

Diffusion of High Technologies

There are no longer any central governmental regulations regarding acquisition of expensive technologies like CT and MRI scanners in public hospitals in Sweden. Each county council can decide to acquire such technology if there is a need and sufficient resources are available. However, central health care think tank agencies influence the diffusion pattern of new technologies by publishing planning, utilization, assessment, and diffusion studies. The first CT scanner was installed in Sweden at university level in 1973. At present, 125 CT scanners are installed, which is about 70,000 inhabitants per CT scanner. CT scanners are available at all acute care hospital levels in Sweden. In Sweden it took ten years from the introduction of CT until this method diffused to the smallest level of acute care hospitals—the local county (community) hospitals. (However, CT scanners are not yet available at all local county hospitals in the country.) It took fifteen years until a private CT scanner was introduced in Sweden.

The first MRI scanner in Sweden was installed in a university hospital in 1984. The diffusion pattern for MRI is as fast as for CT and at present 45 units are installed. This is about 200,000 inhabitants per MRI unit. Most of the MRI units are available at university and county hospital levels, and a few units are installed at the local county hospital level. In Sweden it took eight years from the introduction of MRI until the method diffused to the local county hospital level. It took five years until a private MRI unit was introduced in Sweden.

Regarding research-oriented diagnostic modalities like PET and SQUID cameras, we have at present only two PET scanners and one SQUID camera in Sweden, all at university level. Radiation therapy is very much centralized in Sweden. Radiation therapy equipment like linear accelerators and cobalt units are diffused only to sixteen hospitals (oncology centers) in Sweden.

Telemedicine is a general term and can be defined as "medicine at a distance," which in practice very often means "medical communications via telemedia." Telemedicine refers to a wide range of specific applications, usually named after a particular discipline: teledermatology, telepsychiatry, telecardiology, telesurgery, teleradiology, telepathology, telelogopedics, teleeducation, and teletraining. Teleradiology was introduced in Sweden in the beginning of the 1970s, in cooperation between three acute care hospitals in the most southern health care region in Sweden. In 1979, telepathology was tested between two hospitals, also in southern Sweden. Images were transmitted using television-technology. The transmission of radiology images through the telecommunication network was first introduced in Sweden in 1981. Teleradiology is the most diffused telemedicine method in the Nordic Countries at present with about 104 systems in hospitals and primary health care centers. This makes one teleradiology system per 220,000 inhabitants. Diffusion of teleradiology is most pronounced in Sweden with about 120,000 inhabitants per system.

The following list shows examples of telemedicine tests and applications in Sweden:

Radiology
Pathology
Echo-cardiology
Video-conferencing
Ship to shore
ECG from ambulance
Neurophysiology
Ophthalmology
Dental
Nuclear medicine

The interest for telemedicine is getting significantly larger in Sweden and many county councils are now planning to test telemedicine for different applications to medical, organizational, and economic experience.

Medical Practice

Just over 300,000 people are employed in the health services, that is, about 10% of all employees in the country. This number has diminished during recent years, partly due to the financial squeeze and changes in the work done by the services. There is a tendency that the number of doctors and nurses will increase at the expense of less qualified staff. There is a certain shortage of nurses, especially nurses with certain skills. In the beginning of 1995 there were about 700 unemployed physicians, which corresponds to an unemployment rate of 2.5%. However, at the same time it is difficult to recruit doctors to certain areas and to certain specialist fields.

Reimbursement to Physicians

The Swedish labor market is characterized by a very high degree of unionization, and physicians are no exception in this matter. The Swedish Medical Association, which is the union for the physicians, has during many decades been rather successful in negotiating physician incomes and work conditions. The Association has influenced the admission rate to medical school by arguing that there will be a surplus of physicians in the future. Approximately 50% of the members of the Association are also members of the Swedish Society of Medicine. The Society is a powerful scientific organization for physicians, which has as its main activity continuing medical education.

Most physicians in Sweden, both general practitioners and specialists, work as salaried employees in the primary care centers or hospitals with which they are affiliated. The salary of a hospital doctor with specialist qualification is, on average, SEK 35,400 per month including overtime pay (1993). The salary of a nurse is approximately SEK 14,400 per month including overtime pay (see Table 6). Working hours for Swedish physicians are normally forty hours a week, which are substantially below working hours for physicians in, for example, the United States (income for Swedish physicians is correspondingly also lower.) During the first part of this century, state-employed district medical officers were reimbursed partly by fixed salaries and partly by variable patient fees. Hospital physicians—employed by the state or the county council—received a fixed salary for inpatient care and usually supplemented it with fees from providing private care outside of, or within, the hospital. The fee for an outpatient visit varied according to the doctor's achievement, but after the visit the patient could receive three-fourths reimbursement from health insurance. For inpatient care the patient paid a fixed fee per day.

In 1970, the so-called seven-crown-reform was implemented. This was a health-insurance reform with the effect that the patients paid seven crowns to the county council for each outpatient visit to a physician or other health employee. The county council was then directly reimbursed by the health insurance authority for the remainder. The reform also implied that physicians, both in hospitals and in health centers, could not receive patient fees directly themselves but were compensated by an increase in salary from the county council in relation to qualifications and work schedule. The hospital physicians were put on regulated work schedules with fixed incomes. A result of this, however, was that physicians had no financial incentive to increase the number of patients in ambulatory care. New agreements also gave physicians successively increasing opportunities to be compensated in free time for extra work done when on call and at night.

The demand for health services increased, creating longer waiting periods, particularly within certain specialties (surgery; ear, nose, and throat; and psychiatry) while physicians' work contribution remained unchanged. To satisfy the increase in demand, more physicians were trained. In 1970, Sweden had about 10,600 practicing physicians (770 inhabitants per physician); at the beginning of 1995 there were 27,100 practicing physicians, of which 37% were female. Sweden, with 330 inhabitants per physician in 1995, is among the nations with the greatest number of physicians per population.

Visits to Doctors

Efforts have been made to improve primary care during the last decades. The proportion of visits to doctors taking place at local health care centers rather than at hospital-based clinics has changed from 42% in 1980 to 48% in 1993. The nature of these visits has also changed. An increasing amount of treatment is given by general practitioners employed by the health care center without the patient needing to be taken into hospital. The deliberate emphasis on outpatient forms of care also means that visits to medical staff other than doctors is encouraged. The number of visits to district nurses, nurses, and auxiliary nurses has more than doubled since 1980. During 1993 there were 27 million physician visits of which 5.2 million were done in private practice. This means that on average every Swede goes to a doctor 3.1 times a year, which is relatively low compared to other countries.

During the period 1985–91 the proportion of health care centers with four physicians rose from 15 to 20%, and those with five or more doctors rose from 27 to 32%, whereas the proportion of two-physician centers fell from 26 to 16%. Between 1986 and 1992 the number of inhabitants per existing general practitioner thus declined from an average of 3,160 to 2,550.

Private Health Care

Private health care exists only to a limited extent. The introduction of new reforms, for example, the family doctor and the county council's new obligation to pay for service provided by private

Table A   Visits to Doctors, 1993

	Visits to doctor (1,000s)	Doctor visits per person
Hospital-based physicians	10,641	1.2
Primary care physicians, incl. maternity and child health care	10,921	1.3
(visits to a general practitioner)	(9,529)	(1.1)
Private practitioners, incl. part-time practitioners	5,224	0.6
Total	26,786	3.1

SOURCE: Federation of Swedish County Council (1994).

doctors and physiotherapists, have increased the number of private practitioners. Less then 10% of the physicians work full-time in private practices and in the occupational health field. Besides this, many publicly employed physicians have private practices in their free time. When it comes to dental care, more than 50% of the dentists are working as private practitioners. A large share of the care provided by private undertakings is on the whole financed by public means. Physicians in private practice and in occupational health care receive fees from their patients for treatment and consultations, about the same fee as a visit to a doctor employed by a county council; they receive the remainder from the health insurance via the county councils.

There are only a few private hospitals for short-term care and they are, compared to the county hospitals, relatively small. From 1985 until 1994 the number of short-term beds provided by private hospitals has more than tripled, but still 95% of the total number of short-term beds are provided by the county councils. The private hospitals usually have contracts with the county councils and provide treatments in areas that have long waiting lists, such as coronary bypass surgery and orthopedic surgery. Only a small number of private hospitals are financed by private means such as patient fees and health care insurance. Until recently private health insurance was almost nonexistent, but the dissatisfaction with the waiting time and the service provided by the county councils increased the demand for private insurance. The only private health insurance that exists today is a supplementary insurance for employees in key positions to make sure that they do not have to wait for treatment when they get ill. The total market for private health insurance is only 0.2–0.3% of the total health care financing and only 2% of the total private financing.

Treatments at private hospitals where the patient pays for the whole treatment increased toward the end of the 1980s as a consequence of the long waiting time for some treatments. During the last couple of years these treatments have decreased: the waiting times for public hospital are not that long any more and many people are also in a more difficult economic situation. In a few cases, the county councils have made agreements with private health care providers, who sometimes rent premises from the county councils. The surgeons are mostly employed in public service and carry out private operations in off-duty hours.

During the period 1991–93 private contracts in the elderly care sector have increased fourfold and are now about 4% of the total expenditure for care of the elderly and disabled. About 60% of the municipalities have a contract with a home help service contractor, and about 50% have contracts for running special housing. These private contracts are more common in the big cities and suburbs.

Medical Education and Research

Medical education, like research, is entirely state-supported. Admission to a university medical school requires graduation from secondary school including subjects in natural science. Every year some nine hundred students start medical training programs. The basic study program at the medical schools is 5.5 years and is traditionally divided into preclinical, preparatory, and clinical periods. Doctors are trained at six university medical schools. Teaching hospitals, which also serve as regional hospitals, are affiliated with these schools.

After receiving their medical degree, all doctors must complete a 21-month period of general internship in order to obtain a license to practice. Thereafter most physicians complete postgraduate training programs of four to five years that qualify them as specialists or general practitioners. The National Board of Health and Welfare allocates appointment "blocks" for postgraduate training in accordance with a physician distribution program designed to reflect long-term national needs. There are no compulsory continuing education courses for doctors required. As soon as doctors are licensed they are entitled to practice medicine as long as they wish, unless the National Board of Health and Welfare had taken disciplinary actions. However, all medical specialists' organizations arrange several medical courses in order to enhance the doctors' knowledge and opportunity for promotions.

The program for nurses lasts three years and is available at some thirty nursing colleges, which are normally run by the county councils and which admit some 3,500 new students each year.

Swedish medical research has attracted much international attention and is characterized by close links between clinical and preclinical work. The central government covers half the costs of medical research, which in 1993 amount to almost SEK 4,300 million. Most state grants go to university institutions. The Medical Research Council receives about 10% of state disbursements in this field.

Quality and Safety

Some formal systems exist in health care to "guarantee" a minimum level of quality. These include the educational system, various professional licensing and qualification regulations, the National Medical Disciplinary Board, monitoring activities by the National Board of Health and Welfare, and county council committees (which deal with patient information and complaints). The structural organization of the health services and regulations that define the division of responsibility also serve the same purpose.

If, in connection with medical care or treatment, a patient suffers a serious injury or disease, or is exposed to the risk of injury or disease, the institution providing the care or treatment is obliged to report this fact to the National Board of Health and Welfare. Where faults or negligence are attributable to members of staff, the matter can be referred to the National Medical Disciplinary Board (Hälso- och sjukvårdens ansvarsnämnd), a government agency whose organization is somewhat similar to that of a court. A patient or a relative of a patient can approach the Board if he considers that staff working in the medical services have acted incorrectly. The Board can decide on disciplinary measures (warning and admonition) or remove the person from the professional register. The matter of financial compensation for a patient who has suffered an injury is not dealt with by the Board. There is a patients' insurance that covers such claims. The issue of holding staff responsible for their actions and deciding on sanctions is therefore kept separate from the issue of financial compensation for the patient.

There is no methodical process by which misadventures are identified in the Swedish system. The practical and professional part of quality control is related to supervision and evaluation of clinical work. The interest of staff working in the medical services on issues relating to quality has increased considerably during recent years. Improving quality is considered urgent in a situation in which resources are limited and where it has become all the more important to be able to demonstrate quality in the services that are offered, for example, if there is a purchaser-provider relationship and elements of competition. Quality committees at management level, sometimes with special officers responsible for quality, are working to produce systems to develop and improve quality.

The active follow-up program is one of the monitoring activities by the National Board of Health and Welfare. It is aimed at establishing a basis for assessing the extent to which health and medical care and social welfare objectives are being achieved, as well as identifying obstacles to the fulfillment of such objectives; facilitating the introduction of government measures designed to eliminate obstacles to the effective provision of high quality care; helping and encouraging caregivers to improve resource utilization; and supporting local follow-up and assessment activities.

Another government agency which is engaged in evaluation work is the Swedish Council of Technology Assessment in Health Care (SBU). It contributes toward the rational utilization of the resources allocated to the health services by evaluating both new and established methods from medical, social, and ethical perspectives.

Spri, the Swedish Institute for Health Services Development, is another important organization in the development of quality assurance. It focuses on developing methods and tools to improve quality, effectiveness, and efficiency in health care. This includes efforts to advance the appropriate application of information technology in health care. Spri's development projects involve departments, clinics, and basic organizational units in the health services. These projects have engaged people around the country in a common effort to synthesize experiences and lessons from local initiatives before making central decisions.

Sweden was the first country outside of the United States to adopt the consensus development conference as a method for technology assessment. The format of the Swedish conferences follows the U.S. National Institutes of Health model quite closely. Since 1982, twenty conferences have been arranged jointly by Spri and the Swedish Medical Research Council (MFR). The goal of each conference is to reach consensus among specialists from different disciplines concerning the safety, benefit, cost, and appropriate use of a particular medical technology. Practicing physicians, representatives of the lay public, health care administrators, and politicians often participate.

Dental Care

The Public Dental Service is responsible for the provision of dental services to children and young people, for specialist dental services and for the treatment of adults. The County Councils are also responsible for planning all dental services within their areas. The Public Dental Service includes hospital dental care. All children and young people up to the age of nineteen receive free dental care, with the emphasis on preventive care. The dental health of this group has improved considerably since the 1970s and continues to improve steadily. For adults there is a public dental insurance, which subsidizes dental care exceeding a cost of SEK 500 in any one year.

The national dental services also treats adult patients on the same conditions as do the private dentists. The county councils are responsible for ensuring that sufficient specialist dental care is available to meet the needs of both children and adults. Approximately half of all dentists work in the Public Dental Service, which is run by the county councils; the remainder are private dentists. (In 1992 there were 5,000 dentists, 1,800 dental hyginists, 9,600 dental nurses, and 480 dental technicians employed by the Public Dental Service.) The Public Dental Service also provides practical training for dental staff and still offers first-year residencies for newly qualified dentists.

Public Health

In 1990, Parliament resolved that "greater equality is to be an overriding objective in public health work. Measures improving the situation of the least privileged should be given first priority." Special attention is also to be paid to the health situation of children, young persons, and women. Parliament also resolved that specific health policy aims should be worked out by public authorities. Descriptions of health effects are to be included as far as possible in the decision-making documentation compiled by national authorities and within the cabinet offices and the ministries. The Parliament resolution also set up the National Institute of Public Health (Folkhälsoinstitutet), whose main task is to engage in health promotion and disease prevention at a national level, in close collaboration with the relevant national authorities, local bodies, and popular movements. Primary health care is responsible for public health within a limited scope. Doctors, usually general practitioners, are responsible for medical treatment, advisory service, and preventive care of the population in their area. Primary care also includes clinics for children, vaccinations, health checks, and consultations as well as certain types of treatments provided free of charge to all children under school age. At the maternity clinics there are both midwives and doctors. These clinics are visited by expectant mothers for regular checkups, which are free of charge during the entire pregnancy.

In the following section a short description of responsibilities for the public health work is given. Besides the below-mentioned groups, popular movements and voluntary organizations and enterprises play an important role in public health work.

National government. The role of the state is to guarantee a strategic health policy aimed at creating conditions for good health for all in the long run. By use of research and development several national registers have been created by which the state can monitor the health status of the population. But perhaps the most important instrument at the national level is the frameworks for public health set by legislation and supervision.

National Institute of Public Health. By creating the National Institute of Public Health in July 1992 the government established that practical public health work has a platform of its own. At the same time the development and implementation of public health was separated from the national government's role of legislation and supervision. The most important tasks for the national institute of public health are: (1) health promotion and disease prevention with special emphasis on disadvantaged groups; (2) to actively support local and regional public health work and foster cooperation at the national level; (3) to give public health work a scientific basis aimed at implementing research into practice; and (4) to put together and disseminate knowledge and experiences. By research grants the Institute has created a network with university institutions, county council units of community medicine, and municipalities. The Institute also has the responsibility to foster cooperation between different bodies and has therefore established a group of the chief executive officers of seventeen governmental agencies and the directors of the Federation of County Councils and the Swedish Association of Local Authorities. However, the borderlines of responsibility in public health work can never be clear-cut because of its broad scope, which covers many sectors in the society, county council units of community medicine, and municipalities.

National Board of Health and Welfare. After the establishment of the National Institute of Public Health, the National Board of Health and Welfare acquired the more distinguished role of monitoring the public health activities of county councils and municipalities. Within the Board there is an epidemiological center (EpC) with the responsibility for public health reporting and management of population-based national registers of diseases and causes of death. The Board is also responsible for development and management of recurrent and continuous follow-up and evaluation of the public health work at regional and local levels. Under the heading "Active follow-up" the Board is doing countywide follow-ups: health care, social services, public health, community medicine. Starting in 1994 the Board has issued a national Public Health Report. A decision has been made to publish a report every third year. Both the National Institute of Public Health and the National Board of Health and Welfare pay special attention to how public health work could be effected by the introduction of new ways of financing and organizing health care.

The county councils. The county councils have overall responsibility for the health status of their populations. This entails the responsibility to investigate and identify health risks, disseminate knowledge to various population groups, initiate and implement preventive measures, participate in health planning, document and evaluate public health efforts, as well as provide treatment services.

The municipalities. The wide range of services maintained by the municipalities are important factors governing the public health. Care for children under the age of seven, school education, care for the elderly and disabled, social services, culture and leisure activities are among the responsibilities that belong to the municipalities in Sweden. They are also duty-bound to inform the public of the risks associated with smoking, alcohol and drug abuse, and provide assistance and support for abusers. The World Health Organization–initiated "Healthy City Project" has inspired a network of about thirty-five counties and municipalities in Sweden. This network has put forward some principles for their public health work: Public health shall have political backup, be intersectoral, documented, and followed up, and have a long-range horizon.

Care of the Elderly

Meeting the social service and health care needs of the elderly is one of the cornerstones of the Swedish welfare state and an area that continues to be given priority. Sweden has the oldest population in the world. In December 1993, about 18% of the total population of 8.7 million were 65 and older and almost 2% were 85 and older. At the same time the average life expectancy was for a newborn girl 80.8 years and for a boy 75.5 years. The number of persons in the age group 65 and over will not change significantly between now and the year 2000. On the other hand, the numbers of the very oldest in the population are continuing to rise, as they have done for some time.

The Responsibility for Care

Since 1992 municipalities have had the main responsibility for social services and health care of elderly and disabled persons. The responsibility does not include the attendance of doctors but is

Table B   Old-Age Pensioners Aged 65 and above, 85 and above

	Male		Female		Total		% of total population	
Year	65+	85+	65+	85+	65+	85+	65+	85+
1993	651,142	50,547	884,975	116,259	1,536,117	166,806	17.5	1.9
2000	653,026	67,914	876,047	140,176	1,529,073	208,090	17.0	2.3
2025	926,830	94,480	1,101,756	154,968	2,028,586	249,448	21.2	2.6

SOURCE: Statistics Sweden, Statistical Yearbook of Sweden 1995.

limited to the type of housing and daily activity centers where the municipality is responsible for the activity. Earlier the responsibility was to some extent shared between the municipality and the county council. The government and Parliament have the responsibility of legislation and formulating guidelines for how the elderly shall be cared for and who shall provide the various services.

The purpose of the ÄDEL-reform in 1992 was to create clear lines of accountability and an organizational structure better suited to implementing the goals established by Parliament. The reform included a transfer of about 500 long-term somatic medical care institutions with approximately 31,000 beds from the county councils to the municipalities. The municipalities were also required to reimburse the county councils for the costs of providing continued short-term somatic and geriatric care to patients whose medical treatment had been completed but for whom no municipal housing or institutional care had yet become available ("bed-blockers").

Municipal social services are responsible for home help services, which include shopping, cleaning, cooking, washing, and personal hygiene for those elderly people living at home who cannot cope on their own. The fees charged for home help services vary from municipality to municipality and according to the number of hours of help needed. Help is also available during the evening, at night, and on weekends. Most municipalities today provide night patrols, which usually include both nursing and home help staff.

Housing

The main concept guiding the care of the elderly in Sweden today is that a person should continue living in his or her own home as long as possible. About 80% of persons 80 years and over are living in their own homes, and about 60 per cent are capable of managing on their own or with the help of relatives.

According to the terms of Social Service Act, other forms of housing shall be available to those who are no longer able to live at home. The various "special housing" types (see Table 9) are as follows. *Service buildings* are usually blocks of flats containing twenty to one hundred housing units. These tenants are mainly pensioners who have ordinary rent contracts with the municipality. Help services are available to residents in the same way as they are available to those living in ordinary homes. Elderly people who are unable to live by themselves, even with the aid of home help and home nursing services, usually live in *retirement homes*. Care is provided around the clock by regular staff. At the *nursing homes*, which were transferred from the county councils, you will find the former "bed-blockers" from the acute somatic hospitals. Some nursing homes are now specializing in hospice care, others in respite care, rehabilitation, dementia care, and so forth. In recent years, *group dwellings* for dementia patients have also been established. Group dwelling has no standard definition, but it usually means a small housing collective for six to eight persons, in which each resident has his or her own room, shares communal areas, and has access to service and care provided by resident staff around the clock.

The monthly fees charged to the residents who live in retirement homes, nursing homes, and group dwellings can vary between SEK 3,000 and SEK 10,000. The fee depends on which municipality they live in and is also income-related. The fee includes housing, food, and home help services. If residents need to see a doctor they normally have to pay a fee for each visit. At present only a very small proportion of care for the elderly in Sweden is supplied by privately run organizations. Most of these are foundations or other not-for-profit organizations.

After the ÄDEL reform in 1992 short-term somatic and geriatric care have gone through some extensive changes. One economic incentive with the reform, mentioned above, was to reduce the number of "bed-blockers." The aim is to cure and rehabilitate the elderly patients so they can return home or to a sheltered accommodation as soon as possible. The number of beds at the geriatric wards have decreased by 28%; at the same time the average length of stay has decreased. This development is also due to the difficult economic situation in most counties and municipalities. Stockholm county is the only county that has increased the geriatric care since the ÄDEL reform. The reform has also contributed to making geriatric care more specialized with an increased number of specialized physicians, paramedics, and nurses in the geriatric wards.

Informal Care and Voluntary Organizations

The informal care provided by families and other volunteers is of great significance. A study in 1991 (Johansson 1991) showed that the amount of informal and voluntary help given was at least twice that of formal care. Among the younger elderly (74–84) it was the wife/husband who provided the care, while among the very oldest (85+) it was the children. It is usual in some countries to distinguish between the help given by the family and that which is given by voluntary organizations (such as the Red Cross, the church, and pensioners' organizations). However, the extent of such voluntary work is fairly limited in Sweden and voluntary organizations do not usually give direct care to the elderly. Relatives who take care of their elderly family members can receive payment from the municipality and county council. It is also possible for relatives to take time off work, with compensation from the social insurance system.

More than 30% of all old-age pensioners in Sweden are members of pensioners' organizations. In some places, these have started to run voluntary care facilities, but their main role has been that of advocate for the elderly. Because so many elderly people belong to these organizations in several instances they have been able to exert a direct influence on national political decisions that concern the elderly.

Health Care Costs and Health Insurance

During 1991–93 Sweden was facing its deepest economic recession since the 1930s. The most serious problem of the Swedish health care system was the country's financial situation. A huge gross foreign debt (about 85% of the gross domestic product) and a large national budget deficit (14.7% of GDP in 1993) led to depreciation of the Swedish crown (SEK) and to increased interest rates. These factors led to a difficult financial situation for the county councils, which were forced to make substantial cuts in their budgets. The challenge for the county councils was to maintain the quality of health care with less money. County council taxes are the main source of income for the public health system in Sweden. Nearly three-fourths of the public health care sector is financed through county council taxes.

Costs

Swedish health and medical care holds its own quite well in comparison with other countries as regards the high quality of medicine and the fair distribution of care according to need. In addition, developments over recent years have shown that the Swedish health and medical care system has been quite capable of both adapting expenditure on health and medical care to national economic development and of making operations more efficient. In addition, Swedish administrative costs are low, which means that resources are used primarily for health and medical care. During the same period, costs in some insurance-financed systems in other countries have increased more quickly than the national economy as a whole.

Swedish health care has been hospital-oriented during the last forty years. In 1991 the hospitals accounted for approximately 47% of health care expenditure (dental care excluded) and approximately 18% was accounted for by primary care (including domiciliary care provided by the county councils). The remaining 35% was spent on psychiatric and somatic long-term care.

The major part (75%) of public health care costs in 1993 are covered by the tax levied and administered by the county councils. This tax (or the part that is assigned to health care) must be regarded as comparable with a universal public health insurance covering the individual's costs for medical care. Additional sources are grants from the national government corresponding to 12% of the total health care costs. Patient fees constitute 3% and interests and other income account for 10%. Consumers' out-of-pocket expenses according to the national accounts accounted in 1992 for 14.4% of the total health care expenditures (see Table 10 for a more detailed description of the expenditures). This figure has increased during recent years. However, public coverage differs widely between subsectors and is almost complete for inpatient care, while patient fees for outpatient care, drugs, and dental care have increased. The expenditures for pharmaceuticals have increased rapidly during recent years, especially in relation to other parts of health care. The percentage of total expenditures that went to pharmaceuticals increased from 9.1% in 1990 to 13.7% in 1993.

During the 1970s the county councils' increase in real costs was between 4 to 5% annually. During the first half of the 1980s the increase in costs was about 2.5%, whereas during the last part of the 1980s the cost increase was about 1%. The increase for 1991 was just above 0.0% and for 1992 there was a cost *decrease* in real terms of 1.2%. In 1993 the costs continued to decrease by 2.2%. The county councils' total expenditure in health care (including dental care) per capita was SEK 10,472 in 1993, with a range from SEK 8,714 to SEK 12,472. From 1960 to 1982 health care expenditure in Sweden rose continuously from 4.7 to 9.1% of the gross domestic product. Then there was a decline to 8.6% (excluding the care for mentally retarded) in 1990 and 8.4% in 1991. As a result of the ÄDEL reform in 1992 a total of SEK 15 billion was transferred from county councils to municipalities (Federation of County Councils, 1995); therefore the percentage of GDP decreased to 7.6%. The equivalent figure for 1993 has been estimated to 7.5% (1 SEK = 7.25 U.S. dollars, March 1995).

Sweden has one of the oldest populations in the world (almost 18% are 65 or older) and an increasing proportion of the total resources of the medical services are being consumed by the elderly, especially for inpatient care. In 1979 the percentage of the inpatient short-term care costs for persons 65 years and above was 34.2%. In 1991 this figure had increased to 42.1%. The total cost of public care and services for the elderly is estimated at some SEK 100,000 million. More than half of this goes to various forms of institutions, such as hospitals, nursing homes, and retirement homes.

Table C   Total Expenditure on Health Care, 1960–1993 (% of GDP)

Year	1960	1970	1975	1980	1985	1990	1991	1992	1993
% of GDP	4.7	7.2	7.9	9.4	8.9	8.6	8.4	7.6	est. 7.5

SOURCE: *Statistics Sweden (SCB)*, National accounts.

Productivity and Quality

An expert group on public finance (ESO) under the Ministry of Finance has published a study on productivity and quality change in the public health services in Sweden. It is part of a larger study on productivity in the public sector from 1980 to 1992. The study reiterates the results from an earlier study on productivity change from 1960 to 1980 and the recent study on productivity change 1980–92 in the public health services. Over the years 1960–92 the real cost of the average weighted visit to doctors and nurses and admission to hospital has increased twofold. The report asks if there is an equivalent quality increase, and if the total increase in health care costs is due to more expensive treatments resulting from an aging population and the cost of new technologies.

The study investigates quality change in the health services by sampling twenty-nine diagnoses and asking how the typical patient was treated around 1960 and with what results in respect of diagnostic accuracy, ability to treat various kinds of patients, acute and long-term morbidity, acute and long-term complications, restored physical functions, pains and trouble from treatment, length of treatment, and life quality. The same question is asked about the treatment of the same kind of patient, but concerning treatment in the beginning of the 1990s. The results indicate that there has been a marked increase in quality over the thirty years, and that much of the quality increase has taken place in the 1980s.

Diagnoses, the treatment of which show large increases in quality, are peptic ulcer, fractured hip, prostatic hypertrophy, total hip replacement, cataract, lower limb fracture, cardiovascular disease, and the care of premature babies. Acute morbidity has been decreased by 50% or more, physical functions can be restored almost completely, long-term morbidity has been reduced, treatments involve less pains and trouble, etc. Diagnoses that show hardly any or very small increases in quality are several forms of cancer (in the lungs, ovary, and prostate), glaucoma, and insufficient lung function. There seems to be no correlation between the increase in quality and the increase in costs. Several of these illnesses are treated with higher quality and lower costs today than in the beginning of the 1960s. Other illnesses are treated with both higher quality and higher costs and still others are treated with higher costs but very little quality increase.

Table D illustrates that there has been a shift from a negative to a positive change in productivity from the beginning of the 1990s. The explanation for the high figure from 1993 is probably due to the shift of nursing homes from the county councils to the municipalities (the ÅDEL reform). The Federation of County Councils has made an analysis where only the somatic acute hospitals are included. The results show a positive productivity change: 0.2% increase for 1991, 6.5% in 1992, and 5.1% in 1993, an increase for the period of about 12%.

Insurance and Patients' Fees

The national *health* insurance system, financed by the state and employer contributions, was established in 1955 to provide medical, sickness, and parental benefits. It covers all Swedish citizens and alien residents. The national health insurance system is a principal means of creating socioeco-

Table D   Annual Change in Public Health Productivity Between 1960 and 1993 (%)

Year	1960–80	1980–85	1985–90	1991	1992	1993
%	−3.0	−0.2	−1.4	+0.5	+3.1	(est.) +3.0

SOURCE: Expert Group on Public Finance (ESO), 1994 and Federation of Swedish County Councils (1994).

nomic equality while also functioning as a financing instrument with state control and supervision. Under the national health insurance system, payments are made when a person seeks medical and dental care. During the latest years the *social* insurance expenditures to compensate for loss of income due to illness, early retirement, and work injuries increased markedly in relation to the health care costs. Sickness benefit is the compensation paid for earned income lost due to illness. The employer is responsible for compensation during the first fourteen days of a period of illness; after that the health insurance system takes over.

Health and social services are heavily subsidized, with the recipient usually paying only a fraction of actual costs. Charges may vary between the different county councils and municipalities. These charges (out-of-pocket costs) for health care and social services are rising. Pensioners pay a fee of SEK 75 per day for each day they spend in hospital. For all others except children under the age of sixteen years the fee is SEK 80 per day. For children under the age of sixteen years no fee is charged. The fee for consulting a doctor in the primary health care services, that is to say a family doctor or a district doctor, varies between county councils from SEK 80 to SEK 130. For consulting a specialist at a hospital the fees vary from SEK 100 to SEK 180. These fees cover (both public and private care): the consultation; the issuing of a prescription or doctor's certificate to qualify for sickness benefit; X-ray, radium, and other treatments; referral to a specialist, including the cost of the first consultation. There is normally a fee of SEK 50 for treatments such as physiotherapy, speech therapy, occupational therapy, and psychotherapy, provided they are prescribed by a licensed physician. Birth-control counseling, provided by publicly employed or other authorized specialists, is free of charge. The maximum sum payable at any one time by a prescription holder for pharmaceutical preparations (officially registered drugs) is, as of July 1995, SEK 160 for the first prescribed drug and SEK 25 for each of the following. Life-saving drugs needed for chronic and serious diseases are free of charge.

To limit the cost incurred by patients there is a high cost ceiling. A patient who has paid at least SEK 1,700 for medical care and for medicines is entitled to free care and free medicines for the remainder of the twelve-month period, which is calculated from the first visit to a doctor or the first purchase of medicines. Health insurance covers dental care, both treatment and preventive measures, given by employees of the public dental service as well as the majority of dentists in private practice. Dentists must adhere to an established scale of charges. Children and young people are entitled to free care from the public dental service up to the age of nineteen.

International Perspectives on Health Care in Sweden

During recent years, there has been a great deal of criticism over the long waiting lists for certain medical procedures in some countries, such as hip replacement, cataract, and coronary surgery. During 1991 and 1992 these queues, however, have decreased. There are few incentives toward a rapid adaptation to changing methods for health care. Criticism has also been directed at the lack of services within some parts of the health care system. One study summarizes the main problems in the Swedish health care system in the following way:

> Taken overall, then, the Swedish health care system finds itself under pressure from a series of social and structural factors, few of which are explicitly related to health delivery alone.

These factors include (a) an increased demand for personal service and the satisfaction of individual wants, (b) a ceiling on the growth of health sector revenues, (c) the absence of an adequate mechanism to assess institutional use value and/or organizational failure, and (d) the substitution of intra-organizational and/or employee benefits for use value as a measure of health performance. Combined, these pressures have generated a volatile situation in which a structurally frozen health system can no longer accommodate the demands placed upon it. (Saltman and von Otter 1987)

At the end of the 1980s a strong movement emerged in several counties toward a new way of financing and organizing health care. The main reason for the "paradigm shift" was the tightening economic situation for the counties coupled with a strong demand for health care resources. Several counties are heavily involved in reconstructing their health care sectors. The main features are: separation of production and financing, resource allocation to health districts in relation to the need of the population (number of people, age structure, and socioeconomic variables) and introduction of public competition with purchasing and selling between these health districts and the hospitals. The health district boards are responsible for the health care of the population in their district, hospitals are financed by their activities (for example, through DRGs), and quality aspects are monitored by central authorities.

During March 1988 Professor Alain Enthoven at Stanford University visited Sweden in order to analyze the Swedish health care system's structure and performance. He was focusing on the question "How can incentives for efficiency and equity be improved?" (Enthoven 1989). Earlier Enthoven had done similar studies for the United Kingdom and the Netherlands. One piece of advice Enthoven gave was to implement better management information systems. "How can Swedes pretend to be managing their health care system efficiently without the basic management systems that any successful industrial company in a competitive industry routinely has?" He was also positive on the necessity to decentralize management to clinical departments. But "how can you decentralize if you do not measure the amount and quality of the results departments are supposed to produce? For what are departments being held responsible? Today, the Swedish health care system sets its own standards and evaluates itself."

It is as if we at Stanford University let our students set their own examinations and grade them! What Sweden needs to do, institutionally, is to separate the "demand side" from the "supply side" of health care. That is, Sweden needs to create an institution that determines needs, sets standards and priorities, and measures performance that is independent of the institutions that supply those needs.

Enthoven's prescription to separate the demand and the supply side has been implemented in several counties in Sweden. One rather important impetus in this direction was the experimentation of this concept in former Leningrad (Håkansson et al. 1989 and 1991). Leningrad was the first place in Europe where the purchaser-provider split was implemented and where the hospitals were reimbursed by their activities according to a fixed price list.

On behalf of the Swedish Center for Business and Policy Studies (SNS) five distinguished health economists visited Sweden during the summer in 1991. Their report "Health Care and Health Care Finance in Sweden: The crisis that never was; the tensions that ever will be" was very much discussed in Sweden when the report was translated into Swedish in early 1992.

There is a consensus amongst the authors that there is no Swedish crisis—at least not in the sense that Sweden confronts new problems of a specially intractable kind not commonly found elsewhere. What Sweden has is a set of problems—whose solution is admittedly by no means easy—that are shared with nearly every other country in the developed world. Moreover, Sweden has these in a form that is often less severe than can be found elsewhere and is already containing them in ways that seem superior to the ways adopted in at least some other developed countries. No real crisis, then. But lots of problems, which all interact.

At the end of March 1995 the international health economists' panel led by Professor Culyer from the University of York revisited Sweden. A report will be published this fall.

Health Care Reforms in Sweden

The Swedish health care system has, thanks to its county councils and municipalities (local authorities) a unique opportunity of testing different models and systems in parallel. This opportunity has been utilized to a great extent over the last few years. Most of these reforms have been implemented so recently that it is difficult to know which effects can be attributed to the new control systems. The sector was affected extensively by both financial restrictions and other reforms such as the ÄDEL-reform and the family-doctor-reform during the same period. At the end of this section we shall give one example, out of many, concerning reforms in the county councils: the Stockholm model.

One important purpose behind the process of reforming health care in Sweden, which has been going on for the last twenty years, is to limit national regulation and to encourage local ways of dealing with local conditions. The renewal work can be described as:

- increased influence for the patient who will enjoy full freedom to choose health care provider;
- new methods for political control where the politicians shall act primarily as purchasers and representatives of the patients;
- reformed payment systems for the health care providers;
- establishment of competition and development toward different forms of operation.

The ambitions to separate the responsibility for purchasing and providing care are particularly clear. Furthermore, reimbursement based on contractlike arrangements, competition, and different forms of operation shall be stimulating factors to increase the efficiency of the health care entities.

In 1992 a parliamentary committee, the Committee on Funding and Organisation on Funding of Health Services and Medical Care (HSU 2000), was appointed to analyze and evaluate the resource needs of health services in Sweden until the year 2000, and to consider how health care shall be financed and organized. The considerations of the Committee were to be based primarily on an analysis and evaluation of three finance and organization models: a reformed county council model, a primary care managed model, and a compulsory health insurance model. After the election in September 1994 the directives to the Committee were amended. The Committee's considerations and proposals were now to be based on the current system whereby county councils and municipalities finance and provide health and medical care. The resource needs of health services would now be analyzed until the year 2010, with particular attention given to the significance of demographic growth as regards the requirement for health and medical care for the elderly. This work is to be carried out so that it is completed in its entirely no later than June 30, 1996.

The Role of the Patient in Health and Medical Care

One central aim of the efforts toward reform in Swedish health and medical care over the last few years has been to strengthen the position of the patient by giving individuals more opportunity to choose a care institute, such as in primary care and various types of specialists' care, and to choose a hospital when hospitalization is necessary. Action has also been taken to increase the availability of care by means of guaranteed care undertakings. This development should be viewed against the background of the shift in values, primarily among postwar generations, which places greater demand on influence and options for influencing one's own situation than was previously the case. The option of choosing a care institution is vital for patient influence. There has been a great desire in the care sector to provide clear information, and patients have more and more requested that they be allowed to participate in making medical decisions and decisions on their day-to-day care. However, there is still a long way to go before patients have more general influence.

Purchaser-Provider

In the last few years, several county councils have introduced new financial control systems. One is to separate the buyer and the seller, or usually called a purchaser-provider system. In the beginning of 1995 about half of the county councils had established a purchaser-provider organization. The intent is that elected officials shall concentrate on representing the citizens/consumers, and not participate in operational decisions of the provider units. Several county councils have therefore eliminated their local health care district boards. Special purchasing committees have been instituted where politicians have the responsibility for formulating the requirements that should be made on the hospitals by the county councils and of evaluating quality and prices. The hospitals for their part have become more independent in relation to political bodies. The total effect of the purchaser-provider model is still too early to evaluate, but it is clear that it has led to a greater interest in the performance of health services, in the costs of performance, and in the quality of services provided.

Reformed Payment System

In several county councils the traditional system of fixed annual allocations to hospitals and primary care services have been replaced by contractlike arrangements where the reimbursement is based on the outputs of the health care providers. The measures of output used as a basis for the reimbursement vary, but Diagnosis Related Groups (DRGs) are the most common basis for the reimbursement of hospital care. DRGs are basically a classification system for treatments with regard to medical significance and expected resource requirements. DRGs were developed at Yale University with a view to facilitating comparisons between clinical departments and hospitals.

Conceptually DRGs represent nothing more than a way of thinking about and representing the "products" of a hospital. Their intent originally was to develop a tool that could improve the quality of internal management in hospitals (Kimberly and Pouvourille 1993; Fetter et al. 1991).

In Sweden there has been much experimentation with DRGs, from a rather "passive" way to use as a case-mix instrument to a more "active" way as a basis for payment to hospitals (see Håkansson et al. 1988). Spri has evaluated the DRGs' potential to explain cost variations among inpatients in acute care. The result, by international standards, is very good. After excluding the most costly patients (less than 5% of patients are "outliers") the explained variance is about two-thirds, $R^2 = 0.66$.

Maximum Waiting Time Guarantee

On January 1, 1992, a maximum waiting time guarantee for twelve different medical procedures came into force: coronary angiography, coronary artery bypass grafting (CABG), percutaneous translumnal coronary angioplasty (PTCA), hip replacement, knee replacement, cataract surgery, inguinal hernia operation, cholecystectomy, operation for benign prostatic hyperplasia (BPH), operation for prolapse of the uterus, operation for incontinence (women), and hearing-aid fitting. The aim of the guarantee was to reduce the waiting lists for these procedures. The content of the guarantee is that, after an opinion has been given by a specialist, no patient needs to wait more than three months for treatment. If the waiting time is expected to be longer at the hospital selected, it is the duty of the hospital concerned to ensure that the patient receives treatment at another hospital within three months.

Waiting periods in the fields concerned have been rapidly reduced. At many hospitals the waiting lists were reduced even before the waiting time guarantee came into force. The main explanation for the positive development was partly a result of the extra funds made available but also by applying new technology and reorganizing and rationalizing the care process as such. According to the follow-up reports, only a few departments could not offer their patients treatment within three months. The reports also indicated that when given the choice between waiting longer or receiving treatment at another hospital most patients preferred proximity and continuity to earlier treatment.

A question addressed in the assessment of the waiting time guarantee is to what extent other groups have been crowded out by the guarantee to patients. In the follow-up it was found that this was not a major problem and that the extra funds allocated, together with the rationalization and reorganization, had enabled the waiting list problems in the respective areas to be solved without taking resources from other areas.

The Stockholm Model

Between 1992 and 1995 a new way of financing and organizing health care, the so-called Stockholm model, has gradually been implemented in the Stockholm county council (population 1.7 million). The purpose of the Stockholm model is to strengthen the position of patients and to achieve more effective health care delivery, or, in other words "more and better health care for the money." Fundamental to the new system is that patient needs and their choice of health care provider determine the allocation of resources, that the role of the purchasers (the health district) and providers (the hospitals) are separate, and that hospitals and primary care services (the family physicians) compete in attracting the patients. The patients can freely choose their doctor, health center, or hospital, and may choose a private doctor.

In the Stockholm model, hospital inpatient care is paid by a prospective fixed price per DRG. The prices cannot be exceeded, but agreements about lower prices can be made through negotiated contracts between the local health districts/primary care and the acute somatic hospitals. The payment system was introduced in January 1992 for the departments of surgery, urology, orthopedics, obstetrics and gynecology, and cataract surgery, and has been used since January 1993 for all clinical acute care departments.

A fixed price list for ambulatory services has been introduced. The system includes an ambulatory classification system. Day surgery, for instance, is reimbursed as a percentage (60–80%) of the corresponding DRG price for inpatient care. The costs for teaching and research will continue to be based on a budget allocation principle. In 1994 the Stockholm County Council introduced a family doctor system. At the same time, all funds for primary care, geriatrics, and psychiatry were distributed according to an index based on population and socioeconomic factors (like the RAWP formula in the United Kingdom). A reimbursement system for geriatrics and psychiatry has also been developed.

For the surgical specialties under prospective payments, the number of treated patients during 1992 increased by 8% in inpatient care, day surgery with 50% and outpatient visits by 15%. Taken all together, activities increased by 11%. Because there was a 10% decrease in DRG prices from January 1, 1992, the total costs decreased by 1% due to less personnel.

Data from the first five months in 1993 in comparison with the same period in 1992 show that there has been a decrease in the number of discharges by 1.2%. The number of bed-days has decreased by 5.8%, mainly due to a shorter average length of stay of 4.7% (from 5.8 to 5.5 days). The average case mix index (for the first five months) has increased from 1.04 in 1992 to 1.11 in 1993. This could be due to better coding and documentation but also to what is called ''DRG creep.'' The following results are for all medical and surgical specialties in all somatic acute hospitals in Stockholm county.

During the period 1990 to 1993 the number of physician visits increased by 14% in medical specialties and by 8% in surgical specialties; the number of admissions increased by 16% in medical specialties and by 6% in surgical specialties; the number of bed-days decreased by 13% in medical specialties and by 16% in surgical specialties. In 1990 the average length of stay in medical specialties was 8.7 days and 6.5 days in 1993, a decrease of 25%. In surgical specialties the average length of stay was 5.9 days in 1990 and 4.7 days in 1993, which corresponds to a decrease of 20%.

One major concern that has been put forward when moving from a global budget system for every clinical department to a situation where hospitals are paid according to their activities or output is the problem with total cost control and transaction costs. Högberg (1994) has estimated the increased administration costs caused by the introduction of the Stockholm model to be about 0.5%. In the first two years the problem with total cost control could be handled by successive decreases in the DRG price list. But from 1994 the Stockholm county council has not been able to cope with the increasing cost. The fiscal year 1994 showed an overspending of SEK 853 million, which corresponds to more than 4% of the total budget. This has led to very tough budget cuts for all hospitals for 1995. The equivalent figures for the years before were: a deficit of SEK 84 million (−.5%) for 1993, a surplus of SEK 371 million (+2%) for 1992, a surplus of SEK 47 million (+.2%) for 1991, a deficit of SEK 113 million (−1%) for 1990.

Jonsson (1994) has evaluated the effects of the introduction of the Stockholm model with a group of counties that had not introduced a purchaser-provider split. The evaluation was based on a comparison of the development before (1986–90) and after (1991–93) the introduction of the

Stockholm model. Between 1990 and 1992 the number of discharges for medical and surgical specialties increased by 11 percentage points and patient turnover with 18 percentage points more in Stockholm compared with the control group. At the same time the reduction in hospital beds decreased by 2.5 percentage points more in Stockholm than in the control group. In his conclusion Professor Jonsson pointed to the fact that between 1990 and 1992 the productivity in the somatic acute care sector had increased by 5% in the control group. The equivalent figure for Stockholm county was 18.5%, a difference of 13.5%. This difference was due one-fourth to cost reduction and three-fourths to an increased output.

According to a study by Svensson and Garelius (1994) the average DRG weight increased during 1992. A weak decline can be noted during the second year, which seems to be a trend throughout the data; that is, most of the changes that had occurred since the introduction of the Stockholm model happened during 1992. In the same study the Stockholm county council was criticized for having changed DRG prices several times during the year—even retroactively—which created considerable irritation and made it more difficult to accept the payment system.

The results from the Stockholm model show that physician decision-making has been affected by the economic incentives of the payment system. Patients have been admitted to hospitals more frequently and have been discharged earlier than before the introduction of the Stockholm model. An important factor that made it possible to reduce the length of stay and increase activity is that the municipalities, during the same period under the "ÄDEL" reform, had similar incentives. The study by Svensson and Garelius shows that there was no evidence that the Stockholm model has led to the feared negative effects such as the selection of "profitable" patients or the conscious incorrect registration of diagnoses. However, the respondents expressed fear, both in the question-naire and in the interviews, that such behavior can arise in the future. In conclusion, continuous evaluation of the effects of the Stockholm model is important for the future.

Conclusion

When we look at Sweden's health care system from an international perspective we must say that the scores are quite high: high quality with rather even distribution among its citizens. Very low patient fees assure access even to high-technology medicine. Sweden spends 7.5% of its gross domestic product on health care, which is what can be expected when we make a comparison with the other OECD countries. The system is mostly public (85%), but private initiatives have emerged since the beginning of the 1990s. From an international point of view, the health of the Swedish people is very good, even though there have been signs of an increase in differences in levels of health between different socioeconomic groups over the last few years. Comparisons of what is known as "avoidable deaths"—that is to say, deaths due to causes than can be influenced by health and medical care—is often around 30 to 50% lower in Sweden than in other European countries.

The main shortcomings are: lack of integration between health services, social services, and health insurance (particularly sickness benefits, early retirement pensions, and occupational injury insurance); general practitioners do not act as "gatekeepers," which results in a relatively high proportion of self-referrals to hospital outpatient and emergency departments; there are variations in health care utilizations, which cannot be explained by differences in health problems. There are insufficient incentives for health personnel to improve productivity and efficiency, but improve-ments have been achieved during recent years. But as the international health economists' panel led by Professor Culyer (1991) concluded: "What Sweden has is a set of problems—whose solution is admittedly by no means easy—that are shared with nearly every other country in the developed world. Moreover, Sweden has these in a form that is often less severe than can be found elsewhere and is already containing them in ways that seem superior to the ways adopted in at least some other developed countries. No real crisis, then. But lots of problems, which all interact.''

Sweden's health care system is decentralized among twenty-three counties and three municipalities, which raise income taxes (12%) from the population to finance a comprehensive supply of services. The challenge is to provide a cost-effective health care to an increasing elderly population when the budgets will be reduced just as new technologies are entering the health care market.

Sweden has during the last years experimented with new ways of financing and organizing health care. The most important ingredients are: separation of production and financing, resource allocation to health districts in relation to the need of the population, introduction of public competition with purchasing and selling between health districts and the hospitals, and prospective payments to hospitals by the use of DRGs. Inspiration has come from Leningrad (today, Saint Petersburg) and the United Kingdom (purchaser-provider split); and the United States (DRGs, and health maintenance organizations [HMOs]). The results from these experiments are still preliminary. But one of the major problems lies in the total cost control. When money is "following" the patient there is often a conflict between freedom of choice for the patient and total cost control for the providers. After the recent general government election in September 1994, when the Social Democrats came back to power, the enthusiasm for using purchaser-provider models has diminished. Instead of talking about competition health care officials now are using the term *cooperation*.

Discussion on how the medical services can be made more efficient has begun to concentrate on the structure of the services—and how they can be changed. Sweden has relatively few hospitals, but many beds. At the same time some of the hospitals serve a population that is very small. There are a number of reasons why the structure needs to be changed and there is great interest in this question. The country's bad financial situation is naturally one reason, but issues of quality and safety are nevertheless in the foreground in the ongoing discussion. Examples of issues being studied and discussed are the closing of hospitals, taking care of the acutely ill and severely injured (trauma patients), division of responsibilities and collaboration between hospitals, and the interaction between hospitals and other parts to the health services. The overriding problem for Sweden's health care system is the country's present (1995) negative outlook in financial terms. With a gross foreign debt of 85% of its GDP, high unemployment rate, and a government budget deficit of 15%, very difficult budget cuts are facing all sectors of the health care system.

REFERENCES

Most of the sources used when writing this report are in Swedish and are not included in the references below. Among the sources used are publications from Statistics Sweden (SCB), Swedish Medical Association, the Swedish Institute for Health Services Development (Spri), Federation of Swedish County Councils, Swedish Institute, and National Board of Health and Welfare. If you are interested in the Swedish literature used in this chapter, please do not hesitate to contact the authors.

Anell, A., and P. Svarvar. 1993. *Reformed County Council Model: survey and analysis of organizational reforms in the Swedish healthcare sector.* IHE working paper 3. Swedish Institute for Health Economics, Lund, Sweden.

Culyer, A. J. 1991. *Health care and health care finance in Sweden: the crisis that never was—the tensions that ever will be.* Occasional paper no. 33. Stockholm: SNS.

Culyer, A. J., R. G. Evans, J-M. Graf von der Schulenburg, W. van de Ven, and B. A. Weisbrod. 1991. *International review of the Swedish health care system.* Occasional paper no. 34. Stockholm: SNS.

The Committee on Funding and Organisation of Health Services and Medical Care (HSU 2000). 1993. *Three models for health care reform in Sweden.* A Report From the Expert Group to The Committee on Funding and Organisation of Health Services and Medical Care (HSU 2000). Stockholm: Ministry of Health and Social Affairs.

————. 1994. *International perspectives on health care reform in Sweden: report from a hearing on three models for health care reform*. Stockholm: Ministry of Health and Social Affairs.

Enthoven, A. C. 1989. *Management information and analysis for the Swedish health care system*. IHE working paper 7. Lund: Swedish Institute for Health Economics.

Fetter, R. B., et al., eds. 1991. *DRGs: Their Design and Development*. Ann Arbor, Mich.: Health Administration Press.

Ham, C., R. Robinson, and M. Benzeval. 1990. *Health Check: Health Care Reforms in an International Context*. London: King's Fund Institute.

Håkansson, S. 1994. New ways of financing and organizing health care in Sweden. *International Journal of Health Planning and Management* 9(1):103–24, 15.

Håkansson, S., B. Majnoni D'Intagnano de la Haye, G. H. Mooney, J. L. Roberts, G. L. Stoddart, K. Staehr-Johansen, and H. Zöllner. 1991. *Leningrad Revisited: Report of a Second Visit to the USSR, October 1989*. Copenhagen: World Health Organization.

Håkansson, S., B. Majnoni D'Intagnano de la Haye, J. L. Roberts, and H. Zöllner. 1989. *The Leningrad Experiment in Health Care Management 1988*. Report of a WHO Mission. Copenhagen: World Health Organization.

Håkansson, S., E. Paulson, and K. Kogeus. 1988. Prospects for using DRGs in Swedish hospitals. *Health Policy* 9(2):177–92.

Högberg, M. H. 1994. Hur paverkar fast betalning per prestation och kunkurrens det ekonomiska beteendet pa sjukhusen? (How does performance based case reimbursement and competition influence the economic behavior at the hospitals?). Stockholm: The University of Stockholm (IKE:47).

Johansson, L. 1991. *Caring For the Next of Kin: On Informal Care of the Elderly in Sweden*. Thesis. Uppsala University.

Jonsson, E. 1994. *Har den s.k. Stockholmsmodellen genererat mer vård för pengarna? (Has the Stockholm Model generated more care for the money?)*. IKE report 48. Stockholm University: Institute for Local Government Economics.

Kimberly, J., and G. Pouvourille, eds. 1993. *The Migration of Managerial Innovation: DRGs in Western Europe*. San Francisco: Jossey-Bass.

National Board of Health and Welfare. 1992. *Social Services in Sweden: A Part of the Social Welfare System*. Stockholm: Socialstyrelsen.

————. 1995. *Welfare and Public Health in Sweden, 1994*. Stockholm: Socialstyrelsen.

Saltman, R. B. 1992. Recent health policy initatives in Nordic countries. *Health Care Financing Review* 13:157–66.

Saltman, R. B., and C. von Otter. 1987. Re-vitalizing public health care systems: a proposal for public competition in Sweden. *Health Policy* 7(1):21–40.

Spri. 1992. *The reform of health care in Sweden*. Spri Report 339. Stockholm: Spri.

Svensson, H. and L. Garelius. 1994. *Har ekonomiska incitament påverkat läkarnas beslutsfattande? Utvärdering av Stockholmsmodellen (Have economic incentives affected physicians' decision-making? An evaluation of the Stockholm Model)*. Spri report 392. Stockholm: Spri.

Table 1   Total Population in Sweden by Age and Sex, December 31, 1993

Age	Male	Female	Total	Percent
0–4	312,287	296,326	608,613	7.0
5–9	273,163	258,852	532,015	6.1
10–14	253,750	241,140	494,890	5.7
15–19	267,634	254,512	522,146	6.0
20–24	295,287	284,179	579,466	6.6
25–29	333,540	315,993	649,533	7.4
30–34	302,792	286,487	589,279	6.7
35–39	298,971	286,420	585,391	6.7
40–44	307,677	297,121	604,798	6.9
45–49	341,016	328,897	669,913	7.7
50–54	271,718	261,989	533,707	6.1
55–59	215,102	216,672	431,774	4.9
60–64	196,875	210,592	407,467	4.7
65–69	193,407	218,220	411,627	4.7
70–74	186,213	225,097	411,310	4.7
75–79	132,898	182,493	315,391	3.6
80–84	88,077	142,906	230,983	2.6
85–89	38,350	81,220	119,570	1.4
90 +	12,197	35,039	47,236	0.5
Total	4,320,954	4,424,155	8,745,109	100.0

SOURCE: *Statistics Sweden* (1994), *Population Statistics 1993.*

Table 2   Live Births, Birth Rate, Fertility Rate, and Infant Mortality Rate, Sweden

Year	Live births	Birth rate	Fertility rate	Infant mortality rate
1950	115,414	16.4	74.4	21.0
1960	102,219	13.6	69.6	16.6
1970	110,150	13.7	70.4	11.0
1980	97,064	11.7	57.3	6.9
1985	98,463	11.8	56.4	6.8
1990	123,938	14.5	70.6	6.0
1991	123,737	14.4	70.9	6.2
1992	122,848	14.2	70.8	5.3
1993	117,998	13.5	68.4	4.8

NOTE: Birth rate per 1,000 population and fertility rates per 1,000 women ages 15 to 44 years.
SOURCE: *Statistics Sweden* (1994), *Population Statistics 1993.*

Table 3   Infant Mortality Rate by the Six Most Common Causes, Sweden

Causes of Death (ICD9), 1992[1]	Men	Women	Total	% of total infant death	Mortality rate[2]
Total, under 1 year	369(+9)[1]	269(+10)[1]	638(+19)[1]	100.0	5.35
1. Congenital anomalies (740–59)	134	89	223	35.0	1.82
2. Certain conditions originating in the perinatal period (760–79)	112	94	206	32.3	1.68
3. Signs, symptoms, and ill-defined conditions (780–99) (Sudden Infant Death Syndrome [798])	59 (58)	35 (31)	94 (89)	14.7 (13.9)	0.77
4. Infectious and parasitic diseases (1–139)	11	11	22	3.4	0.18
5. Diseases of the Nervous System and Sense Organs (320–89)	9	12	21	3.3	0.17
6. Diseases of the Circulatory System (390–459)	9	5	14	2.2	0.11
All other causes	35	23	58	9.1	0.62

[1]The figures in Table 2 and Table 3 are not from the same year so the total number of infant mortality differs by 19 deaths.
[2]Per 1,000 live births, own calculation.
SOURCE: *Statistics Sweden (1994):* Causes of Death 1992.

Table 4   Death Rates for the Fifteen Leading Causes of Death in Sweden, 1990, 1991, and 1992

Cause of Death (ICD9) Men	Death Rate 1990	Death Rate 1991	Death Rate 1992	% of Total Death 1992
	49,050	48,997	48,221	100.0
1. Ischemic heart disease (410–14)	14,882	14,548	14,059	29.2
2. Cerebrovascular disease (430–38)	4,284	4,448	4,293	8.9
3. Other forms of heart disease (415–29)	3,197	3,333	3,271	6.8
4. Malignant neoplasm of other and unspecified sites (140–49, 155–56, 158–59, 170–73, 181, 184, 186–99)	2,652	2,673	2,672	5.5
5. Malignant neoplasm of prostate (185)	2,093	2,163	2,131	4.4
6. Pneumonia (480–86)	2,156	2,031	2,065	4.3
7. Other diseases of circulatory system (440–59)	2,058	2,096	2,033	4.2
8. Malignant neoplasm of respiratory and intra-thoracic organs (160–65)	2,041	2,036	2,006	4.2
9. Bronchitis, emphysema, and asthma (490–93, 496)	1,268	1,212	1,251	2.6
10. Malignant neoplasm of lymphatic and hematopoietic tissue (200–208)	1,028	1,002	1,027	2.1
11. Suicide (E950–E959)	1,020	1,036	936	1.9
12. Malignant neoplasm of small intestine, including duodenum and colon (152–53)	773	829	881	1.8
13. Other diseases of digestive system (540–70, 572–79)	766	755	817	1.7
14. Mental disorders (not alcoholic psychoses and syndrome) (290, 292–302, 304–319)	751	783	808	1.7
15. Diabetes mellitus (250)	707	718	742	1.5
All other causes	9,374	9,334	9,229	19.2

Women	Death Rate 1990	Death Rate 1991	Death Rate 1992	% of Total Death 1992
	46,091	45,939	46,005	100.0
1. Ischemic heart disease (410–14)	10,937	10,835	10,964	23.8
2. Cerebrovascular disease (430–38)	6,010	5,998	6,034	13.1
3. Other forms of heart disease (415–29)	4,015	4,030	4,003	8.7
4. Malignant neoplasm of other and unspecified sites (140–49, 155–56, 158–59, 170–73, 181, 184, 186–99)	2,642	2,535	2,546	5.5
5. Pneumonia (480–86)	2,215	2,283	2,273	4.9
6. Other diseases of circulatory system (440–59)	2,395	2,326	2,176	4.7
7. Mental disorders (not alcoholic psychoses and syndrome) (290, 292–302, 304–19)	1,439	1,501	1,557	3.4
8. Malignant neoplasm of female breast (174)	1,477	1,515	1,518	3.3
9. Malignant neoplasm of respiratory and intrathoracic organs (160–65)	884	994	1,024	2.2
10. Other diseases of digestive system (540–70, 572–79)	917	956	981	2.1
11. Malignant neoplasm of small intestine, including duodenum and colon (152–53)	949	896	938	2.0
12. Malignant neoplasm of lymphatic and hematopoietic tissue (200–208)	851	867	905	2.0
13. Diabetes mellitus (250)	828	818	813	1.8
14. Other symptoms and incompletely described conditions (780–799)	771	778	799	1.7
15. Bronchitis, emphysema, and asthma (490–93, 496)	777	800	788	1.7
All other causes	8,984	8,807	8,686	19.1

SOURCE: *Statistics Sweden (1994):* Causes of Death 1992.

Table 5 Selected Operative (Surgical) Procedures and Average Length of Stay in Hospital for Each Type of Operation, Sweden

Operation	Number of Procedures (Thousands) (1993)	Procedures per 100,000 inhabitants (1993)	Number of clinics (1992)	Average Length of Stay in Days (1992)
Coronary angiography	14,807	169	15	—
Coronary artery bypass grafting (CABG)	6,405	75	7	9.9
Percunteous translumnal coronary angioplasty (PTCA)	3,698	43	7	—
Hip replacement	11,434	132	85	13.3
Knee replacement	5,802	66	78	12.8
Cataract surgery	39,106	450	40	2.4
Inguinal hernia operation	19,286	222	94	3.0
Cholecystectomy	11,181	129	94	8.1
Operation for benign prostatic hyperplasia (BHA)	14,539	340	89	5.8
Operation for prolapse of the uterus	6,037	133	65	8.3
Operation for incontinence (women)	1,926	45	66	9.7

SOURCE: National Board of Health and Welfare (1994): Maximum Waiting-Time Guarantee in 1993.

Table 6   Average Monthly Salary including Overtime Pay (before Personal Income Taxes) of Doctors, Nurses, and Dentists in the County Councils, 1993

Category	Average Salary in SEK	
	Women	Men
Chief Medical Officer	36,700	40,000
District Medical Officer	32,800	35,000
Ward Physician	29,500	31,300
Intern and Assistant Physician	20,000	21,000
Chief Dentist	28,400	29,400
District Dentist	19,900	21,300
Chief Nurse	16,500	16,600
Registered Nurse and Midwives	14,400	14,600
Assistant Nurse	12,200	12,000

SOURCE: *Statistics Sweden (1994):* Employees in county councils, 1993.

Table 7 Number of Acute Short-Term General Hospitals Broken Down by the Number of Beds

County Council and Municipalities	0–100	101–200	201–300	301–400	401–500	501–700	701–900	901–1,200	Total
County Councils									
Stockholm	2[1]	2	1	1	1	1	3		11
Uppsala		2						1	3
Sörmland		1	1		1				3
Östergötland	1	1			1		1		4
Jönköping			1	1		1			3
Kronoberg		1			1				2
Kalmar		1	1		1				3
Blekinge		1		1					2
Kristianstad	1	1	1			1			4
Malmöhus		3			1			1	5
Halland				1	1				2
Bohuslän	1	1		2					4
Älvsborg	1	2			1	1			5
Skaraborg	1		1			1			3
Värmland		4				1		5	
Örebro		2					1		3
Västmanland	2	1			1				4
Dalarna	2	1				1			4
Gävleborg	1	2	1	1					5
Västernorrland	1	1	1			1			4
Jämtland					1				1
Västerbotten		1	1				1		3
Norrbotten	1	4		1					6
Municipalities									
Göteborg							1	1	2
Malmö							1		1
Gotland			1						1
Total	14	32	10	8	10	8	8	3	93

Average short-term beds broken down by county council and regional hospitals: Regional hospital ($n = 9$): 936 beds per hospital; Central county hospital ($n = 28$): 460 beds per hospital; District county hospital ($n = 56$): 148 beds per hospital.
SOURCE: Federation of Swedish County Councils (1994).

Table 8 Number of Acute Care Hospital Admissions per Year, and the Overall Average Length of Stay in Acute Care Hospitals (hospital service, 1993)

Main group/Area 1993	Number of beds	Beds per 1,000 inh.	Admissions	Bed-days (1,000s)	Number of occupied beds (%)	Average length of stay (days)	Visits to the doctor in hospital (1,000s)	Of which primary health care (%)
Medical short-term care	13,204	1.5	676,937	4,154.1	86.2	6.1	3,692.6	5.8
Surgical short-term care	14,108	1.6	762,437	3,855.3	74.9	5.1	5,506.8	3.0
Undistributed short-term care	562	0.1	39,381	190.9	93.1	4.8	69.5	—
Somatic long-term care	10,691	1.2	64,941	3,793.9	97.2	—	109.9	0.3
Psychiatric care	10,865	1.2	107,250	3,526.0	88.9	32.9	714.9	—
General care	—	—	—	—	—	—	9,528.7	100.0
Other specialized care	3,561	0.5	52,246	537.0	—	—	924.0	0.1
Total	52,991	6.1	1,703,192	16,057.2	83.0	9.4	20,546.4	48.2
Total short-term care	31,435	3.1	1,531,001	8,737.3	—	5.3	10,192.9	—

SOURCE: Federation of Swedish County Councils (1994), *Statistical Yearbook 1995*.

Table 9 Number of Persons Living in Nursing Homes and Related Types of Facilities and the Average Number of Beds per Facility

Year	Retirement homes	Service buildings	Group dwellings	Nursing homes	Special Housing	Total
1985	48,916	35,949		34,865		119,730
1990	37,150	52,261		29,941		119,352
1991	34,515	52,488	5,105	30,346		122,454
1992				2,443	118,618	121,061
1993					127,443	127,443

NOTE: The changes in 1992 are effects of the ÄDEL reform (See text ''Care for the elderly'').
SOURCE: National Board of Health and Welfare (1994): The ÄDEL reform.

Table 10 Detailed Survey of Current Outlays on Medical Care and Health, SEK Million, Current Prices

	1985	1988	1990	1991	1992[1]	1993
Private consumption	7,244	9,697	11,488	13,841	15,746	17,910
Medicines	1,630	2,300	2,704	3,067	3,658	4,298
Other pharmaceutical products	795	929	1,043	1,136	1,116	1,158
Eyeglasses and other therapeutic products	1,095	1,552	1,818	1,958	1,860	1,972
Services by doctors, etc.	3,724	4,916	5,923	7,680	9,112	10,482
Compensation for services from doctors in public health service	1,213	1,358	1,470	2,166	2,574	2,627
Doctors in private practice	354	485	715	—	—	—
Doctors, etc. in private practice	—	—	—	4,263	5,063	6,421
Dentists in private practice	1,632	2,354	2,760	—	—	—
Fees to the national dental service	498	713	978	1,246	1,475	1,434
Dental care in central government	27	6				
Public consumption	57,833	71,163	88,553	90,594	74,845[1]	—
Health and medical care	57,833	71,163	88,553	90,594	74,845[1]	—
of which: expenditure by social insurance offices	12,759	12,426	14,442	15,143	13,070	5,836
Total consumption for health care	65,077	80,860	100,041	104,435	90,591[1]	—
Investments	5,329	6,107	5,167	5,075	4,631	4,161
Private investments	262	628	604	882	614	565
Public investments	5,067	5,479	4,563	4,193	4,017	3,596
Total consumption and investments	70,406	86,967	105,208	109,510	95,222[1]	—
% of GDP	8.13	7.80	7.74	7.57	6.61	—
Subsides to the pharmacies for medicines	3,830	4,449	6,862	7,774	8,764	9,517
Subsides to doctors and dentists in private practice	2,462	3,599	4,432	4,996	4,956	4,634
Total current outlays for health and medical care	76,698	95,015	116,502	122,280	108,942[1]	—
% of GDP	8.9	8.5	8.6	8.4	7.6	est. 7.5
GDP in Sweden	866,601	1,114,502	1,359,879	1,447,327	1,441,723	1,442,182

[1]As a result of the ÄDEL Reform 1992 a total of 15 billion SEK was transferred from county councils to municipalities.
SOURCE: *Statistics Sweden (1994)*: Expenditure of GDP 1980–1993, The National Accounts.

The Health System of the United Kingdom*

Peter R. Hatcher

Introduction

Political System

The United Kingdom is both a constitutional monarchy with the queen as the head of state and a unitary parliamentary democracy with the prime minister exercising the executive powers of government through the cabinet appointed by the prime minister from members of the legislature. There is a bicameral legislature, the Parliament composed of a lower house, the House of Commons, and an upper house, the House of Lords, with legislation requiring approval of both houses and royal assent to become law. The upper house cannot prevent, but can delay, the passage of legislation approved by the House of Commons, and royal assent is virtually a constitutional formality.

There is effectively no separation of the executive and legislative branches of government as the prime minister must command a majority of the votes in the House of Commons to remain in power. This support is usually ensured through a tradition of strict party discipline with members of House of Commons belonging to the prime minister's political party being expelled from the government parliamentary caucus if they do not vote in favor of legislation the prime minister declares to be a matter of confidence in the government. If such a legislation is defeated, the prime minister and his cabinet are constitutionally required to resign and the queen usually calls a general election; otherwise general elections must be held every five years.

*I thank Professor Gordon Hatcher for his assistance in developing the tables. Andrew Wall and other colleagues at the Health Services Management Centre have been most helpful in commenting on the text. Thanks also to Luigina Garden for inputting the tables.

These constitutional provisions are particularly relevant to the current process of reform of the health system that has been under way in the United Kingdom since 1990 with the passage of the National Health Service and Community Care Act. This has been followed by the Health Authorities Act 1995, which completes the legislative programme of U.K. health reforms. This effective control of Parliament by the prime minister's administration has greatly facilitated the rapid implementation of the most radical reform of the health system in the United Kingdom since 1948. This differs from the situation in countries such as the United States where there is a clearly defined separation and balance of powers between the executive and legislative branches of government—which is why it was more difficult for President Clinton to have significant national health reforms legislation enacted.

Central and Local Government

Another factor that has facilitated implementation of the health reforms is the unitary rather than federal structure of the U.K. government, which means it does not share powers with state or provincial governments. As a unitary state the United Kingdom has one elected central government, Parliament, based in London which is supreme and responsible for governing four nations: England, Wales, Scotland, and Northern Ireland. It also has exclusive power to levy income, corporate and sales taxes, and duties. Only Northern Ireland had its own elected legislative assembly, but this has been replaced by direct rule by Parliament due to the political instability of the past twenty-five years. The administrative structure for implementation of central government policies is different in each nation reflecting the differing history, traditions, and legal systems. Each country is responsible for managing its health system and there are organizational differences, but the fundamental principles and functions of the health system, and of the reforms since 1990, are the same throughout the United Kingdom. For the purposes of clarity and simplicity this chapter will focus on the health system in England as representative of the United Kingdom, although important differences will be described. Health data is collected separately by each country, but where possible statistics given will be compiled for the United Kingdom as a whole.

Local governments are elected assemblies with the power to levy a locally fixed tax on every household within the limits set by central government. Local government is subsidiary to central government and is granted responsibility by central government for specified functions including housing, primary and secondary education, social services, and residential care homes. The central government makes grants to local governments to help finance these services, as the local government taxing capacity is not sufficient, nor intended to be sufficient, to finance all of the services for which local government is responsible.

The National Health Service and the 1990 Reforms

Most health care in the United Kingdom is provided by the National Health Service (NHS) and funded by central government from tax revenues. The exception to this is long-term residential nursing care, which is funded through local government and the private charitable and for-profit sectors. Acute and elective care is also available in private hospitals and clinics which, in 1992–93, was estimated to constitute about 8% of total expenditures in the United Kingdom for acute and elective hospital care, including specialist fees.[1] Consequently, a review of the development of the NHS is essential to an understanding of the U.K. health system and its current reforms.

The underlying principles of the NHS were set down in the Beveridge Report of 1942, which called for the establishment of a comprehensive, universally available, publicly financed system of health care in order to improve the living standards of the population. By "comprehensive," the report meant medical treatment available on the basis of need, regardless of the ability to pay, provided both in the home and in hospital by general practitioners, specialists, dentists, opticians, nurses, and midwives, and including the provision of medical appliances and rehabilitation services. The National Health Service bill was passed in 1946 and called for the establishment of "a comprehensive health service designed to secure improvement in the physical and mental health of the people . . . and the prevention, diagnosis and treatment of illness." The bill incorporated the principles of the Beveridge Report and on July 5, 1948, the NHS was born.

Then, as now, the principles of freedom and choice were maintained by enabling doctors to practice privately and patients to see doctors outside the NHS on an out-of-pocket or privately insured basis. All local government and voluntary hospitals were nationalized and brought under the control of appointed Hospital Management Committees supervised by the thirteen Regional Hospital Boards newly appointed by the Ministry of Health. Teaching hospitals were separately administered directly under the Ministry of Health. A full range of community, environmental, and preventive health services were provided and administered locally; general practitioners were contracted on a capitation basis; and specialists were hospital-based and contracted on a salary basis.

Since its establishment the NHS has gone through three statutory reorganizations, one in 1974, a second in 1982, and the last initiated in 1990 with the passage of the National Health Service and Community Care Act. The 1990 act constitutes the most controversial and far-reaching set of reforms yet undertaken. The reforms initiated then are now in the final stages of implementation.

Up to 1990 NHS hospitals and community health care units had been state-owned and operated by the NHS through the Regional and District Health Authorities in England and Wales, Health Boards in Scotland, and Health and Social Services Boards in Northern Ireland (Health Authorities). These Health Authorities employed most NHS health services staff, including the doctors. The exceptions were the general practitioners, dentists, pharmacists, and optometrists who provided Family Health Services under contract with the NHS. This was a classic public integrated-model health system with hospital services provided to patients in kind, prospectively financed through the NHS Health Authorities with funding of the NHS by the national government from general tax revenues and national insurance payments from employers and employees.

Unlike the previous reorganizations, the 1990 act constitutes a fundamental conversion of the NHS to a public contract model health system by separating the funding bodies, or purchasers, from the provider organizations. The 1990 NHS reforms have created an "internal market" with Health Authorities and fundholding general practices (Fundholders) acting as purchasers contracting prospectively with hospital and community health care providers for defined services. The independent contractor status of the community-based Family Health Service practitioners was not changed. Hospital and community health care organizations have become semi-autonomous, self-governing public trusts (Trusts) that compete with one another for contracts with purchasers. Health Authorities have been functionally and organizationally redeveloped to commission health services for the population within their boundaries. They can now contract with both the NHS and private for-profit and not-for-profit voluntary or charitable providers. Trusts are also able to contract with private insurers and provident funds.

The Health Authorities no longer manage hospitals or community care units, but are responsible as purchasing organizations for assessing the health needs of their area population, determining the priority health services required and contracting with the NHS and private providers to deliver these services. Fundholders are responsible for purchasing a restricted list of common hospital services and a full range of community care services to meet the needs of their registered service population. Hospital and community care Trusts are able to contract with Health Authorities, private insurers, and provident funds to treat patients from other districts. Health Authorities and Fundholders can contract with Trusts and independent providers outside their district.

The eight Regional Offices of the NHS Executive in England have replaced the Regional Health Authorities and now have the responsibility to monitor and regulate this "internal market" to ensure that the purchasers and provider organizations are effectively discharging their respective responsibilities. The Offices are responsible to the NHS Executive for regional implementation of national health policies and for ongoing regional development in the areas of education and training, research and development, and public health. The NHS Executives of other U.K. countries do not have the population to justify regional offices, but work directly with the Health Authorities.

The NHS Executive in England is responsible for national health policy development and implementation and manages the NHS at the strategic level through the Regional Offices.[2] The NHS Executive forms part of the Department of Health, which is accountable to the secretary of state for health, a government cabinet minister. There is similar accountability of the NHS to a government cabinet minister in the other three countries of the United Kingdom. Although the administrative structure of the NHS in each of these countries differs, the roles of the purchaser and provider organizations are the same.

Hospital and Community Health Services in the Reformed National Health Service

The 1990 NHS and Community Care Act provided for hospitals and community care units to become self-governing NHS Trusts as provider organizations in the new "internal market." Hospital Trusts are increasingly multihospital unit organizations providing services to a catchment area population. Community care Trusts provide a range of specialized community nursing services as well as community-based chiropody, dental, psychiatry, and physiotherapy services in health centers and GP practices. Small community hospitals may also be part of the community care Trusts. Some Trusts vertically integrate hospital and community care units.

The 1990 act called for the development of purchasing organizations that contract with providers in the "internal market." Health Authorities became purchasers no longer responsible for the management of providers that became Trusts. Fundholders also developed as purchasers of Community Health Services and some hospital care.

Self-Governing NHS Trusts

The establishment of NHS self-governing Trusts as semi-autonomous NHS organizations with new corporate boards has introduced a greater degree of freedom for hospitals to manage their affairs. This has included the responsibility to establish budgets, set policy, appoint the chief executive, employ staff and doctors, own and sell property, raise capital, and contract with NHS purchasers and private purchasing organizations. These freedoms are circumscribed by a series of provisions that regulate the operation of Trusts as part of the NHS in areas including the appointment of the board chairman and members, annual efficiency saving targets, prior approval of major capital borrowing, and capital asset disposal. Trusts are encouraged to be innovative, but the ability to develop new services, purchase major equipment, and expand bed capacity is limited by the operating and capital funding available from the NHS purchasers, who provide most of the Trusts funding.

The NHS can take over the management of a Trust if it is not considered to be operating in a fiscally responsible manner or in the interests of the public. In the case of the dissolution of a Trust, ownership of the assets is retained by the NHS.

The opportunity for local representatives to serve on Trust boards is limited by the statutory provision for only five nonemployee board positions, excluding the chairman, on a board restricted to eleven members. These five positions are paid, part-time appointments that tend to be offered to those considered to have the requisite business experience or community involvement. The chairman is also appointed from outside the Trust on a part-time, paid basis. The remaining five board positions are reserved for the chief executive officer, the financial, nursing, and medical directors, and one other senior executive staff member.

It is not compulsory to apply for Trust status, and organizations can only become Trusts when they have demonstrated satisfactory financial and managerial viability as well as local support for the change. However, it is government policy that virtually all hospitals and community care units become Trusts by 1996 and this goal has been 95% achieved with the creation of 528 NHS hospital and community Trusts in the United Kingdom since 1990. Most of the remaining directly managed NHS provider organizations are to become Trusts in 1997.

Greater local autonomy to enable Trusts to compete effectively has been one of the major benefits advanced by the supporters of the NHS reforms. However, the potential for increased efficiency through competition only works if patients and their referring GPs agree to treatment by different Trusts, possibly outside their district. If a Trust is not able to compete effectively enough to secure sufficient funding through service contracts, it will hypothetically have to close or merge with another Trust. For political reasons the rationalization and merger of Trusts serving similar areas has been the preferred option. The opportunity for competition amongst Trusts is limited by the number of organizations able to provide the same services to a specified population. This is particularly true of district hospitals and community care units, which historically have been developed to serve total local populations.

Acute Hospital Services

Acute hospital services are predominantly provided by district and regional specialty hospitals. Since 1962 the NHS policy has been to develop district general hospitals in each Health Authority and progressively to close smaller hospitals. District hospitals are often multihospital Trusts with bed numbers ranging from 300 to 1,200 beds, but with most having 600 to 700 beds. These institutions provide a full range of secondary care including the major diagnostic and treatment specialties of radiology, pathology, general and orthopedic surgery, anesthesia, medicine, obstetrics and gynecology, pediatrics, and psychiatry, and at least some of the subspecialties including opthalmology, geriatrics, and cardiology. All care is provided by specialists with no provision for general practitioners (GPs) to admit and treat their patients. A 24-hour emergency care service is also provided by the district hospital, including treatment of major trauma in centers without a regional tertiary care hospital readily available. The emergency department is usually staffed by junior doctors supported by consultant specialists.

Tertiary care is provided mostly by specialty referral hospitals, which are usually affiliated with a medical school for teaching and research. These hospitals are generally located in regional centers that serve several districts. There are also hospitals that have historically developed as supra-regional or national centers of excellence in particular specialties. Care requiring expensive, specialized technology is generally limited to these tertiary centers, including sophisticated diagnostic imaging (NMR [that is, MRI] scanners) and reference laboratory analysis, open heart surgery, organ transplantation, burn treatment, plastic surgery, neurosurgery, and radiotherapy. A regional referral hospital is usually designated as a major trauma center equipped and staffed to handle multisystem trauma. There are some pediatric and maternity hospitals functioning as regional centers, but these specialty services are generally provided both by district hospitals and regional referral hospitals.

Although there is not a national policy to control the dissemination of specialized technology, these major capital investment decisions have historically been determined at the Regional Health Authority level. Trust hospitals now have much greater control over such decisions, although the Health Authorities will determine from which hospitals they will purchase these specialized services.

In 1975 NHS policy was developed to support the role of community hospitals in the provision of local medical and nursing care that cannot be provided in the home for patients who do not require the specialized services of a district hospital. Although community hospitals have not been systematically developed under this policy, their potential continues to be to contribute to the provision of a more cost-effective, progressive spectrum of care provided as close to patients' homes as possible. Community hospitals are more commonly found in smaller communities and range in capacity from 10 to 100 beds. They are staffed predominantly by general practitioners, with visiting specialists often providing outpatient care. Basic medical and surgical care is usually provided along with a minor injuries unit. Obstetric care is now centered at district hospitals, although there is currently pressure to provide more community-based services.

The advances in medical technology, including the development of ambulatory day surgery, diagnostic procedures, and improved surgical and medical treatment techniques, complemented by a broader range of follow-up health care services available in the community have reduced the need for acute and maternity hospital beds. The average number of NHS acute beds available in England decreased by an average of 2.5% per year, from 142,000 to 110,000, between 1983 and 1993.[3] During the same period in England the bed throughput increased by an average of 4% per year.[2] Similarly, in England over the same period the number of NHS maternity beds decreased by an average of 3.4% per year, from 18,000 to 13,000, and the bed throughput increased by an average 5.7% per year.[3] In Great Britain (England, Wales, and Scotland) since 1959 there has been a steady reduction in NHS acute beds excluding maternity to 2.3 beds per 1,000 population and in all NHS hospital beds including psychiatry to 4.8 beds per 1,000 population estimated by 1995, which is quite low compared to most OECD countries.[4]

Acute bed occupancy in Great Britain, excluding psychiatry, declined from 86% in 1988–89 to 81% in 1992–93 while the average acute length-of-stay dropped from 7.5 days in 1988 to 5.7 days in 1993.[5] These changes reflect in part the closure of beds that had been occupied by longer-term geriatric patients who were discharged to other institutional or community care settings as a result of the health service reforms.[5]

Hospitals generally have six- and four-bed rooms with a few single beds on each ward. The older hospitals still have large, open wards of twenty-four or more beds. Priority access to single rooms is based on clinical need with a provision also made for patients wanting to pay for a private room. Some NHS hospitals have developed private wards for these patients to raise additional revenue. Patients can decide at any time during their stay to change status to a private patient and pay both the doctor and the hospital for all services received.

Long-Term Hospital Care

Long-term hospital care has traditionally been provided by the NHS, often in buildings over a century old. This care is provided at no cost to the patient upon referral and assessment that the care is needed. Over the past ten years the trend has been to reduce long-term care provision by the NHS and substitute less intensive level of care at home or in nursing homes. The policy of closing long-term care hospitals and providing more care in the community is a key element of the 1990 NHS reforms, which also transfer much of the financial responsibility for long-term care to local government and patients. However, there is justifiable concern that insufficient resources have been committed to provide adequate care in the community for those who cannot pay for themselves.

Long-term hospital care for the mentally ill has been traditionally provided in large public psychiatric hospitals, most of which were built as asylums in the last century and are still found in some districts. Since 1962 it has been a policy goal to close these large hospitals and place many of the patients in supported community settings with small district hospital acute psychiatric units serving to provide short-term specialist care. In England between 1983 and 1993 there was a 48% reduction in NHS psychiatric beds to 43,000 and the annual bed throughput increased by an average of 8.1%.[3] This has been achieved with the development of district hospital–based short-term inpatient, day care, and outpatient units and improved home and community services for the mentally ill. Multidisciplinary mental health teams have developed in hospital and community settings supported by improved levels of medical, nursing, and social work staffing. However, there is considerable disquiet that inadequate alternative provision has been made for the patients with long-term psychiatric problems who previously had formed the majority of the large psychiatric hospital population.

The mentally retarded, or people with learning disabilities as they are now described, have traditionally been cared for in large institutions. Since 1971 it has been government policy to provide care for those with learning disabilities, particularly children, in more appropriate environments including residential homes, their own homes, and modified hospitals with improved staffing to improve the standards of care. In England between 1983 and 1993 there was a 65% reduction in NHS hospital beds for the learning disabled to 16,000 beds and the annual bed throughput increased by an average of 13.7%.[3] However, the majority of those still in hospital do not medically require this level of care.

Learning disability without medical complications requiring active treatment is no longer considered to be a health care responsibility. Under the community care provisions of the 1990 act it is now the responsibility of local government Social Service Departments to arrange more appropriate placements. However, this transition has been slow, in part because of the need to shift funding from the NHS to Social Services while ensuring continued interim financing for the large existing NHS institutions until this process is complete.

The elderly constitute the largest single category of patients, with about 15% of the population 65 years of age and over. Although this proportion is projected to decrease, the number of those 75 years of age and over will continue to increase. The development of geriatric medicine as a recognized specialty and the establishment of a geriatric assessment unit in most district hospitals since 1962 has ensured the provision of specialized hospital care for the elderly. The holistic approach of these units focuses on patient health in relation to their environment and with the purpose of rehabilitating the patients to minimize their dependence. Many hospitals also provide day care and ambulatory care services to the elderly living in the community.

However, hospitals have also provided long-term care for the elderly that could be provided more appropriately and at lower cost in nursing homes, residential care homes, or at the patient's home supported with home and community-based services. For these patients, once this level of institutional dependence has been established, it is very difficult to transfer an elderly patient successfully to a lower level of care. The policy of moving these patients to alternative care settings also transfers the financial responsibility for much of this long-term care from the NHS to local government and the patients themselves. As with care for the mentally ill, there is considerable concern that inadequate alternative provision has been made for the long-term, chronically ill elderly patients who previously formed the majority of the large geriatric hospital population and who cannot pay for their care.

The 1990 Act requires Social Service Departments to assess elderly people not requiring active hospital treatment and to arrange more suitable care placements on a means-tested basis, if necessary. Nursing home care is provided primarily by the independent profit and not-for-profit sectors and residential care is provided both by local government on a means-tested basis and by the independent sector. Private insurance for nursing home care is unusual, so this creates a financial barrier for many elderly patients who end up staying in hospital inappropriately for long-term care despite their wish to live in a less institutionalized setting. Despite this, between 1983 and 1993 in England there was a 32% reduction in NHS geriatric hospital beds to 38,000, the annual bed throughput increased by an average of 9.7% and the average length of stay dropped from 38.5 days in 1988 to 23.5 days in 1992.[6] This trend accelerated since 1990 and has particularly afffected the large, long-term care geriatric institutions.

The physically disabled requiring ongoing hospital medical and nursing care tend to be treated in acute hospitals, an unsuitable environment, particularly for younger disabled patients on wards with elderly, confused patients. From 1970 it was government policy to build special care hospital units for the younger disabled with the intent of providing early, multidisciplinary rehabilitation to maximize the degree of function. However, there have not been more than 2,000 such beds developed; subsequently the priority has been to provide this care in voluntary sector residential care homes or in the patient's home with NHS community health service support. The disabled person living at home is usually eligible for a broad range of physical aids and house adaptations from the NHS and the local Social Service Department. An attendance allowance is also provided by the government Benefits Agency based on an assessment of individual daily care needs and is not means-tested.

District Health Authorities

The Health Authorities have also undergone significant functional and organizational changes as a result of the 1990 NHS reforms. This is particularly the case in England where the number of District Health Authorities has been reduced from more than 200 to about 100, thus covering larger areas and populations. The District Health Authorities have also merged with the ninety-eight Family Health Service Authorities in England and Wales. Now the funding and regulation of Family Health Services (general practice, dentistry, pharmacy, and ophthalmalic services) is the responsibility of the Health Authorities in all four countries of the United Kingdom.

As hospital and community health units have increasingly become Trusts, so the Health Authority's responsibility for the management of these organizations has shifted to the Trust boards. It is now the Health Authority's primary responsibility to ensure that the health needs of the district population are met by assessing, prioritizing, and purchasing a comprehensive range of accessible health services; by ensuring that effective health promotion and disease prevention policies are in place; by setting population health targets and monitoring the performance of providers in achieving them.

A key element in the reformed Health Authorities is the role of the district director of public health in establishing the priority health needs of the district population based on sound epidemiological research and analysis. The director as an employee member of the Health Authority provides an objective, independent assessment of the nature and degree of the district's health needs in an annual report. Progress toward both nationally set and locally determined population health targets must be reported. The Health Authority uses this report to determine its health care funding priorities for the following year, focusing proactively on strategies to achieve measurable health gains in the population.

The Health Authority membership has also changed significantly to a smaller group less directly representative of the community. Prior to 1990 the Health Authority had a maximum membership of twenty, including local representatives of a range of hospital and community health professionals and four or more local government representatives. From 1990 the Health Authority was restricted to a corporate model of eleven members like the Trust boards with only five nonemployee board positions, excluding the chairman, being appointed on a part-time paid basis mainly for their business and community experience.

This change has increased the importance of Councils in representing the views of health service users. The Councils are statutory bodies established in most districts in 1974 and consisting of voluntary members nominated primarily by local government and voluntary organizations and appointed by the NHS. Community Health Councils are organizationally part of the NHS with the duty to advise Health Authorities and Trusts on consumer views and to inform consumers generally on local NHS issues and assist them in utilizing the NHS complaints procedure. Despite this lack of independence, the Councils have the ability to bring the consumer's view to bear on the effective use of resources to meet local health needs.

GP Fundholders

The 1990 reforms have created a new purchasing role for larger GP practices, initially those with 11,000 or more registered patients. This minimum limit has been progressively reduced by 1995 to 5,000 registered patients to make the fundholding option available to more practices. Fundholding general practices annually negotiate funds to purchase Community Health Services, drugs, and listed appliances and most elective and outpatient hospital services for their registered patients. Fundholders also negotiate an annual fund to pay for the salaries or fees of administrative staff and health professionals including nurses, physiotherapists, and specialists providing services for the practice. The hospital care that can be purchased by Fundholders is limited to elective surgical procedures and investigations generally costing less than £6,000, which constitute about a third of the hospital care provided. The Community Health Services purchased must include home care and community nursing, and can include a full range of specialized therapy services including chiropody, psychiatric nursing, physiotherapy. Health Authorities purchase similar services for the registered patients of non-Fundholders, as well as all of the care that Fundholders are not able to purchase including emergency and nonelective care.

Savings made by a Fundholder from the funds for hospital services, drugs, community care services, or salaries and fees can be retained and spent on additional patient care services or on practice equipment and materials or building and furnishing improvements that enhance the service, comfort, and convenience of patients. None of these funds can be used to pay GPs of the fundholding practice for the comprehensive range of general medical services that they are already paid to provide under contract with the NHS. However, there is an incentive to increase the value of the practice assets by diverting the funds intended for patient care services into the development of the practice premises. General practitioners, as independent contractors, are partners in the practice and benefit directly by increasing the value of their business. The use of the funds provided to Fundholders are regulated by the NHS Executive, which can withhold or claim back any funds it believes are being misused.

Fundholding was introduced to enable GPs to respond more effectively to their patients' needs and preferences by enabling them to fund directly a combination of health care personnel, drugs, and hospital and community care services and to reallocate any savings. Fundholders are also able to shift resources from the secondary to the primary care sector without the prior agreement of the hospitals. For example, a Fundholder may pay a specialist to provide ambulatory care in the practice rather than paying a hospital to provide this outpatient care. By purchasing care directly from both NHS and private care providers, some Fundholders have been able to give their patients faster access to care by avoiding some waiting times faced by the patients of non-Fundholders. Fundholding also introduces a financial incentive for low-risk patient selection by Fundholders. Although Fundholders are regulated, the inequalities in service access resulting from the introduction of fundholding have led to strong criticism that fundholding is promoting development of a two-tier system of care within the NHS.

Fundholding is a voluntary option for GP practices, which must apply and qualify by demonstrating sufficient organizational development and management expertise. Financial, contracting, and information systems must be sufficiently developed, and a satisfactory annual business plan is required prior to being granted fundholding status. If the practice is not able to manage within the agreed resource levels or supply the necessary financial and management information, fundholding status can be withdrawn. In order to reduce the financial risk to fundholding practices there is a maximum cost for each hospital care episode, which was £6,000 in 1995. Costs in excess of this limit are paid by the Health Authority.

It is government policy to foster the development of fundholding practices, but GPs have become Fundholders at a much slower rate than hospitals, and community care units have converted to self-governing Trusts. The government has less influence with GPs who are independent contractors managing their own businesses. By April 1995 more than a third of all GPs in England and Wales serving 40% of the population were working in fundholding practices. Fundholding has not been so popular in Scotland where 22% of the population is served by 17% of the GPs who are fundholders or in Northern Ireland where 31% of the population is served by 27% of the GPs who are fundholders.

In 1994 two new forms of fundholding were introduced to increase the availability and interest in fundholding. Community Fundholding enabled practices with a minimum of 3,000 registered patients to purchase most of the services as other Fundholders except inpatient elective hospital care. Total Fundholding was introduced on a pilot basis for large, well-developed Fundholders, enabling them to purchase all health services for their registered patients. About fifty practices are involved in this pilot scheme.

Financing of Hospital and Community Health Services

The 1990 NHS reforms make the financing of hospital and Community Health Services for a district population the responsibility of its Health Authority whether the patient is treated within or outside the district. The Health Authority is required to contract with providers to pay for a comprehensive range of services within the funds annually allocated to it by the Regional Offices. Current allocations from the NHS Executive take population-based health needs into account and target resources to meet national health targets.

Operating funds are allocated to Health Authorities on a weighted capitation basis, which takes into account the age, sex, and health-risk factors of the population and geographical cost differences. Funds allocated to GP fundholders to purchase hospital and community services are deducted from the Health Authority allocation. It is then the responsibility of the Health Authority to ensure that it purchases services that address the priority health needs it has identified in the district.

Prior to 1990 resources were allocated to regions according to a formula developed in 1975 by the Resource Allocation Working Party (RAWP) to allocate resources more fairly based on the health needs. The RAWP formula calculated regional target operating funding allocations that took into account the age, sex, morbidity and mortality rates and socioeconomic deprivation of each region's population. Regions then used the RAWP criteria to guide the allocation of funding to districts. Historical imbalances were being reduced using the RAWP formula, particularly between London and the rest of the country. However, the formula was a slow and difficult process to implement and was discontinued as part of the 1990 reforms before achieving its full potential.

Contracts between purchaser and provider organizations are not legally binding but constitute service agreements for specific services with the Region arbitrating in the case of a dispute. Initially these agreements were mostly annual block contracts that did not specifiy the volume of services. Increasingly, cost-volume and cost-per-case contracts for each clinical specialty are being negotiated, including some service-quality specifications such as waiting times. The Health Authority pays hospitals on a prospectively agreed basis rather than on a case-specific reimbursement basis and the price is required to be the actual cost of providing the service. The cross-subsidizing of services between different contracts is not permitted.

Although a diagnostic-related group classification system is being developed, it has not been introduced as a standard basis of payment. Prices are negotiated with individual Trusts rather than being set or regulated at district or regional level and can vary significantly for the same service. Consequently, there is price competition where two or more hospitals are able to provide the same services to the same population.

Capital funding for hospital and community care Trusts is also provided by the Health Authority based on its annual allocation from the Region. Capital planning is undertaken to ensure that funds are distributed to renew the building stock across the region rather than distributing capital funds equally to each district. However, by 1990 capital planning had been severely compromised by lack of funding and the condition of hospital buildings was quite poor compared to other countries. The 1990 Act encouraged Trusts to maximize the use of their assets by requiring them to value their assets in current real terms and to achieve a 6% annual return on these assets. Previously the value of assets had been written off for accounting purposes as having no current value.

Under the 1990 Act additional sources of capital funding became available to self-governing Trusts including public donations, revenue-generating enterprises including parking charges and commercial space rental, sale of redundant property, and borrowing on the capital market. Subsequently, provision has been made for joint public and private ventures to fund capital development. Hospitals may also generate revenue by charging for private room accommodation, but they are limited by having to meet the performance criteria of their NHS contracts, particularly those relating to waiting times.

Hospital Admission, Discharge, and Utilization

The decision to admit a patient to hospital is made by a specialist on the staff of the hospital, unless it is a community hospital where a general practitioner working for the hospital will make this decision. Admissions are usually made following referral of the patient by the general practitioner to the hospital specialist for an appointment in the outpatient department. Following one or more outpatient visits and diagnostic tests, the specialist decides whether to schedule the patient for admission. Urgent or emergency referrals from the general practitioner may be directly admitted by the specialist. Patients appearing at the hospital emergency department without a GP referral may be admitted under the care of the appropriate specialist on call.

There are no financial barriers or co-payment requirements to limit patient access to hospital care. All Health Authorities fund emergency hospital care for their residents regardless of where in the United Kingdom it is provided. However, if a GP wishes to refer his patient for nonemergency care at a hospital the Health Authority has not contracted with, the prior agreement of the responsible Health Authority is usually required. These requests for extracontractual referrals (ECRs) are reviewed on an individual basis and district hospitals are generally responsive to special circumstances. If approved, an ECR treatment is paid for by the responsible district hospital at an individually negotiated price; however, this is the exception, as most care is provided on a previously contracted basis.

A hospital risks not being paid by the responsible Health Authority for treating an extracontractual referral without advance authorization, nor can the patient be charged. Health Authorities consult with GPs regarding which hospitals they contract with and are increasingly sensitive to GPs' recommendations, which has tended to reduce requests for extracontractual referrals. GP fundholding practices also reduce the demand for ECRs by contracting independently with providers for the more common elective treatments.

There are substantial waiting times for elective patients requiring hospital treatment, although these times have been reduced over the past few years. Following referral by their GP to a hospital specialist, elective patients must wait for their first outpatient clinic appointment. The current national targets for this are a maximum waiting time of 26 weeks with 90% of patients waiting no more than 13 weeks. In the third quarter of 1994, 83% of patients in England had waited less than 13 weeks, 96% of patients had waited less than 26 weeks, and 4% of patients had waited more than 26 weeks for their first outpatient clinic appointment. Orthopedics and plastic surgery had the longest waiting times and general surgery, general medicine, and gynecology had the shortest times. The second waiting time is for admission to elective inpatient care after being referred from the outpatient clinic. The current national target is to ensure no patient waits more than 18 months. In March 1995 this target had been virtually met in England with 97% of patients waiting less than 12 months for elective admission. The waiting times tend to be longest for the most common elective operations including those for hernias, varicose veins, cataracts, and hip replacements.

Patients referred to hospital for urgent care are supposed to be seen by a specialist in a month, but this is not nationally tracked. Emergency hospital referrals are seen in the emergency department and admitted or transferred based on clinical need. GPs are required to provide a 24-hour primary medical care service to their registered patients, including home visits if needed. Given this service patients generally contact their GP first if they are ill rather than going directly to the hospital emergency department. Patients who inappropriately bypass their GP are seen in the emergency department, but are referred back to their GP for follow-up care. GPs who send their patients unnecessarily to the emergency department without first seeing them may be reported for being in breach of their contract.

Since 1991 under the 1990 act local government Social Service Departments have been made responsible for assessing patients with continuing care needs prior to discharge and developing individual care plans that take into consideration the level of care dependency and the financial and social circumstances. These plans are developed, costed, and implemented collaboratively with the hospital and with the Health Authority. A patient should not be discharged from hospital until a care plan has been developed and agreed with the parties concerned.

This system was developed in part to address the community care needs of the elderly, the physically and mentally handicapped, and the mentally ill patients and to prevent them from being discharged before appropriate care has been arranged. Concerns have been raised that the resources provided to the Social Service Departments and Health Authorities for undertaking these new responsibilities and for implementing the deinstitutionalization process have been inadequate. This problem of transitional funding combined with the involvement of the local government Social Service Department in the hospital discharge process has contributed to delays in the discharge of patients, but has also provided greater protection against inappropriate community placement. The cost of these additional days in hospital are not charged to the patient, but are paid for by the NHS.

Contracts are increasingly specifying the cost and volume of care, the waiting times and the development of clinical protocols that help to ensure the effective and efficient utilization of resources. However, hospital utilization review programs are not well developed in part due to a lack of timely and accurate clinical activity information. Although case-mix systems have been piloted, they are not in general use. The national standards for reducing waiting times and the pressure from purchasers to meet contract performance requirements is encouraging hospitals to implement improved clinical activity and utilization review systems.

Quality and Accreditation

The need to improve quality of service to patients has been a major focus of the 1990 reforms. In order to qualify as a Trust, a hospital had to include a quality strategy in its business plan. The NHS requires Health Authorities to include quality statements in contracts with providers. A range of quality strategies has been implemented by hospitals including Total Quality Management, Continuous Quality Improvement, patient-focused care, process reengineering and benchmarking with other similar Trusts. The Regions monitor the compliance of Health Authorities and Trusts to agreed quality targets including the national Patient's Charter standards set by the NHS. Patient's Charter standards relate to access, availability, and choice, including maximum waiting periods for GP appointments, inpatient admissions, outpatient appointments, and community care visits; having a named, qualified nurse responsible for nursing care; choosing and changing the GP.

The 1990 NHS reforms also required medical audit programs to be instituted by doctors both in hospital and community practice. The purpose of these programs is not regulatory but educational, with support provided locally to assist doctors to develop guidelines for clinical practice, monitor practice, and provide feedback through continuing education. A national annual survey, the Confidential Enquiry into Perioperative Deaths, examines and makes recommendations on surgical care based on all deaths occurring up to thirty days after a surgical procedure. Clinical guidelines are also developed by the various medical Royal Colleges for particular conditions. These recommendations and guidelines have informed the medical audit process. The impact of these medical audit programmes on clinical practice is indirect, as compliance with clinical guidelines is voluntary. Trusts are responsible for ensuring that doctors, nurses, and other health professionals are appropriately qualified, licensed, trained, and supervised, although the mechanism for disciplining consultant specialists is cumbersome.

Over the last five years a voluntary acute hospital accreditation program has developed under the auspices of the King's Fund, a charitable foundation supporting health care management innovation. The accreditation program is based on the Australian hospital accreditation program modified for the U.K. environment with the participation of the various national health professional colleges and organizations. In 1990 this program started as a confidential hospital organizational audit service assisting hospitals to apply accreditation standards, but not offering an accredited status. By 1995, some 115, or about 25%, of NHS acute hospital Trusts and 70 private hospitals from all parts of the United Kingdom had participated in this program. The demand for a public accreditation status led to the addition of an accreditation component to the program using recently updated standards that is now being piloted in ten hospitals. An organizational audit program without accreditation status has also been developed by the King's Fund for GP practices and about 100 practices have participated so far. Programs for community and mental health services, nursing homes, and for Health Authority and GP purchasing organizations are also being developed.

NHS hospitals and health centers, most of which are in NHS Trusts, are permitted to operate under the ultimate jurisdiction of the Department of Health and the responsible government minister. The Department, through the NHS Executive, issues and enforces directives and procedures in accordance with the legislation and regulations to ensure reasonable operating standards. However, private hospitals, clinics, and nursing homes must register under the Registered Homes Act, which is administered through the NHS. Inspection of these private facilities to ensure compliance with regulatory standards is the responsibility of the NHS.

Private Hospital and Clinic Care

The major reasons for people to chose privately financed health care are to avoid the NHS waiting lists, to be able to chose their hospital, specialist, and admission date and to have more comfortable, private accommodation.[7] Elective care waiting times both for seeing a specialist and for hospital or clinic treatment are usually less than a month, well below most NHS providers. The most common elective conditions treated on a private pay basis include hernias, gall-bladder disease, ulcers, hysterectomies, varicose veins, and hip replacements. These are also the conditions with the longer NHS waiting times. About 20% of all nonemergency operations are paid for privately and many uninsured people pay out-of-pocket for private care to avoid the waiting times.

Urgent and emergency treatment for serious conditions that are life-threatening are also treated privately, but this is less common and usually done in NHS hospitals, particularly when intensive care is required. Some acute psychiatric care and treatment of substance abuse is also provided privately, usually funded locally by the Health Authority, to care for patients discharged from the large psychiatric hospitals. Screening and diagnostic services primarily to meet occupational health requirements are privately funded. Lastly, fertility regulation (IVF and AID) and abortion services are funded both by the NHS and privately.

In the United Kingdom the private hospital and clinic expenditures, excluding specialist fees, were estimated to be £950 million in 1992 and private hospital care provided by the NHS, excluding specialist fees, were estimated to be £150 million. The specialist fees for this care were estimated to total £600 million. The other elements of private and clinic care expenditure (acute psychiatric and substance abuse care; screening and diagnostic services; fertility regulation and abortion) were estimated to be £122 million. This is a total of £1.67 billion excluding NHS receipts. This compares with net NHS expenditure on hospital services, excluding community health services, of £19.2 billion, or 8% of total U.K. hospital service expenditures for 1992–93.[1]

Private hospitals with an operating theater are classified as acute and these hospitals accounted for about 7% of total U.K. bed capacity in 1992–93. Of the 11,306 beds reported available in 221 private acute hospitals in 1993, approximately 2,000 beds were for day cases only. However, it appears that about 50% of surgical cases in private hospitals are done on a day-care basis. The private hospital average occupancy rate is believed to be about 60%. From 1979 to 1993 there was a 71% increase in the number of private beds and a 49% increase in the number of private hospitals.[7] The volume of private elective and acute health care, including that provided by the NHS, increased at a rate of 6.9% per annum from 1985–86 to 1990–91, but declined by about 1% in 1991–92.[1]

The three leading private hospital companies are General Healthcare Group (formerly AMI), the British United Provident Association (BUPA) Hospitals Limited, and Nuffield Hospitals, which together were responsible for 49% of the total private acute turnover. About 70% of the procedures performed in private acute hospitals are classed by them as minor (for example, grommet insertion, manipulation of leg joint) or intermediate (ligation of varicose veins, surgical removal of impacted tooth), with the remaining being classed as major (hip replacement, hysterectomy, replacement of coronary arteries).[7]

Since the establishment of the NHS, a proportion of the beds in an NHS hospital are authorized for use as "pay-beds," which means consultants can admit and treat patients in these beds and charge private fees and the hospital can charge these patients privately for the hospital services. In 1991 there were about 3,000 NHS pay-beds in the United Kingdom used for private patients about a third of the time. However, these beds are being replaced by NHS Trust hospitals with building-dedicated private patient units, which increased from 25 to 80 units between 1991 and 1993. NHS private patient revenue also increased by an estimated 50% from 1989–90 to 1992–93 to £150 million.[7] There is competition among private hospitals and clinics, increasingly, involving NHS Trust hospital private care units.

Most private medical services are provided by specialists whose main commitment is to their NHS work, so most private practice is undertaken in addition to NHS working hours. Most private practice is concentrated in central London, southeast and central England, and the principal cities of Scotland, Wales, and Northern Ireland. Patients want private hospital and clinic facilities to be as close to their homes as possible and specialists want to do their private work close to their NHS hospital; consequently, private facilities are generally located in or near reasonably large urban populations and NHS hospitals.

The increase in private elective and acute care has been matched and strongly influenced by the growth in private medical insurance. The main player has been BUPA, with a market share declining in the face of strong competition from virtually the only company in the 1970s to 44% in 1992. The other large companies are the Private Patients Plan at 28% market share, the Western Provident Association at 5%, other provident associations at 4%, and commercial insurers (for example, Norwich Union Healthcare, Prime Health, Sun Alliance) at 19%.[7] The percentage of the U.K. population covered by private health insurance peaked in 1990 at 11.6% and declined to 11.1% by 1992. Economic recession accounted for much of this reduction as 61% of all subscribers in 1990 were on company-paid schemes, but growth is expected to resume in 1995 at an annual rate of over 5% per year resulting in a 16.5% coverage of the U.K. population by 2000.

Medical Practice

Medical practitioners consist mainly of general practitioners (GPs) providing community-based primary care and consultant specialists with their teams of junior doctors providing hospital-based care. In addition, public health medicine specialists fulfill a public health role, maintaining surveillance of the population's health-assessing need for health service interventions and evaluating outcomes. Finally, a small group of specialists provide community-based specialty care.

In 1992 the UK had 32,003 fully qualified GPs and 2,840 GPs in various staff and training positions; 20,094 qualified, hospital-based senior specialists, called consultants, and 32,741 hospital specialists in a range of staff and training positions; 4,309 public health and community-based specialists, including staff and training positions. The ratio of doctors to population in the United Kingdom for 1992 was one doctor to 631 persons, a rate of 1.6 doctors per 1,000 population. This compares with more than 2.0 doctors per 1,000 population for most European and North American OECD countries in 1989, 1990, and 1991.

By 1996 there are estimated to be 36,380 GPs, 57,073 full-time-equivalent hospital-based doctors and 3,429 full-time-equivalent public health and community services doctors. This is a ratio of 59% hospital-based FTE doctors to 41% FTE GPs and other community-based doctors; 1.65 FTE doctors per 1,000 population.

General Practice

GPs are independent contractors with the predominant form of practice being partnerships of two or more GPs. In 1994 only 10% of GPs in the United Kingdom practiced single-handed, 13% practiced in partnerships of two, 17% practiced in partnerships of three, 18% practiced in partnerships of four, 16% practiced in partnerships of five, 26% practiced in partnerships of six or more principals, with very few in partnerships exceeding eight unrestricted principals. The NHS reforms have encouraged development of group GP practices by granting them greater management autonomy and additional management resources through the GP fundholding scheme to GP practices of at least three to four principals.

Virtually all practicing GPs have a full- or part-time contract with the NHS and full-time private practice is unusual because there is very little difference in the level or availability of GP service provided privately. The NHS GP contract is uniform across the United Kingdom, is nationally negotiated and pays GPs for general medical services, primarily on a capitation basis. There are additional payments made for achieving specified target levels of immunization and cervical screening among the population registered with each GP. Additional payments are also made for each session of minor surgery, childhood development monitoring, for providing health promotion and chronic disease management for cardiovascular disease, asthma, and diabetes and for serving predominantly socioeconomically deprived populations.

The GP is the patient's access point to most NHS primary and secondary care services and must ensure provision of a full range of general medical services and 24-hour a day medical service coverage, including house calls, for all registered patients. A community-based primary care team is coordinated by the GP to provide practice-based and home visiting nursing care, particularly for the elderly and young families. GP practices provide limited diagnostic and treatment services, but refer patients to hospital for laboratory, X-ray, ultrasound, ECG investigations and physiotherapy, speech therapy, and minor surgical treatment. As a result of the NHS reforms GPs have been increasingly able to provide services in the practice, including physiotherapy, counseling, and specialist outpatient clinics.

Any resident of the United Kingdom can register with one GP of his choice in his service area, and most residents do register. Patients may also change their GP without prior notification. The GP may decide not to accept a patient on his list, but provision is made through the Health Authority, the Family Health Services regulatory and funding body, to ensure access to a GP for every resident who wants one, although choice may be limited. There is no charge or co-payment for the patient for care provided by the GP. For emergency care, patients also have the right of direct access to hospital accident and emergency departments and admission for treatment without charge or co-payment.

The GP acts both as a care provider and as a gatekeeper, controlling access to NHS specialist and hospital care, a common feature of managed-care health systems. With the exception of some small community or cottage hospitals located in more isolated areas, GPs do not admit or treat patients in hospital. Hospital care is provided by consultants and their specialist medical teams. The NHS reforms encourage an increasing shift of clinical care from the hospital to GPs in the community, particularly for postdischarge, follow-up care and the management of diabetes and asthma. Shared and integrated care protocols are being negotiated between referring GPs and consultants for the management of particular conditions that previously would have been undertaken by consultants only. The incentive for GPs to reduce the amount of hospital care provided per case is to increase the resources available to their practice for provision of primary or secondary care services. However, unless there is greater provision made in their contract for GPs to be paid for this additional work, there will continue to be a financial disincentive for GPs to accept this transfer of care from the hospital.

Although the distribution of GPs is generally good across districts, their distribution within districts does not match population health needs, particularly in socioeconomically deprived rural and inner city areas. In 1993 the average number of patients in England and Wales registered with a GP (average list size) varied from 1,669 to to 2,103. An independent body called the Medical Practices Committee classifies areas with an average list size over 2,100 as overdoctored and areas with an average list size under 1,700 as underdoctored. In 1993 approximately 2.5 million people in England and Wales lived in underdoctored areas and 9.25 million people lived in overdoctored areas. The Health Authority controls the number of GPs practicing in each area, restricts doctors from moving into overserved areas and encourages GPs to develop practices in underserved areas by providing advice and funding for training, facility development, and staff.

Under the GP contract the intended average net (pre-tax earnings net of expenses) remuneration target for full- and part-time GPs for 1993–94 was £40,610 plus the payments for achieving specified targets worth an average of £3,000. The average allowance for practice expenses per GP in 1993–94 was £22,190. A survey of GPs in 1992–93 showed that a GP worked an average of 40.5 hours per week providing general medical services. Differences in GPs' income is related to the GP's list size and the amount of private work undertaken. Actual average gross or net incomes of doctors are not available so that it is not possible to determine the average income of doctors.

Specialists

Consultants and their medical teams are hospital-based and staff the outpatient, emergency, day case, and inpatient services. These doctors now have employment contracts with the hospital and community Trusts. This is a recent change as previously these doctors were employed by the Regional Health Authorities who also controlled the number of consultant and other specialist positions. Trusts will decide the number and mix of specialists they employ in accordance with the contracts they secure for providing care, but also within nationally set NHS human resources policy. The pay scales for hospital doctors is currently standard across the United Kingdom for all specialties. This may change as Trusts now are able to negotiate directly with their doctors. The full-time consultants' pay scale in 1992–93 ranged from £38,475 to £49,680 per annum with 35% of consultants also receiving a distinction award ranging from £9,750 (21% of consultants) to £46,500 (1% of consultants) per annum. Consultants may be employed on a full-time contract or varying levels of part-time contract. By 1995–96 the consultants' pay scale had increased to £40,620–£52,440. A full-time consultant may also earn an additional salary income for managerial or clinical responsibility equivalent to one-eleventh, and sometimes two-elevenths of his salary.

Most private practice is undertaken by consultants whose main commitment is to the NHS. Full-time NHS consultants are limited to earning an additional gross private practice income of 10% of the sum of his or her salary plus distinction award. The private practice income of a part-time NHS consultant is not limited and most consultants with a private practice have a maximum part-time contract (ten-elevenths of a full-time contract). Private medical services are paid on a fee-for-service basis, usually according to British Medical Association (BMA) Guidelines or BUPA benefit maxima.

Based on a self-reporting survey of consultants, the Monopolies and Mergers Commission into Private Medical Services concluded that in 1992 the median total net earnings (pre-tax earnings net of expenses) from the NHS and private practice for maximum part-time consultants earning more than £1,000 a year from private practice were £59,000, the upper decile total net earnings were £127,000, and the average total net earnings were £77,000. These figures reflect the skewed distribution of private practice earnings toward high earners. The average total net earnings of a senior lawyer in private practice are £186,000 and the median is £149,000, or approximately two and a half times that of a consultant.

This survey also reported the distribution of median net (pre-tax earnings net of expenses) private practice earnings in 1991–92 by specialty with plastic surgery in the £50,000 to £74,999 band; orthopedics in the £30,000 to 49,999 band; ear, nose, and throat (ENT), urology, ophthalmology, general surgery, and ob-gyn in the £20,000 to £29,999 band; anesthesia, cardiothoracic surgery, oral surgery, radiology, neurosurgery, and psychiatry in the £10,000 to £19,999 band; and general medicine and pathology in the £5,000 to £9,999 band. This reflects the role of private practice in elective surgery where waiting lists for NHS patients are greatest.

The number of hours spent by consultants on NHS and private practice according to the 1992 survey reflected the terms of the full-time or part-time NHS contract and the extent of commitment to, and demand for, private practice. The mean weekly hours spent by full-time consultants on NHS work was 53 hours and on private work was 6 hours; by maximum part-time consultants on NHS work, 51 hours and on private work, 11 hours; by less than maximum part-time consultants on NHS work, 45 hours and on private work, 16 hours.

Professional Organizations

The Provincial Medical and Surgical Association was founded in 1832 and changed its name to the British Medical Association (BMA) in 1856. As the professional association and trade union for doctors in the United Kingdom, it aims "to promote the medical and allied sciences and to maintain the honour and interests of the medical profession.'' Membership is voluntary and approximately 75% of doctors practicing in the United Kingdom are members of the BMA.

The early Association advocated a single licensing authority and a single professional qualification of doctors in order to curb unqualified practice, which resulted in passage of the Medical Act by Parliament in 1857. This act established the General Council of Medical Education and Registration, later renamed the General Medical Council, as the body funded and organized by the profession and responsible for its regulation. The BMA and the General Medical Council (GMC) are independent of the government and of each other.

The GMC membership comprises representatives of the Royal Colleges, university medical schools, the government, and the medical profession at large. It maintains a register of doctors licensed by the recognized authorities, supervises the educational standards of training institutions and disciplines doctors it finds responsible for professional misconduct including removal from the Medical Register for serious offenses. Royal Colleges or other equivalent medical corporations have been established for each speciality, including general practice. In practice, the universities are responsible for the standards of undergraduate training and licensure and the Royal Colleges for the standards of postgraduate and specialist training and licensure. All postregistration training programs in hospitals and other health care organizations must be accredited by the responsible Royal College or equivalent medical corporation.

The BMA is the body with which the government negotiated the role of the medical profession in the NHS when it was established in 1948. The BMA had already established through a professional code of ethics the continuing responsibility of the GP for patients registered on his list and the responsibility of the specialist for episodic diagnosis and treatment of patients referred by their GP. The 1990 NHS reforms were also negotiated with the BMA, although these reforms were introduced despite BMA opposition to many aspects of the reforms because of its concern that their effect would be detrimental to patient care.

The BMA is the recognized organization representing the interests of doctors in national and local negotiations with NHS and other employers. It has sole bargaining rights for NHS doctors employed under national agreements and is also recognized by the independent Review Body on Doctors' and Dentists' Remuneration. The BMA has established committees to negotiate on behalf of the five main groups of doctors: general practitioners, hospital consultants and specialists, public health doctors, medical academics, and doctors in training. These BMA committees act autonomously of the BMA governing council, each taking complete responsibility for the interests of all the doctors it represents, which includes non-BMA members. The BMA also has a network of regional offices with industrial relations specialists to advise individual doctors on employment issues and help resolve problems with employers. The BMA's Legal Department supports the regional offices in these activities.

There are also a number of BMA committees dealing with matters affecting the medical profession as a whole, including medical ethics and the impact of U.K. membership in the European Union on mobility of doctors and on prescribing practices. In 1968 the BMA established a Board of Education and Science to produce reports on key health issues and support the BMA in areas of public health reform such as cervical cancer screening, compulsory seat belt legislation, and banning tobacco advertising.

There are other organizations that have developed to protect the interests of doctors, but their memberships are relatively small compared with the more than 100,000 members of the BMA. Although the BMA is generally regarded as the foremost organization representative of the medical profession as a whole, the BMA leadership has not always been seen by doctors as being in touch with their interests or as adequately presenting the position of the profession. This situation is compounded by the existence of three different, and at times competing, professional bodies: the BMA, the GMC, and the Royal Colleges or other professional medical corporations.

Medical Education

All doctors have common preclinical and clinical training leading to qualification after five or six years followed by a preregistration year working in a hospital as a house officer in general medicine and general surgery. Following registration, doctors training as specialists undertake a training program accredited by the responsible college or faculty that consists of two to four years as a senior house officer, two to four years as a registrar, and up to four years as a senior registrar. The candidate must also pass the specialty examinations set by the college or faculty for certification as a specialist.

If a senior registrar has not been appointed to a consultant position upon completing the maximum four years of training at this level, it may be impossible to obtain a consultant appointment in future. The medical profession, in consultation with the Department of Health, attempts to ensure that the total number of senior registrar posts do not exceed the number of consultant positions coming available. However, trainees are not assured of gaining a consultant appointment in the wide range of specialties where vacancies are few or in the geographical area they wish to practice. The number of positions in public health medicine is controlled by the Health Authorities and RHAs, which employ virtually all of these specialists. Each district and region has a director of public health and at least one other qualified consultant in public health medicine.

Doctors training to become general practitioners require three years of postqualification training consisting of experience in relevant hospital specialties, including general medicine, pediatrics, and obstetrics, a supervised training period in a GP practice and an elective training period of the candidates choice. Since 1948 about half of all qualifying doctors have consistently chosen to train in general practice, which has had the effect of increasing both the numbers of general practitioners and the ratio of GPs to population. In 1995 this ratio was estimated to be one GP to approximately 1,800 resident population in the United Kingdom, which is well within the target range of 1,700 to 2,100 patients per GP set by the Medical Practices Committee. About a quarter of GPs are women and this proportion is increasing as half of medical school admissions are women. Upon completion of training, each graduate must find a position in a general practice. The NHS limits the number of GPs permitted to practice in each area according to the average GP registered patient list size.

Undergraduate and postgraduate medical training is publicly funded. The number of undergraduates entering medical schools is limited through the University Funding Council in consultation with the medical schools, the Department of Health, and the BMA. The number and specialty of postgraduate training and consultant positions has been controlled by the Department of Health in consultation with the BMA and Regional Health Authorities through the Joint Planning Advisory Committee. Medical manpower planning has been facilitated through these consultative mechanisms, but has also been complicated by the emigration of overseas doctors and, more recently, by doctors emigrating from the other European Union (EU) countries. The ability of hospital and community Trusts to employ their own consultants may also affect demand.

In 1993 the Calman Report recommended reducing to seven years the length of training for postregistration specialty training required to become a fully qualified consultant, which would bring the United Kingdom in line with EU directives. The implementation of these measures is expected to increase the supply of U.K.-trained specialists.[8]

Continuing education for doctors is not a requirement for continued licensure, but Central Councils for Postgraduate Medical Education in each county monitor standards and advise Regional Postgraduate Committees on continuing medical education. The Regional Postgraduate Committees ensure continuing education programing is organized, financed, and delivered at district level through postgraduate training centers that have been developed at district general hospitals. A program of peer review assessment of competence for all doctors every five years is under active consideration.

Other Health Practitioners

Dentists

Dentists train for four to six years to obtain a diploma or degree from an approved school of dentistry before being licensed to practice by the General Dental Council. The Council keeps a register of all professionally qualified and licensed dentists, supervises the standard of dental teaching and examinations, and disciplines dentists it finds responsible for professional misconduct including removal from the Dental Register for serious offences.

There are about 22,000 dentists in practice of which the largest group are general dental practitioners. The number of practicing dentists per 1,000 population was 0.3 in 1993, which is lower than North American and most European OECD countries. In 1994 about 18,500 dentists worked at least part-time for the NHS as independent contractors. A second small group of dentists are employed as specialists by NHS Trust hospital dentistry departments and provide orthodontic, oral surgical, or restorative treatments not provided by general dental practitioners. A third group of dentists are employed by NHS community health Trusts to provide dental care to people who do not have access to general dental practitioners, such as the elderly and handicapped in residential care. The fourth group of dentists are those in full-time private practice.

A new NHS dental contract implemented in 1990 for general dental practitioners doing NHS work emphasized the need for continuing dental care and provided incentives to provide preventive care rather than only restorative treatment. This was achieved by the NHS paying a continuing care payment to the dentist for each adult patient who agrees to register with the dentist for continuing care over a two-year period. This fee entitles a patient to a written treatment plan and emergency dental care (previously only available at the discretion of the dentist). Most of the treatments for adults must be paid for by the patient on a fee-for-service basis according to a nationally agreed fee schedule that takes into account practice expenses. For children under eighteen who have registered with a dentist, the NHS also pays the dentist a capitation fee that includes the costs of most treatments. About 20% of a dentist's NHS income is made up of the continuing care and capitation payments, with the rest generated by fee-for-service payments. In addition, dentists may provide private dental care, paid for by the patient and for which private dental insurance is available. As with medical doctors, data on average private and NHS income of dentists is confidential.

Many patients are exempted from having to make payments for NHS dental care including children under eighteen, pregnant mothers, and people on social security support. For these people the NHS makes the applicable fee-for-service payments to dentists. In 1995 patient dental charges constituted about 30% of the total gross cost of NHS dental services.

Nurses

Nursing in the United Kingdom was united as one profession in 1979 by the Nurses, Midwives, and Health Visitors Act. In 1983 the U.K. Central Council for Nurses, Midwives and Health Visitors replaced all previously separate registering bodies and became responsible for establishing and improving standards of training and professional conduct, regulating registration and maintaining a single professional register of nurses, and protecting the public from unsafe practitioners.

Historically three years of study and supervised practice in an approved hospital was required for qualifying as a registered nurse, and two years of training program for qualifying as an enrolled nurse. The reform of nursing training under the Project 2000 proposals of 1986 led to the development of university certificate nursing qualification consisting of core training of 18 months for all nurses followed by a further 18 months training specializing in adult, pediatric, mental health, or learning disabled nursing. This program trains all nurses to work both in hospital and community settings and also provides enrolled nurses with the opportunity to upgrade their qualification to registered nurse level. Midwives have maintained a separate three-year university diploma training program.

Community nurses, including district nurses and health visitors, work in the community more independently of doctors and require additional training. These nurses care for the elderly, mothers and children in the home and residential care settings, in health centers and GP practices. They require a year of postregistration training at university diploma level, and may qualify at degree level, although less than 5% of nurses hold degrees. Since 1990 several master's-level courses have been developed for training nurse practitioners, although licensing has not been developed for this specialty.

Pharmacists

Pharmacists must register with the Pharmaceutical Society after completing training in order to practice. The NHS employs registered pharmacists to prepare and dispense medicines prescribed by hospital doctors to inpatients and outpatients. There is no charge to the patient for medicines prescribed by the hospital.

Retail registered pharmacists are independent contractors paid by the NHS to dispense medicines prescribed by GPs. The practice of retail pharmacists is regulated by the NHS at district level to ensure compliance with the Medicines Act and drug formulary and guidelines regarding proprietary and generic drugs. The NHS pays for all medicines prescribed by GPs and the patient must contribute to this cost at a flat fee in 1995 of £5.25 per item. Children under eighteen, pregnant mothers, the elderly, and people on social security support are exempted from this charge.

Opticians

The Opticians Act in 1958 restricted the prescribing and dispensing of eyeglasses to ophthalmic medical practitioners and ophthalmic opticians registered and regulated by the General Optical

Council. In 1984 the Health Services Act revoked the monopoly granted to opticians to supply eyeglasses; thus private retailers as well as opticians can now sell, but not prescribe, eyeglasses. The NHS pays for eye tests and a specified range of eyeglasses and contact lenses for children, people who need complex lenses or are at high risk, the registered blind or partially sighted, and people on social security support.

Others

The Council of Professions Supplementary to Medicine was established in 1960 and oversees seven Boards, one each for chiropodists, dieticians, medical laboratory technicians, occupational therapists, physiotherapists, and radiographers (radiology technologists) and orthoptics. Each Board maintains registers of qualified practitioners, prescribes qualifications for state registration, approves training programs and institutions, and disciplines practitioners for professional misconduct.

Continuing Health Care Services

Continuing health care is provided through hospitals, nursing and residential care homes, hospices, family health services, and community health care services. As described above, there has been a significant shift of continuing care delivery in the past decade from hospital to less-intensive care settings.

Following introduction of the NHS reforms, the continuing health care services to be purchased by Health Authorities and Fundholding GPs to meet local needs have been specified to include care requiring regular specialist clinical supervision in a hospital or nursing home. For patients at home, in hospital, and in nursing or residential care homes, Health Authorities and Fundholders must fund a full range of professional rehabilitation, convalescent, palliative, respite, and community health care services, specialized health equipment, and ambulance transport. These health services include care by a full range of health professionals, including GPs and medical specialists, physiotherapists, chiropodists, dentists, speech therapists, and nurses specializing in areas such as home care, stoma, diabetic and palliative care, and mental health. The patient's GP is responsible for organizing and coordinating individual care programs for the patients registered with them whether they live at home or in an institution. These health services are fully funded by the NHS and provided on the basis of clinical need.

The NHS is not responsible for social care that includes accommodation, meals, and custodial or personal care provided at home or in nursing and residential care homes. Social care is paid for by the individual resident or the local government Social Services Department based on a social needs assessment and on the financial means of the applicant. For patients with both health and social care needs, responsibility for funding of an integrated care plan is negotiated on a case-by-case basis between the Health Authority and the Social Services Department. The elderly, mentally ill, physically disabled, mentally handicapped, and drug- or alcohol-dependent who are assessed as requiring social care and have assets totaling less than £8,000 may qualify for income support to help pay for the cost of their social care. Any personal income source including pensions must be contributed to the cost of this care.

Nursing home care is provided by the private and voluntary sectors and is defined as care with a component that must be supervised or provided by a registered nurse. Nursing homes register by type and number of beds with the local Health Authority, which sets staffing and quality standards and inspects the homes. Nursing home residents' medical care and other specialized health care needs of nursing home and residential home residents are met by their GP and other NHS or private health services.

The nursing home average length of stay was 2.2 years in 1993 and had been dropping due in part to the reduction of long-term hospital beds, which led to inappropriate discharging of terminally ill patients. The NHS subsequently issued directives to hospitals to prevent this practice.

Public Health

The Department of Health, and the equivalent government departments in the other U.K. countries, is responsible through its chief medical officer for ensuring that the full range of public health services are financed and functioning effectively. In England the chief medical officer, as the government's most senior public health official, advises the secretary of state for health and other government ministers on medical matters and works through the regional and district directors of public health to support implementation of a comprehensive national public health program. This program includes development and implementation of national health strategy and meeting national health targets; health needs and outcomes assessment; control of communicable disease and non-communicable environmental exposures to microorganisms, chemicals and radiation; monitoring and surveillance including surveys, cancer registries, and national confidential inquiries into mortality and morbidity; public health protection, health promotion and disease prevention in areas including screening, smoking, substance misuse, immunization, coronary heart disease, stroke, and accident; safety of drugs and medical devices, blood, blood products and tissues. Similar programs are in place in Scotland, Wales, and Northern Ireland.

In carrying out these activities the health departments work closely with other government departments and publicly funded, public health-related agencies including the Public Health Laboratory Service, the Communicable Disease Surveillance Centre, the Health Education Authority, the Office of Population Census and Surveys, the National Radiological Protection Board, local government Environmental Health Departments and the Occupational Health and Safety Directorate. At the Health Authority level, each Department of Public Health has a director of public health, a consultant in communicable disease control, other consultants in public health medicine and qualified support staff to assist in implementing a locally focused public health program. The director of public health is an executive member of the Health Authority and as the senior public health official also serves as its medical adviser. Similar public health teams and roles are established elsewhere in the United Kingdom.

Health Costs and Private Health Insurers

Total health expenditure in the United Kingdom as a proportion of the gross domestic product (GDP) was 6.9% in 1993 and is projected to drop to 6.7% by 1995 and 6.4% by 1997. This compares with a figure for all EEC countries of 8.3% of GDP in 1992 projected to drop to 8.0% in 1995 and a figure for all OECD countries of 9.9% of GDP in 1992 projected to rise to 10.4% by 1995.

The disparity in health expenditure between the United Kingdom and most major industrialized countries is also reflected in total health expenditure per capita, with the United Kingdom spending in 1992 about 60% of the average for all OECD countries and about 74% of the average for EEC countries. Projected expenditures based on the close association between per capita GDP and health spending indicate that the difference between U.K. and other OECD and EEC countries' total health expenditure will continue.

Government, or public health expenditure in the United Kingdom has been about 85% of total health expenditure since 1985 and is projected to stay at this level. This compares with the average EEC level of public expenditure of about 77% since 1990 and the average OECD level of about 60% since 1990. Total U.K. health expenditure rose 48% between 1989 and 1993, with public health expenditure increasing more slowly by 46% and private health expenditure by individuals and insurers increasing more rapidly, by 62%. NHS administration costs in 1987 were 2.5%, and this is the target for Trusts to achieve.

The factors responsible for the increase in total health expenditure during this period were population growth (3%), health inflation (67%), and increased utilization (30%). The rise in health sector pay and prices account for much of the inflation and the increase in utilization is attributable to changes in demographic structure, technology, and medical practice. The aging population, increased availability and utilization of technology, higher expectations and greater demand for health services all contribute to increased utilization costs. The projected percentage increase in U.K. total health expenditure from 1993 to 1997 is a modest 17%, reflecting a very optimistic anticipation of cost savings to be generated in part by the NHS reforms.

In the United Kingdom, private elective and acute health expenditure includes patient payments for NHS prescriptions, dental and ophthalmic care, health appliances and payment for private care in NHS hospitals, as well as payments for care in private hospitals, private prescriptions, and medical equipment paid by patients or their insurers. All expenditures on NHS services, including patient payments, represented about 88% of total health expenditure in 1993, with the remaining expenditure made in the private sector. This is a decrease from 1985 when 90% of total health expenditure was on the NHS and represents an increase in the relative size of the private sector. This ratio of private to NHS health sector expenditure is projected to remain unchanged.

Although nursing home, residential home, and at-home personal care services are not privately insured or provided by the NHS, they are a rapidly expanding area in the private sector. These services are paid for by individuals or local governments on a means-tested basis. This market was worth £6,032 million in 1994.

The sources of finance for the NHS in 1993 were central government general tax revenue (84.2%), National Insurance Scheme employee and employer compulsory contributions (12.2%), and payments by patients (3.6%). Patient payments consisted of statutory charges, mostly for NHS prescriptions and dental treatment (57%); the rest were NHS hospital charges mainly for discretionary private services. The revenue from NHS statutory charges for prescriptions and dental services more than doubled in real terms between 1979 and 1993, in part because the annual rate of increase in these charges was in excess of general inflation.

During the period from 1984 to 1993 public funding from general tax revenue and National Insurance contributions fluctuated between 96% and 96.4% of total NHS revenue with patient payments financing the remaining proportion. In 1995 public funding is projected to finance 96.6% and patient payments 3.4% of total NHS revenue.

Private health care insurers set their own premiums and schedule of benefits, subject to review under the 1973 Fair Trading Act. The British Medical Association (BMA) also started publishing medical fee-for-service rate guidelines in 1989 because the fee schedule for the largest medical insurer had not been increased for three years. In 1993 an investigation by the Monopolies and Mergers Commission found that the use of the BMA Guidelines resulted in doctors' private fees being higher than they otherwise would have been and that their publication was against the public interest. The publication by insurers of benefit schedules, however, was encouraged as it promoted competition and was a legitimate means of informing policy-holders of the extent of the benefits they could claim under their policies.

Private health insurers do not have to accept individual applicants for health insurance coverage, but 60% of subscribers are covered by employer-paid schemes that pool risks. In the highly competitive company private health insurance market, insurers generally accept liability for preexisting conditions.

Conclusion

The reforms of 1990 have transformed the NHS from a compulsory health insurance system with integration of the public payer and provider organizations (public integrated model) to a compulsory health insurance system with prospective contracting between the public purchaser and provider organizations (public contract model). This creation of an internal market with Health Authority and Fundholder purchasers and Trust, Family Health Service, and private providers has resulted in the decentralization of NHS organization and management from a detailed central command-and-control system to a more autonomous, self-regulated system. The lack of excess NHS provider capacity and consumer resistance to more distant providers has limited actual competition.

More important has been the focus of the NHS reforms on achieving gains in population health status by funding programs to achieve locally relevant health targets. This has been combined with increased emphasis on improving the quality, availability, and efficiency of health services through contract performance targets. The NHS has set national health gain and provider performance targets and these have been addressed and augmented through the local contracting process. The most significant change has been the involvement of GPs working with directors of public health in the determining of local priorities for purchasing community and hospital services. In summary, the funding of health services is focusing more on health needs and outcomes and becoming more quality- and cost-explicit.

The NHS reforms have been implemented in phases over a six-year period with full implementation to be completed in 1996. It is too early to assess the medium- and long-term results of these reforms, but the transitional consequences have not all been positive. GP Fundholding has enabled some Fundholders to offer earlier access to a broader range of health services than non-fundholders, thus introducing a preferential level of care within the NHS. Fundholding also creates an incentive to select lower-risk patients; thus GP practices serving higher-risk patients are less financially able to meet the health needs of their patients.

In the United Kingdom health status is closely related to socioeconomic status, but by fragmenting purchasing responsibility among Fundholders and the Health Authority the reforms have made it more difficult for Health Authorities to purchase the health care required by those with the greatest health needs. Contracting has also introduced new transaction or administrative costs to the health system, although these have partially been compensated for by reductions in health authority staffing. Public accountability of NHS organizations to the local population has become less direct with the exclusion of local government representation on Health Authorities and the lack of local government or other elected local representation on Trust or Health Authority boards.

The rate of increase in total NHS expenditure does not appear to have been reduced by the reforms. For 1985–89 the growth in NHS gross expenditure was 41% compared to the growth of 46% for 1989–93; however, productivity increased during this latter period resulting from lower pay and price inflation and a greater increase in volume of services provided. The projection for 1993–97 is for an NHS gross expenditure increase of 16%, although this seems based on overoptimistic assumptions.

The development of the NHS reforms has been strongly influenced by the U.S. and Dutch experience with managed competition between purchasers and providers of health services, which was reflected in Alan Enthoven's report on the NHS. Fundholding incorporates elements of U.S. Health Maintenance Organizations, fostering competition among both purchasers and providers.

However, if the Opposition Labour Party wins the general election in 1997, it may phase out the independent purchasing role of Fundholders, substituting longer-term, consolidated service agreements between the Health Authorities and providers in order to reduce transaction costs and increase equity in service provision without losing the benefits of the public contract system. If the current Conservative Government is reelected, the fragmentation of purchasing among Fundholders is likely to continue making it more difficult for Health Authorities to ensure limited resources are focused effectively to meet high-priority health needs.

NOTES

1. Private Medical Services, Monopolies and Mergers Commission. 1993. 8–11.

2. Managing the New NHS, Functions and Responsibilities in the New NHS. July 1994. *NHS Executive, 3.*

3. *Statistical Bulletin 12/94.* October 1994. NHS hospital acitivity statistics: England 1983 to 1993–94. Department of Health, 8.

4. Compendium of Health Statistics, Office of Health Economics. 1995. 9th ed., 30–31.

5. Ibid., 30–31, 33, and 36.

6. *Statistical Bulletin 12/94.* October 1994. NHS hospital activity statistics: England 1983 to 1993–94. Department of Health, 14.

7. Private Medical Services, Monopolies and Mergers Commission. 1993. 14–19.

8. DHSS, BMA Joint Consultants' Committee, RHA Chairman. July 1987. Hospital Medical Staffing: Achieving a Balance. London.

In addition to the above references, the following books are recommended. The Reorganised National Health Service has been an invaluable source of information for this chapter:

Baggott, R. 1994. *Health and Health Care in Britain.* Macmillan.

Levitt, R., A. Wall, and J. Appleby. 1995. *The Reorganised National Health Service.* 5th ed. Chapman and Hall.

Ranade, W. 1994. *A Future for the NHS? Health Care in the 1990s.* Longman.

Robinson, R., and J. Le Grand. 1994. *Evaluating the NHS Reforms.* King's Fund Institute.

Yates, J. 1995. *Private Eye, Heart and Hip: Surgical Consultants, the National Health Service and Private Medicine.* Churchill Livingston.

Table 1A United Kingdom Population by Age and Gender, 1994 (in millions)

	Male	Female
<5	2.02	1.92
5–9	1.95	1.85
10–14	1.88	1.78
15–19	1.79	1.69
20–24	2.12	2.02
25–29	2.39	2.31
30–34	2.32	2.27
35–39	2.02	2.01
40–44	1.90	1.91
45–49	2.02	2.03
50–54	1.61	1.62
55–59	1.46	1.49
60–64	1.37	1.45
65–69	1.25	1.42
70–74	1.06	1.36
75–79	0.71	1.09
80–84	0.44	0.85
>85	0.25	0.75

SOURCE: *Compendium of Health Statistics,* Office of Health Economics, 9th ed., 1995.

Table 1B United Kingdom Population by Gender and Political Subdivision, 1994 (in millions)

	Male	Female	Both Genders
England and Wales	25.28	26.32	51.60
Scotland	2.49	2.65	5.14
Northern Ireland	0.80	0.83	1.63
United Kingdom	28.56	29.80	58.37

SOURCE: *Compendium of Health Statistics,* Office of Health Economics, 9th ed., 1995.

Table 1C Elderly (65+) and Very Old (75+) Population, United Kingdom

	1983		1993	
Percentage of Total Population	65+	75+	65+	75+
England	15.8	7.0	9	12
Wales	17.2	7.6	14	19
Scotland	15.1	6.5	6	15
N. Ireland	12.1	5.2	5	14
United Kingdom	15.7	7.0	9	13

SOURCE: *Compendium of Health Statistics,* Office of Health Economics, 9th ed., 1995.

Table 1D   Dependency Ratios, Populations under 15 and over 65 as % of Working Population

	1994	Projected 2025
United Kingdom	54.2	57.2
European Union	49.1	57.8
OECD	50.5	57.4
World	62.4	53.0
United States	52.5	57.0

SOURCE: *Compendium of Health Statistics*, Office of Health Economics, 9th ed., 1995.

Table 2A   United Kingdom Birth, Fertility, Infant and Childhood Mortality Rates

	Live Births	Birth Rate[1]	Fertility Rate[2]	Infant Mortality Rate[3]	Childhood Mortality Rates[4]
1993	762,000	13.1	62.1	5.9	0.3
1994[5]	773,000	13.2	—	5.1	0.2

SOURCE: *Compendium of Health Statistics*, Office of Health Economics, 9th ed., 1995.
1. Per 1,000 population.
2. Live births per 1,000 females age 15–44 years; calculated from OHE data.
3. Deaths under one year per 1,000 live births.
4. Deaths between ages 1–4 per 1,000 population.
5. Estimated.

Table 2B   United Kingdom Political Subdivisions— Selected Regions' Infant Mortality Rates

	1992	1993
England	6.5	5.8
East Anglia[1]	4.6	4.2
N. W. Thames	5.5	5.1
N. E. Thames	7.1	6.7
W. Midland[2]	8.2	8.0
Wales	6.0	5.5
Scotland	6.8	5.6
Northern Ireland	6.0	5.6

SOURCE: *Compendium of Health Statistics*, Office of Health Economics, 9th ed., 1995.
1. Lowest regional rate.
2. Highest regional rate.

Table 3   United Kingdom Political Subdivisions—Infant Deaths and Rates by Most Frequent Causes

ICD-9 Codes		1992 England and Wales		1993 Scotland		1993 Northern Ireland	
		Deaths (under 1 year)	IMR	Deaths	IMR	Deaths	IMR
740–49	Congenital anomalies	370	0.54	133	2.1	72	2.89
760–79	Certain conditions originating in perinatal period	218	0.32	174	2.75	62	2.49
E-code	Injuries, accidents, poisonings, etc.	83	0.12	10	0.16	4	0.16
480–93	Pneumonia and bronchitis, asthma	75	0.11	7	0.1	18	0.72
000–139	Infections and Parasitic Disease	77	0.11	5	0.08	6	0.24
	Live Births	689,307		63,337		24,909	

SOURCES: Department of Health, England; NHS, Scotland; Welsh Office; Department of Health and Social Services, Northern Ireland.

Table 4 Crude Death Rates by Leading Causes of Death, United Kingdom, 1992 and 1993, (Both Sexes) per 1,000 population

	1992	1993
	Actual	Estimated
1. All below heart disease and hypertension	302	290
Ischemic heart disease	259	250
Diseases pulmonary circulation and other heart	33	31
Chronic rheumatic heart disease	4	4
Hypertensive disease	6	4
2. All neoplasms	258	253
Malignant neoplasms of trachea, bronchus and lung	59	57
of Breast	24	24
of Stomach	14	15
of Uterus	5	5
Leukemias	6	5
3. Cerebrovascular disease	117	113
4. Asthma, pneumonia, bronchitis and emphysema	62	61
Asthma	3	3
Pneumonia	48	48
Bronchitis and emphysema	11	10
5. All accidents and violence	30	29
Motor vehicle accidents	7	7
Suicide and self-inflicted injury	7	7
6. Mental disorders	22	22
7. Diabetes mellitus	14	14
8. Ill-defined conditions	9	10
9. Ulcer of stomach and duodenum	8	7
10. Chronic liver disease and cirrhosis	5	5
11. All infectious and parasitic diseases	5	5
Influenza	1	1
Tuberculosis of lung	1	1
12. Hernia of abdominal cavity and other intestinal obstruction	4	4
13. Nephritis, nephrosis, nephrotic syndrome (*ESRD*)	4	3
14. Congenital anomalies	3	3
15. Hyperplasia of prostate	1	1

SOURCE: *Compendium of Health Statistics*, Office of Health Economics, 9th ed., 1995.

Table 5A Selected Surgical Procedures (Diagnostic Procedures Exclusively), United Kingdom, 1992 (Rate per 1,000 population)

1. Endoscopic exam of upper G.I. tract	5.6
2. Endoscopic exam of bladder (cystoscopy)	2.9
3. Biopsy of cervix uteri	0.9
4. Endoscopic exam of colon (colonoscopy)	1.0
5. Endoscopic exam of peritoneum (laparoscopy)	0.8
6. Endoscopic exam of knee joint (knee arthroscopy)	0.7
7. Endoscopic exam of lower bowel (colonoscopy)	0.7
8. Diagnostic spinal puncture	0.6
9. Endoscopic exam of sigmoid colon (sigmoidoscopy)	0.5
10. Endoscopic exam of bronchus (bronchoscopy)	0.4

SOURCE: *Compendium of Health Statistics*, Office of Health Economics, 9th ed., 1995.

Table 5B Selected Surgical Procedures (Primarily Therapeutic Procedures), United Kingdom, 1992 (Rate per 1,000 population)[1]

1. Evacuation[2] of contents of uterus	6.2
2. Curettage of uterus (D & C)	5.7
3. Excision of skin lesions (including subcutaeneous tissue)	2.6
4. Cataract surgery (lens extraction)[3]	2.3
5. Tonsillectomy plus operations on adenoid	1.9
6. Myringectomy (incision of eardrum)	1.4
7. Primary repair of inguinal hernia	1.4
8. Abdominal hysterectomy	2.4
9. Transurethral prostatectomy (endoscopic resection outlet of male bladder)	1.0
10. Endoscopic ligation of fallopian tubes	1.9
11. Varicose vein ligation and other varicose vein operations	1.2
12. Emergency appendectomy	0.8
13. Excision of vas deferens (vasectomy)	0.8
14. Circumcision	0.8
15. Endoscopic exterpation lesion of bladder	0.7
16. ''Total hip'' prosthetics	0.5
17. Cholecystectomy	0.5
18. Operations on nasal septum	0.5
19. Carpal tunnel (release of nerve entrapment)	0.4
20. Destruction of lesion of cervix uteri (female)	0.8

SOURCE: *Compendium of Health Statistics*, Office of Health Economics, 9th ed., 1995.
1. Where exclusively for female sex, per 1,000 female population but rates for males (e.g., TURP) are per 1,000 *total* population.
2. Other than by D and C.
3. About three-fourths included insertion of lens prosthesis.

Table 5C   Selected Surgical Procedures (Hospital Length of Stay [Days][1] for Selected Operative Procedures), United Kingdom, 1992

	1992	1992–93
1. Cataract surgery	3	
2. Tonsillectomy		2
3. Prostatectomy (non-malignant)	8	
4. Inguinal hemiorrhaphy		3
5. Appendectomy (appendicitis)	6	
6. Varicose Veins	4	
7. Hip Arthroplasty		18

SOURCE: *Compendium of Health Statistics,* Office of Health Economics, 9th ed., 1995; Department of Health, England.

1. These may include preoperative days and some cases where there was no surgery.

Table 6   Doctors' and Dentists' Average Net Income Before Personal Income Taxes (£) (after office and other professional expenses)

1. Dentists[1]	36,352
2. General practitioners[2]	45,090
3. Full-time NHS consultant[3]	51,216
Plus allowable 10% private practice earnings	56,338
4. Part-time NHS consultant	50,000
Plus private practice earnings[4]	77,000
5. Part-time NHS consultant plus private practice earnings by speciality[5]	
Plastic surgery	92,000–116,999
Orthopaedic surgery	72,000–91,999
ENT, urology, ophthalmology, general surgery, obstetrics & gynecology	62,000–71,999
Anesthetics, cardiothoracic surgery, oral surgery, radiology, neuro-surgery, psychiatry	52,000–61,999
General medicine, pathology	47,000–51,999
Others	52,000–61,999

SOURCE: Private Medical Services, Monopolies and Mergers Commission, 1993.

1. Target average net income, 1993–94, Review Body on Doctors' and Dentists' Remuneration, 23d Report, 1994.

2. Intended average net remuneration, 1994–95, Review Body on Doctors' and Dentists' Remuneration, 23d Report, 1994.

3. Mid-range NHS salary plus weighted average distinction award, 1993–94, Private Medical Services, Monopolies and Mergers Commission, 1993.

4. NHS Maximum Part-time Consultant average earnings plus estimated average net private practice income for 1992, Private Medical Services, Monopolies and Mergers Commission, 1993.

5. NHS Maximum Part-time Consultant median earnings for 1992 plus median estimated net private practice earnings for 1991–92, Private Medical Services, Monopolies and Mergers Commission, 1993.

Table 7   Number of Acute NHS Hospital Beds, Acute Finished Consultant Episodes and Acute Average Length of Stay for Great Britain[1]

	1992/93	1994/95[2]
Average daily available acute beds[3]	177,000	169,000
Acute Finished Consultant Episodes[4]	8,319,000	8,670,000
Acute average length of stay[5]	5.7 days	—
Acute bed occupancy[6]	81%	80%

SOURCE: *Compendium of Health Statistics,* Office of Health Economics, 9th ed., 1995.
1. England, Wales, and Scotland.
2. Estimated.
3. Excluding all psychiatric, geriatric, and mental handicap patients.
4. Replaced discharges and deaths after 1987–88; excludes day cases, psychiatric, geriatric, and mental handicap patients.
5. Excluding obstetrics and psychiatric patients.
6. Excluding psychiatric hospital beds; in England also excluding mental handicap and psychiatric patients in any hospital.

Table 8   Hospital and Community Trusts[1] in the UK by Total Beds,[2] 1995

Bed Size	<100	100–199	200–399	400–599	600–799	800–999	1000–1499	1500–2000	>2000
No. of Trusts	21	34	95	98	80	67	62	11	2

SOURCES: *The Fourth Newchurch Guide to NHS Trusts,* Newchurch and Co., 1994; *Health Service Directory,* Institute of Health Service Managers, 1995.
1. Bed figures available for 470 of 528 Hospital and Community Trusts; some Community Trusts have no beds.
2. All types of beds including psychiatric, geriatric, mental handicap; one or more hospital units per Trust.

Table 9A   Registered Nursing Home and Private Residential Home Beds in the United Kingdom

	1989	1994
Registered Nursing Home Beds[1]	89,766	181,124
Registered Residential Home Beds[2]	176,528	210,655

SOURCE: *Review of Private Healthcare 1994,* Laing and Buisson.
1. For elderly care only.
2. Excludes local government residential home beds.

Table 9B   Registered Nursing Homes in England, 1993–94

Number of registered nursing homes	5,132
Registered nursing home beds	165,021
For the elderly	147,904
Average number of beds per nursing home	32

SOURCE: Department of Health, England.

Table 10A NHS Expenditures by Type of Expenditure, United Kingdom (£ millions)

	Gross Expenditure		Net Expenditure		Patient & Insurer Payments	
	1993	1995e	1993	1995e	1993	1995e
Hospitals	20,784	22,489	20,205	22,034	579[1]	455[1]
Community health services	3,286	3,570	3,286	3,570		
Total family health services	9,297	10,475	8,528	9,634	769[2]	841[2]
Pharmaceutical	4,091	4,364	3,832	4,061	259	303
General Practice	3,081	3,266	3,081	3,266		
General Dental	1,528	1,563	1,066	1,084	462	479
General Ophthalmalic	227	242	227	242		
Other	370	394	370	394		
Other Expenditures[3]	4,844	4,983	4,844	4,983		
Total	38,211	41,517	36,863	40,221	1,348	1,296

SOURCE: *Compendium of Health Statistics,* Office of Health Economics, 9th ed., 1995.
1. Includes payments for Community Health Services.
2. Including unallocated pharmaceutical and dental payments.
3. Costs not financed by the other NHS Services including Health Authorities/Boards administration, central administration, ambulance services, mass radiography services; public health laboratory, vaccines, research and development costs.

Table 10B Acute and Elective Private Health Care by Type of Expenditure (£ millions), United Kingdom, 1994 (Paid by Patients and Insurers)

Hospitals and clinics total[1]		1,163
Medical and surgical inpatient and outpatient care	1,061	
Medical/Physical rehabilitation	12	
Psychiatric and substance dependency care	79	
Screening and diagnostic tests (including medical fees)	31	
Fertility regulation (termination of pregnancy and fertility treatment including medical fees)	25	
Medical specialist fees		641
Pharmaceutical products and medical equipment		2,700
General practice		55
Dentistry		200
Eye tests, eyeglasses, and contact lenses		700
Trained therapists and complementary medicine		500
Total		5,959

SOURCE: *Review of Private Healthcare 1994,* Laing and Buisson.
1. Excludes total NHS payments of £45 million for acute care services included in detailed acute care figures below.

Table 10C Long-Term Care Expenditures (£ millions), United Kingdom, 1994 (by Patients and Local Government)

Nursing Homes	3,151
Residential Homes[1]	2,411
Non-residential Care	470
Long Term Care Total	6,032

SOURCE: *Review of Private Healthcare 1994,* Laing and Buisson.
1. Excludes local government residential homes.

The Health System of the United States

Marshall W. Raffel and Norma K. Raffel

Introduction

The United States is a republic with a federal system of government consisting of a federal (national) government and fifty state governments. The original thirteen colonies revolted against the British Crown in the latter half of the eighteenth century, and on winning their independence joined to establish the federal government. They created a federal government with limited powers, seeking to avoid the excesses they saw practiced by the European powers of that day. The delegation of powers from the original thirteen states to the federal government was specified in a written constitution.

The federal government consists of three independent branches: executive, legislative, and judicial, each serving as a check on the other. The President, who heads the executive branch, is independently elected, as is the Congress (the legislative branch), which consists of a Senate and a House of Representatives. Laws must be approved by both houses and signed by the President. Though the President can reject (veto) legislation passed by the Congress, Congress can override that veto if two-thirds of both houses approve. The judges of the independent judiciary—the Supreme Court and lower courts—are appointed for life by the President but their appointments must be approved by the Senate. State governments have a similar structure; the executive in the states is known as the *governor* and the legislative branch is typically known as the *legislature.*

Today, each state and the federal government have written constitutions that specify what each government, and each branch of government, can and cannot do. Each government has the power to tax, build roads, maintain peace, and so on, but the federal government has exclusive powers over interstate and foreign commerce, foreign affairs, and war. Neither the federal government nor the states have the power to interfere with free speech, what the press writes, the practice of religion, the right of the people to assemble peaceably, and to petition government for redress of grievances.

While there is a consensus that the United States is one country and that the various governments must work together, a state of tension exists between the state and federal governments, and between government and the people, tension over what is best for society and over who should assume responsibility for various policies—the federal government, state governments, or the private sector. Political discussions throughout society and elections resolve most issues, and the judiciary resolves others.

When it comes to health services, each level of government and the private sector has a role to play; some have exclusive rights and responsibilities, some shared responsibilities. The federal government provides health services for military personnel, veterans with service-connected disabilities, Native Americans (American Indians and Alaskan Natives), and the inmates of federal prisons. The Constitution of the United States does not refer to health services but it does grant the federal government authority to raise taxes and to provide for the general welfare. By interpretation, therefore, the federal government has the power to allocate monies to the states and the private sector to carry out functions the federal authority desires for the general welfare of the population. This grant of constitutional authority legitimizes appropriations for biomedical research, medical and nursing education, and since 1966 money to pay doctors, hospitals, nursing homes, and others for care of the elderly and the poor.

It should be emphasized, however, that most money for support of the health system comes not from government but from the private sector. Only 43% of all monies spent during 1993 came from the government: 33% from the federal government, and 10% from the state and local governments. That the federal government accounts for only 33% of national health expenditures moderates the extent to which the federal government is able to regulate health affairs and why it must be responsive to the concerns of the state governments, private hospitals, medical associations, health insurance companies, and others who have a role in the health system.

Hospitals, universities, voluntary (nonprofit, nongovernmental) agencies, and state governments receiving federal monies must conform to federal regulations governing the use of those monies. Since money also comes from other sources, if a state, hospital, university, or other agency chooses not to use federal money, it is free of much federal control. But not to use federal money when it is available presents a challenge when money is in short supply; hence agencies try to get federal money whenever possible. As a consequence, the federal government increasingly sets the agenda for much of what goes on today. Nonetheless, the extent of federal control is moderated because, as just noted, the federal government pays only a small part of national health expenditures. Further, if its policies or regulations are perceived by the states or the people as excessive or too rigid, public pressure can lead Congress to force the executive branch to moderate its policies so that they are more acceptable to the states and the affected people. It does not serve the federal government's objectives, moreover, if the states and others refuse to apply for federal monies because the federal monies are there to promote the general welfare as the federal authorities believe appropriate.

The powers of the states are limited by their respective constitutions and by the federal government in the areas where the federal government has exclusive authority. State legislatures can raise their own revenue; there is no federal limit on state taxing powers. State money is raised within the states by various taxes including taxes on income, business enterprises, retail sales, and so forth. Different states tax different items and at different rates. States also get various types of grants from the federal government. State powers are either spelled out or implied in their constitutions or are inherent in the police powers of government. Thus, licensure of hospitals and various types of health professionals (including physicians, dentists, nurses) is a function of state government; traditional public health activities such as food and water quality, sanitation, public health nursing, vital statistics, have also historically been a function of state governments as well as mental health and mental retardation services. State government activity in the delivery of health services does not prohibit or exclude the private sector from also engaging in these activities, with or without state financial support.

The states vary as a result of different traditions and styles, and different wealth. Federal transfer payments via formula grants tend to serve as an equalizing force to some extent by taking into account the wealth and special needs of each state. While state governments are, in a certain sense, sovereign because they exist independently of the federal government and cannot be abolished or have their borders changed without state consent, local governments do not have such independence. They are creations of the state governments; as a consequence the powers of local governments vary. In some states local governments have broad taxing powers, in other states limited powers. Local governments generally carry out many of the state-mandated public health activities, which are typically financed by a combination of local and state monies, and occasionally with some federal grant support. Some local governments also run general and special hospitals. There are often strong disagreements between the larger local governments and their state governments, disagreements over finance and over policies. Large cities typically argue that they are not getting a fair share of state government revenues, and this is debated every year in the various state legislatures.

The organization and delivery of most health services is largely in the domain of the private sector. The private sector's independence of government is increasingly compromised by a growing dependence on federal and state monies that finances medical care for the elderly, the disabled, and the poor. With government financing comes the imposition of government policies and regulations: for example, family planning clinics during the administration of George Bush were not allowed to discuss abortion if they were recipients of federal monies. Clinics that continued to do abortion counseling had as a consequence to forgo federal money, getting their money from state government or the private sector.

Between the private sector and both state and federal governments there has always been an uneasy relationship stemming from a historical distrust of government. The private sector consists of hospitals, physicians, dentists, nursing homes, home care agencies, and mental health (MH) and mental retardation (MR) services, to name just a few. While the nonprofit sector dominates, many of the institutional services are also provided by for-profit enterprises. The private sector also includes health insurance companies, both nonprofit and for-profit, medical supply and pharmaceutical manufacturers, universities, as well as an enormous number of professional and business interest groups.

Medical Practice

Rapid changes are occurring in the practice of medicine. The growth of Health Maintenance Organizations (HMOs) and other managed-care alternatives designed to contain costs has resulted in a decline of professional autonomy, increased competition, and changes in the methods of payment for medical care services. The oversupply of physicians in some parts of the country is another factor facilitating changes in medical practice. There were 607,339 practicing physicians in the United States in 1993 or 258.6 per 100,000 people—more than ever before and the number is expected to increase throughout the 1990s. Of these, 37% are primary care physicians and 63% are specialists. (Primary care is defined as specialists in family medicine, internal medicine, and pediatrics.) The increasing physician-population ratio has intensified competition among physicians for patients, and between physicians and hospitals that provide care in ambulatory settings.

These pressures have resulted in more physicians forming group practices, taking salaried positions in hospitals, and participating in managed-care arrangements.

Historically most physicians practiced alone and were paid a fee-for-service, but now the majority are in group or hospital-based practices that are either of the same specialty or of multiple specialties. Typically, groups share offices, personnel, equipment, and other expenses. They may be paid on a fee-for-service basis, a salary, or a share of the group's income. The most recent survey of physician-practice types by the American Medical Association showed that 33.4% of physicians who were involved in patient care were in group practice; 34% were in solo or two-physician practices; 32.6% were in other types including employment by hospitals, medical schools, public health departments, and private industry. More and more physicians are being employed by others (39% in 1994), with almost half of the younger physicians being in that category. Approximately 55% of all nonfederally employed physicians are still self-employed in private solo or group practice.

Most groups, as well as individual physicians still practicing by themselves, have contracts with one or more managed-care programs to treat their members at a reduced rate. These physicians will also usually treat other patients, charging their usual fee for their services. In 1994, 77% of all physicians had managed-care contracts and derived on average over one-third of their income from them.[1] Some physicians derive all of their income from managed-care arrangements.

Managed Care

Managed care includes a variety of programs ranging from HMOs and Preferred Provider Organizations (PPOs) to preapproval of hospital admissions, which is required by many traditional health insurance companies. All have a common goal: to reduce health expenditures while maintaining quality of care. About 51% of all insured people are in some type of managed-care arrangement though it should be noted that those insured where only preadmission authorization for hospital care is required have only nominal managed care, being completely free to choose their primary care physician, specialist, and hospital.

HMOs are a major type of managed-care arrangement that have experienced dramatic growth in recent years with enrollments expected to reach 65 million Americans in 1996, almost 25% of the population. They provide comprehensive services for members for a fixed, prepaid fee. There are several models (types) of HMOs and they are constantly changing to remain competitive. They use a variety of cost-containment procedures to control unnecessary use of medical resources such as requiring a primary care physician to approve referral to specialists, for diagnostic tests, and for hospital admissions. The services provided by individual HMO physicians are frequently compared to those of other physicians in the HMO who are treating similar conditions to compare clinical outcomes and costs. Some HMOs as well as specialty groups are adopting clinical guidelines for treating specific symptoms. HMO physicians may be salaried, paid a fee-for-service, or a capitation fee for each patient on their list, and are often provided with financial incentives to reduce the amount of unneeded services. HMOs may own their own hospitals or contract with hospitals for services. For-profit HMOs are the fastest growing type of managed care.

PPOs are managed-care arrangements in which a limited number of health care providers—physicians, hospitals, and others—agree to provide services to a specific group of people (for example, employees of a company) at a negotiated fee-for-service rate that is less than their normal charge. PPOs are a phenomena of the 1980s when they grew rapidly as an alternative to the restrictive features of HMOs. PPOs provide a choice of health care provider for patients.

Though encouraged to use a PPO physician and hospital, patients are permitted to go to other physicians and hospitals but pay a larger co-payment. In addition, in most PPOs patients are not required to see a primary care physician first but are free to consult specialists whenever they choose to do so. Physicians like the PPO's feature of maintaining fee-for-service, office-based medical practice, and many regard PPOs as a way to compete with HMOs and increase the number of patients in their practice because of the greater choices available to patients. Many physicians have contracts with more than one PPO as well as with HMOs, and also see other patients who are not in a managed-care arrangement. PPOs, like HMOs, depend upon cost-saving activities such as prior authorization for nonemergency hospital admission, utilization reviews, mandatory second opinions for surgery, and studies that compare the treatments provided by their physicians with those in other practice settings. In PPOs, as in HMOs, physicians lose some of their autonomy and must accept some controls. Utilization reviews may be designed and carried out by hospitals, insurance companies, or outside physician groups with varying amounts of input by the PPO health providers. PPOs face increasing competition from HMOs, some of which also offer the option of treatment outside of the organization. For this option, known as a Point-of-Service HMO, the premium is typically higher and the patient incurs a co-payment when using a non-HMO provider. Competition has forced PPOs and HMOs to change benefits and programs to respond to the demands of health care purchasers (particularly businesses and government). Both PPOs and HMOs are expected to continue to grow at the expense of the traditional form of medical practice because they cost less and are increasingly accepted by the public and medical providers.

Notwithstanding, as managed care programs grow, and particularly HMOs, there is concern that in their efforts to contain costs, quality of care will suffer: patients may have to wait longer for appointments, fewer referrals will be made for specialist consultations and diagnostic testing, and patients will not get the type of care they (rightly or wrongly) believe they need. Quality of care has thus become a very significant issue for the public as competition and cost-containment efforts increase. Methods for determining quality include more rigorous peer review and the development of standard diagnostic and treatment guidelines for common conditions. Comparing clinical outcomes is also becoming an important measure of quality of care. Although many physicians have resisted attempts to evaluate their clinical treatments, medical organizations are concerned that those outside the medical profession will impose quality assessment measures and are thus urging their colleagues to take a major role in developing procedures to measure quality of care.[2]

Monitoring quality of care is not easy. Surveys of HMO enrollees show overall satisfaction although the satisfaction rate varies from one HMO plan to another. A survey of Medicare (which finances care of the elderly and disabled) beneficiaries found overall satisfaction with their medical care but those beneficiaries who chose to enroll in an HMO were less satisfied than the Medicare fee-for-service beneficiaries who had unlimited options.[3] Hard quality-of-care data is difficult to come by. According to a recent study by the General Accounting Office (GAO) of the U.S. Congress, in the private sector, businesses and other organizations that offer HMOs to their employees do a better job in their efforts to monitor quality of care than does the government's Medicare program. Increasingly the private sector requires that the HMO be accredited by a nongovernmental agency which publicizes the results of its accreditation reviews; some large employers require specific information from the HMOs about their quality of care when deciding which HMO they will sponsor for their employees.[4] The GAO report found the government's monitoring of HMOs to be lax.

Primary Care Physicians and Other Specialists

The demand for primary care physicians is growing mostly because of expanding managed care systems—primarily HMOs—that use primary care physicians as ''gatekeepers'' to treat patients and refer them to specialists for hospital admission when appropriate. Part of the recent emphasis on primary care is an effort to control costs by encouraging the use of primary care doctors rather than the more expensive specialists who tend to order more diagnostic tests, write more prescriptions, and hospitalize patients more often.[5] Despite the increased demand and incentives, the number of medical graduates entering the primary care fields is beginning to rise but only very slowly in part because of the disparity in income between them and other specialists, and the absence of primary care role models for students in many medical schools. Other reasons are that specialties are intellectually appealing and specialists are more highly regarded by the general public. Thus far, efforts to decrease the number of medical graduates entering specialties, instead of the primary care fields, have had limited success.

In the United States patients may consult specialists directly rather than be referred by a primary care physician except in some managed-care arrangements. Both primary care physicians and specialists can admit and treat patients in most hospitals except teaching hospitals. Often even after the primary care physician has referred patients to other specialists, they continue to visit their patients in the hospital, confer with the specialists, and charge a fee for their services.

The average physician in 1993 spent about 53 hours a week in direct patient care and had an average of 110 patient visits a week. The average net income for physicians in 1993 after expenses and before taxes was $189,300; the median income was $156,000.[6] In 1994 the median physician income dropped 3.8% to $150,000 because overhead costs have been increasing, Medicare reimbursements have remained stable, and managed-care companies have been negotiating lower payments. There is a great disparity in earnings depending upon the specialty (see Table 6). Physicians are the highest-paid professionals in the United States; their average income is over ten times that of the average production worker who is paid on an hourly basis. Physician incomes are a subject of debate even within the medical profession. Internists have argued that their skills are undervalued compared to surgical skills and technological procedures. To correct the wide variation in physicians' fees and to encourage more medical graduates to enter the lower-income primary care specialties, the federal government in 1992 began to pay physicians who treat Medicare patients on a relative value–scale basis that relates each medical procedure to others. The scale increased the amount paid for cognitive services and decreased the amount paid for invasive procedures and diagnostic tests. Some insurance companies and managed-care groups are also using the relative value scale to revise physician payments.

Rural and Inner-City Medical Practice

Rural and poor inner cities have considerable difficulty in recruiting and keeping physicians. In rural areas some of the obstacles are professional isolation, inaccessibility to hospitals, and lack of educational and cultural opportunities for physician families. Programs that provide generous living and educational subsidies have not been effective. Neither have federal government programs to finance part of medical education for those who practice in rural areas. Some rural areas unable to attract physicians are using nurse practitioners or physician's assistants who treat patients under the supervision of a physician with whom they consult, usually by telephone. Historically people in the poor inner cities have used hospital outpatient departments, hospital emergency rooms, and city health department clinics rather than private physicians to meet their medical needs.

Quality of Care

The quality of medical care in the United States is safeguarded by the licensure requirements of each state government, which are roughly similar, requiring graduation from an accredited medical school, passing a national examination, and some postgraduate training in a hospital before a person can practice medicine. State government licensing authorities will usually grant reciprocity to physicians from other states and Canada. Those seeking certification as a specialist must complete a residency program in that specialty, which lasts three to seven years, depending on the specialty, and pass an examination approved by each specialty board. Specialty status is granted by nongovernmental specialty boards, not by state government. Continuing medical education of all physicians is required by the specialties and most state governments. Nearly all specialties now require periodic recertification in the specialty by examination.

Other quality safeguards include Professional Review Organizations, composed of nongovernment physicians, which are required by the federal government to monitor quality and utilization, as well as to review patient complaints under Medicare. Medical societies have attempted to discipline incompetent physicians, but have not been very effective. State licensing authorities have in recent years become more diligent in dealing with such cases following much public criticism. Hospitals may be legally liable for malpractice that occurs in their hospitals and are therefore monitoring quality of care more vigorously. They are aided in this process by the compilation of data concerning the result of treatments by each physician who practices in their hospital. In the past if physicians were disciplined or had hospital privileges revoked they could go to another hospital or state and continue to practice without the new hospital knowing of their past record. Federal legislation recently established the National Practitioners Data Bank that stores information on disciplinary actions against individual physicians. Hospitals are required to report to the Data Bank all disciplinary actions taken as a result of their internal reviews and to refer to the Data Bank before hiring or granting hospital privileges to physicians.

Medical Societies

Some physicians find it valuable to belong to their state and local medical societies, which sponsor continuing education programs, medical journals, and services such as relatively inexpensive malpractice insurance. Also, they provide an organized representation of physicians' views to government or industry on matters that affect them. Although less than half of all practicing physicians are members of the national American Medical Association (AMA), the AMA plays a key role in shaping federal health legislation through testimony before congressional committees, direct lobbying with members of Congress, and contributions to political campaigns. The AMA is widely recognized as one of the most effective lobbying groups in the nation's capital. However, its power is being somewhat diminished as many specialty societies set up lobbying groups to concentrate on their particular interests, which are not necessarily those of the AMA. The AMA publishes one of the world's leading medical journals, several specialty journals, and a weekly newspaper. It collects data on physicians and medical education and works with other national organizations on issues affecting the public's health and the health system.

Hospitals

The large majority of acute care, general (community) hospitals in the United States are nonprofit, which means that they do not distribute any leftover monies to persons or groups, but reinvest them in the hospital. These hospitals are built and financed by citizens and religious groups without government mandates. The money to build a hospital comes from many sources: private contributions, money borrowed by floating tax exempt bonds, and occasionally state and local government grants. The federal grant program for acute care hospital construction no longer exists. Hospitals must have a license from their state government, which may be issued after the hospital meets state standards. In addition, most hospitals apply for accreditation from a nongovernmental organization, the Joint Commission on Accreditation of Healthcare Organizations (JCAHO), which periodically inspects and evaluates the physical plant, hospital rules and procedures, and more important, quality of care indicators. Most insurance companies and government programs will only pay for care in an accredited institution.

Most acute care hospitals have between 100 and 300 beds with two and sometimes four beds to a room (see table 7). Private rooms are available for the very ill or at an extra cost for those who prefer them. Hospitals owned by local government, common in some of the nation's larger cities, are much larger and tend to provide services for lower-income people who do not have private health insurance. In rural areas there are hospitals with as few as 25 to 50 beds, but they usually have financial problems and account for most of hospital closures.

The average occupancy rate in acute care hospitals is 60 to 70%. The low rate is due to a combination of factors: the growth of ambulatory surgery and other outpatient services, some overbuilding in the 1970s, and the current efforts to contain costs, which have reduced inpatient hospital stays to an average of seven days in 1993. Large city and medical school–affiliated hospitals are, however, usually full.

About 15% of acute care hospitals are for-profit institutions usually owned by corporations that distribute any profit to their stockholders. These investor-owned hospitals maintain that it is possible to provide efficient quality of care at costs comparable to or below those of other hospitals and make a profit as well. The nonprofit hospitals contend, on the other hand, that these for-profit hospitals tend to be small and are thus able to handle only the less complicated cases on which they can make a profit, leaving the more difficult and more expensive kinds of care to the nonprofit institutions. This, the nonprofit hospitals argue, forces their average costs up. Not only do they have to be structured to handle the more complicated cases but they also lose the "profit" from some of the less complicated cases, which they do not get and which would be an offset against their losses on the expensive cases and the charity care they have to provide. Most of these for-profit hospitals are located in four states: California, Florida, Tennessee, and Texas.

The low occupancy rate of hospitals persists because hospitals are reluctant to close beds officially. Each hospital is licensed by the state for a specific number of beds. To close beds officially requires notification of the state, which then reduces the hospital's licensed bed complement accordingly. If in the future the hospital sees a need for additional beds, it has to go back to the state licensing authority for permission to reopen the beds that had previously been closed. Rather than deal with the bureaucratic procedures and uncertainties that that entails, hospitals instead close unneeded beds unofficially, reduce staffing for those beds, and are free to reopen them whenever they choose. When they do this, however, the record shows a low occupancy rate.

Patients are admitted to hospitals by their primary care physician or a specialist. Prior approval of the admission from the insurance company, if required and if not an emergency, is usually done by telephone. Unless enrolled in a managed-care organization that limits their choice, patients can select the hospital where they will be treated. In most cases they will choose a hospital where their physician has privileges. Other times they may choose a hospital renowned for special types of treatment. Some HMOs, PPOs, and private insurance companies allow enrollees to go to hospitals outside of the approved ones if the patient agrees to pay a significant percent of the costs. Approved hospitals are those where the organization has negotiated a fee usually lower than the normal fee.

Responsibility for nonprofit hospitals rests with an elected board of trustees, which develops and implements policies, hires and evaluates the hospital administrator, assesses the hospital's financial status, decides which physicians can admit and treat patients, monitors quality of care, and develops long-term plans. Trustees typically serve without pay.

Hospital Finance and Competition

Hospitals are financed by payments from private insurance companies, from business corporations that are self-insured, from Medicare for the aged, Medicaid for the poor, by patient payments when the insurance does not cover the costs, and by philanthropic organizations. Government-run hospitals also collect money from these sources with deficits covered from tax revenue. About 40% of a hospital's income is from Medicare and is based on Diagnosis Related Groups (DRGs). This method of payment was introduced initially by the federal government in 1983 for payment of Medicare admissions as a way to control hospital costs. Hospitals are paid a specific amount for inpatient services according to the patient's diagnosis. If the hospital can provide care at a cost lower than the DRG payment, it keeps the difference. However, if the cost of care exceeds the DRG payment, the hospital must bear the additional cost in all but exceptional cases. The DRG system, or a modification of it, is being used increasingly by private insurance companies and Medicaid programs. The DRG system of payment has resulted in a reduction in hospital admissions, length of stays, and a transfer of patients to outpatient and rehabilitation services not yet covered by DRGs.

Hospitals, especially in large-population areas, compete for patients, and they advertise in newspapers, on radio, and on television emphasizing the expertise of their medical staffs, and the breadth and sophistication of their technologies. Hospitals have considerable freedom to innovate, purchase equipment, develop new services, and adjust the number of beds. Government efforts to control the expansion of facilities and high-technology equipment have not been successful. As a result, hospitals try to purchase the latest equipment to lure patients, to recruit physicians for their medical staffs who will bring with them their patients, and to increase the number of insured patient admissions. More than 70% of the hospitals have CT scanners, about 25% have MRIs, and increasingly hospitals are performing more sophisticated and more profitable types of surgery (e.g., coronary bypass surgery). While there is a growing trend for hospitals to have salaried physicians providing their services, in most cases care is still provided by physicians who are independent of the hospital.

Emergency and Outpatient Departments

One of the components of an acute care general hospital is the emergency department. Although small hospitals in rural areas may use physicians who have admission and treatment privileges on a rotating basis to cover emergencies, most hospitals have staffed their emergency departments with full-time physicians twenty-four hours a day. Most of these physicians have either special training or specialty certification in emergency medicine. The emergency department also treats minor conditions on nights and weekends when the patient's physician is not available or when the patient has no physician. It is common for emergency departments to treat earaches and sore throats as well as severe trauma injuries and heart attacks. Any person can go to the emergency department and by law they cannot be refused treatment. Many attempts have been made to decrease the use of emergency departments for minor, nonemergency conditions because they overload the departments and are a very expensive way to treat such conditions. Until recently many of the larger hospitals sought to upgrade their emergency departments to be certified as trauma centers. This involved additional training, a highly skilled support staff, and special equipment. The cost of operating these centers is so great that they almost always operated at a deficit. As a result, some hospitals have been forced to discontinue them.

Another component of many acute care hospitals is the outpatient or ambulatory care department. Historically only teaching hospitals and other large hospitals provided specialty consultation services for those who could not afford such consultations. Recently, many smaller general hospitals have developed and expanded their ambulatory care services to accommodate the enormous increase in outpatient surgery. More than 90% of community hospitals now have ambulatory care and ambulatory surgical services, with the physician services provided mostly by private emergency medical groups. Some hospitals are also establishing primary care clinics in the community to increase the number of patient referrals needing hospital outpatient and inpatient services. This is another way hospitals compete for patients.

Special Hospitals

In addition to community acute care hospitals, there are psychiatric and mental retardation hospitals sponsored by state governments and private organizations; federal hospitals for the armed forces, veterans with military service–connected disabilities, and Native Americans; public and private long-term care and rehabilitation hospitals. The occupancy rate at state government psychiatric hospitals has declined dramatically because of a policy of deinstitutionalization. Community groups and church groups also own and operate psychiatric hospitals, but recently most have been developed by for-profit organizations.

State government, and some local governments, provide care for the mentally retarded and also operate some long-term care hospitals. There is an increasing number of rehabilitation hospitals in part because acute care hospitals are discharging patients earlier and in part because of the aging of the population with the accompanying medical problems that require rehabilitation services. Most of the rehabilitation hospitals and outpatient services are for-profit.

Medical Education

To obtain a license to practice medicine in the United States typically requires four years of postsecondary school study at a university to obtain a baccalaureate degree, four years of additional study at an approved medical school to obtain either a Doctor of Medicine (M.D.) degree or a Doctor of Osteopathic Medicine (D.O.) degree, plus residency training and passage of the U.S. Medical Licensing Examination. The 127 medical schools offering the M.D. degree accept about 40% of those who apply based on university grades, performance on the Medical College Admission Test, recommendations, and an interview with the candidate. In addition there are 15 schools offering the D.O. degree. The training programs offering the M.D. and D.O. degrees are virtually the same, and graduates from both types of schools can be fully licensed in all states.

Medical schools usually concentrate studies of the basic sciences in the first two years and clinical experience in the third and fourth years. Although there have been many calls to decrease the use of didactic lectures and increase the use of alternatives in which the student is more active in the learning process and assumes more responsibility for the acquisition of information, computer-assisted instruction and independent learning, although increasing, still play only a minor role in most medical schools. About half of the medical schools use small-group teaching as a major format.[7] Medical schools are being pressured by state governments and by the federal government to produce more graduates who choose primary care specialties, but with little success. Medical school costs continue to increase at the same time as federal, state, and local government appropriations have decreased. Even so, government monies constitute close to half of medical schools' revenue. Income from medical services provided by medical school faculty make up most of the rest; this includes income from insurance companies, Medicare and Medicaid, as well as supplementary charges to privately insured and uninsured patients. Some income also is derived from grants and contracts. Student tuition payments account for only 4% of medical school revenues. Because of the large amount of government support, it is easy to understand why government feels it should be able to exercise some influence on medical schools to graduate physicians who will choose specialties that meet society's needs.

Graduate medical or residency training consists of a period of supervised clinical training in an approved setting following graduation from medical school. Hospitals provide almost all residency programs, but ambulatory clinics, health departments, and mental health agencies have programs. Residency programs are accredited by each specialty's national review board. At the end of the training period physicians become board-certified after passing a written and usually also an oral examination. The length of training required for certification varies from three to seven years depending upon the specialty. Virtually all specialties require recertification within ten years. There are twenty-two general specialties, including family medicine, and many more subspecialties. The general practitioner (GP) as such is being replaced by the specialist in family medicine, the residency training program for which lasts three years. Continuing education in the form of regional and local programs, hospital courses, videotapes, and computer programs are required by most states for retention of the license and by medical specialties to retain certification in the specialty.

Medicare adjusts its rates at teaching hospitals to allow for the additional costs associated with residency programs and is a major source of funding for graduate education. Insurance companies absorbed some of the cost of residency programs, which were included in hospital charges for patient services. While they were willing to subsidize residency programs when funds were plentiful and there was a shortage of physicians, insurance companies and government are now seeking ways to reduce their support for what many think costs too much and produces an imbalance in the types of specialties. Limited future funding is causing a careful reexamination of graduate medical education and its financing.

Dentists, Nurses, and Physician Assistants

People desiring to become dentists are required to complete a university baccalaureate degree before commencing four years of dental school training. Upon successful completion of dental school studies, they are licensed by the respective state governments upon successful passage of a national qualifying exam. Most dentists are general practitioners who have private practices although some dental HMOs are emerging. Some employers offer dental insurance, but the majority of the population has none. The mean annual income of dentists in 1993 was $98,140.

The nursing profession is undergoing significant change in its educational and training programs, its professional responsibilities, and its relationship to physicians. There are three pathways to become a registered nurse. One path is training for three years in a nursing school associated with a hospital. Another is training in a university for four years to earn a baccalaureate degree. The third path is training at a community college for two to two and a half years to earn an associate degree in nursing. All have an academic component, use hospital facilities for clinical training, and take the same state examination to become a registered nurse. Currently most nurses train in community colleges. As new procedures and techniques evolve, nurses are taking more responsibility for patient care and want to be more involved along with physicians in decisions affecting medical care. A growing number of nurses pursue advanced clinical studies, receiving a master's degree on completion. There are in addition a number of doctoral programs in nursing, designed primarily for administrative and academic roles.

Physician assistants have been trained since the 1960s to extend physicians' services by performing comprehensive physical examinations, providing basic treatment for common illnesses and some emergency care under the supervision of a physician who assumes responsibility for their performance of duties. To become a physician assistant one must graduate from an approved two-year program and take a certifying examination. They are required to take continuing education courses and pass a recertifying examination every six years. The majority of physician assistants work with physicians in primary care, but they also work in hospitals taking on some of the duties of residents.

Medical Services for the Frail Elderly and Disabled

Numerous services are provided both in communities and institutions for those unable to cope with the daily tasks of living for extended periods of time because of physical or mental impairment. Most of these services are consumed by persons with functional disabilities who are 85 years of age and older. Most people who are unable to cope with the daily tasks of living are helped by families, friends, or neighbors, not by an organized service or agency. For a growing number of others, home care and other community-based services are relied upon and are a significant alternative to institutional care. However, an increasing number of people—the chronically and mentally ill, impaired children, and especially the frail elderly—need some level of institutional care. This is typically available through long-term care facilities that provide inpatient care for those who need it over a longer period of time than the acute care general hospital provides. Long-term care institutions include nursing homes, psychiatric and mental retardation facilities, chronic disease hospitals, and rehabilitation hospitals. The majority of long-term care institutions are nursing homes that primarily care for the frail elderly.

Nursing Homes

About 73% of the more than 15,000 nursing homes in the United States are owned and operated by for-profit groups. Nine large chains operate more than 100 homes each and the largest chain operates about 800. Nonprofit secular and church-related groups own about 20% and 5% are owned by government. They all have occupancy rates of 95% or more and there is a need for more beds. Federal and state standards must be met for licensure and there are regular inspections. The federal government recognizes two levels of care and with different payments for each under its programs. A skilled nursing facility provides 24-hour nursing service, regular physician supervision, and rehabilitation therapy. Typically, it provides care for convalescent patients and those with long-term illnesses. An intermediate care facility provides less extensive health-related care and services. It provides care for those who are not able to care for themselves, but who are not sick enough to need 24-hour nursing care. Most nursing homes provide both skilled and intermediate care. There are about 53 nursing home beds per 1,000 persons over 65 years of age and most beds are for skilled nursing care. The average length of stay in a nursing home is two years, but varies greatly according to the type of patient. The average length of stay for those recovering from an illness is 57 days, but for those receiving unskilled care the average is twenty times longer. More than 90% of nursing home patients are 65 years of age or older. The remaining are younger people who cannot care for themselves because of chronic disease or accidents. Medical care in nursing homes is provided by individual physicians or by HMO organizations.

Government health insurance programs, mainly Medicaid, paid for about 55% of nursing home care while residents paid out-of-pocket for about 45%. Most nursing home residents deplete their own financial resources within one year after entering and apply for Medicaid benefits. Medicare pays only about 5% of nursing home care because it narrowly targets those persons requiring skilled care during recovery from an acute illness; it does not cover intermediate care. Private long-term care insurance pays for less than 4% of nursing home care, but more such insurance is being purchased and some states have programs that make the purchase of long-term care by individuals more attractive. A few employers sponsor long-term care insurance plans so employees may purchase it at less expensive group rates.

It is estimated that 20 to 40% of the nursing home population could be cared for at less intensive levels if adequate community-based services were available. Although home health services are expanding, there is no definitive study to show it can be justified on the basis of health benefits or cost savings.[8] Home health care includes a variety of medical and social services such as monitoring medications, changing bandages, help with bathing and dressing, changing bed linens, cooking, and shopping. It also provides some or all of the following: part-time skilled nursing care, physical therapy, speech therapy, and some medical supplies and equipment (e.g., crutches, walkers, wheelchairs). Agencies providing home health care can operate under various names, have varying organizational ties, and offer differing services. Agencies can be independent, hospital-operated, or managed by a health department. Close to 50% of the agencies are for-profit and are financed by Medicare, Medicaid, government grants, insurance company payments, patient's fees, and charitable contributions. Adult day care and Meals-on-Wheels are other available community-based services.

Public Health

Public health in the United States emphasizes prevention of disease, disability, and premature death. Its "core functions" include health status monitoring and disease surveillance; investigation and control of diseases and injuries; protection of the environment, workplace, housing, food and water; laboratory studies to support disease control and environmental protection; health education and information; community mobilization for health-related issues; targeted outreach and linkage to personal services; health services quality assurance and accountability; training and education of public health professionals; and leadership, policy development, planning and administration.[9] Public health involves an interplay among federal, state, and local governments. Although the federal government provides some services, its principal role has been to stimulate the development of new or improved services by providing funds for acitivities it wants to promote. Except in certain specific areas, the federal government has no authority to provide direct health services for people, this being the domain of the states and the private sector. Public health programs are developed at the state and local levels. Through a variety of preventive measures state and local health departments have assured the population of safe drinking water, milk and perishable food products, and an environment relatively free of harmful substances. They have initiated environmental and personal prevention programs to deal with various illnesses.

States determine how to organize public health activities at the local level. Some public health services are administered directly by the state (state psychiatric and mental retardation hospitals; licensure of professional personnel, hospitals, nursing homes, and other health facilities), but most states encourage local health departments to deliver services under state standards. Local health services are usually partly subsidized by the state. The mix of programs, the sophistication, and the population served vary from state to state. All states offer some personal preventive services in areas relating to maternal and child health, school health, and immunizations. In some states public health agencies provide to the poor many of the services provided by hospitals and private physicians. The financing of state and local public health actitivies is a combination of state and local funding plus federal funding in the form of grants and contracts. The Public Health Service of the federal government is administered by the assistant secretary for health in the Department of Health and Human Services. It consists of agencies that provide biomedical research grants to universities and hospitals and maintain biomedical research laboratories, provide technical assistance to states and local health agencies, disseminate information, ensure the safety of foods and drugs that cross state lines, maintain laboratories for the study of infectious and communicable diseases, provide training for state and local public health personnel, gather and disseminate national health statistical data, provide grant support for educational and health projects, and run a comprehensive medical care system for Native Americans and Alaska Natives. Also in the Department of Health and Human Services is the Health Care Financing Administration (HCFA), which oversees the Medicare and Medicaid programs.

A number of other federal agencies are involved with health services including the Environmental Protection Agency (EPA), Occupational Safety and Health Agency (OSHA), Department of Veterans Affairs, and Department of Defense.

Health Costs

Health spending rose in 1993 to 13.9% of the GDP, totaling $884.2 billion.[10] The rate of increase has slowed somewhat, which may reflect the efforts of the private sector and government to contain health costs. As in most countries, the rise in costs can be attributed largely to technological advances, increased population (especially the elderly), and inflation. There are many complex factors that account for the rapid rise in costs in the United States. The most significant factor is the expanding use of high-technology procedures for diagnosis and treatment. Magnetic resonance imaging is commonplace and readily available. One county in California with a population of about 2.5 million people has more MRIs than all of Canada; one county area in Pennsylvania with slightly over 100,000 people has two MRI units and the units advertise for business. Coronary artery bypass surgery is about five times more frequent in the United States than in the United Kingdom, and more than twice as frequent as Canada, Australia, and the Netherlands. There is also a high rate in the use of other expensive procedures. In addition to the cost of the original equipment, highly trained personnel and well-paid specialists are required to perform the procedures. Some experts question whether all of these expensive high-tech procedures are medically indicated and whether some could be replaced by less invasive, less expensive procedures that would have the same clinical outcome.

The increase in the population of those over 65 years, and especially of those over 85 years, also contributes to the increased health costs. These people are most likely to suffer the complications of chronic illnesses and have more frequent hospital stays as well as higher surgical rates than younger patients. The elderly are treated more aggressively in the last years of their lives than they are in many other countries.

Inflation is another factor in rising health costs. The rising costs of fuel, food, electricity, telephones, and labor are hard to control and particularly so for the health sector. Another aspect of inflation is medical inflation, which includes the cost of equipment and its operation, drugs, and the cost of highly skilled professional personnel. Medical inflation exceeds the rate of general inflation.

Some of the other factors that increase health costs are the high costs of administration, litigation, malpractice insurance costs, and the oversupply of specialists. The costs of administration need special attention because they are enormous. As Table 10 shows, in 1993, $48 billion went into program administration and the net cost of private health insurance. That accounts for 5.4% of national health expenditures. But that figure represents only a small amount of the costs. Table 10 reports what government and charitable institutions spent for administration and the balance of the insurance company receipts after paying benefits. What is not included are the costs incurred by physicians, hospitals, home care agencies and others in personnel, telephone, and numerous other costs to meet insurance company requirements before treatment (e.g., securing permissions prior to hospitalization), to justify procedures and charges, to file claims on behalf of patients, to appeal Medicare/Medicaid/insurance company payment decisions on denials and underpayments, to bill patients for deductibles and coinsurance payments, and to file claims for those Medicare patients who have supplementary insurance that covers deductibles and co-insurance liabilities. The appeal of other health systems is in part their simplicity and the lower administrative costs, thus freeing funds for patient care. The American proclivity for cost analysis, while it has some merits, is costly in itself: the DRG payment system and fee-for-service payments require extensive cost analyses that are largely avoided by global budgeting and salaried systems.

The money that fuels the health sector comes from many sources as Table 10 indicates. Some 82% of all health costs are paid as follows: by private health insurance, 34%; government programs, 43%; and other private sources such as charitable groups, 5%. Patient out-of-pocket payments accounted for 18%, a figure that represents insurance deductibles and co-payments as well as items not covered by insurance such as hearing aids, nearly half the cost of dental care, nonprescription drugs and other over-the-counter items such as aspirins and vitamins. Also included in these patient payments are the payments made by people who do not have health insurance but are able to pay some of the costs. Categorizing who pays for health services is, however, somewhat misleading; in a very real sense all people pay medical care costs through taxes, reduced wages, and in the price of goods they purchase.

Slightly less than 86% of the nation's 268 million people have health insurance or health cost coverage by some government program. An estimated 38–40 million people, more than 14% of the population, have no health insurance or protection by a government program. Most of the uninsured are employed, often in low-paying jobs where the employer does not provide coverage or in part-time positions where the employer seeks to avoid the necessity of providing health insurance and other benefit packages that are available to the employer's full-time employees. Some of the insured, an unknown number, are covered by health insurance policies that do not adequately meet the major costs of health care. Though uninsured, most of the 38–40 million are able to get needed medical care through hospital emergency departments, which, by law, are not permitted to deny care. Although the services of a private physician may be difficult to secure, the inability of a patient to secure access to care is therefore the exception rather than the rule.

Most people secure their health insurance through their place of employment where the employer may pay part or all of the cost of the insurance. Employer payment for health insurance represents a form of nontaxable income to the employee. Families of the insured are also typically covered through the employee's workplace. The cost of health insurance policies to the employer are tax-deductible as a business expense and the rest of the cost to the employer is reflected in the price of goods and services provided by the employer. Thus, as the cost of insurance rises, the added cost to the employer is passed along to the consumer. The added cost can have an adverse effect on the employer's business, making their products either too expensive for potential purchasers or noncompetitive.

Employers have tried to deal with the problem of rising insurance costs in several ways. They have shifted more and more of the costs to their employees by requiring them to pay higher deductibles and co-payments. Many of the largest employers have also opted to self-insure, assuming the risks of only their employees and their families and not any of the risks in the larger community. Where employers do this they anticipate that their costs will be lower than the community average. The net effect is that since they are not contributing to the community risk pool, they force the insurance premiums for others to rise more than they would have otherwise.

Employers have also turned to various forms of managed care and managed competition to control costs. Businesses in various parts of the country have formed business coalitions or alliances to share information about hospitals and individual physicians and to identify those that have lower charges and provide care comparable in quality outcomes to higher cost hospitals and physicians. This has led some businesses and business coalitions to negotiate with hospitals and physicians to limit their charges and to become *preferred providers*. Employers have also been encouraging their employees to enroll in HMOs.

Many of the larger employers now offer their employees a choice of health insurance options: an HMO, a PPO, and the traditional fee-for-service type policy. Employees select each year which type of policy they prefer. The HMO is typically the least expensive, the employee having to contribute more for a PPO, and an even greater amount of money for the traditional insurance policy. It might be noted that these three options, and the negotiating power of business coalitions, were at the core of the health reform proposals advocated by the Clinton administration in 1994 but which were not adopted by Congress. In a way the Clinton plan is being adopted incrementally throughout the country without federal legislation except that there is no solution to providing coverage for the uninsured as President Clinton had proposed.

Governments—federal, state, local—have also been affected by the rising cost of health care. As employers, they face increasing health insurance costs to cover their employees just as by private businesses, and they have responded as have businesses by offering their employees HMOs, PPOs, and traditional insurance options. Governments have also, like businesses, raised their charges for their services by increased taxation, made cuts in other government programs, and required employees to pay higher deductibles, co-payments, and premiums. Governments have also been impacted by the rising costs of care because they finance the medical care of the elderly, the disabled, and the very poor through Medicare and Medicaid. As the number of elderly and poor increase, the costs to government go up and each is faced with the alternatives of increasing taxes, shifting the costs to the providers and patients, or cutting other worthwhile programs. The political debates at the federal level are intense because, as Figure 1 shows, Medicare pays 17% of all health costs in the country, and the federal share of Medicaid expenses is 46% of the $73.2 billion spent in 1993. The remaining 54% of Medicaid costs was borne by state governments and some local governments, an enormous amount for those states with a disproportionate number of eligible poor. State governments have sought to deal with this problem by changing eligibility criteria to keep as many poor off the Medicaid roles as possible, thereby shifting the burden of costs for their care to the private sector. Medicaid typically pays hospitals much less than the actual cost of care. Because of these factors, hospitals in particular seek to recover their losses by increasing their charges to others (cost-shifting), which encourages large employers to self-insure and which in turn drives up health insurance premiums for smaller employee groups and individual policy-holders, forcing many to join the ranks of the uninsured. Hospitals compete with each other to attract cases on which they can make money to offset their losses, and they develop services on which they can also make a profit. They acquire the latest technology for profit-making procedures and increase ambulatory care services, particularly same-day surgery. They also compete by developing their own health care networks such as HMOs, primary care clinics, and merging with other hospitals to assure an increased flow of paying (insured) patients for outpatient and inpatient care. Physicians cope by increasing their charges wherever possible, and by increasing the volume and intensity of their services.

Patients share responsibility for increased health care costs because they want the very best treatment for themselves: the latest technology and freedom to choose their own doctor and the hospital in which they are to be treated. The hospitals and the medical profession have been very responsive to consumer demands. State legislatures have, ironically, also contributed to increased costs by mandating that all insurance policies cover specific procedures (mammograms, Pap smears, immunizations). As laudable as the state mandates are, they increase the cost of health insurance premiums because the initial insurance rates never anticipated coverage for these mandated benefits.

At the same time as these things are occurring, hospitals—as already noted—are providing a large amount of free care to people who have no insurance. The costs of free care incurred by hospitals are significant, and pose enormous economic problems for hospitals: How can hospitals simultaneously survive financially, serve their communities, and provide the highest quality care? This is in part the reason why hospitals in some states went into court to force their state governments to pay for the full cost of care under Medicaid. Some of the smaller hospitals have closed because of financial pressures. Some merged with other hospitals. More and more hospitals are restructuring themselves along the lines of a corporation to provide fiscal flexibility with monies earned from profit-making enterprises they have developed, removing—in other words—from the hospital budgets income from consulting services, management services of smaller hospitals, drug rehabilitation programs, and so forth.

The precarious financial position of some nonprofit hospitals is exacerbated where there is competition from a for-profit acute care hospital. For-profit acute care hospitals tend to target cases on which they can make a profit, removing this source of income from the nonprofit hospitals. The nonprofit hospitals would have used the earned income from such cases as an offset against lower-than-cost payments from Medicaid and to cover costs of care they provide for the uninsured.

Figure 1   The Nation's Health Dollar, 1993

Where It Came From

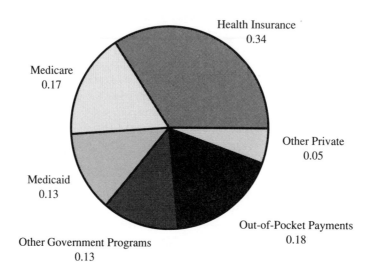

Where It Went

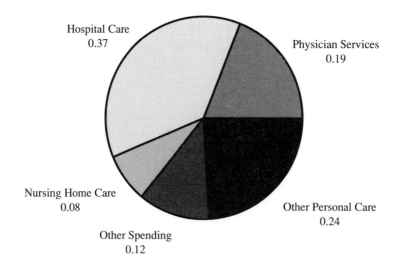

Health Insurance

Health insurance is available on a group and nongroup (individual) basis. Group policies are purchased by employers and are generally less expensive than nongroup policies because with groups there is a pooling of health risks whereas with nongroup policies the insurance company is at greater risk of adverse selection; that is, getting poorer health risks because those are the people most inclined to take out such insurance. Health insurance policies are offered by both nonprofit and for-profit insurance companies. Among the nonprofit companies are Blue Cross (which pays hospitals) and Blue Shield (which pays physicians and other professionals), Kaiser-Permanente (the nation's largest nonprofit HMO), and the Health Insurance Plan of Greater New York (also a nonprofit HMO). Among the larger for-profit insurance companies are CIGNA, Metropolitan, and Prudential.

Blue Cross was started by hospital leaders and Blue Shield by leaders in the medical profession in the late 1920s and 1930s. Companies of each exist all over the country but each is independent of the others. They cooperate through a national organization that grants each Blue Cross and Blue Shield plan the privilege of using the Blue Cross and Blue Shield names and symbols. The two organizations generally work closely, Blue Cross usually being the sales agent for Blue Shield policies. As nonprofit organizations they are more tightly regulated by the various state government insurance departments. Significantly, they are usually considered the insurers of last resort in that they will insure any group, even those avoided by other insurance companies because of poor risk experience. Because of the very competitive environments in which they operate and the restrictions imposed as a consequence of their nonprofit status, some Blue Cross and Blue Shield Plans are planning to give up their nonprofit status and to meet their competitors on what they believe will be a more level playing field.

Historically, Blue Cross and Blue Shield sold their policies on a community rate basis, charging the same rate for all groups regardless of their expected risk. Over the years, however, as for-profit insurance companies entered the market and offered lower premiums to groups with a lower risk experience, Blue Cross and Blue Shield were forced to abandon the community rate approach and meet the competition by experience rating as well. This tended to drive up the insurance costs for small employer groups that were not large enough to attrack the for-profit insurance companies. For small employers, the rising premium costs are forcing many to stop offering health insurance for their employees.

Generally, group health insurance, and Blue Cross policies for the nongroup-insured, cover all acute care hospital costs for at least 21 or 30 days for each admission. The hospitals are paid one of three ways: costs per day, a DRG payment based on the admitting diagnosis, and in fewer and fewer instances by what the hospital charges. Charges are typically higher than costs, and the profit is used by the hospital to offset losses incurred from charity care and from less than cost payments by Medicaid, but this practice of paying charges is decreasing as insurance companies and employers negotiate payments. Nongroup insurance, other than Blue Cross, typically pays a fixed amount which may or may not cover all of the hospital bill.

Insurance generally covers 80 to 100% of physician charges. Where the physician is salaried, the physician's employer will bill the insurance company. The amount of coverage for ambulatory medical care varies, but increasingly coverage is available after the patient pays the first $100 or $200 of charges, the insurance policy then covering 80% of the additional costs, the patient responsible for the balance. For a growing number of policies, after the patient bears one or two thousand dollars of expenses, the insurance typically picks up all of the additional costs. Patients in HMOs have virtually no costs to pay for either hospital or doctor care. Sometimes there is a nominal charge for ambulatory care visits. Patients in PPOs usually pay a lesser co-payment than those under the more traditional types of insurance.

Most large corporations today are self-insured, avoiding the cost of using insurance companies (except perhaps to administer the payment of claims). These large companies will typically negotiate payment rates directly with hospitals and physicians. Hospitals and physicians must accept what the corporation believes is reasonable or the companies will send their employees to other hospitals and doctors who will accept their payments. Those who agree to accept the payment schedule become preferred providers and it is said that the corporation has a PPO. This system enables these large employers to avoid costs shifted by hospitals to cover the hospital's cost associated with care of the uninsured and from underpayments by Medicaid. Also, the self-insured employers are not contributing to the pool of funds necessary to finance health care for the community, which leads to increased hospital deficits and forces up the insurance premiums for others. PPO payments for doctors limit the amount doctors get for various services. However, the doctors continue to do well financially because, being preferred providers for a business corporation they generally have an increase in the number of patients.

Most people and their families, as has been noted, are covered by insurance secured through their place of employment. The elderly—those 65 years and older—and some who are permanently disabled are covered by Medicare, and the poor by Medicaid.

Medicare is financed by the federal government and by those who are covered. Hospital coverage (Part A) is an entitlement, the money for which comes from social security taxes paid by all workers. There is an annual deductible for inpatient care, but otherwise Medicare covers virtually all inpatient hospital care. Part B of Medicare for physician care, outpatient hospital treatment, and some other nonhospital services is financed by monthly premiums paid by enrollees and by annual federal appropriations. There is an annual deductible for physician services and some co-payments for some of the other services. Hospitals are paid by DRG for inpatient care. Physicians are paid a fixed relative value scale fee and may charge the patient a limited amount over and above the Medicare payment. Many Medicare enrollees have supplementary insurance to cover the deductibles and co-payments. Medicaid is financed by federal and state governments and administered by each state government. Physicians who agree to treat Medicaid patients may not charge over and above the Medicaid payment. The costs of both Medicare and Medicaid are rising rapidly and are of concern to public policy makers—how to control the rise in costs without compromising on quality of care and on access. One approach being tried is to encourage, but not force, people to join HMOs.

National Health Care Reform

Debates over the need for health care reform have intensified due to the rapid rate of growth in health care costs and the fact that so many Americans are either uninsured or are covered by government insurance plans. There is a widespread conviction that something must be done to moderate the increase in health care costs and that something must be done to make certain that everyone has easy access to needed services. Unfortunately, there is no consensus on which approach to take.

While we tend to think of this as a new issue facing Americans, it bears remembering that in the

1930s and again in the 1940s there were major national proposals for reforming the health care system by instituting some form of national health insurance. In 1932 the Committee on the Costs of Medical Care issued its report calling for the provision of medical care by organized groups of physicians, dentists, nurses, pharmacists, and others and that these services be financed by some form of a prepayment mechanism. Prominent among the unenacted bills in Congress was the Wagner-Murray-Dingell bill in 1943, which also proposed a compulsory system of health insurance, financed from payroll taxes and providing comprehensive health and medical beneifits. Subsequently, in the late 1940s, President Truman took a strong position in favor of national health insurance and sent proposed legislation to the Congress for a comprehensive insurance plan to be financed through Social Security. Opposition from the American Medical Association (AMA) was largely responsible for failure of Congress to adopt any of the legislative proposals. Health insurance for those over the age of 65 captured the attention of national leaders during the 1950s and 1960s, culminating in the Medicare and Medicaid legislation but these programs helped only a small segment of the population.

Although each successive U.S. president has proposed changes in the health care system, the most comprehensive attempt at recent health care reform was the Clinton administration's proposed Health Security Act, which was defeated by Congress in 1994. The proposal was considered by many health experts to be technically sound but it proved to be politically disastrous because of its length and complexity. Powerful interest groups (e.g., small business, medical, and health insurance associations), inept political leadership, disinformation, and a lack of public understanding contributed to its demise. Another important factor is that the great majority of Americans are currently insured and satisfied with their health care and were apprehensive that changes would adversely affect them. The potential threat of such a sacrifice on the part of the insured Americans for the sake of the uninsured weakened the political support for the president's proposal so that in the end the interest groups were able to dominate.

Although the Clinton plan with its managed-care component was defeated, many aspects of managed care are working without legislation. Businesses and other groups are organizing to negotiate health benefits similar to Clinton's proposed purchasing cooperatives, and they are demanding insurance packages that can be meaningfully compared in terms of benefits, costs, and quality of care.

When national health care reform was defeated in 1994, many believed that states would develop their own plans to extend health insurance coverage to the uninsured and to develop models that could be used nationally. Some state governments, frustrated by national inaction, did in fact initiate their own approaches. Most common was the "play or pay" approach where the state mandated that all employers play by paying for health insurance for their employees or pay a payroll tax to the state government so the state can purchase the insurance for those employees and their families. Unfortunately, most of these state plans have been delayed because of political pressures to reduce taxes and budget deficits. Meanwhile, the number of people without health insurance continues to increase.

State governments have tried many other innovative approaches to secure additional funds for medical care. Early in the decade many latched onto the idea of levying taxes—sometimes referred to as mandated donations—on health care providers. These "donations" were used to support the Medicaid program. This increased the amount the state allocated to Medicaid and in turn increased federal matching monies. The increased federal matching funds enabled these states to pay the providers more (thus a return of their "donation"). The federal government viewed this as an open-ended raid on the federal treasury and eventually Congress limited the amount states could raise in this manner to 25% of the state's total Medicaid expenditures. To control medical costs many states are trying to move the Medicaid recipients to HMOs. Some states also assist hospitals by paying for some of the costs of care provided to the uninsured with money from general tax revenues, special taxes on alcohol and tobacco, as well as hospital surcharges on all admissions of insured patients.

An innovative approach was developed by the State of Oregon. Oregon proposed to extend Medicaid benefits to all residents who were below the federal poverty level ($13,944 for a family of four in 1992). This would add many more people to the Medicaid roles. To pay for the cost of care of these new Medicaid enrollees, Oregon proposed to mandate managed care for all Medicaid patients and developed a list of medical services in priority order based on the effectiveness of the services. It proposed not to pay for those procedures that had little or no beneficial effect. The list of medical treatments and their prioritization were developed by a broadly representative commission of health professionals and community leaders. The plan offered a basic benefit package that stressed prevention and would cover most, but not all, of the usual Medicaid treatments. The federal government approved the plan in 1993 for a five-year demonstration period. Federal approval was necessary because federal funds would partly finance the project. The implementation of the plan has been delayed for political and financial reasons.

Hawaii took a somewhat different approach. It simply mandated universal coverage: employers were required to provide health insurance coverage for all who worked more than twenty hours a week. Those not falling under that rule—the unemployed, seasonal workers, and others—were provided coverage by the state government from general revenues. Initiated in 1974, its approach has been very successful. Other states that had hoped to use Hawaii as a model have been thwarted by federal legislation that protects self-insured businesses from state regulations so that states cannot require them to insure workers. Hawaii is exempt because the law was enacted after Hawaii's plan was implemented.

Although state governments are trying to lead health care reform along with the private sector in the immediate future, their ability to address problems of access to care and its costs is limited. Therefore, the role of the federal government is essential. For the immediate future changes will be incremental due to the current conservative political climate. However, the basic problems persist; only when insured Americans conclude from personal experience that health care reform is worth its undesirable risks will the federal government be forced to act.

Notes

1. Emmons, D. W., and C. J. Simon. 1995. *Managed Care: Participation, Revenues, and Risk: Socioeconomic Characteristics of Medical Practice*. Chicago: American Medical Association.

2. Birdman, A. B. 1994. Primary and Medical Care: Ingredients for Health Care Reform. *Western Journal of Medicine* 161 (1):78–82.

3. Adler, G. S. 1995. Medicare Beneficiaries Rate Their Medical Care—New Data From the MCBS. *Health Care Financing Review* 16(4):175.

4. Medicare: Increased HMO Oversight Could Improve Quality and Access to Care. 1995. Washington, D.C.: General Accounting Office, 2.

5. Greenfield, S., et al. 1992. Variations in Resource Utilization Among Specialties and Systems of Care. *Journal of the American Medical Association* 269(12):1624–30.

6. Moser, J. W. 1995. *Physician Earning Trends: Socioeconomic Characteristics of Medical Practice*. Chicago: American Medical Association.

7. Jonas, H. S., S. I. Etzel, and B. Barzansky. 1994. Educational Programs in U.S. Medical Schools, 1993–1994. *Journal of the American Medical Association* 272(9): 694–701.

8. Weissert, W. G. 1991. A New Policy Agenda for Home Care. *Health Affairs* 10(2):67–77.

9. Office of Disease Prevention and Health Promotion. 1993. Health Care Reform and Public Health: A Paper on Population-Based Core Functions. Washington, D.C.: U.S. Public Health Service.

10. Levit, K. R. et al. 1994. National Health Expenditures, 1993. *Health Care Financing Review* 16(1):247–93.

Table 1 Total Population by Age, Race, and Sex, 1990 Census (in millions)

Population, 1990 census: 248.7: 121.2 males, 127.5 females, 199.7 white, 30.0 black, 2.0 Native American, 7.3 Asia or Pacific Islander, 9.8 other race
Population, 1993 estimate: 268.0

Age, 1990 census	
Under 5 years	18.4
5–17 years	45.2
18–20 years	11.7
21–24 years	15.0
25–44 years	80.8
45–54 years	25.2
55–59 years	10.5
60–64 years	10.6
65–74 years	18.1
75–84 years	10.1
85+ years	3.1
Median age: 32.9 years	

SOURCE: U.S. Bureau of the Census.

Table 2 Live Births, Birth Rate, Fertility Rate, and Infant Mortality Rate, 1994
(Birth rate is the number of live births per 1,000 population; fertility rate is the number of live births per 1,000 women age 15–44 years; infant mortality rate is the number of deaths under 1 year per 1,000 live births.)

	Number	Rate
Live births	3,979,000	15.3
Fertility	—	67.1
Infant mortality	31,400	7.9

SOURCE: Centers for Disease Control and Prevention, *Monthly Vital Statistics Report: Births, Marriages, Divorces, and Deaths for 1994* 43 (12): June 13, 1995.

Table 3 Infant Mortality Rate by the Six Most Common Causes per 100,000 Live Births, 1994

Cause of death	Number	Rate
1. Congenital anomalies	6,740	169.9
2. Disorders relating to short gestation and unspecified low birth weight	3,820	96.3
3. Sudden infant death syndrome	3,730	94.0
4. Respiratory disease syndrome	1,620	40.8
5. Intrauterine hypoxia and birth asphyxia	600	15.1
6. Pneumonia and influenza	390	9.8

SOURCE: Centers for Disease Control and Prevention, *Monthly Vital Statistics Report* 43 (12): June 13, 1995.

Table 4 Estimated Deaths, and Death Rates per 100,000 Population, for Fifteen Leading Causes, 1994

Cause of death	Number	Rate
All causes	2,298,000	882.4
1. Disease of heart	736,270	282.7
2. Malignant neoplasms, including lymphatic and hematopoietic tissues	540,790	207.7
3. Cerebrovascular disease	153,560	59.0
4. Chronic obstructive pulmonary diseases and allied conditions	102,300	39.3
5. Accidents and adverse effects	88,840	34.1
6. Pneumonia and influenza	82,870	31.8
7. Diabetes mellitus	55,470	21.3
8. Human immunodeficiency virus infection	40,210	15.4
9. Suicide	30,680	11.8
10. Chronic liver disease and cirrhosis	25,390	9.7
11. Nephritis, nephrotic syndrome, and nephrosis	24,400	9.4
12. Homicide and legal intervention	24,010	9.2
13. Septicemia	20,280	7.8
14. Atherosclerosis	17,380	6.7
15. Certain conditions originating in the prenatal period	14,320	5.5

SOURCE: Centers for Disease Control and Prevention, *Monthly Vital Statistics Report* 43 (12): June 13, 1995.

Table 5 Selected Operative Procedures, Average Length of Stay, and Rate (per Thousand Population), 1992

	Number (in thousands)	Rate	Average length of stay (days)
Episiotomy with or without forceps or vacuum extraction	1,611	6.4	
Cardiac catheterization	1,000	4.0	4.5
Caesarean section	921	3.6	4.0
Repair of current obstetric laceration	790	3.1	2.1
Artificial rupture of membranes	729	2.9	
Hysterectomy	580	2.3	4.1
Cholecystectomy	525	2.1	4.9
Coronary artery bypass graft	468	1.8	
Oophorectomy and salpingo-oophorectomy	464	1.8	
Open reduction of fracture with internal fixation	417	1.6	7.7

SOURCE: *Socio-Economic Factbook for Surgery 1995,* American College of Surgeons, Chicago.

Table 6 Average Net Physician Income, 1993 (before taxes, after professional expenses)

Specialty	Income (in thousands of $)
General/family practice	116.8
Surgery	262.7
Radiology	259.8
Anesthesiology	224.1
Obstetrics/Gynecology	221.9
Pathology	197.3
Internal Medicine	180.8
Pediatrics	135.4
Psychiatry	131.3

SOURCE: AMA, *Socioeconomic characteristics of medical practice*, 1995.

Table 7 Acute Care General Hospitals, by Bed Size, 1993

Total number of beds	5,261
Urban	3,012
Rural	2,249
Under 100	2,302
Urban	699
Rural	1,603
100–200	1,337
Urban	847
Rural	490
200–299	730
Urban	609
Rural	121
300 +	895
Urban	857
Rural	38

SOURCE: American Hospital Association, *Community hospital trends*, 1995.

Table 8 Selected Measures in Acute Care Hospitals, 1993

	1993	% Change 1983–93
Number of hospitals	5,261	−9
Number of beds (in thousands)	919	−9.8
Average number beds per hospital	175	−0.8
Admissions (in thousands)	30,748	−14.9
Average daily census (in thousands)	592	−21.0
Average length of stay, days	7	−7.1
Inpatient days (in thousands)	215,889	−21.0
Outpatient visits (in thousands)	366,885	+74.7

SOURCE: American Hospital Association, *Community hospital trends*, 1995.

Table 9 Nursing Home Data by Type of Owner, 1991 and 1994

	Government		Church-Related		Secular nonprofit		Profit		Average
	1991	1994	1991	1994	1991	1994	1991	1994	1991
Facilities	5.0%	4.4%	5.5%	6.1%	14.9%	16.4%	74.5%	73.1%	
Bed distribution	14.4%		8.0%		22.1%		74.2%		
Occupancy	95 %	97.3%	97 %	93 %	95.8%	95.2%	94.9%	91.3%	95.4%
Patient mix									
Medicare	6.2%		2.4%		4.9%		6.1%		4.9%
Medicaid	70.1%		44.9%		53.0%		64.7%		58.2%
Private pay	25.0%		52.9%		45.5%		29.5%		38.2%
ALOS (days)									
Medicare	67.9		40.2		58.1		56.9		57.2
Medicaid	1,162.9		1,120.3		1,379		941.6		1,151
Private pay	1,192.1		1,045.9		962.0		964.6		993

SOURCE: Marion Merrell Dow, Kansas City, Mo., 1992 and 1994.

Table 10 National Health Expenditures, by Source of Funds and Type of Expenditure

Year and Type of Expenditure	Total	Private					Government		
		All Private Funds	Total	Consumer		Other	Total	Federal	State and Local
				Out of Pocket	Private Insurance				
1993									
National Health Expenditures	884.2	496.4	453.6	157.5	296.1	42.8	387.8	280.6	107.3
Health Services and Supplies	855.2	484.3	453.6	157.5	296.1	30.7	370.9	268.6	102.4
Personal Health Care	782.5	445.5	415.5	157.5	258.0	30.0	337.0	259.0	78.1
Hospital Care	326.6	143.7	126.9	9.1	117.8	16.8	182.9	149.2	33.7
Physician Services	171.2	113.1	110.3	26.2	84.1	2.7	58.1	45.0	13.1
Dental Services	37.4	35.6	35.5	18.7	16.8	0.2	1.7	1.0	0.8
Other Professional Services	51.2	40.6	37.0	21.2	15.8	3.6	10.6	7.3	3.3
Home Health Care	20.8	9.4	6.9	4.3	2.5	2.5	11.4	9.8	1.5
Drugs and Other Medical Non-Durables	75.0	65.8	65.8	47.4	18.4	—	9.2	4.7	4.4
Vision Products and Other Medical Durables	12.6	8.5	8.5	7.6	0.9	—	4.2	4.0	0.2
Nursing Home Care	69.6	26.0	24.7	23.0	1.7	1.3	43.6	28.3	15.3
Other Personal Health Care	18.2	2.8	—	—	—	2.8	15.3	9.5	5.8
Program Administration and Net Cost of Private Health Insurance	48.0	38.8	38.1	—	38.1	0.7	9.2	6.3	2.8
Government Public Health Activities	24.7	—	—	—	—	—	24.7	3.3	21.4
Research and Construction	29.0	12.1	—	—	—	12.1	16.9	12.0	4.9
Research	14.4	1.2	—	—	—	1.2	13.1	11.1	2.1
Construction	14.6	10.9	—	—	—	10.9	3.8	0.9	2.8

NOTE: 0.0 denotes less than $50 million. Research and development expenditures of drug companies and other manufacturers and providers of medical equipment and supplies are excluded from research expenditures, but are included in the expenditure class in which the product falls. Numbers may not add to totals because of rounding.
SOURCE: *Health Care Financing Review* 16(1): Fall 1994.

Dominant Issues: Convergence, Decentralization, Competition, Health Services

Marshall W. Raffel

Ten countries—democratic, industrialized, and affluent with educated populations, well-trained health professionals, and high health standards—all facing a series of problems that stem from the rising costs of health care. These costs affect the amount of money available in the economy not only for health care, but also for consumer spending, education, social services, agriculture, defense, and other activities. Because of rising health care costs, and the requirements of other sectors in the economy, limits have been or are being placed on the amount of money available for health care—limits placed by government, employers, and insurance companies, as well as by individual citizens in terms of how much they are willing to pay for health insurance and out-of-pocket. As monetary limitations occur, ready access to health services inevitably becomes limited for some. Such rationing occurs in all countries and Victor Fuchs was correct when he said that "every nation chooses its own death rate by its evaluation of health compared with other goals."[1]

Costs are a paramount problem for countries because, unlike pre–World War II times, more and more can now be done to improve the public's health and to treat the maladies that afflict it. There is almost no limit to what can be done to keep people alive. New antibiotics (largely unknown before 1940) and immunosuppressives and other drugs are being developed each year. Organ transplants, joint replacements, and life-support systems are available. We have developed an enormous capacity to prolong life and increase its quality with the latest technology, but to use this capacity indiscriminately is costly and would have adverse social and political consequences.

Assume for a moment that an artificial heart is developed that is no larger than the human heart, and can be maintained by a small, flashlight-size battery that could be easily replaced. Imagine the cost to each nation's economy if all who could benefit from it were to get it! Heart disease is, after all, the major cause of death in all developed countries today. Where would the money come from? From education? From disaster relief? Defense? Social services? Decreased consumer spending?

Complicating the issue is that as we acquire new knowledge we learn that many other factors influence health—smoking, alcohol, air pollution, and a wide variety of other environmental prob-lems—the controls of which are costly and can affect a nation's economy. We have also come to recognize the importance of education and employment in maintaining health, enabling people to apply the knowledge we have for healthful living through nutrition, exercise, good housing, and so forth.

The problem facing political leaders is to find a solution that will be acceptable to the electorate, not an easy thing to do because the elements of a nation's economy today are interdependent. Changes in one sector affect other sectors. A concrete example of this was presented in the United States during the debate on President Clinton's health care reform plan in 1994 when small busi-nesses argued that mandating that they provide health insurance for their employees would make the price of their goods noncompetitive and force many of them to go out of business. Going out of business would result in unemployment, which would have widespread implications for the localities in which they were located. Their opposition was not to health care reform per se but rather to the economic burden it would place on them.

It is interesting to note that in most countries, in their search for ideas on how to provide the most effective, efficient health care, political leaders, insurance executives, and business people all appear to try similar approaches. The most popular reform among the countries is to limit or reduce the amount of money available to the health system. The health sector is said to be inefficient, doing unnecessary procedures, and manipulating such things as surgical waiting lists in order to pressure the politicians for additional resources. There is an element of truth in this: in *all* societal systems in all countries inefficiencies develop and strategies are employed by all to secure addi-tional resources. Tightening the money supply forces organizations to eliminate the frills and, more important, the desirable but not absolutely necessary services. Frequently decreased are services that contribute to improved quality of life. However, increasing efficiency by restricting the money available to the health sector realizes only a short-term goal—a one-time-only gain; it does not solve the major problem of rising costs. Tight money policies whether dictated by government, insurance companies, or employers remove the room for the health sector to maneuver, the opportu-nity to experiment, to try out new ways of doing things, and to cope adequately with inflation and, most important, the increased demands resulting from population growth, aging of the population, quality of life considerations, and new capabilities resulting from new knowledge. This is one reason why *per-case* payment for hospital care may be relatively more harmful to patient care than global hospital budgeting. With global budgeting clinicians and administrators in hospital have at least some room to maneuver though as Pomey and Poullier note there is some evidence that global budgeting "overallocated resources to some hospitals by as much as a fifth of their revenue whereas other hospitals had to do with a shortfall." When a shortfall occurs under global budgeting, how-ever, as Claudia Scott points out in the New Zealand chapter, "Tight budget constraints in public hospitals raise, if anything, concerns about underservicing rather than overservicing." Wolfgang Greiner and J.-Matthias Graf v.d. Schulenburg correctly observe in the German chapter that the "old system" of full payment for hospital care on a cost-price basis had an important advantage in that "the treatment of patients and the relationship between the patient and doctor in the hospital were not influenced by economic considerations." This "old system" was once the practice also in the Netherlands, the United States, and France. However, the need and desire of hospitals to secure additional revenue, and physicians to augment their incomes when paid on a fee-for-service basis, caused this "old system" to crumble and fall increasingly, if not completely, by the wayside. Getting organizations and individuals to exercise restraint in the face of opportunities to increase their revenue flow is extremely difficult. Fee-for-service is, of course, a two-edged sword. On the one hand, it may increase costs by generating discretionary and unnecessary services. On the other hand, it is a safety valve, enabling and encouraging both physicians and hospitals to provide services more promptly and conveniently for the patient. The rise of private health insurance and private hospitals in New Zealand and the United Kingdom makes this point.

A certain disingenuousness is evident in the rhetoric justifying limitations on health budgets whenever it is said that the most important factors contributing to health are not medical but rather individual: self-discipline, good nutrition, exercise. While true, what is not stated is that these nonmedical factors apply mainly to the future. The effects of unhealthy lifestyles are already in the system, and their medical costs are largely unavoidable. Smoking may indeed be injurious to our health and in the long run nonsmoking will contribute to reduced rates of lung cancer and heart disease and the costs associated with those conditions. However, enormous costs associated with those conditions are already built into the immediate future because of the adverse effects caused by those who have been smoking until now.

After limiting funds, governments have turned to changes in the health system. Most countries are looking at other countries to see which mechanisms might be tried out, as well as which should be avoided. The countries in this book are especially inclined to look at one another's efforts at reform because of the economic and social similarities and ties that exist among them. The Nordic countries are a case in point: they are in regular consultation and use the Nordic Council to facilitate this process. New Zealand has historically looked to the United Kingdom for leadership and many of its health care reforms were, and still are, adaptations of what the United Kingdom was doing. Government agencies in the United States have increased their study of the leading industrialized societies as witnessed by dedicated issues of the *Health Care Financing Review* (a journal published by the Health Care Financing Administration of the U.S. Department of Health and Human Services,[2] and by reports from the General Accounting Office (an agency of the U.S. Congress) on Canada, Sweden, the United Kingdom, France, Germany, and Japan.[3] Private professional journals such as the *New England Journal of Medicine, Journal of the American Medical Association, Health Affairs,* the *Journal of Medical Practice Management,* and the *Journal of Health Politics, Policy and Law* have also printed accounts from time to time of the health systems in various industrialized countries.

In recent years the United States, for example, has looked very closely at Germany for health care reform ideas because the Germans rely, as in the United States, on the insurance mechanism to finance their health system and also rely upon fee-for-service payments to doctors in ambulatory care. The United States has also looked closely at the Canadian system because of the long historical, economic, and cultural ties between the two countries, and the fact that until the latter part of this century the two health systems developed along almost identical lines.

The closer two nations are economically and culturally, the more their health systems, and other systems, are likely to converge, to become more alike. To the extent the countries are dissimilar, then convergence may not be as evident though the sharing of ideas may still provide, as a Swedish government publication put it, "seeds . . . to enrich the gene variation."[4]

Health System Convergence

Because countries face similar problems, adopt similar solutions, and are clearly influenced by the ideas developed in other countries, the notion that the health systems of the industrialized world are converging, becoming more and more alike, is an intriguing concept. Jeremy Hurst, in a report prepared for OECD on seven European countries (Belgium, France, Germany, Ireland, Netherlands,

Spain, and the United Kingdom), noted that "in several respects, the seven countries seem to be converging in their health care policies and institutions. This is evident in: the continuing moves towards universal public coverage; the strengthening of control over total health expenditure by governments; the universal adoption of global budgets in hospital markets; and in the movements towards the contract model in several countries. However, there is currently divergence on the subject of regulation. Whereas at the beginning of the 1980s, six of the seven countries relied on a highly centralized command-and-control approach to regulation, by the end of the 1980s the Netherlands and the United Kingdom had followed Germany, by moving towards a greater measure of self-regulation."[5]

A number of developments in Western industrialized countries reinforces the notion of convergence. Sweden, the Netherlands, and the United Kingdom have been strongly influenced by the ideas set forth by Alain Enthoven of Stanford University in California particularly as regards competition, incentives, and managed competition.[6] New Zealand has also been influenced if not directly then at least indirectly by the Enthoven influences on the United Kingdom and the Netherlands. The health systems of these countries are adapting some aspects of Enthoven's proposals, which gives some credence to the notion of health systems convergence. Enthoven's idea of managed competition also influenced the Clinton health care reform proposals in the United States and even without legislation is being adopted by many employers and insurance companies throughout the nation. Another example of convergence is in hospital financing where the American mechanism for paying hospitals based on DRGs has influenced France, Germany, and Sweden, and appears to be on the verge of emerging in the United Kingdom as fundholding GPs negotiate with hospitals. It has also influenced some changes in Japan.

Brian Abel-Smith in his analysis of seventeen OECD countries noted that "while a considerable amount of convergence can be found among these 17 countries, the extent of it should not be exaggerated. . . . In one respect, it may seem that there is some movement in contrary directions."[7] The countries included in this study were different from the preceding OECD publication but did include all five Nordic countries.

Marie-Pascal Pomey and Jean-Pierre Poullier in the French chapter also see signs of convergence in the European Union, though they correctly note that convergence does not translate into cultural or complete health system homogeneity. As they put it,

> The European Treaties exempt social protection from a drive toward legislative harmonization, thereby safeguarding the wealth of multiple approaches to enhancing health status. . . . There is no single path to health, but unique experiences. Among those described in this volume, there have been over the years strong convergence features amid great institutional diversity. None were dictated by a single theoretical model or by an intergovernmental harmonization process. Shared problems and often also solutions are perceived through heterogeneous information infrastructures. No amount of goodwill can channel these analyses in a rigorously identical synopsis.

Later they observe that "in many walks of life, the European Union . . . may be viewed as a single entity. Healthwise, a strong informal convergence pervades but little formal harmonization has taken place. Institutions, incentive mechanisms, benefit baskets, finance are still largely country-specific."

Although convergence may exist among some countries and may well emerge between others over time, both Hurst and Abel-Smith suggest that the evidence is not yet conclusive, and the situation bears watching. Contrary movement, as both note, also bears watching. Despite the proximity of the United States and Canada, and the parallel development of their health systems, in recent years Canada has diverged as it mandated universal, publicly administered health insurance, assumed its own accrediting processes, and exercised control both on charges to patients and physician fees. While Denmark and Sweden share many common approaches, Sweden seems to be diverging as patients are called upon to pay nominal fees for *hospital* care, a practice not found yet in Denmark. What is not known is whether these Canadian and Swedish policies are real divergences, or the setting of new directions for health sector development that in turn will be followed respectively by the United States and Denmark. Some convergence may be occurring on at least one score in the United States as controls are imposed increasingly on both physician charges and fees through Medicare, Medicaid, and Preferred Provider Organizations.

In the enthusiasm to solve a problem by adopting some other country's policies one risks not examining closely enough the experiences of the other country. How well are the policies really working? How much of the policy's success is due to unique political, economic, and cultural factors in that country? The danger is that insufficient critical examination will occur and will bring about results that are not desirable and that may make things worse. The industrialized democracies of the West tend to follow that cautionary practice routinely, though some might conclude from the New Zealand chapter that New Zealand leaped into adopting reforms inspired from abroad without adequate consideration of all key factors. Some Europeans undoubtedly feel this way about managed competition and DRGs. The advice, however, is particularly applicable today to the health care reform efforts in Central and Eastern Europe where euphoria over their newfound freedoms coupled with pressures to develop market economies may lead to inappropriate reforms.

Apart from current cross-national influences there are also historical influences that have shaped health systems, influences resulting from commercial interactions, colonial policies, and wars. Japan was influenced in the 1870s from ties to Germany, and following the Second World War by the American Occupation forces. The American system of medical education was influenced by early ties to Scotland, and during the nineteenth century by visits of American physicians to the United Kingdom, France, Germany, and Austria.[8] The Canadian system developed jointly and parallel with the U.S. system due to their economic and cultural proximity, and diverged only in recent years. The Dutch insurance system was established by the German occupation forces during the Second World War, and has continued. The British influence on New Zealand, as already noted, has been enormous as professionals from both countries moved back and forth for training and employment.

Decentralization and Freedom to Experiment

Stefan Håkansson and Sara Nordling note in the Swedish chapter that with decentralization there are increased opportunities to experiment as there are many more actors who can devise ways to overcome some of the obstacles they face—more trials, more failures, but also more chances for success. Decentralized government has historically been strong in Sweden and Denmark. County and local governments have paid most of the Swedish and Danish health care costs, but as those authors note even greater authority is devolving upon them as a way to increase health system efficiency and deal more effectively with rising health costs. The Swedish system in particular had to address considerable public dissatisfaction over limitations on patient choice of physician and hospital. Some of the reasons behind Swedish reform were also implicit in Canadian reform although there may not have been the same degree of Canadian public dissatisfaction. Peggy Leatt and Paul Williams note, "A key direction for reform at the provincial level is devolving authority for management of the health system down to local and community levels and increasing citizen participation in decision-making. Such reforms are motivated by democratic values and by a desire to make the health system more open and accountable to the people it serves."

The United Kingdom is perhaps making the most radical change as it abandons what appeared to many to have been a highly centrally controlled system to one that is very decentralized. This occurs as it allows hospitals to become self-governing trusts and free to set many of their policies, and GPs to become Fundholders with opportunities to augment their primary care services and the power and money to purchase hospital care for nonemergency hospital admissions for their patients. New Zealand, like the United Kingdom, is also decentralizing with its creation of Crown Health Enterprises which, like the U.K.'s self-governing hospital trusts would, in the words of the New Zealand author, "operate according to commercial objectives."

Some form of decentralization is also occurring in the Netherlands, France, and Japan. The United States, of course, has been constitutionally decentralized from the very beginning and the opportunities to experiment are manifest today in many states as the states and the private sector seek to bring about health care reform in the absence of a federal solution.

Where decentralization occurs in countries following decades of central government leadership and control, there is greater chance of error as different approaches are tried, as the Swedish authors have observed. Because errors may be costly and may sometimes have unanticipated and unintended results, decentralization requires a level of tolerance and restraint on the part of central governments. This is a very serious problem in the United States where Congress is all too often inclined to impose new restrictions on all states and the private sector whenever practices in only one or a few states turn out not as intended, thereby decreasing the opportunities for others to experiment and find new and better ways to do things.

Decentralization typically has an added advantage in that it establishes a competitive structure whereby local units can be challenged to do better than their neighbors. The challenge comes from each unit's constituency—its public, its patients—who pressure their county or local government or their hospital to provide the benefits and services of people in the neighboring region. Such pressure, however, has many cost implications.

Competition

Hans Maarse notes in the Dutch chapter that competition assumes some excess capacity. Can one compete on quality and costs without some excess capacity? Competition requires an alternative, a choice of ways to deal with a problem. In Sweden and Denmark if the county hospital cannot provide a service promptly, the patient has the right to go to some other hospital be it private or in another county, and the patient's home county hospital has to pay. Similarly in the United Kingdom this is likely to occur whenever the fundholding GP may try to satisfy the patient on his or her list (and thereby retain the income for their primary care) by negotiating with hospitals not only the amount to be charged for care but also how long the patients may have to wait. If the local hospital is unable to meet the GP's preferred timetable, or charges too much, the GP can send the patient to a hospital that has a more acceptable arrangement. One hospital's revenue stream would thus be reduced; this would pose a challenge for it to do better. Sometimes this practice may lead to additional costs because it may force the hospital to hire more people or acquire new equipment.

Where the competition is based solely on a monetary difference one needs to be careful that the difference does not also translate into lesser quality.

Competition is also evident in the Netherlands, France, Germany, Japan, and the United States where insurance systems are dominant. The more patients the hospital treats, the more revenue it gets. In these countries, it can be financially advantageous for a hospital to seek out and make room for cases on which it can make money. The money earned would give the hospital some flexibility, some room to maneuver. But to compete in those systems, as Maarse notes, may require some excess capacity. The excess capacity can occur naturally from having more beds than ordinarily needed, as in the United States, or can be created either by avoiding certain types of money-losing cases and/or by discharging patients from hospital sooner than would ordinarily occur. American hospitals have been accused of discharging patients ''quicker and sicker'' as a result of insurance company and Medicare-limited, fixed payments per each patient's hospital admission.

Excess capacity can, however, have a negative effect on both quality and costs. In three countries—the United States, Japan, and Germany—many ambulatory physicians have a significant amount of sophisticated, diagnostic equipment in their private practice offices. The equipment costs money, and those costs must be written off. The easiest way to accomplish this is to use the equipment more and be paid for its use. The concern with physician-owned equipment is not only as regards unnecessary utilization but also over quality, being certain that the physician is fully qualified to carry out the tests and interpret the results. When the equipment is part of an institution—a hospital or an independent freestanding ambulatory care specialty unit—and the patient is referred by the family physician, there is some control, providing that the family physician does not have a financial investment in either the equipment or the institution. This potential for excessive use exists, however, even for hospitals in some of the countries, particularly if they are in financial straits and are struggling to survive: depending on how they are paid, extra tests, X-rays, and other outpatient services can be a way to alleviate their financial problems, and additional money-making inpatient admissions whenever possible could help especially if they are paid on a fee-for-service or *per diem* basis. Avoiding the admission of cases on which the hospital is likely to lose money is strategy for financial survival in all systems.

While competition may challenge all to do better, it can also be excessive and have negative consequences as the U.S. experience seems to be demonstrating in the competition among health insurance companies, between physicians and the hospitals on which the physicians depend for inpatient care, and between hospitals as they struggle to survive in an environment that some believe has become too competitive and not in the best interests of the larger community.

Health Services

Cost-Shifting

In Sweden, New Zealand, France, and the United States costs are being shifted to individuals by government, insurance companies, hospitals, and/or physicians. This is being done in several ways: increasing premium charges, deductibles, co-payments, and for other items of service such as for catering or hotel costs in hospital. The practice of shifting costs to the individual becomes more attractive as national economies decline. Asking patients to pay something for ambulatory care has some merit to it, especially for primary care. The objective is to discourage frivolous use of the health services. The amount charged in theory should be high enough to cause patients to exercise good judgment in deciding whether or not to see the physician or to have a certain test, but not so high as to deter the patients when they should visit the physician or have the test. Finding the appropriate policy balance is not easy. However, the trend toward increasing deductibles and co-payments is likely to produce adverse effects by encouraging more patients to gamble and not see the physician when in fact they should. (Where such patient charges are made, the burden is at least moderated for some because there is typically a limit as to the amount of costs the insured patient will have to incur, after which no additional charges are made.) Asking the patient to pay hospital catering or hotel costs is somewhat troubling because it assumes that the patient no longer has to pay any of those costs at home (which is often not true). Increasing the premium charges where the insurance is voluntary as in the United States can also be counterproductive, though from an insurance point of view necessary: as premiums go up, more and more employers and individuals drop their health insurance. Patients take a chance, pay out-of-pocket for ambulatory care, and/or simply rely on the hospital to contribute to their care.

In Denmark, France, Germany, the Netherlands, New Zealand, Sweden, and the United Kingdom (and increasingly in the United States) where there are limitations on salary, capitation, or fee payments to physicians, physicians are usually able to augment their incomes by caring for patients who are privately insured or self-paying. Except for the United Kingdom and Sweden, they can also enhance their incomes by increasing the number of their services. PPO physicians in the United States can get around the limitation by increasing the number of patient services provided to PPO patients as well as by seeing other patients who are not in the PPO to whom they can charge their regular fees as well as maintain a volume of services. The practice of increasing the volume of services can occur in Canada although, as in Germany, the practice styles of ambulatory care physicians are monitored to make certain that they exercise restraint and there is a penalty if physicians go too far in this regard.

Cost-shifting is not confined to shifts to the individual citizen. It also occurs between levels of government, and between the public and private sectors. In France, Canada, and the United States, hard-pressed central governments have shifted financial responsibilities to other levels of government. Sometimes the initial transfer is eased by a transfer of money as well, but usually a source or base of taxation is not transferred so that over the years the receiving political jurisdiction will have to bear the burden of additional costs. This shift between levels of government may also be occurring in Denmark, Sweden, and the United Kingdom, where local governments have had to assume increased financial responsibilities for nursing homes and home care. In the United States when government policies restrict the number of poor people eligible for Medicaid and where Medicaid payments to physicians and hospitals are well below costs, government is effectively shifting those costs to the private sector. The private sector then has to find the money by charging other patients more if they can, by increasing the volume of services provided to these other patients, by trying to avoid money-losing cases, and by developing new services and programs that will produce new revenue. Such acts of "musical chairs" serve primarily to relieve the financial burden from one part of government to be placed upon another agency while rarely solving the problem of patient needs and associated costs.

The private for-profit hospital sector, in a reverse sort of situation, tends to make certain that it does not have the capability to handle cost-losing cases and thus avoids that risk, a situation clearly evident in both France and the United States. Where public and nonprofit hospitals have excess capacity, as in the United States, then the for-profit hospitals gain revenue at the expense of the nonprofit and public hospitals. On the other hand, the for-profit hospitals often offer amenities not always available in some of the other hospitals, amenities that make the difference in their appeal to well-insured patients.

Quality Assurance

The Canadians and Americans were pioneers in quality assurance. The Flexner Report in 1910 led to the reform of medical education in both countries. Years later with the Joint Commission on Accreditation of Hospitals, initially serving both countries, an accreditation process for hospitals began with its strong reliance on professional peer review and sanctions. Specialty organizations progressively strengthened their procedures for review of institutions, setting standards for specialty training programs, mandating periodic additional training, and lately retesting of individual physician qualifications. While the Canadians now have their separate organizations, the communications and professional interactions between both countries are so pronounced that at times it is difficult to determine who is influencing whom.

Although most countries have instituted activities to improve the quality of care, it has been difficult to measure objectively the impact of those activities. Only recently has there been the technology and data available to measure quality meaningfully. The latest American efforts at quality assurance have sought to identify key clinical factors that indicate the appropriate treatment of various ailments and the measurement of clinical outcomes. Clinical guidelines have been and continue to be developed by specialty groups for the diagnosis and treatment of specific symptoms. Periodic competence retesting of primary care physicians and other specialists and the requirements for continuing education are further positive steps in the United States. It is interesting to note that guidelines (protocols) have been initiated in the Netherlands to improve the quality of GP care. Steps have also been taken by the Netherlands to reregister GPs every five years. Canada, New Zealand, and the U.K. have also begun to develop guidelines, and other European countries have shown a great interest in improving the measurement of clinical outcomes.

Peter Hatcher reports a particularly interesting U.K. development where leverage is increasingly in the hands of fundholding GPs: "Shared and integrated care protocols are being negotiated between referring GPs and consultants for the management of particular conditions that previously would have been undertaken by consultants only." This should go a long way toward dealing with the problem common in many countries where communications between hospital specialists and GPs are weak at best, to the detriment of patient care.

In Germany, though progress is being made particularly as regards the educational requirements for medical services, the guidelines developed "are not very precise about the care-giving itself." Quality-assurance efforts seem to be largely absent in Japan where the author notes that "there has been no formal quality check system of medical care such as peer review or the PRO system in the United States, except the assessment, guidance, and auditing system from social health insurance administration. There remains the traditional emphasis among the medical profession for professional freedom and individual professional independence." The French quality assurance system appears to be hampered by an absence of key clinical data from its hospitals.

The authors of the German chapter make an interesting observation regarding quality assurance in ambulatory care: quality in that setting "is not permanently monitored." What goes on in the ambulatory care setting should be of particular concern in all countries particularly where the ambulatory physicians have significant amounts of equipment at their disposal. The amount of equipment available to physicians in nonhospital ambulatory settings is fairly excessive in the United States, Germany, and Japan. The concern, as noted previously, is not only excess utilization where payments are made for use of the equipment but more important the competence of the physician to administer the test properly and to interpret test findings. Where the technological armamentarium is limited in nonhospital ambulatory care settings, the concern for what is done for the patient is somewhat less troubling. The primary—but not exclusive—concern here is that the primary care physician knows when to refer the patient. As noted earlier, the requirements for continuing education and the periodic retesting of physicians in the United States are steps to assure high-quality care in both primary care and other settings. In the United Kingdom the new medical audit program for physicians in both hospital and community practice also addresses the need for quality assurance.

The quality of care in all of the countries in this book is believed to be high because the physicians are well trained and they have access to the latest scientific knowledge. Moreover, each nation's health statistics are among the best in the world. But there are still weaknesses in their surveillance systems, and when the costs are so high, those who pay understandably want some assurance that they are getting value for their money. In the United Kingdom, Denmark, and Sweden this is occurring where there are efforts to separate the purchaser of care from the provider. In the United Kingdom, however, it might be suggested that the fundholding GP has a vested interest in keeping patients out of hospital and in some cases this may prove not to be an adequate separation. What is encouraging in this regard is that the British because of their large population have ample opportunity to experiment, and are trying different approaches to fundholding. In the United States, by way of contrast, there is some movement toward eliminating the separation that prevails in those cases where the HMO or PPO is owned by the hospital, insurance company, or the self-insured employer. Complete separation still exists in Canada.

Hospital Waiting Lists

Waiting lists for outpatient consultation and for admission to hospital are the subject of much patient irritation and much public debate in most countries in which patients must line up for treatment. Waiting lists have been reduced significantly where governments—the United Kingdom, Sweden, New Zealand, and Denmark—have provisions entitling those who wait more than a specified period of time the option of going to another hospital. Sometimes patients have the right to go to another county hospital or even a private hospital. Whoever would have to pay for care in the hospital for which the patient waits, has to pay for care in the other hospital. This encourages hospitals and physicians to treat patients more promptly. This policy could well have advantages for patients enrolled in HMOs in the United States where delays have been reported in getting an appointment for primary care as well as delays and/or denials in seeing a specialist and getting costly tests. A solution to this U.S. problem could well be to entitle HMO patients with the right to go outside the HMO if the requested service is not provided within a specified, agreed-upon reasonable time, the HMO having to pay for that outside service. A variation of this already exists in the United States for HMO patients who have the Point-of-Service HMO option but the patient in these instances still has to pay some portion of the outside service. Someone once observed that in the United Kingdom the length of waiting lists seemed to grow as budget time approached. The most recent reforms in the United Kingdom seem to have made this approach to budget enhancement less likely.

Those who resist change in the United States often refer to the dangers and inconveniences that would arise from the waiting lists that would inevitably develop if certain reforms are instituted. What they fail to note is that waiting lists are mostly either for nonemergency treatment (emergency cases are handled promptly in all countries) or in transplant cases from a shortage of organs. There are some indirect costs associated with waiting lists for which there is no known accounting as the Dutch author notes. These are the costs that result from lost working days and lost earnings. He might also have noted the costs associated with decreased worker efficiency.

The Danish and Swedish authors all report that patient decisions to wait for hospital admission were not affected by offering patients free choice of hospital. People in both countries still tended to wait and be treated at their local hospital. This suggests an important point about waiting lists: they are an irritant, but bearable by most. The freedom to opt for a hospital other than the one for which they are waiting—and this is also true now of the United Kingdom and New Zealand—is a safety valve for the impatient, articulate persons who would complain. The safety valve always existed before this reform in New Zealand where there were private hospitals for inpatient care and to a lesser extent in Sweden and the United Kingdom where the private hospital sectors were not so large. Those patients who did not want to wait but who were willing to pay, could opt for private hospital care. This led to the growth of private health insurance to the extent that in the United Kingdom today an estimated 11.1% of the population has private health insurance; in New Zealand, some 50% of the population has private health insurance. The private sector offered an alternative to those on waiting lists. To be sure, it was only for those who could afford to pay or who had private health insurance. What this option did, however, was to remove some of the pressure on government to provide additional resources to the health sector to enable it to hire additional staff and open more beds and surgical theaters.

Average Lengths of Stay and Occupancy Rates

The average length of stay, excluding nursing home–type patients, has decreased in nearly all countries. The data can give a distorted picture, however, since different countries have different mixes of patients in their hospitals. Toshitaka Nakahara notes, for example, that Japanese hospitals have many nursing home–type patients, which skews the average length of stay data. More meaningful is the average length of stay for specific conditions as some countries have reported in Table 5 of their chapter.

The occupancy rate and average length of stay in the acute care hospitals tends to go down. As noted in the U.S. chapter, low occupancy rates can be misleading. Once licensed by government for a given number of beds, if the need for those beds no longer exists, the better part of wisdom is not to tell but simply to close off the rooms and the sections, turn off the lights and heat, and reduce the staff that serviced those beds. In this way, if the need for those beds arises in the future, they can be opened without having to argue with government as to whether the beds are needed or not. As one hospital administrator put it: "a licensed bed is a licensed bed; you never give up a licensed bed!" The argument for closure of unneeded beds is based on the belief that because it costs so much to maintain a hospital bed, closure will reduce hospital costs. What these advocates fail to recognize is that the hospitals have already cut their costs by the unofficial closure of beds and that little will be gained in cost reduction by formal closure.

Home Care

Countries look to home care on the assumption it is less expensive and more sensitive to patient needs. The Dutch and Danish authors, as well as a U.S. study, have questioned that assumption. The U.S. study found "that the expansion of case management and community services beyond what already exists does not lead to overall cost savings. But it does yield benefits in the form of in-home care, reduced unmet needs, and improved satisfaction with life for clients and informal caregivers who bear most of the burden. Whether these benefits are commensurate with its costs is a decision for society to make.''[9] When the intensity of home care services is less than optimal, then home care might be less costly. One should always be careful that a hospital's decision to discharge a patient to home care is in fact a decision based on patient clinical needs and not an effort to shift costs to others. This could be a problem in both Denmark and Sweden where the hospital is county-financed and home care is financed by local government, as well as in the United Kingdom and Germany. Under the DRG and limited payment systems in the United States, hospitals have an incentive to discharge patients as soon as possible but home care services are sometimes not adequate and finance of those services often has to be borne by the patient.

Declining Influence of Medical Profession

The influence of the medical profession on health policy is declining in most of the countries of this book. Allan Krasnik and Signild Vallgårda note in the Danish chapter that this reflects the general reduction in the physician's authority in society as well as internal divisions among various groups of doctors, factors common in most countries today. In some countries (for example, Germany, Netherlands, and the United States) only half of the physicians belong to the national medical association. There are some understandable reasons for such low representation, the most important of which is that physicians are increasingly finding that a national body representing all physicians does not really represent *their* interests. They are finding that their specialty associations are more important for both their professional growth and for representing their interests to government, the private sector, and the public. This was vividly apparent in the United States in the debate over the Clinton health reform proposal, which was vigoroously opposed by the American Medical Association but supported in the main by many other medical associations. The AMA, perhaps the largest lobbyist in Washington and a heavy contributor to political campaigns, prevailed in this debate largely because it teamed up with a large number of other non–health sector opponents.

The declining influence of the medical profession—as a group as distinct from an individual's personal physician—has also occurred as a result of actions taken by the profession either to protest or protect how it is paid, and the amount it is paid. Strikes and other pressure tactics have generally undermined the credibility of the profession, even when the efforts they undertook succeeded. As Uwe Reinhardt remarked, referring to a recent controversy in Germany, ''You can appeal to quality and free choice, but finally all appeals lose their power and people yawn. The German doctors had drawn their account down to where they had little political leverage.''[10]

The above-mentioned factors of course contributed to the declining influence of the profession in many nations. The decline, however, was and continues to be inevitable because of health sector cost pressures on national economies. Because physicians are the driving force behind health care costs—for they are the ones who order tests and determine who needs treatment and what kinds of treatment—the more health care costs impinge upon other sectors in a nation's economy, the more government, business leaders, interest groups, and others insist on having a say in determining the shape of the health system.

Conclusion

Ten countries—similar but very different—displaying elements of convergence, of their trying some of the same procedures to deal with the problems of rising costs and equity. However, that does not mean that a homogenization process is occurring. Nonetheless, as countries continue to struggle to deal with the health sector problems confronting them, information and ideas on possible solutions continue to be exchanged across national borders. This has been most apparent in the financing of the health systems, the movement for greater decentralization, and the drive for more competitive environments. However, a Swedish government publication had a pertinent observation in this regard: "The grass is definitely greener on our side, but let us get some seeds from our neighbor to enrich the gene variation, seems to be a basic strategy. Countries tend basically to keep their cultural system heritage, but the growing need for urgent 'solutions' and the diffusion of ideas is increasingly followed by imports of methods from other systems. Evidently, the risks in such haste imports is that you do not investigate enough the experiences of the imported elements. You may cure the immediate problems, but bring other unwanted effects."[4]

As each country struggles to cope with the health sector problems, enormous political dilemmas must be faced. Public outrage at prospective changes can inhibit necessary efforts at reform. The French protests toward the end of 1995 motivated partly because of a proposed reduction in social benefits illustrate this point as does the difficulty the U.S. Congress is having in 1996 in trying to balance the budget in part by savings and changes in Medicare and Medicaid. Public outrage in both countries is very evident and effective. People may agree that some changes are needed but they also want fewer taxes and more money for personal spending. They do not want change to adversely affect them personally, nor do they want to see change alter the values they hold regarding care of the elderly, the poor, and the other social safety nets which exist.

Whatever the choices, whatever the decision on health sector reform and on budgets, everyone needs to bear in mind constantly that few health sector problems are permanently solved because of the dynamic nature of health care. Today's solutions often become tomorrow's problems. Societies are dynamic entities, constantly changing, constantly evolving. The process of reform in health care is thus a neverending process but reform proposals are often honed and facilitated by examining the thinking and experiences of other countries.

NOTES

1. Fuchs, V. 1974. *Who Shall Live?* New York: Basic Books, 18.

2. International Comparison of Health Care Financing and Delivery: Data and Perspectives. 1989. *Health Care Financing Review,* supplement.

International Comparisons of Health Systems. 1992. *Health Care Financing Review* 13(4).

Physician Payment and Cost Containment: Perspectives from the U.S. and Abroad. 1993. *Health Care Financing Review* 14(3).

3. Health Care Spending Control—the Experiences of France, Germany, Japan. November 1991.

1993 German Health Reforms—New Cost Control Initiatives. July 1993.

German Health Reforms—Changes Result in Lower Health Costs in 1993. December 1994.

Primary Care Physicians—Managing Supply in Canada, Germany, Sweden, and the United Kingdom. May 1994.

4. Olsson, S. E., H. Hansen, and I. Eriksson. 1993. Social Security in Sweden and Other European Countries—Three Essays. Finans-Departementet. Stockholm, 150.

5. Hurst, J. 1992. *The Reform of Health Care.* Paris: OECD, 151.

6. Enthoven, A. 1993. The History and Principles of Managed Competition. *Health Affairs* 12: 24–28.

Enthoven, A., and R. Kronich. June 5 and 12, 1989. A Consumer Choice Health Plan for the 1990s. *New England Journal of Medicine* 320 (1–2).

7. Abel-Smith, B. *The Reform of Health Care Systems.* 1994. Paris: OECD, 49.

8. Raffel, M. W., and N. K. Raffel. *The U.S. Health System: Origins and Functions.* 4th ed. Albany, N.Y.: Delmar, 4–6.

9. U.S. Department of Health and Human Services. 1987. The Evaluation of the National Long-Term Care Demonstration: Final Report Executive Summary. Washington, D.C.

10. *American Medical News,* February 15, 1993.